Teacher Education in Taiwan

Before the Teacher Education Act was passed in 1994, student teachers were educated through diverse educational institutions instead of the traditional normal schools (Taiwan's equivalent of teachers' colleges). But such market-based teacher education has been altered by politics, society, and culture in the direction of government-controlled teacher education, particularly in the evaluation of quality in teacher education. Taiwan maintains teacher education quality by controlling the number of teachers, using assessment to eliminate teachers who are not up to standard, evaluating teacher education institutions, and evaluating the professional development of teachers to raise elementary and secondary teacher quality. This book uses Taiwan as a case study to analyze the transformation of teacher education in a country going through political, economic, and societal transitions along the axis of state regulation versus marketization. It analyzes the uniqueness of Taiwanese teacher education for international reference, and draws implications for teacher education policies in the context of education reform.

The book covers, among others, the following areas:

- formation of two approaches to teacher education;
- teacher education policy and policy direction in Taiwan;
- ideology, implications and applications of teacher profession standards;
- teacher education strategic alliances in Taiwan.

This book will also be of interest to policy-makers, researchers, and students in the field of education, especially in teacher education and comparative education.

Shen-Keng Yang is a ROC National Chair Professor and a Professor at the National Taiwan Normal University.

Jia-Li Huang is a Professor, Office of Teacher Education and Careers Service at the National Taiwan Normal University and Deputy Secretary-General, Teacher Education Society of the ROC.

Routledge Research in Teacher Education

The Routledge Research in Teacher Education series presents the latest research on teacher education and also provides a forum to discuss the latest practices and challenges in the field.
Books in the series include:

Preparing Classroom Teachers to Succeed with Second Language Learners
Lessons from a Faculty Learning Community
Edited by Thomas H. Levine, Elizabeth R. Howard and David M. Moss

Interculturalization and Teacher Education
Theory to Practice
Cheryl A. Hunter, Donna K. Pearson and A. Renee Gutiérrez

Community Fieldwork in Teacher Education
Theory and Practice
Heidi L. Hallman and Melanie N. Burdick

Portrait of a Moral Agent Teacher
Teaching Morally and Teaching Morality
Gillian R. Rosenberg

Observing Teacher Identities through Video Analysis
Practice and Implications
Amy Vetter and Melissa Schieble

Navigating Gender and Sexuality in the Classroom
Narrative Insights from Students and Educators
Heather McEntarfer

Teacher Education in Taiwan
State Control vs Marketization
Edited by Sheng-Keng Yang and Jia-Li Huang

Critical Feminism and Critical Education
An Interdisciplinary Approach to Teacher Education
Jennifer Gale de Saxe

The Use of Children's Literature in Teaching
A Study of the Politics and Professionalism within Teacher Education
Alyson Simpson

Teacher Education in Taiwan
State control vs marketization

Edited by Shen-Keng Yang
and Jia-Li Huang

LONDON AND NEW YORK

First published 2016
by Routledge
2 Park Square, Milton Park, Abingdon, Oxfordshire OX14 4RN
711 Third Avenue, New York, NY 10017

Routledge is an imprint of the Taylor & Francis Group, an informa business

First issued in paperback 2017

Copyright © 2016 S.K. Yang and J.L. Huang

The right of the editors to be identified as the authors of the editorial material, and of the authors for their individual chapters, has been asserted in accordance with sections 77 and 78 of the Copyright, Designs and Patents Act 1988.

All rights reserved. No part of this book may be reprinted or reproduced or utilised in any form or by any electronic, mechanical, or other means, now known or hereafter invented, including photocopying and recording, or in any information storage or retrieval system, without permission in writing from the publishers.

Notice:
Product or corporate names may be trademarks or registered trademarks, and are used only for identification and explanation without intent to infringe.

British Library Cataloguing-in-Publication Data
A catalogue record for this book is available from the British Library.

Library of Congress Cataloging-in-Publication Data
Names: Yang, Shenkeng, author. | Huang, Jia-Li.
Title: Teacher education in Taiwan : state control vs marketization / Shen-Keng Yang and Jia-Li Huang.
Description: Abingdon, Oxon ; New York, NY : Routledge, 2016. |
Series: Routledge research in teacher education ; 8
Identifiers: LCCN 2015041180| ISBN 9781138804302 (hardback) |
ISBN 9781315753102 (ebook)
Subjects: LCSH: Teachers–Training of–Taiwan. | Education and state–Taiwan.
Classification: LCC LB1727.T28 Y36 2016 |
DDC 370.71/10951249–dc23
LC record available at http://lccn.loc.gov/2015041180

ISBN: 978-1-138-80430-2 (hbk)
ISBN: 978-0-8153-6084-1 (pbk)

Typeset in Galliard
by Cenveo Publisher Services

Contents

List of figures and tables vii
List of contributors ix
Foreword xiii

Introduction: the formation of two approaches to teacher education 1
CHUN-PING WANG

PART 1
Historical background 15

1 Development of teacher education policies in Taiwan during the Dutch and Spanish occupation, the Zheng and Qing period and the Japanese colonial period 17
   CHUNG-MING LIANG

2 Teacher education policy and policy direction in Taiwan 42
   YUNG-MING SHU

3 Ideologies and theories influencing the development of teacher education in Taiwan 67
   SHEN-KENG YANG

4 The ideology, implications, and application of teacher profession standards 87
   JIA-LI HUANG

PART 2
Developing teacher education — 107

5 The development of pre-service teacher education courses — 109
YU-FEI LIU

6 The education practicum from the development of teacher education in Taiwan — 135
WEI-LING TANG

7 Teacher professional development in Taiwan — 157
BO-RUEY HUANG

PART 3
Improving teachers' professional performance — 177

8 Development of teacher education institutions in Taiwan — 179
CHOU-SUNG YANG

9 Evaluation of the professional development of school teachers — 197
FENG-JIHU LEE

10 Teacher education strategic alliances in Taiwan — 216
SHENG-YAO CHENG

11 The evaluation of teacher education for quality assurance in Taiwan — 238
JIA-LI HUANG

12 State control vs the market mechanism: Taiwan's experience with teacher education — 260
JIA-LI HUANG

Name index — 275
Subject index — 277

List of figures and tables

Figures

0.1	Comparison of the two approaches to teacher education	9
1.1	Education system during the Kingdom of Tungning	25
1.2	Taiwanese education system during the Qing dynasty	26
1.3	History of Japanese schools and normal schools	36
7.1	Promotion strategies of teacher professional development	164
10.1	Educational policy analysis model	218
10.2	Research procedure	220
10.3	Research framework	222

Tables

1.1	Courses for Dutch missionary and teacher education in 1642	21
1.2	Student allowances provided to normal school students during the Japanese colonial period in Taiwan	34
1.3	Development of the teacher education system in Taiwan and education policies	38
2.1	Number of applicants and qualified elementary school teachers	44
2.2	Number of secondary school teachers who took pre-service training courses and their educational degrees	48
2.3	Educational degrees of provincial junior high school teachers in Taiwan	48
2.4	Enhancement Programme for Teacher Education Quality	56
2.5	Evaluation criteria and results for teacher education evaluation	57
2.6	Number and current employment status of certified teachers according to the Teacher Education Act 1994	61
4.1	Prioritized specialty and employment of people with a teaching license issued by the revised Teacher Education Act of 1994	88

4.2	Number of new teachers developed between 2008 and 2012 in Taiwan	89
4.3	Comparison of contents of the three types of teacher profession standards in Taiwan	97
5.1	Development of pre-service teacher education courses in Taiwan	111
5.2	Professional education subjects and minimal required credits for pre-service teacher education classes: 2013 academic year	118
7.1	Systematic teacher in-service training framework	167
7.2	The number of teachers and schools participating in the evaluation of teacher professional development	169
10.1	Research subjects	221
10.2	The response and return rate of the survey	222
10.3	Analysis of the different opinions on important indicators	229
10.4	Analysis on the different opinions on feasible indicators	233
11.1	Accreditation criteria and utilization of results	244
11.2	Comparison of the first cycle and the second cycle of the teacher education evaluation system in Taiwan	246
11.3	Two different versions of indicator contents of teacher education evaluation for the second cycle	249
11.4	Overview of institutions withdrawing from the teacher education market	251

List of contributors

Sheng-Yao Cheng is Professor in the Graduate Institute of Education and Center for Teacher Education at National Chung Cheng University in Taiwan. Dr Cheng also serves as the Director of Institute for Disadvantaged Students' Learning at Yonglin Hope School since 2009, Board Member of Chinese Comparative Education Society-Taipei and Taiwan Association of Sociology of Education, Program Chair of Comparative and International Education Society (CIES) SIG: Higher Education (2009-2013), International Advisor at the National Center for University Entrance Examinations in Japan since 2009, Affiliated Faculty in the Institute of International Studies in Education at University of Pittsburgh since 2008, and Fulbright Visiting Scholar at University of Pittsburgh from 2011 to 2012. Dr Cheng got his degree at UCLA in 2004 and his recent research interests are disadvantaged students and remedial teaching, teacher education, comparative education and sociology of education.

Bo-Ruey Huang is Associate Professor in the Department of Education at the Chinese Culture University, Taiwan. His research interests are in comparative education, philosophy of education, sociology of education and teacher education. He was the vice CEO of Xiofon College at Chinese Culture University and is responsible for the Teaching Excellence Project in CCU funded by the Ministry of Education. Dr Huang also serves as secretary member of the Taiwan Association of Sociology of Education, and executive editor of the *Journal of Comparative Education*. He has published in the field of comparative education, teacher education and sociology of education.

Jia-Li Huang holds a PhD in education from National Taiwan Normal University. She serves as Professor in the Office of Teacher Education and Careers Service at National Taiwan Normal University in Taiwan. Dr Huang is the current Deputy Secretary-General, Teacher Education Society of ROC. She served as the Director of Division of Interns Programs and Supervision at NTNU. Her research and teaching focus on teacher education, teacher professionalism, curriculum and teaching design, sociology of education and history of education. She has published two books, *Teacher Quality and Teacher*

Credential Governance and *The Ideas and Practice of Standards-based Teacher Education*, and over 60 journal and book articles about teacher education in Chinese, English and Japanese and edited and co-edited over 20 books about teacher education.

Feng-Jihu Lee, Professor of the Graduate Institute of Education, National Chung Cheng University, Taiwan, is a philosopher of education who completed his PhD at the University of Reading, England. Dr Lee's major areas of inquiry include philosophy of education, comparative education, critical pedagogy, meta-ethics, moral and character education and teacher education. Dr Lee has authored three books, and more than 160 research articles, book chapters and seminar/conference papers. He has also edited and co-edited seven books, which are all focused on the field of comparative and international education, and teacher education. Dr Lee has served on professional associations such as Executive Director of WCCES (twice), President of Chinese Comparative Education Society-Taipei (twice), and Director of the Association of Taiwan Sociology of Education and Association of Normal Education of Taiwan. Dr Lee was a Fulbright Visiting Scholar at University of Pittsburgh, August 2013 to July 2014.

Chung-Ming Liang is Professor in the Department of Education, National Taitung University, Taiwan, ROC. Since 1994 he has taught in Tohoku University. He received his PhD from Tohoku University, Japan, in 1997. In 1999 he returned to Taiwan, he has been head of the Continuing Education Department, head of the Teacher Training Centre, Dean of the College of Education and Vice Chancellor. He has published *The formation and development of modern Japanese vocational education* and *The characteristics of Japanese education* (both in Japanese) and *Modern moral education in Japan* (in Chinese). He specializes in Japanese education, teacher education and comparative education. He is also a board member on many of Taiwan's TSSCI journals.

Yu-Fei Liu is Assistant Professor and Vice Dean of the Center of Teacher Education at Chinese Culture University, Taipei, Taiwan. She obtained her PhD at Tohoku University in Japan. While studying in Japan (2002–2009), she was awarded scholarships from the Interchange Association, Japan (公益財団法人交流協会) and DENTSU Scholarship Foundation. She also was a member of a research project, regarding comprehensive study on career education in schools, of the National Institute for Educational Policy Research, Japan's main official education research organization. She also holds secondary school teacher's certificates, both in business management and Japanese, and has taught in Taiwan and Japan. Her research focuses on upper secondary education, school systems, career education and teacher education from a comparative and sociological view. Since 2012, she has been participating in two large research teams on comparative education, both in Taiwan and Japan, and she is mainly responsible for the comparative study of education between Taiwan and Japan.

Yung-Ming Shu is Professor in the Department of Education and Learning Technology, National Hsin-chu University of Education, Taiwan, ROC. He was a secondary school teacher for three years and then a school inspector for local government. He majored in philosophy of education and got his degree from Nottingham University in 1995. He published *Contemporary Educational Thought* (in Chinese) in 2015. He is also a board member on many of Taiwan's TSSCI journals. Professor Shu has also been a teacher educator for more than ten years.

Wei-Ling Tang is Associate Professor of the Department of Education at the National Pingtung University, Taiwan. Since receiving her PhD from the National Taiwan Normal University in 1996, she has taught graduate students at the National Taitung Teachers College, following her career as a junior high school teacher and an assistant researcher in the Ministry of Education. She has been a visiting scholar in the Institute of Education, University of Sheffield, UK, and in the Department of Curriculum and Instruction, University of Maryland at College Park, USA. She has published many research papers in academic journals and books. She is also a board member of Taiwan's TSSCI journals. She specializes in teacher education, curriculum and instruction. Her research interests include comparative education, professional development school for teacher education, e-learning and remedial instruction.

Chun-Ping Wang is Associate Professor of the Graduate School of Curriculum and Instructional Communications Technology at National Taipei University of Education (NTUE), where he is also Dean of the Center for Teacher Education and Careers Service. Dr Wang serves as an editorial board member of Eco-Justice Press, Oregon, USA, the editor-in-chief of the *Journal of National Education Quarterly* and executive editor of *Journal of Comparative Education* since 2015. He has studied the philosophy of education, political philosophy, ecological ethics and teacher education. His current research focuses on capabilities approach theory and related educational issues.

Chou-Sung Yang is Professor in the Graduate Institute of Curriculum Instruction and Technology at National Chi Nan University (NCNU) in Taiwan, where he is also Vice Dean of Academic Affairs and Director of the Center for Teaching Development. Dr Yang has served as Editor-in-Chief of *Journal of Comparative Education* (JCE) since 2014 and is Board Member of the Taiwan Association of Sociology of Education. Dr Yang got his degree at National Taiwan Normal University (NTNU) in 1998 and his recent research interests are cultural studies, philosophy of technology, media literacy education, teacher education, comparative education, philosophy of education and sociology of education.

Shen-Keng Yang, whose PhD is from Athens University, Greece, is currently Chair Professor at National Taiwan Normal University and one of the Life-Long

National Chair Professors selected by the Ministry of Education, Taiwan. He has served as President of the Chinese Comparative Education Society-Taipei (1983–1985, 1995–1996, 1997–1999, 2005–2007, 2007–2008), China Education Society (Taipei) (1990–1992), Vice-President of Comparative Education Society of Asia (2001–2005) and Vice-President of National Chung Cheng University (2006–2007) in Chiayi, Taiwan. His main publications include *Comparison, Understanding and Teacher Education in International Perspective, EinevergleichedeStudiezurTheorie der MestotesbeiAristotles und Konfuzius, Theories of Sciences and Development of Educational Sciences* (in Chinese) and four more books. He has also authored/co-authored or edited more than 30 books and more than 200 research articles, book chapters, monographs and technical reports on comparative education, teacher education and philosophy of education.

Foreword

Teachers and their education/training are key components of high-quality education for fostering not only sound individual person formation, but also social, economic and political development and thus leading to world peace. In view of the crucial role of teachers in developing humanity to a perfect ideal, international agencies and many countries in the world put the enhancement of teacher quality as their policy priorities. In the 1996 UNESCO Special Intergovernmental Conference on the Status of Teachers, a resolution was passed to acknowledge the teachers' professional status and their right to participate in professional discourses. UNESCO further launched its *UNESCO Strategy on Teachers, 2012–2015* in 2012 aiming to promote teachers' quality through setting up professional standards. For improving teacher's quality in European countries, the European Union established Teacher Education Policy in Europe Network which held annual conferences in 2009 and 2010 with the themes of Quality in Teacher Education and Developing Quality Cultures in Teacher Education respectively. The OECD published *Teachers for the 21st Century: Using Evaluation to Improve Teaching* proposing to set up professional standards framework for managing teacher qualities.

For guaranteeing high quality of teachers, many countries exert their state powers in regulating teacher education in various ways. In some countries, e.g. France, Germany, the state power intervenes in the teacher education institutional organization, curriculum design, even in the teachers state exam and their recruitment. In other countries, e.g. the UK and the USA, the state's power in regulating teacher education is not as strong as that in France and Germany. The state in the UK and the USA has power only in accrediting teacher education programs and licensing teachers. Recently most countries in the world strengthen their state powers in monitoring education, specifically teacher education, in order to outstrip the rivals in the highly competitive arena of international social, political and economic development.

Concomitant to the centralized tendency of state-controlled teacher education, there emerged also international moves of market-driven teacher training. The neoliberalism has recently dominated teacher education discourse. The neoliberals deem education and teacher education as services and products which can be traded in the marketplace. Deregulation in teacher education is thus required to promote competition among higher education institutions, private for-profit training agencies and school districts.

The pendulum swinging between strict state control and free marketization in teacher education can be observed also in Taiwan. Teacher education was thought to be one of the most important spiritual national defense force under the Martial Law, which was promulgated in 1949 when the government of the Republic of China moved its site to Taiwan after military defeat. The teacher education, from institutional organizations, training programs, practicum to recruitment and in-service training, was under strict state control in order to strengthen nationalism and patriotism. After the lift of Martial Law in 1987, various social forces pressed for pluralizing and diversifying teacher education. Different kinds of teacher education theories and various alternative teacher training programs were introduced in Taiwan. Diversity and competitiveness of teacher education theories, institutes and programs between universities had been further strengthened, for the market-driven logic and neoliberal "deregulation" ideology had been interwoven in the discourses of the 1996 Final Consultation Report for Education Reform and the 2002 Ammended Teacher Education Act. Nevertheless, the government had never given up its responsibility to maintain teacher quality at the highest possible level. The government of Taiwan had initiated and launched many policy strategies to raise professional standards even confronting many servere challenges from different social forces and stakeholders.

As Honorary Professor at National Taiwan Normal University and former Minister of Education, Taiwan (2009-2012), I had not only studied, but also involved myself personally in the initiation and enactment of teacher education reform in Taiwan. I am very confident that I have a very clear picture of Taiwan teacher education. After reading the drafts, I found that the analysis: of different aspects of teacher education in the chapters of this book are much more profound and penetrating than I imagined. This is perhaps due to the fact that most of the authors of this book belong to a joint research group rich in the experience of teacher education studies leaded by Prof. Shen-Keng Yang and Prof. Jia-li Huang. The research group had jointly done many cooperative research projects financed by the Ministry of Science and Technology since 1992. The studied results have been published in the following books: *A Comparison of Probationary Teacher System in Various Countries* (1994), *Systems of Teacher's In-Service Education in Different Countries* (2001), *The Development of Teacher's Professional Organizations and Professional Rights in Different Countries* (2003), *Systems of Teacher Quality Management in Various Countries* (2008) and *Institutional Organizations of Teacher Education and Teacher's Quality in Different Countries* (2011). In addition, most of the authors in this book have been involved in policy making consultation and practice of teacher education. Some of the authors were the members of Ministrial-level Committee of Teacher Education Review. The editor-in-chief Professor Shen-Keng Yang is life-long National Chair Professor selected by the Ministry of Education who has been involved many times in the consultation work of teacher education.

Prof. Jia-li Huang, another editor-in-chief, as section chief of the Department of Teacher Education and Teacher Practicum at Taiwan Normal University and Deputy Secretary-General of the Chinese Teacher Education Society, Taipei, ROC has rich experience in supervising student teachers. She participated also in the drafting of the important teacher education policy document White Book of Teacher Education in ROC issued in 2012. The authors' profound studies in teacher education and their rich experiences in teacher education practice converge in the writing of this book and thus make it very valuable for those who wish to understand the uniqueness of Taiwanese teacher education for international reference. Based upon the above-mentioned observation, I strongly recommend this book to the international audience of teacher education researchers, policy-makers and practitioners.

Ching-Ji Wu PhD

Former Minister of Education, Taiwan, ROC
Chancellor, Taiwan University of Education

Introduction

The formation of two approaches to teacher education

Chun-Ping Wang

Introduction

Globalization in the twenty-first century has offered humanity the promise of a bright new future, but it has also introduced numerous complex and often unforeseen challenges. Some of the more pressing topics related to globalization include the world's exponentially increasing population, low and sometimes falling birth rates in developed countries, modernization in developing countries, environmental crises and sustainable ecological development, advances in information technology, changing values in society, economic globalization and national competitive advantages, decentralization and localization of political power, and individualization and democratization of societies. The diverse nature of globalization has led to distinct effects, both positive and negative, on the nations of the world, and certain aspects of the impacts of globalization on the world's nations are more far-reaching than others. Some countries are focused on solving existing development issues; other countries, meanwhile, are investing their energy in sustainable development capabilities in order to stay competitive. Despite the disparities in the strategies different states are adopting to respond to globalization, their rationale when analyzing the issues is remarkably consistent. That is to say, these countries believe that improving the quality of teachers is the most fundamental strategy for dealing with the challenges of globalization. The emphasis placed on teacher quality is due to the enormous influence teachers exert on enhancing student learning efficacy, which in turn is directly linked to the quality and competitiveness of a nation's labor force and potential future development. The economy of a country will naturally become more competitive as the quality of its labor force improves (Wolhuter, 2011, pp. 68–76). It is clear that the quality of a nation's teachers plays a crucial role in determining its future prospects. This is why states around the world have by and large come to emphasize the quality of teachers and are continuing to ramp up efforts to reform their teacher education system. When examined more closely, we realize that teacher education systems and the icons of ideal teachers in each nation inevitably imply their unique context or social culture. Examples include the extremely famous "teachers as researchers" model in Finland, the standard-based model that emphasizes "professional knowledge and implementation ability" in the United States, the goal of cultivating "teachers that demonstrate new professionalism" in the United Kingdom, the framework of "Value-Skill-Knowledge" underlying the professionalism required of teachers in Singapore, and the requirement for the professional development of teachers to be capable of consolidating the sustainability of Hong Kong as a whole in global competition (Wang, 2014a). A stated aim in Taiwan's White Paper of Teacher Education released in 2012, "take advantage of your teaching assets to educate students over the lifetime", also follows the same representative logic. The White Paper emphasizes the core values of "teaching assets, responsibility, exquisiteness, and sustainability" in the hopes of building a teacher education system that is both highly professional and standards-based and rooted in the belief of ultimately realizing the vision of "nurturing mentors for a new era who provide world-class high-quality education" in the field of teacher education (Ministry of Education, 2012, p. 4).

In response to the economic globalization and political democratization trend, Taiwan's teacher education system has gone through extreme changes for the past nearly 20 years. It has transformed from the original planned model that was available to only a few educational institutions to the current market-oriented competitive model where ordinary universities are able to take part. In addition, in terms of the credentials required of teachers, Taiwan has evolved from its original concepts of "teacher education" (often anachronistically referred to as "normal education") and "competence-based" concepts to more broadly encompass a standards-based set of requirements for teachers. When compared with other major Asian states, Taiwan certainly has its own unique background and features. For example, although Japan, Korea, Singapore, and Hong Kong all have declining birth rates, the issue is particularly severe in Taiwan. Taiwan's aging society is accordingly impacting its school governance, distribution of educational resources, and control over the supply and demand of teachers. There is no hiding the fact that despite the contextual uniqueness in the reform of Taiwan's teacher education system, reform measures should serve as a valuable reference to other countries. This book collects advanced discussions about the experience and issues in Taiwan from scholars investigating the local teacher education from perspectives such as the development history of teacher education, important changes to policies and regulations, important thoughts and theories affecting the reform of the teacher education system, adjustment of the organization in teacher educational institutions, planning of pre-service teacher education programs, establishment of the standards-based approach and professional teacher evaluation, teacher education and advanced strategic alliance.

Due to the transformation of teacher education in Taiwan from a state control model to a free market system, the centralized controlled pattern of planned education was completely adopted under the original system, ranging from the regulations governing the establishment of educational institutions, students screening system, planning of competence-based pre-service programs, to practicum and placement following graduation. Later, as a result of the lifting of

Martial Law and social democratization, the system in Taiwan switched toward marketization featuring open competition. Ordinary universities were able to take part in teacher education while the quality of teachers and talent was ensured and controlled through the mechanism of free competition. For the past few years, however, the teacher education system has been impacted by neo-liberalism and neo-professionalism in Taiwan. As such, the emphasis has gradually shifted toward standards and performance-based teachers' quality control strategies. In other words, unlike polarized state control and free market approaches on the same spectrum, a new trend of modifying toward the center has appeared. This article aims exactly to analyze the two approaches – state control and free market – which will serve as the reference framework in the issue analysis provided in papers under different titles herein.

Conceptual origin and transformation of the two approaches

In "Addresses to the German Nation", Johann Gottlieb Fichte asserted that the government must provide its people with new education given the contemporary moral turpitude and ethical corruption. That is, new education should be used as a means to re-gather the collective spirit of a nation state, instill self-awareness of obligations and responsibilities into its citizens, and accordingly accomplish the ideal of restoring Germanic culture, civil ethics, and national spirit. This is the only way that he believed for the life of the new generation to connect with true and eternal traditional spirit, to guide higher social order, and make restoration of the Deutschland nation possible (Moore, 2008, p. 36). In his publications entitled *Education and Sociology* and *Moral Education*, Émile Durkheim also expressed a similar idea of "connect with traditional spirit" as that indicated by Fichte. He believed that moral education should be defined as the "influence of a mature generation on one yet to be fully capable of living in society" because morals have to be a community of various specific norms. They are like dies with many determinant borders and each person's behavior is kept within these dies. Moral norms can be refrained because they themselves carry certain authoritative traits. Without these traits, there is no way they could be called "moral". In other words, moral norms are a form of order and nothing else. This is exactly why morals command people and accordingly contribute to the realization of disciplines throughout society (Durkheim, 1956, 1961). Simply put, regardless of whether it is to "gather the collective spirit of a nation state" or to "signify collective disciplines in society through moral education", the assertion actually reflects the functional "education – civic identity – state formation" link in education.

> The original function of educational systems was to cultivate social integration and cohesion, forging new notions of national citizenship and identity. This continued to be the case with the development of new nations since 1971 and among the old nations in periods of national crisis and war.
>
> (Green, 1997, p. 4)

There is a clear link between the emergence of teacher education (often still officially translated as "normal education" in Taiwan) and state formation by a specific ethnic group (i.e. education – civic identity – state formation). It is an extremely natural development when a nation state cultivates prospective teachers to promote national education. It not only helps enhance the quality of its people but also exercises the effect of gathering national awareness within the state. The history of Western education development shows that besides Prussia, which proactively promoted compulsory education in the early eighteenth century, French enlightenment thinkers in the mid-eighteenth century, such as Rolland and Condorcet, called for the establishment of a state education system. Elementary education was promoted in states such as Massachusetts of the US in the early nineteenth century and after the mid-nineteenth century in the United Kingdom. The establishment of elementary schools by the state quickly spawned an increasing demand for teachers. As a result, "normal schools" (teachers colleges) flourished in the mid-nineteenth century to educate a new wave of teachers to support elementary education (Cubberley, 1948; paraphrased quote from Peng, 2008, p. 81).

Without a doubt, education based on the concept of "eternal spirit and tradition" or "social moral values" always carries some semblance of ethnic nationalism. In other words, if education through standardized schooling is considered the most effective means of forming a nation state (e.g. training patriotic soldiers, strengthening national identity, or promoting national language, etc.) (Green, 1990, 1997; Green and Janmaat, 2011), then teacher education must be considered "a type of spiritual national defense over which the state maintains supreme control" (Lee, 2008, p. 57; Wang, 2011). In the case of Taiwan, Liu Mingchuan set up a "Normal School" (teachers college) during his term as provincial governor of Taiwan during the late Qing Dynasty. In 1895, Taiwan was ceded and became a colony of Japan because of the "Treaty of Shimonoseki" entered into by and between China and Japan after the defeat in the First Sino-Japanese War. The Normal School was abolished right after the Japanese came to Taiwan (Wang, 2014b). The Japanese government assigned Izawa Shuji to be the first head of the Department of Academic Affairs under the Office of the Governor General in Taiwan. He started to plan academic systems at respective levels in order to generalize elementary education. He also started to set up public schools in Taiwan for compulsory education in 1898 as well as teacher education in the following year. After the "Normal School Rules" was promulgated in 1919, public schools and teaching colleges in Taiwan were able to educate Taiwanese people more systematically on new knowledge from the Western world and instill Japanese awareness in Taiwanese (Lee, 1997; Wu, 1983). A review of the ruling policy adopted in Taiwan during the Japanese colonial period reveals that Japanese language and "ethics-based character building" classes accounted for a very high ratio of weekly hours in public education. The mission of such courses was clearly aimed at enhancing national identity (i.e. imperialization) (Tsurumi, 1977, pp. 133–45). Teachers who received their education at "normal schools" (e.g. junior teachers colleges) were of course under the full control of the Japanese colonial government.

After the end of World War II, and particularly the early period after the relocation of the Nationalist government in Taiwan, school education appeared to be another means of political correction to turn imperialization into Chinese identity and instill anti-communism beliefs and patriotic values. After the Nationalist government took over Taiwan in 1945, it set up the Governing Council under the Province of Taiwan. The Council had jurisdiction over the Provincial Education Office that was in charge of education and thought reform. The education measures emphasized "promoting the Three Principles of the People and developing the nation's culture" (Huang, 1999, p. 20; Peng, 2008, p. 81). When the nine-year compulsory education was first implemented in 1967, for example, the contemporary government indicated, in the form of the president's draft order, that moral education was meant to "develop an active good student that will sufficiently demonstrate the moral culture of the Chinese nation and be a true Chinese". It goes without a doubt that although imperialization, re-localization of Chinese culture, or the subsequent Taiwanese awareness reflect the generational relay of culture and value in society, they also reflect the fact that national divine education and moral education are effective ruling tools. This is exactly the basis on which the state will naturally have complete control over an effective teacher education system that helps promote spiritual national defense.

Compared to the model of teacher education controlled entirely by the state, liberal marketization appears to present a drastically different policy rationalization mechanism and teacher education model (Bonal, 2003). This model generally originates from the culture and tradition of egoism as indicated in Adam Smith's *An Inquiry into the Nature and Causes of the Wealth of Nations*. Smith (2009, p. 15) indicated that the baker worked so hard every day to prepare pastries not because he was worried that people would have no bread to eat but because he needed to make money. It completely portrays the nature of humanity to pursue self-interest. Smith first introduced the theory of modern economics (now known as classical economics) in his book *An Inquiry into the Nature and Causes of the Wealth of Nations*. Later, in the nineteenth century, Alfred Marshall further expounded on Smith's theories and models to establish neoclassical economics. Both of these pioneering economists asserted that the market should be considered "an open field" consisting of numerous sovereign enterprises or individuals and that only when the market price of a certain item could be determined by adjusting supply and demand could it be completely open. As far as the interaction between a state and a market is concerned, classical economists hold that the "invisible hand", that is the supply and demand mechanism, on the market should be empowered to determine the price of an item.

Although the term "free market" is a popular concept and believed by most to be able to bring about happiness (Wringe, 1994), its full implementation can cause a high centralization of capital and even lead to monopolized markets. In the panic triggered by the Great Depression in 1930, for example, liberalism emphasized in classical economics made unemployment even worse. As a result, in as early as 1920 John Maynard Keynes and other scholars indicated that the market of a capitalist economy will eventually result in sluggishness. In other words, governments must relinquish their original free market policies and instead seek to proactively take responsibility for regulating market operations and guiding economic development. Simply put, Keynes reversed the relationship between a state and a market, that is governments must adopt the perspective of planned economy and change their classical economics perspective to the "large state-small market" one. Basically, Keynes' perspective challenged the classical liberalism theory with socialism. In other words, it is not beyond our imagination that the "large state-small market" approach would solicit the criticism of excessive control of the state machine over its people and the market. As such, Friedrich A. von Hayek and Milton Friedman switched toward neo-liberalism; they held that socialism-planned economy featuring state ownership or centralization should be abandoned, which, however, does not equal the return to the free stance typical of classical liberalism. Compared to these two theories, neo-liberalism was based on the belief that the government's responsibility was only to accomplish the goal of maintaining an ultimate proactive and effective market mechanism through tax reduction, reduced government expenditure, and streamlined administration, among others. Neo-liberalism defines the relationship between a government and a market as that between a large market and a small yet capable government, the keynote of neo-liberalism.

Margaret Thatcher, one of the most dominant figures in the UK's Conservative Party, took office in 1979 and immediately adopted the neo-liberalism policy. On the one hand, she cut taxes, reduced government expenditure, and controlled monetary supply in an effort to inhibit inflation; on the other hand, she included labor as part of her social welfare policy in order to compensate for the low wage on the labor market through the social security system. She also tried to bring down capitalist production costs and increase employment. Ronald Reagan also promoted investment and the willingness to work through tax reduction and streamlined administrative efficiency, initiated decentralization, and reduced social welfare expenditure, the three policies to accordingly realize a "small and efficient government" in 1981 (Dai, 2001, pp. 313–14). Unlike the state-control model, marketization means that the characteristics of a market mechanism are demonstrated through the Law of Demand between consumption and production, external free competition, and internal quality improvement under the free economic system (Gai, 2004). In other words, the developments in the US and the UK obviously demonstrated market-state governance characteristics and the changes to education policies and systems compared to the welfare-state governance model (Ainley, 2004). From the perspective of macroeconomics, when the government adopts practices such as deregulation, de-monopolization, privatization and de-nationalization, school education and teacher education systems will develop toward perfect competition under the leadership of the government. In addition, when looked at from the marketing concept, education is commoditized; that is, with consumers at the heart of organizational production and distribution, the quality of education must be determined through market segmentation, product position, selling price, and distribution channel, and should be based on how many needs of consumers are fulfilled (Gai, 2004, p. 39; Mok and Lo, 2001, p. 336; Pollitt, 1993; Dai, 1999, pp. 235–36).

Because under the state-control model, state nation spirit or collective moral norms in society are often adopted as education objectives, objective setting as such must mean public goods. Public goods, however, are unlike private goods or profitable commodities in nature (Tooley, 1994). In other words, the so-called neo-liberalism follows the operating principle of market competition and individual selection freedom (Apple, 2006, p. 11; Huang, 2013, p. 47) in order to turn education from original public goods to be completely private (Zeichner, 2008, p. 12). The lifting of government control is of course the only way to maintain transparency of the market mechanism and protect the equal rights of people to pursue self-interests. As indicated in the White Paper of Education published by the Ministry of Taiwan in February 1995 or the four issues of the Advisory Report between April 1995 and December 1996, education reforms in Taiwan exactly resemble the developments in Europe, America, and Japan and also followed the operating logic of marketization (Dai, 1999, p. 245). Ever since the government of Taiwan lifted Martial Law and began promoting new educational reforms one after the other, the underlying concept has shifted away from the previous state control toward marketization which is typical of neo-liberalism. The most important belief behind deregulation of education in the very beginning, for example, was not just a passive principle to prevent authoritarianism from interfering with education in an inappropriate way but also a reminder that the relationship among the state, market, and education should be reviewed proactively, with market freedom as the premise or paramount value based on the proactive assertion that the state should minimize its intervention with education affairs (Chu and Dai, 1996).

Methodological foundations for the two approaches and the establishment of a comparative framework

These two approaches are based on totally different foundations, compared to the state-control model, which pursues educational public goods, such as national spirit or collective moral norms, but the market orientation of neo-liberalism, on the other hand, follows the operating rules of market competition and individual free choice (Apple, 2006, p. 11; Huang, 2013, p. 47). Therefore, the logic of neo-liberalism reallocates education from being a public good to a private good (Zeichner, 2008, p. 12). The lifting of government control is of course the only way to maintain transparency of the market mechanism and protect the equal rights of people to pursue self-interests.

Teacher education in Taiwan is based on the Normal Education Law promulgated in 1979. The Law specifically consolidated the unified teacher education system and protected the employment of students who graduated from so-called "normal schools" (Lee, 2001, pp. 124–25). Saying that the education system was "unified" merely meant that "normal schools" and institutions were able to cultivate teachers to support elementary and high-school education. The government established these institutions for educating new teachers for the express purpose of implementing compulsory education as laid out in the "Three Principles of the People" established by Dr Sun Yat-sen (National Construction and Planning Committee, 1970, p. 31). The unified teacher education model lasted for quite some time. After Martial Law was lifted in Taiwan in 1987, normal education that was originally reputed as "spiritual national defense" was ridiculed as a mechanism for exclusivity and creating a monopoly. To change the existing teaching structure and break the monopolized and exclusive normal system, the Legislative Yuan approved the Teacher Education Act in 1994. The Act marked the fact that the unified, closed, controlled, and state-sponsored teacher education policy under the Normal Education Law was officially replaced by the new pluralistic, open, liberal, and self-sponsored policy (Ministry of Education, 2010, 2012).

To better understand the feasibility of the methods for understanding human social behavior, we can refer to the concept of the "ideal type" as put forward by Max Weber in his *Basic Concepts in Sociology*. Weber believed that the ideal type was a model created through experiential observation and logical hypotheses. It is like an ideal scale that helps us gain greater understanding of the subject being observed. From the perspective of social action, on the other hand, Talcott Parsons believed that action taken by players in the social system is selective between pattern alternatives of value orientation, that is the pattern variables by Parsons' definition. An overview of the two approaches to teacher education in Taiwan as mentioned in the foregoing, that is state control and market orientation, reveals that they are also concept-oriented spectral segments (see Figure 0.1).

- *Public good vs private interest.* If it is determined that the aim of the teacher education system is to achieve a social function for maintaining cultural values and national traditions and teachers are expected to serve as highly moral "clergies" then it follows that "restoring the national spirit" or "creating a better nation through better teachers" will be the ideals of the teacher education system. If teachers are considered purely an occupation intended to serve their own interests, teachers of course are entitled to negotiate their working conditions and reasonable treatment. This is about protecting private interests. It has nothing to do with moral issues.
- *Closed system vs open system.* If only a few schools (such as "normal schools") are in charge of cultivating teachers, the minority chartered system is closed. If ordinary universities can decide on their own if they want to devote to the development of teachers, the system is pluralistic and competitive.
- *Socialism (conservatism) vs (neo-)liberalism.* When the pursuit of common goods or overall social welfare is at the core of the operation of the overall teacher education system, it is determined that social interests are placed higher than individual interests; this is socialism or conservatism. If one's efforts and contributions are used to evaluate the value or status, and

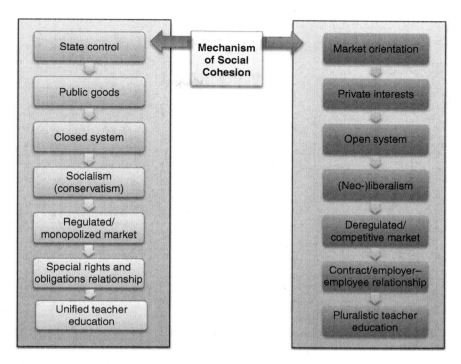

Figure 0.1 Comparison of the two approaches to teacher education

standards are established through reasonable procedures accordingly, and the standards are used to evaluate individual professional performance, this is realizing (neo-)liberalism.

- *Regulated/monopolized market vs de-regulated/competitive market.* If teachers are trained under the planned education model and regulatory establishment, demand and supply on the market, screening, training, and placement are all strictly controlled by the government, the teacher education model is of the oligopoly market type and is, in other words, completely controlled by a few "normal schools". If system-related regulations are lifted and competitive teachers are selected completely through the free market mechanism, this meets the principle of the free market approach.
- *Special rights and obligations relationship vs contract employer–employee relationship.* If teachers are considered quasi-civil servants, the relationship between teachers and the state is like that between military people or public servants and the state. Teachers are protected by special laws and regulations and are entitled to special benefits and treatment. They are, however, also assigned special obligations at the same time; they have to be absolutely loyal to the state, are prevented from going on strike, or are not entitled to

free association, for example. Teachers in the special rights and obligations relationship are often required in order to implement state control. If the relationship between teachers and schools (or the government) is considered simply as that between the employer and the employee, working requirements and protection of rights for teachers can only be ensured through a private contract. In other words, it is simply a contract relationship.

- *Unified normal education vs pluralistic teacher education.* The unified normal education in the past in Taiwan was more like the state-control model and the current pluralistic teacher education is relatively similar to the market-oriented model in either the set social functionality, basic ideas about systematic operation, systematic control, and extent of monopoly.

In summary, teacher education implemented in the past in Taiwan consisted of planned, state-sponsored education with the highly codified mission of passing down common goods in society. The current teacher education system, on the other hand, aims to attract the most outstanding talent to devote themselves to education through the marketized free competition mechanism. Obviously, the former appears to be closed and monopolized due to its planned education nature while the latter is open and competitive because of the marketization mechanism. In terms of the difference in the role of teachers, teachers are protected as quasi-civil servants because of the special rights and obligations relationship if the supply and demand of teachers at schools is completely controlled by the state. On the contrary, if the government does not adopt the state-sponsored teacher education model but lets the market decide the supply and demand of teachers, the relationship between teachers and the government will become a contract relationship similar to that which exists between an employer and an employee.

Orientation and challenges facing Taiwan in the context of globalization

Unquestionably, although neo-liberalism is an effective strategy for dealing with the challenges of globalization (Furlong, 2013), neo-liberalism greatly increases the function of individualism. Because market logic is highly individual, particularly in terms of success which is considered a facet of personal accomplishment, it reflects a high performance-oriented principle or characteristics of social Darwinism. In addition, the concepts of neo-liberalism are internalized as a personal philosophy of life, e.g. individualism, competitiveness, efficacy, and self-enhancement, by most members through education. These values, however, are likely to offset common goods in society (Chiang, 2012, p. 46). In other words, it is inevitable that the value of marketization is unable to encompass all civic virtues and will also limit personal autonomy (McLaughlin, 1994). It is emphasized that the competitive efficacy of marketization is without a doubt white-washing the ethical challenges inherent in the notion of social Darwinism (Buchanan, 1985) and will force teachers to be tool-oriented since operating efficacy is used as a means of control (Ball, 2003). When contrasting the two models of state control and market orientation, the teacher education mechanism in Taiwan seems to completely abandon the original normal education tradition and completely welcome the free market model, that is a movement from unified education to diverse sources of teachers. The facts, however, are not so straightforward.

In terms of a free labor market, during early debates over whether or not a market-oriented reform policy should be adopted, scholars indicated that – if teachers are "available on the open market" – high-quality teachers would more likely be attracted to work for private enterprises because the latter tend to offer better treatment (i.e. higher salary and benefits) during economically prosperous times. However, because such circumstances would compromise the quality of teachers or result in insufficient labor or resources, it was determined that allowing teachers to be employed on the open market could indirectly result in a range of latent dangers (Liu, 1990, pp. 5–6). It is fortunate that Taiwan has not succumbed to an "educational brain drain" of its outstanding teachers being lost to private enterprises. Nevertheless, Taiwan's notoriously low birth rate has resulted in a drastic decline in the demand for teachers. A stagnant market naturally results in supply exceeding demand. Faced with this difficulty, despite the claim that the teacher education model in Taiwan is still technically based on the market-oriented model, the Teacher Education Act still contains detailed requirements with regard to the configuration of education programs, curriculum planning, and teacher certification which reveals that the state still maintains strict control over the operation of the market for employing teachers (Lee, 2008, p. 57).

Even if Taiwan's Ministry of Education were to repeatedly emphasize that it would continue to possess a diverse source of teachers and would only adjust its education policy to maintain good quality and an adequate quantity, the marketization mechanism and unified education standards in fact would not necessarily lead to enhancing the quality of teachers. Moreover, it would be dangerous to brashly modify the education policy without giving serious consideration to the underlying issues of marketization and unified standards (Apple, 2001; Cochran-Smith, 2005). Marketization policies such as school selection by parents and inter-school competition would result in hierarchical opposition among students and schools being tagged for their level (Ball, 1993). Hence, we can clearly see that the assertion of "adequate quantity and exquisite quality" as part of teacher education policies in Taiwan at least indicates that education policies are no longer based on the traditional "large market – small state" free market principle. In other words, the original "diverse sources of teaching talent" market principle is no longer maintained. Perhaps a more apt description would be to say that, despite the fact that the value of marketization has not been wholly abandoned, the current form of teacher education in Taiwan no longer comprises a wholly competitive market. Furthermore, to address the declining reputation of teachers and the criticism that the newest generation of teachers are not competent enough, the return to the teaching culture and tradition emphasizing "stricter teachers", "respect for teachers", and "educating with love" was proposed in the

White Paper of Teacher Education released in 2012 to emphasize that teaching should be looked at as a cause instead of an option on the job market (Wang, 2014a). Under the mainstream force of neo-liberalism, current teacher education policies in Taiwan not only reflect neo-conservatism but also exercise the re-regulation effect on the state-control approach in the name of professional labor quality management as supported by the framework for standards-based education. Simply put, from the era of Dutch rule to the Japanese colonial period and finally to the relocation of the Nationalist Party in Taiwan after World War II, the teacher education system in Taiwan more or less remained entirely state-controlled, and the situation did not change until the 1990s. If the Teacher Education Act approved in 1994 represents a new turn of events, then the "relaxation" idea adopted in the very beginning – despite the fact that it is a standard saying for marketization – is of course impacted by globalization and the influence of neo-liberalism. To address the serious imbalances in the supply and demand of teaching talent in an open market, the government later established institutional evaluation, certification, and exit mechanisms as part of its dismantling efforts. In other words, the government retains its administrative rights over the review of educational institutions' programs and teaching certification while at the same time starting to develop the "standards-based" approach in order to accomplish total quality control in the professional career development of teachers. It is clear that aside from the state-control approach, the teacher education system in Taiwan, despite having ostensibly undergone liberalization, has not completely followed the free market approach, but is rather still in a trial-and-error stage. In this regard, Taiwan remains focused on adjusting its approach to education in order to achieve a more balanced solution that will satisfy all perspectives of society.

References

Ainley, P. (2004) "The new 'market-state' and education," *Journal of Education Policy*, 19 (4): 497–514.

Apple, M. W. (2001) "Markets, standards, teaching and teacher education," *Journal of Teacher Education*, 52 (3): 182–96.

Apple, M. W. (2006) *Educating the 'Right' Way: Markets, Standards, God, and Inequality*. New York: Routledge.

Ball, S. J. (1993) "Education markets, choice and social class: the market as a class strategy in the UK and USA," *British Journal of Sociology of Education*, 14 (1): 3–19.

Ball, S. J. (2003) "The teacher's soul and the terrors of performativity," *Journal of Education Policy*, 18 (2): 215–28.

Bonal, X. (2003) "The neoliberal educational agenda and the legitimation crisis: old and new strategies," *British Journal of Sociology of Education*, 24 (2): 159–75.

Buchanan, A. (1985) *Ethics, Efficiency, and the Market*. Oxford: Clarendon Press.

Chiang, T. H. (2012) "The impact of neoliberalism on the development and management models of higher education", *Tsinghua University Education Research*, 33 (4): 39–46 (in Chinese).

Chu, C. and Dai, H. (1996) *Educational Deregulation*. Taipei: Yuan-Liou Publishing (in Chinese).
Cochran-Smith, M. (2005) "The new teacher education: for better or for worse?" *Educational Researcher*, 34 (7): 3–17.
Cubberley, E. P. (1948) *The History of Education*. London: Constable.
Dai, X. X. (1999) "Market orientation and its impact on higher education," *Journal of Education Research*, 42: 233–54 (in Chinese).
Dai, X. X. (2001) "Globalization and changes in the relationship between nation and the market: the context of the marketization of higher education," *Journal of Education Research*, 47: 301–28 (in Chinese).
Durkheim, E. (1956) *Education and Sociology*. Glencore, NY: Free Press.
Durkheim, E. (1961) *Moral Education*. Glencore, NY: Free Press.
Furlong, J. (2013) *Education: An Anatomy of the Discipline: Rescuing the University Project?* London: Routledge.
Gai, C. S. (2004) "Examination of the marketization policies of Taiwan higher education", *Journal of Education Research*, 50 (2): 29–51 (in Chinese).
Green, A. (1990) *Education and State Formation: The Rise of Education Systems in England, France and the USA*. Basingstoke: Palgrave Macmillan.
Green, A. (1997) *Education, Globalization and the Nation State*. Basingstoke: Palgrave Macmillan.
Green, A. and Janmaat, J. G. (2011) *Regimes of Social Cohesion: Societies and the Crisis of Globalization*. Basingstoke: Palgrave Macmillan.
Huang, J. L. (2013) *The Idea and Practice of Standards-Based Teacher Education*. Taipei: National Taiwan Normal University Press (in Chinese).
Huang, Y. T. (1999) "Cultivation of National School Teachers in the Early Years of Taiwanese Retrocession (1945–1949)". Unpublished Master's thesis, Department of History, National Taiwan Normal University (in Chinese).
Lee, F. J. (2008) "Centralization and the education market: a study into England's transformation of the teacher education system," *Journal of Educational Research and Development*, 4 (1): 55–82 (in Chinese).
Lee, Y. H. (1997) *Normal Education System of Taiwan During the Japanese Colonial Period*. Taipei: SMC Publishing (in Chinese).
Lee, Y. H. (2001) *History of Taiwan Normal Education*. Taipei: SMC Publishing (in Chinese).
Liu, S. H. (1990) "Research on teacher education policies in Taiwan", *Educational Psychology and Research*, 13: 1–33 (in Chinese).
McLaughlin, T. H. (1994) "Politics, markets and schools: the central issues," in D. Bridges and T. H. McLaughlin (eds), *Education and the Market Place*. London: Falmer Press, pp. 153–68.
Ministry of Education (2010) *National Conference of Education Issue 7: Teacher Education and Professional Development*. Taipei: MOE (in Chinese).
Ministry of Education (2012) *White Paper of Teacher Education in R.O.C.: Promoting the Teaching Profession to Cultivate Future Talent*. Taipei: MOE (in Chinese).
Mok, K. H. and Lo, H. J. (2001) "The marketization and evolution of university management models: a comparative study of Hong Kong and Taiwan," *Journal of Education Research*, 47: 329–61 (in Chinese).
Moore, G. (2008) *Fichte: Addresses to the German Nation*. Cambridge: Cambridge University Press.
National Construction Planning Committee (1970) *How to Improve Teacher Education in Taiwan*. Taipei: National Construction and Planning Committee (in Chinese).

Peng, H. S. (2008) "Development of and challenges in teacher education in Taiwan after World War II (1946–2006)," *Journal of Education Research*, 165: 81–92 (in Chinese).

Pollitt, C. (1993) *Managerialism and the Public Sector: The Anglo-American Experience*. Oxford: Basil Blackwell.

Smith, A. (2009) *The Wealth of Nations*. Blacksburg, VA: Thrifty Books.

Tooley, J. (1994) "In defense of markets in educational provision," in D. Bridges and T. H. McLaughlin (eds), *Education and the Market Place*. London: Falmer Press, pp. 138–52.

Tsurumi, E. P. (1977) *Japanese Colonial Education in Taiwan, 1895–1945*. Cambridge, MA: Harvard University Press.

Wang, C. P. (2011) "An analysis of legitimate foundation of 'mentor model,'" *Educational Resources and Research*, 102: 19–44 (in Chinese).

Wang, C. P. (2014a) "Is it *the perfect recipe*? Or walking around blind? Issues in Taiwan's teacher training in comparison with the reform experiences of other nations," *Teacher Education Research*, 3: 20–38 (in Chinese).

Wang, C. P. (2014b) *Taipei Historical Documents Quarterly: Educational Administration, 1981–2011*. Taipei: Taipei City Archives Committee (in Chinese).

Wolhuter, C. (2011) "Globalization and teacher education," *Journal of Comparative Education*, 71: 55–82.

Wringe, C. (1994) "Market, values and education," in D. Bridges and T. H. McLaughlin (eds), *Education and the Market Place*. London: Falmer Press, pp. 105–16.

Wu, W. X. (1983) "A study of Taiwan teacher education under Japanese occupation," *Special Issue of the National Taiwan Normal University's Graduate Institute of History*, 8 (in Chinese).

Zeichner, K. (2008) "Neoliberal ideology and reform in American teacher education," trans. J. G. Liu, *Elementary Education*, 6 (4): 7–12 (in Chinese).

Part 1
Historical background

1 Development of teacher education policies in Taiwan during the Dutch and Spanish occupation, the Zheng and Qing period and the Japanese colonial period

Chung-Ming Liang

Introduction

In this chapter, the development of teacher education policies during the Dutch and Spanish occupation of Taiwan, the Kingdom of Tungning, the period of Qing dynasty rule of Taiwan and the Japanese colonial period is explicated. By using a historical research method and literature analysis, we explore the development of teacher education systems in Taiwan during the early modern period (approximately 320 years ago). The history of Taiwan from the early modern period of Taiwan until the end of the Second World War can be briefly described as follows. Taiwan was first occupied by the Dutch (38 years, 1624–62) and then the Spanish in the northern regions (17 years, 1626–42), collectively known as the Dutch and Spanish Era. The Zheng dynasty (i.e. the Kingdom of Tungning, 23 years, 1662–84) established by the rulership of Koxinga and his son during the Ming and Qing dynasties of China followed next. Taiwan was later reclaimed by the Qing dynasty (1684–1895), followed by the Japanese colonial rule (50 years, 1895–1945). In 1945, the Republic of Taiwan reclaimed the island. The teacher education system of Taiwan over these periods is explored.

In 1622, a Dutch fleet invaded Penghu and constructed fortresses, intending to conduct long-term occupation of Taiwan. The Fujian authorities of the Ming dynasty requested the Dutch to leave Penghu. In 1624, under the mediation of Li Dan, who was engaged in Sino-Japanese trade, the Dutch moved to Southern Taiwan and created Provintia at Tayouan, which is now Anping District, Tainan City (Tsau, 2010, p. 18). The Dutch established a cordial relationship with the local Siraya people at Sinckan, and missionaries actively undertook missionary work centred around Tainan. The Spanish were concerned about the Dutch occupation of Southern Taiwan and feared that the Dutch would influence trade with China and the Philippines. In 1626, a Spanish fleet moved north along the east coast of Taiwan and established strongholds in Northern Taiwan. In 1628, the Spanish constructed Santo Domingo. Consequently, the Spanish and Dutch occupied Northern and Southern Taiwan, respectively. In 1642, a Dutch fleet moved north, attacked Keelung, and ended the Spanish occupation of Northern Taiwan, which had lasted for 17 years. The Dutch claimed the Spanish assets and occupied all of Taiwan, and Taiwan became the base of Dutch trade in Asia (Kann, 2001, p. 12; Tsau, 2010, p. 19).

In 1661 (the late Ming dynasty), Koxinga directed his troops across the Taiwan Strait. In 1662, Koxinga and his troops defeated the troops of the Dutch East India Company stationed at Tayouan and began the 23-year (1662–84) rule of Taiwan under the Zheng family. The Qing dynasty contemporaneously imposed a ban on maritime activities (i.e. the Haijin order), causing Southern Taiwan to become the main focus of development. In the twentieth-third year of the reign of the Kangxi Emperor (1684), Shi Lang commanded the conquest of the Kingdom of Tungning and persuaded the Qing dynasty to include Taiwan in the territory of Qing (Cheng, 2000, p. 112). Tainan was still the political and economic centre of Taiwan, and Keelung remained undeveloped. Only aboriginal people and a small population of Han resided in Keelung (Cheng, 2000, p. 113). According to a report published in June 1684 by the Taiwan Affairs Office established by the Cabinet of Japan, the education system in Taiwan during this period included four official school systems, namely village-level schools (*xiangxue*), county-level schools (*xianxue*), city-level schools (*fuxue*) and government-level schools (*dufu*), as well as private schools such as free schools (*yixue*) and study schools (*shufang*). Children of high socio-economic status attended official schools while children of average socio-economic status attended free schools or study schools. Instructional materials comprised the Four Books and the Five Classics though no teacher education system existed.

After the Treaty of Shimonoseki was signed on 8 May 1895, Taiwan became a part of Japan. Following the First Sino-Japanese War, Izawa Shuji (1851–1917), who emphasised that nationalism as an educational philosophy was critical for governing, became the first Director of the Bureau of Educational Affairs of Taiwan. He served as the principal of Aichi Prefectural Normal School. From 1875 to 1878, he was dispatched to the United States to investigate the US teacher education system. After he returned to Taiwan, he actively implemented assimilation education policies based on nationalism, and established the direction and foundation of Japanese education in Taiwan.

Compared with the periods of Dutch and Spanish occupation, the Kingdom of Tungning and the rule of the Qing dynasty, the Japanese colonial period in Taiwan (approximately 50 years) yielded substantial educational results. According to the *Rapport sur Formose* by the French scholar Kann (2001), the Japanese school system not only prevented young people from being assimilated into Japan, but also prevented them from evading Japanese rule. Students learnt the basic skills required to be an assistant. This type of assistant was helpful and reliable, and therefore only elementary school education was developed. Taiwan, then known as Formosa, contained three types of schools: Japanese schools, local schools and aboriginal schools (Kann, 2001, p. 43). In addition, from 1895 (the military period), 12 Japanese language schools were founded, providing courses that lasted from six months to three years for the locals to learn the Japanese language.

This system required using interpreters as teachers. The schools did not produce favourable results for the first three years after founding. By 1898, numerous teachers at the Japanese schools understood and spoke the Formosan dialect and used the dialect to teach students. In addition, local people sufficiently understood the Japanese language and could help teachers. Language therefore provided tremendous convenience for education. Accordingly, 74 schools were founded based on Japanese elementary education (Kann, 2001, p. 44). "By 1906, 153 public schools for local residents existed, employing 620 teachers comprising 242 Japanese teachers and 387 local teachers, and enrolling 23,346 male students and 2,734 female students. Students were not required to pay tuition fees and could attend classes freely" (Kann, 2001, p. 44). Students in the normal school were divided into two groups. One group consisted of 50 Japanese people, who attended a 15-month programme and were aged between 18 and 25 years. The other group consisted of 158 local people, who attended a four-year programme and were aged between 14 and 23. The subjects taught included ethics, pedagogy, Chinese literature, Japanese, history, geography, arithmetic, geometry, algebra, physics, chemistry and natural history. In addition, calligraphy, painting, Formosan crops and physical education courses were also taught. Elective courses included arts and crafts and basic business concepts. Thirty sessions were conducted per week (Kann, 2001, pp. 44–5).

From the rule of the Qing dynasty in Taiwan until Taiwan became a part of Japan in 1895, approximately 5 per cent of Taiwanese children received elementary education. However, immediately before the end of the Second World War (1945), 70 per cent of Taiwanese children received elementary education (Yamamoto, 1999, p. 6), indicating that an excellent teacher education system was a critical factor in the increase in elementary education levels among Taiwanese children.

Teacher education policies during the Dutch and Spanish occupation of Taiwan

Teacher education policies during the Dutch occupation of Taiwan (1624–62)

In 1624, the Dutch occupied Southern Taiwan and erected a strong fort, Zeelandia, at Tayouan. Zeelandia became the ruling centre for the Dutch in Taiwan. The Dutch occupied Taiwan and used Zeelandia as a transhipment centre to obtain silk from China and conduct business with Japan. However, China did not permit the Dutch to enter into China for business trade. Therefore, using Tayouan as a base, the Dutch convinced Chinese merchant ships to transport silk to Taiwan for business trade. However, pirates were active in the Taiwan Strait. Japan ceased business with the Dutch because of the Hamada Yahyoue incident (Tsau, 2010, p. 24). Therefore, during the first several years after the Dutch occupied Taiwan, Taiwan could not successfully function as a transhipment centre.

In the 1630s, the pirate Zheng Zhilong yielded to the Ming dynasty. He became an admiral, defeated the pirates in the Taiwan Strait (Tsau, 2010, p. 23) and pacified those waters. Subsequently, Japan resumed doing business with the Dutch, and Chinese vessels continued to transport silk to Taiwan for business trade. Using Zeelandia as a transhipment base, the Dutch began conducting business with China, Japan and Batavia (now the capital of Indonesia, Jakarta, which was the headquarters of the Dutch East India Company in Asia). The Dutch East India Company, which controlled Taiwan, considered cultivation and education to be more effective than coercion and therefore adopted propaganda and education policies (Lee, 1970, p. 2). Concurrently, the Dutch East India Company attempted to gain the favor of indigenous leaders to educate residents through preaching and missionary work and control their thoughts and actions (Lin, 1977, p. 84). Administrative staff were placed in various regions, but no administrative officials were installed; a few troops were stationed in Taiwan and only simple equipment was provided. In addition, although people were designated as business members, referees, preachers, teachers or medical personnel, they were actually support personnel to the administrative staff, the numbers of which were insufficient (Lin, 1977, p. 84). The governor of Taiwan was responsible for the educational administration. Schools were associated with churches. A management policy that unified religion and education was adopted. Thus churches were responsible not only for missionary work, but also for implementing education practices (Lee, 1970, p. 2).

To smoothly conduct missionary work, Dutch missionaries first learnt the indigenous languages, used them to preach and translated various classics (Yamazaki and Nogami, 1990, p. 40). The policy adopted by the Dutch authorities was not to assimilate people but to educate them through religion. In addition, with religious education and Christian doctrines (i.e. respect for the Lord and loyalty to the country), the Dutch authorities aimed to rule the aboriginal people and make them recognise the Netherlands as their country (Lee, 1970, p. 3).

In 1636, the Dutch acquired Northern Taiwan, which was originally occupied by the Spanish, and began to erect schools. The Dutch founded the first school in Sinckan (near the current Tainan City). At first, teachers were selected from among soldiers, and the quality of teachers and teaching was uneven. Subsequently, the Dutch constructed community churches at Mujialiuwan (now Anding District, Tainan City), Soulangh (now Jiali District, Tainan City), Madou (now Madou District, Tainan City), Tavocan (now Sinhua District, Tainan City) and Tapuyen (now Lujhu District, Kaohsiung City)(Lee, 1970, pp. 1–2). Missionaries served as teachers, undertook missionary work and taught students. Initially, schools admitted students aged 10–13 years. The students were taught Roman characters, the Lord's Prayer, the Apostles' Creed, the Ten Commandments, the Doctrina Christiana, Morning Prayer, Evening Prayer, grace before meals, grace after meals, hymns and choruses, the Gospel of Matthew, the Gospel of John and the Catechism. Later, the Dutch also educated adults aged 20–30 years and used various languages to teach the indigenous people. Initially, Siraya was the main language used to teach the indigenous people (Lee, 1970, p. 1; Lin, 1977, p. 84; Nakamura, 2001, p. 114). Aboriginal people were then taught to use Roman letters to write their own languages. The documents written in Roman letters were called the Sinckan Manuscripts, in which aboriginal people in Taiwan used written words for the first time. According to the statistical data provided by the Dutch authorities, more than 400 children attended schools and approximately 1,849 people were baptised in 1639 (Lin, 1977, p. 86). In addition, approximately 1,000 couples received Christian weddings (Yamazaki and Nogami, 1990, p. 40).

In 1642, the Dutch designated aboriginal people who were knowledgeable about Christianity and literate as teachers to educate indigenous tribes. In addition, to train high-quality aboriginal teachers, the Dutch founded missionary schools at Sinckan and Soulangh and used part of the church as classrooms (Yamazaki and Nogami, 1990, p. 44). A summary of the establishment of schools is as follows (Lee, 1970, p. 1; Lin, 1977, p. 84):

1. The number of students per class was 30.
2. Students were 10–14 years old, orphans, gentle and possessed excellent memory and comprehension.
3. School staff included a principal, a vice principal and administrators.
4. Every Thursday was a school holiday.
5. Table 1.1 shows the courses taught in school.

The school rules were as follows (Lee, 1970):

1. Students must get up, dress, prepare and say grace before breakfast before sunrise.
2. Students must obtain permission before leaving school.
3. The vice principal cannot excessively punish students physically.
4. Students who do not return to school on time are punished.
5. Every month, two students are selected to record students' mistakes and occurrences of speaking languages other than Dutch within a specific period of time.

Table 1.1 Courses for Dutch missionary and teacher education in 1642

Time	Activity	Course content
0600–0800	Lesson	Catechism
0800–0900	Breakfast	Grace before and after meals
0900–1000	Lesson	Copybook
1000–1100	Lesson	Catechism
1200	Lunch	Grace before and after meals; translating and reading the Bible in turns
1400–1700	Lesson	Dutch
1800	Dinner	Grace before and after meals

Source: Yamazaki and Nogami (1990, p. 4) and Lee (1970, pp. 4–5).

6. The cleanliness of the school environment must be maintained; personal hygiene must be developed.
7. School workers responsible for cooking and laundry must be employed.

Although the aforementioned summary appeared simple, the education provided by teachers resembled missionary education. By 1643, the number of students increased to more than 600. Numerous students could write Roman characters fluently and could recite the Ten Commandments and the Lord's Prayer, among other prayers.

After the Dutch had governed Taiwan for more than 20 years, 300 or more aboriginal tribes in the plains of Taiwan were under the nominal rule of the Dutch. The Dutch governor in Taiwan convened the Landdag at Fort Provintia every year and gathered submissive tribal elders and leaders at a designated location to meet Dutch officials, who used the opportunity to announce decrees and to enquire about political achievements (Lin, 1977, p. 84). In every meeting, indigenous people were persuaded to demonstrate loyalty to the Dutch. Approximately 700–800 people participated in the meetings (Yamazaki and Nogami, 1990, pp. 40–3). However, numerous missionaries were originally soldiers and often exhibited illegal behaviour; therefore, indigenous people in Southern Taiwan gradually separated from the missionaries. In addition, in 1651, the director of the missionaries Hans Olhoff died from epidemic disease as did numerous missionaries. Consequently, no pastor was willing to undertake missionary work in Southern Taiwan. Although missionaries travelled to Southern Taiwan to undertake missionary work in turns by drawing lots, indoctrination work was not effectively performed (Lin, 1977, p. 88). However, by 1656, 6,078 people were familiar with the Catechism (Nakamura, 2001, p. 128). In 1657, a school was founded in Madou to train aboriginal teachers. The scale of this school was limited. Before the school was completely constructed, the Dutch were defeated by Koxinga and withdrew from Taiwan.

The Dutch began to occupy Taiwan in 1624 and yielded to Koxinga in 1662. During the 38-year occupation of Taiwan, the Dutch mainly undertook missionary work and trading operations. Several people still understood written words in the Roman alphabet 100 years after the Dutch withdrew from Taiwan. Documents written in the Roman alphabet during that period can currently be located (Lin, 1977, p. 87; Yamazaki and Nogami, 1990, p. 44).

Teacher education policies during the Spanish occupation of Taiwan (1626–42)

The Spanish occupied Taiwan because they intended to fight against the southward policy of Toyotomi Hideyoshi in Japan. In 1622, the Dutch dispatched a fleet to Penghu and constructed fortresses, intending to occupy Penghu for the long term. In 1624, the Dutch occupied Southern Taiwan and threatened the Spanish who occupied Luzon in the Philippines. The Spanish feared that the Dutch would interfere in the trade routes between Luzon and Japan and threaten the trade between China and the Philippines. In 1626, a Spanish fleet moved north along the eastern coast of Taiwan, bypassed Santiago, entered the port of Keelung, occupied Sheliao Island (now Hoping Island) and constructed San Salvador, effectively establishing a base in Northern Taiwan. In 1628, the Spanish occupied Hobe and constructed Santo Domingo (now Fort San Domingo).

Although the economic value of Taiwan was insignificant to the Spanish, Taiwan was a relay station and foothold for trade between China and the Philippines and for missionaries who secretly travelled to China and Japan. In 1626, a Spanish fleet departed from Luzon, landed in Sheliao Island, erected San Salvador at the southwest corner of the island and constructed fortresses to protect the port of Keelung. Aboriginal and Han streets existed on Sheliao Island and around Dashawan. People in Keelung frequently communicated with others overseas, causing Keelung to become a trade centre between Southern China and Manila, where 22 Spanish merchant ships once simultaneously entered Keelung harbour. After the Spanish occupied Northern Taiwan, they attempted to use the influence of religion to govern the aboriginal people and actively promoted Catholicism (Lin, 1977, p. 48; Yamazaki and Nogami, 1990, p. 44). They erected Catholic churches and schools in Keelung, Jinshan, Tamsui and Santiago, actively advocated Catholicism to aboriginal people and implemented indoctrination policies. Because religion was integrated with education, missionaries often served as teachers and administrative staff did not belong to a specific division but rather were associated with religion. In other words, school education was operated by the church (Lee, 1970, p. 2; Lin, 1977, p. 48; Yamazaki and Nogami, 1990, p. 44). Spanish priests used the Roman alphabet to record an aboriginal language spoken in Tamsui, studied the aboriginal language and compiled the renowned books *Tamsui Language and Vocabulary* (*Vocabulario de la lengua de los Indios Tanchui en Isla Hermosa*) and *Christian Doctrine in the Tamsui Language* (*Doctrina Cristiana en la lengua de los Indios Tanchui en Isla Hermosa*) (Nakamura, 2001). The priests also translated holy books about religion and Christian miracles, which were then used as missionary textbooks (Lee, 1970, p. 2). During the Spanish occupation of Taiwan, more than 4,000 aboriginal people were Catholics (Cheng, 2000, p. 65). The shogunate in Japan banned religion and practised isolationism strictly, only allowing Chinese and Dutch vessels in at specified locations in Japan for business trade while forbidding Spanish vessels from entering the territory of Japan. Accordingly, the Spanish were not permitted to trade with Japan or to undertake missionary work there (Tsau, 2010, p. 58). Because Taiwan could not be used as a trade base, the Spanish gradually disregarded the value of Taiwan and reduced the number of defensive soldiers stationed there. In 1636, aboriginal people in Tamsui fought against the Spanish and burned Fort Santo Domingo. In 1638, the Spanish left Tamsui. Concurrently, unrest in the Southern Philippines occurred and Spain redeployed most of the troops originally stationed in Taiwan to Luzon to pacify the area. The Dutch were aware of the weak defences in Northern Taiwan and in 1642 dispatched a fleet to attack Keelung and ended the 17 years of Spanish occupation of Northern Taiwan. Because the Spanish occupied Northern Taiwan primarily to undertake missionary work in China and Japan and to trade with China and Japan, they mainly propagated Christian doctrine to local residents and educated them. Consequently, numerous aboriginal people understood Spanish and Catholicism (Nakamura, 2001, p. 181).

Overall, the Spanish and Dutch did not actively develop an education system in Taiwan nor did they substantially contribute to teacher education. Instead, the Spanish and Dutch focused on operating businesses and undertaking missionary work, and considered business interests and missionary success crucial. Except for exploring gold and coal mines, the Spanish and Dutch did not contribute greatly to Taiwan.

Kingdom of Tungning and Qing dynasty rule of Taiwan

Kingdom of Tungning (1862–84)

In 1661, Koxinga directed troops to cross the Taiwan Strait. In 1662, he and his troops defeated the troops of the Dutch East India Company at Tayouan and commenced the Kingdom of Tungning, which lasted 23 years (1662–84). Koxinga was an intellectual and Confucian; he was concerned about education and established Chuxianguan (cultivation-of-sage house) in the 11th year of Emperor Shunzhi to cultivate talented people. Koxinga died before founding any schools. His son, Zheng Jing, commissioned Chen Yonghua to construct a temple and school and to educate talented people. In the 15th year of Emperor Kangxi (1666), a temple was erected and the Minglun Hall was established beside the temple to educate students. In addition, Zheng Jing ordered local authorities to establish schools. Children aged eight years were required to attend elementary school to learn classical literature and history. A county-level examination was conducted every year. Students who passed the county-level examination were admitted to a city-level school. Every three years, a city-level examination was conducted and those who passed the city-level examination were admitted to a college. College students were offered meal allowances each month. After studying for three years, college students undertook a major examination. Students who passed the major examination were designated government officials (Lee, 1970, p. 8; Lin, 1977, p. 159). It is likely that the education administration system during the Kingdom of Tungning originated from the system established during the Ming dynasty. Protocol officers were considered the highest authority for education administration. Colleges were responsible for education practices and examination work. Various local schools were designated for elementary education. City-level schools were secondary education institutions. Colleges were the highest institutions of learning in ancient times in China. The Imperial College of the Ming dynasty resembled a contemporary higher education institution, was the highest education institution in the Kingdom of Tungning and belonged to the protocol officer system. Figure 1.1 shows the education system.

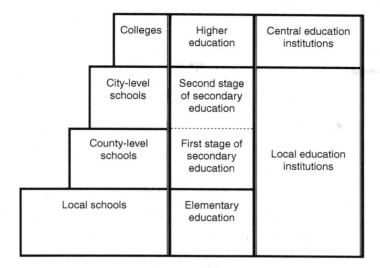

Figure 1.1 Education system during the Kingdom of Tungning
Adapted from Lin (1977, p. 160) and Lee (1970, p. 2).

During this period, scholars from mainland China or retired academics of the Ming dynasty as well as the gentry who sought refuge in Taiwan were invited to teach students (Lee, 1970, pp. 6–8).

Zheng's purpose for establishing schools during the Kingdom of Tungning can be understood by analysing the proposal of Chen Yonghua, who was the chairperson of the advisory committee during Zheng Jing's reign and who was responsible for the college. The proposal stated that Taiwan covered a vast territory, was far from China and contained a population of several hundreds of thousands of people. The people were simple, but if talented people were discovered, they could compete with Central China after being educated. Therefore the purpose of establishing schools was to teach people the meaning of shame and how to fight enemies: in other words, to teach people to learn from failure and thus learn how to fight the Qing dynasty and restore the Ming. The objective of education was to cultivate talented people for the Kingdom of Tungning and to improve and strengthen the kingdom (Lee, 1970, p. 6).

Qing dynasty rule of Taiwan (1684–1895)

In the 23rd year of Emperor Kangxi (1684), Zheng Keshuang (son of Zheng Jing) accepted the title given by the Qing dynasty and the Kingdom of Tungning (1662–84) ended (Lin, 1977, p. 240). Taiwan was then included in the territory of the Qing dynasty and was governed by Fujian Province. Because Taiwan was isolated from mainland China, a senior official in Taiwan occupied a concurrent position and served as an education governor responsible for education practices. Various senior officials were appointed as education governors, causing numerous changes to the education administration system. In the 15th year of Emperor Guangxu (1889), Taiwan became a province. Liu Mingchuan was designated the first Governor of Taiwan and was also responsible for education practices (Wang, 1978, p. 19). The education administration system comprised three levels: provincial, city and county. An education governor, who was ranked below the governor of Taiwan, was responsible for education practices at the provincial level. A chief city magistrate, ranked below the education governor, was responsible for city-level schools; teachers at city-level schools were called professors. The county magistrate was ranked below the chief city magistrate and was responsible for county-level schools. Teachers at county-level schools were called instructors (Lee, 1970, pp. 3, 14). According to the imperial examination system in the Qing dynasty, the imperial examination was conducted in the capital. The central government, located in the capital, managed higher education. Therefore, during the Qing dynasty, the highest education institutions in Taiwan were city-level schools, which were equivalent to contemporary secondary education institutions. Types of schools in Taiwan included city-level schools and academies, and county-level schools and academies. The level of an academy was between an official school and a village school. Academies compensated for the inadequacy of an official school. An academy was public or private and was established in a city, county or other region. Elementary education institutions included free schools, local schools, aboriginal local schools and study schools. Figure 1.2 shows the education system.

City-level and county-level schools were managed by the state. Academies, free schools, local schools and aboriginal local schools were public, private, semi-public or semi-private. All study schools were private. Free schools, study schools and local schools existed in various regions in Taiwan. Unlike current elementary education which aims to convey knowledge to children, the purpose of these schools was to help students prepare for the imperial examination

		(Beijing)	Higher education	Central education institutions
	Academies	City-level schools	Second stage of secondary education	Local education institutions
	Academies	County-level schools	First stage of secondary education	
Free schools	Local schools	Study schools	Elementary education	

Figure 1.2 Taiwanese education system during the Qing dynasty

(Lee, 1970, pp. 3, 16–17). Most professors at city-level schools were senior licentiates, people who had passed a triennial examination or people who passed the highest imperial examination (Lee, 1970, pp. 18–23).

During the reign of Emperor Tongzhi, theological colleges and schools were founded in Tainan and Tamsui because Dr James Laidlaw Maxwell (an English Presbyterian missionary), Pastor Hugh Ritchie, W. Campbell (a missionary), and George Leslie Mackay (a Canadian Presbyterian missionary) intended to cultivate missionaries. Subsequently, new-style education was initiated. In Taiwan, official new-style education began in the third year of Emperor Guangxu (1887) when Liu Mingchuan adopted a Western education system. New-style schools such as Western schools, telegraph schools, foreign schools (Wang, 1978, p. 20) and teacher schools (Wang, 2014, p. 1) were established to educate people about current affairs. In 1890, Liu Mingchuan resigned from his position because of illness and various Western schools were abolished by the Governor of Taiwan Shao Youlian (Lin, 1977, pp. 316–17; Wang, 1978, p. 21).

In 1895 (the 21st year of Emperor Guangxu), the Qing dynasty ceded Taiwan to Japan and ended its governance of Taiwan, which had lasted for more than 210 years. The education system of city- and county-level schools, academies and private local and free schools established for the imperial examination system was generally complete. Although Japan abolished city- and county-level schools and academies after occupying Taiwan, private study schools for elementary education still existed. According to the Japanese Governor General of Taiwan, in 1897 (the 30th year of the Meiji period), 1,127 study schools existed and 17,066 children attended a study school (i.e. 5 per cent of children of school age in Taiwan) (Wu, 1994, p. 65). Therefore, when the Qing Dynasty governed Taiwan, the education system in Taiwan was established mainly because of the imperial examination system that aimed to recruit talented people for the country. Because of this education system, limited results were achieved in elementary education. Study schools resembled private *terakoya* or *zyuku* (private teaching), widely established during the early Meiji period. Thus, during Japanese colonial rule of Taiwan, Japan also adopted a traditional policy and transformed private schools into public schools. Around the 31st year of the Meiji period, approximately 1,707 schools, which admitted 29,941 students, existed. Numerous students became prospective teachers in education centres or Japanese schools, and were offered government grants (10 maces for daily allowance and 5 maces for living allowance (Kaminuma, 1974, p. 289). The traditional policy helped Japan introduce the modern school education system into Taiwan.

Teacher education policies during the Japanese occupation of Taiwan

On 17 April 1895 (i.e. the 21st year of Emperor Guangxu and the 28th year of the Meiji period), the Treaty of Shimonoseki was ratified and Taiwan was ceded to Japan. By 1945, when Japan surrendered unconditionally, Japan had ruled Taiwan for 50 years. While Japan ruled Taiwan, Japan implemented an authoritarian and assimilationist colonial policy (Kobayashi, 1994, p. 227), which advocated that the government must be united with the people to produce homogeneous nationals (Chen, 2008, p. 11). On 17 June 1895, the inauguration of the first Governor General of Taiwan occurred in Taipei. The admiral Kabayama Sugenori (1837–1922) was designated as the first holder of that office. At the Civil Affairs Bureau, the Bureau of Educational Affairs was established. Izawa Shuji (1851–1917) was designated as the director of the bureau and founded a Japanese school. Izawa had studied in the United States during the early Meiji period and had served as the principal of Tokyo Higher Normal School. Izawa was a nationalist and advocated assimilating Taiwan into Japan and obeying the Mikado (Kobayashi, 1994, p. 228); he believed that this goal could be achieved through education (Komagome, 1994, p. 299). When Japan captured Taiwan in 1895, the teacher education system in Japan was thoroughly developed. Therefore, Japan was highly capable of formulating education policies and developing a teacher education system in Taiwan. According to previous experience in education, Japan believed that mental assimilation was the optimal method for ruling Taiwan (Kobayashi, 1994, p. 227). To popularise education in the Japanese colony of Taiwan, Japan designed two systems for teacher education policies. One system was the Japanese-school system. This system aimed to cultivate teachers in various fields. The other system was the normal-school system. The goal of this system was to cultivate teachers for elementary education. In addition, to recruit outstanding students and to cultivate excellent and loyal teachers, the Japanese government offered student grants. Accordingly, these teachers helped teach people Japanese and indoctrinate people into Japanese imperial ideology. These two systems existed simultaneously in the early stages but by 1919, these two systems were integrated into one teacher education system for cultivating teachers.

Teacher education during the Japanese-school period (1896–98)

At the beginning of the Japanese colonial period in Taiwan, Japan attempted to obtain agricultural products and mineral resources in Taiwan through economic development by adopting a coercion policy. To smoothly govern the Japanese colony of Taiwan, Japan developed education to a minimal degree and implemented the "assimilation and Kominka (the imperialisation of subject peoples)" policies (Ōkōuchi et al., 1973, p. 89; Yamamoto, 1999, p. 5). Izawa, who was the director of the Bureau of Educational Affairs of Taiwan, wrote a letter to Kabayama, the Japanese Governor General of Taiwan, proposing two ideas regarding education in Taiwan: (a) establishing a normal school at the place where the Governor General of Taiwan was located and establishing an affiliated exemplary elementary school; and (b) gradually establishing normal schools and affiliated exemplary elementary schools in various prefectures. In addition, Izawa stated that establishing a teacher education institute for providing six-month short-term training to candidates for principal and teaching positions of elementary schools in various regions was crucial (Compilation Committee for the History of Education, 1941, p. 535). Izawa immediately began to develop a teacher education program for establishing a Japanese school and education centre under the Governor General of Taiwan. In December 1895 (the 28th year of the Meiji period), Izawa also established a Japanese school (teacher training centre) in the building that belonged to the Chihshanyen Student Affairs Department. In January 1896, Izawa stipulated regulations for Japanese teachers (Compilation Committee for the History of Education, 1941, pp. 536–7), and afterwards returned to Japan. After returning to Japan, Izawa established a temporary branch office of the Bureau of Education Affairs at the Ministry of Education and recruited 36 Japanese teachers and nine students from a Japanese school. Izawa commissioned experts to investigate hygiene and first-aid methods as well as animal and plant research and collection methods, and to educate the participants. In addition, Izawa purchased teaching books and equipment. After completing preparation, Izawa, along with 13 teachers and 45 students, arrived in Taipei on 11 April.

According to Taiwan Governor School-System Royal Decree No. 94 announced on 31 March 1896 (the 29th year of the Meiji period), a Japanese school and a Japanese education centre were founded. The purpose of the Japanese school was to train Taiwanese people to become Japanese teachers and other related professionals (Compilation Committee for the History of Education, 1941, pp. 538–9). Following the announcement of the Taiwan Governor School System, the Chihshanyen School was renamed the "Chihshanyen School Affiliated with Japanese Schools" on 13 April and commenced operation on 15 April. On 21 May, the locations of 14 Japanese education centres were determined. Japanese education centres provided Japanese elementary education to Taiwanese people and offered two classes (A and B). In Class A, six-month Japanese express training was provided to Taiwanese adults aged 15 years or above. In Class B, a four-year elementary education programme was implemented to educate people aged between 8 and 15 years (Ōkōuchi et al., 1973, p. 90). Japanese education centres rapidly popularised the Japanese language in Taiwan, and Japanese schools cultivated teachers for Japanese education centres (Lee, 1981, p. 149). On 1 June, Chihshanyen School Affiliated with Japanese School was renamed the "First School Affiliated with Japanese Schools", and later produced teachers who specialised in the Japanese language. A graduation ceremony was held on 1 July. These new teachers became the first group of teachers to promote Japanese education in Taiwan (Compilation Committee for the History of Education, 1941, pp. 538–40).

On 25 September, the Regulations for Taiwanese Governor Japanese schools (Government Decree No. 38) were stipulated. The regulations defined the types of Japanese schools and their purposes (Chapter 1), school systems (Chapter 2), teaching summary and course levels (Chapter 3), admissions, withdrawals and attendance (Chapter 4), and examination and graduation (Chapter 5)

(Compilation Committee for the History of Education, 1941, pp. 538–9). Notable regulations included the following:

- The first regulation stipulated that a Japanese school must include a teacher education division and a language division, and must establish an affiliated school.
- The second regulation stipulated that the teacher education division of a Japanese school must cultivate native Taiwanese teachers for normal schools affiliated with Japanese education centres and principals or teachers for elementary schools, and must investigate general education methods in Taiwan.
- The third regulation stipulated that the language division of a Japanese school must teach Japanese and related dialects as deemed necessary.
- The fifth regulation stipulated that students admitted to the teacher education division must be Japanese people aged 18–30 years with a fourth-year high-school level or above education, and that students admitted to the language division must be Japanese people aged 15–25 years who graduated from advanced elementary schools or Taiwanese people aged 8–25 years who graduated from schools affiliated with Japanese schools or from Japanese education centres.
- The ninth regulation stipulated that students at the teacher education division must study for two years and students at the language division must study for three years.

Therefore, at the beginning of the Japanese colonial period in Taiwan, the first teacher training institution was a Japanese school. The teacher education division of the Japanese school was originally created to cultivate native Japanese teachers for the school affiliated with the Japanese school; the purpose of the language division was to cultivate both native Japanese and Taiwanese teachers and provide higher general education to Taiwanese people. On 27 September, the regulations for student allowances offered to stipendiary students at Taiwanese Governor Japanese schools and education centres (Government Decree No. 40) were stipulated. Students at Japanese schools and education centres received food allowances (25 maces per day for Japanese people and 10 maces per day for Taiwanese people) and living allowances (15 maces per day for Japanese people and 5 maces per day for Taiwanese people). In addition, Japanese students were offered travel and medical allowances and were provided clothing. The amounts of allowances were adjusted several times according to social development (Lee, 1981, pp. 814–25). The sixth school rule specified that the subjects for the teacher education division were ethics, education, Japanese, Chinese, native dialects, geography, history, mathematics, bookkeeping, science, music and gymnastics. Therefore students of the teacher education division, who were mainly Japanese students, were required to learn methods for teaching Japanese and to master Chinese and native dialects through which they communicated with local people to understand local customs.

The establishment of Japanese schools aimed to cultivate not only teachers for Japanese education centres but also various professionals. Japanese schools were the highest education institutions in Taiwan, and their purpose was mainly to cultivate native Japanese teachers (Compilation Committee for the History of Education, 1941, p. 572). Therefore the Regulations for Taiwanese Governor Japanese schools (Government Decree No. 38) were critical regulations for Japan for developing the teacher education system in Taiwan.

In 1898 (the 31st year of the Meiji period), Japanese education centres were integrated into the six-year public school system (Ōkōuchi et al., 1973, p. 90). In April 1898, according to the regulations for the third school affiliated with the Taiwanese Governor Japanese School, the branch school of the First Affiliated Girls' School was changed to the Third School Affiliated with a Japanese School, which included a general division and a crafts division, and recruited Taiwanese girls as students. The general division recruited female students aged 8–14 years and the study period was six years; the crafts division recruited female students aged 14–25 years and the study period was three years. Over half of graduates became teachers at public schools.

In March 1902 (the 35th year of the Meiji period), the Third School was renamed the "Second School Affiliated with a Japanese School". In April 1906 (the 39th year of the Meiji period), according to the regulations for the Second School Affiliated with the Taiwanese Governor Japanese School, the general division was abolished and teacher education, express teacher education and arts divisions were established. The study period was three years for the teacher education and arts divisions and two years for the express teacher education division. The teacher education and express teacher education divisions recruited students who were aged 14–25 years and had graduated from a public school or possessed a similar level of education. The arts division recruited students who were aged 13–25 years and completed four-year courses at a public school or possessed a similar level of education. The Second School became the main institution for cultivating female Taiwanese teachers. Therefore, in May 1910 (the 43rd year of the Meiji period), the Second School was renamed the "Affiliated Girls School" (Lee, 1981, pp. 2559–60).

Although the regulations regarding Japanese schools were modified and new regulations were formulated, general policies did not change. By 1918, a Japanese school was renamed as Taipei Normal School. After the Taiwan Education Decree and the Taiwan Governor Normal School system were announced on 1 April 1919 (the 8th year of the Taisho period), the Japanese-school system was officially abolished (Compilation Committee for the History of Education, 1941, p. 568). The Girls School Affiliated with a Japanese School was renamed "Taiwan Public Senior Girls General School", which was no longer affiliated with a Japanese school.

Normal-school system and teacher education (1899–1945)

In 1868, the Meiji Restoration started in Japan, and Japan implemented compulsory education shortly after. In 1872 (the 5th year of the Meiji period), the first Normal School for cultivating teachers was founded in Tokyo. Within a few years, seven national normal schools were established nationwide to cultivate teachers for teacher education institutions in various cities and prefectures. In 1879 (the 12th year of the Meiji period), Japan announced a revised Education Act, which specified that public normal schools must be established for various cities and prefectures. In 1880 (the 13th year of the Meiji period), Japan modified the Education Act and specified that various cities and prefectures must establish normal schools to cultivate teachers for elementary schools. In 1881 (the 14th year of the Meiji period), the guidelines for normal schools were formulated. In 1886 (the 19th year of the Meiji period), the Normal School Decree was announced, indicating that the normal school system was officially established in Japan. According to the Normal School Order, normal schools were classified into two types: advanced and general. An advanced normal school was supervised by the Ministry of Education and was located in Tokyo. General normal schools were established in various cities and prefectures. The graduates of general normal schools mainly served as principals or teachers in public elementary schools. The graduates of the advanced normal school mainly served as the principals or teachers of general normal schools. In addition, the advanced normal school contained male and female teacher education divisions. The male teacher education division admitted the graduates of general normal schools, the study period of this division being three years. The female teacher education division admitted those who completed two years of study at general normal schools, the study period for this division being four years. In 1890 (the 23rd year of the Meiji period), an advanced women's normal school was founded. In 1894 (the 27th year of the Meiji period), industrial teacher education and apprentice schools were established to cultivate teachers for industrial cram schools. Subsequently, an agricultural teacher education school affiliated with the University of Agriculture at Tokyo Imperial University, a business teacher education school affiliated with the Commercial Training School, and an industrial teacher education school affiliated with the Tokyo Technical School were founded (Hosoya et al., 1990, pp. 517–18). When the Meiji regime ruled Taiwan in 1895, the school system and the teacher education system in Japan were thoroughly developed. Japan rapidly applied its experience and methods to develop the school and teacher education systems in Taiwan.

Like most suzerains, the purpose of Japan's occupation of Taiwan was for political and economic interests. To achieve this goal, school education was the typical method for training dutiful and obedient citizens and workers.

As the teacher education system in Japan developed, the teacher education system in Taiwan also changed. In 1897 (the 30th year of the Meiji period), Japan announced the Normal School Order, and the development of the normal-school system advanced. In 1898 (the 31st year of the Meiji period), the Taiwan Education Act was announced, which mandated compulsory education for Taiwanese people; public schools were widely established and native Taiwanese teachers for public schools were trained. Consequently, normal schools started to be established (Lee, 1997, p. 8).

On 31 March 1899 (the 32nd year of the Meiji period), the Governor General of Taiwan announced the Taiwanese Governor Normal School System (Royal Decree No. 97) and stipulated that a Taiwanese Governor normal school was the place for cultivating teachers for Japanese education centres, public schools, study schools and free schools. In addition, the Taipei Normal School, Taichung Normal School and Tainan Normal School were established in Taipei, Taichung and Tainan, respectively (Compilation Committee for the History of Education, 1941, pp. 608–9). The teacher education system in Taiwan then began to cultivate teachers. On 12 April 1899, the Taiwanese Governor Normal School Rules (Government Decree No. 31) were announced and specified that normal schools must cultivate teachers for Japanese education centres and public schools. Accordingly, the normal-school system that originally cultivated native Japanese teachers was divided into the Japanese school teacher education division for cultivating native Japanese teachers and normal schools for cultivating native Taiwanese teachers. The courses for a normal school included ethics, Japanese, writing, reading, arithmetic, bookkeeping, geography, history, science, penmanship, music, gymnastics and pedagogy. The study period for normal schools was three years; these schools recruited students aged 18–25 years. The first semester began on 1 April of each year. The academic year ended on 31 March of each year. An academic year comprised three semesters (from 1 April to 10 July, from 1 September to 28 December 28 and from 4 January to 31 March). An academic year comprised 40 weeks (34 hours per week). Students attended classes for six hours per day. The number of students in a class was between 25 and 35 (Compilation Committee for the History of Education, 1941, pp. 610–11).

Because public schools did not develop as rapidly as expected, there appeared to be an excess of native Taiwanese teachers. In 1902 (the 35th year of the Meiji period), the Taipei and Taichung Normal Schools were closed. Students from these two normal schools were admitted to Japanese schools or the Tainan Normal School. By 1904 (the 37th year of the Meiji period), Tainan Normal School students were admitted to Class B of the teacher education division of Japanese schools. Normal schools for cultivating native Taiwanese teachers were closed and Japanese schools became the main teacher education institutions again (Compilation Committee for the History of Education, 1941, pp. 625–6).

During the Taisho period (1911–25), the education system in Taiwan progressed substantially. Taiwanese people were willing to receive education and the demand for public schools increased. In addition, because of the influence of democratic ideology, Taiwanese people were dissatisfied with Japan's application of racial segregation in education strategies for Japanese and Taiwanese people. To appease the escalating unrest of the Taiwanese people, the Governor General of Taiwan announced the Taiwan Education Act in 1919, stipulating that normal schools be institutions for implementing teacher education, and changed the Japanese school in Taipei to the Taipei Normal School, with other normal schools to be established later. The elementary school teacher education division of Japanese schools and the teacher education division of public schools were abolished. In addition, the Governor General of Taiwan announced the Normal

School Rules (Government Decree No. 23) and specified courses, rules, textbooks, critical events during academic years, guidelines for admission and withdrawal and punishment methods for normal schools. The fourth regulation stipulated that according to the Imperial Descript on Education, teachers with ethical capacity and dignity should be cultivated (Compilation Committee for the History of Education, 1941, p. 632). In addition, the regulations for providing student allowances to Taiwanese Governor normal school students (Japanese and Taiwanese students) were formulated. Accordingly, policies regarding the provision of tuition fees, accommodation fees, and meal and living allowances continued. However, an additional rule was included. If students were expelled from school because of misbehaviour or voluntarily withdrew from school, the students or their guarantors were required to repay tuition fees in full or in part. This rule encouraged normal school students to earnestly receive teacher education and comply with the regulations. Based on the data obtained several years before the surrender of Japan in the Second World War, Table 1.2 shows student allowances provided to normal school students during the Japanese colonial period in Taiwan.

As shown in Table 1.2, student allowances for normal school students were adjusted according to social development. Particularly at the end of the war, although student allowances did not substantially decrease, student allowances were flexibly allocated to students. As mentioned previously, Taiwanese people were unsatisfied with differential treatment of Japanese and Taiwanese people regarding the Japanese education system and normal-school system, and Taiwanese people did not necessarily enjoy their teaching jobs. However, living and economic conditions were extremely unfavourable for Taiwanese people;

Table 1.2 Student allowances provided to normal school students during the Japanese colonial period in Taiwan (unit: yen)

Type	Course type	1940	1941	1943	1944
Class A student allowances (Japanese students)	Preparatory course			≤ 300	
	Lecture course (3 years)	144	≤ 360	≤ 300	
	General course	140	≤ 300		
	Practical course	240	≤ 360		
	Research course	240	≤ 360	*Uncertain	
	Professional course			≤ 360	
	Lecture course (1 year)	240	≤ 360	≤ 360	
Class B student allowances (Taiwanese students)	Preparatory course			≤ 240	
	Lecture course	108	≤ 288	≤ 240	
	General course	108	≤ 240		
	Practical course	108	≤ 288		
	Research course	168	≤ 288	*Uncertain	
	Professional course			≤ 280	
	Lecture course (1 year)	168	≤ 288	≤ 280	
Youth Normal School					≤ 480

Source: Lee (1981, pp. 2198, 2214–15).

therefore, government grants, the job assignment system and secure income helped the normal-school system develop smoothly and attract outstanding Taiwanese students.

In 1922 (the 11th year of the Taisho period), the Taiwan Education Act and Normal School Rules were modified. In the same year, a lecture division on the teacher education course was established at Changhua Advanced Girls' School (now National Changhua Girls' Senior High School) to cultivate female teachers for public schools. Students who completed four years of study at an advanced girls' school or possessed a similar level of education were admitted to Changhua Advanced Girls' School, the study period being one year (Compilation Committee for the History of Education, 1941, p. 115; Lee, 1981, p. 2561). In 1928 (the 3rd year of the Showa period), Taipei First Normal School provided a girls' practical course division and the lecture course division was abolished. In 1944 (the 19th year of the Showa period), a compulsory youth school was established, and teachers for the youth school were required urgently. In April 1944, the Taiwanese Governor Normal School System was modified and Changhua Youth Normal School was established to cultivate teachers for youth schools. Changhua Youth Normal School recruited high-school graduates or students who possessed a similar education level, the study period being three years. In addition, because of the special requirements of Taiwan, a lecture division was provided for which the study period was one year (Lee, 1981, p. 2563). Because of insufficient funding, Changhua Youth Normal School did not possess school buildings and used other buildings temporarily. After Taiwan's retrocession, the Changhua Youth Normal School was the predecessor of the National Changhua University of Education (which was named the Taiwan Provincial College of Education in August 1971, renamed the National Taiwan College of Education in July 1980 and again renamed the National Changhua University of Education in August 1989) (Chong, 1993).

In March 1942 (the 17th year of the Showa period), the Taiwanese Governor School System was modified, a temporary teacher school affiliated with the Taipei Advanced School was founded and the regulations for the temporary teacher school affiliated with the Taipei Advanced School were announced. The temporary teacher school was created to cultivate teachers for high schools and advanced girls' schools affiliated with normal schools. Courses provided by the temporary teacher school included mathematics, physics and chemistry. The temporary teacher school admitted normal school or high-school graduates and the study period was three years (Lee, 1981, p. 2654). The Youth Normal School and the temporary teacher school also offered government grants and financial assistance to prospective teachers.

The Taiwanese normal-school system changed and developed according to the development of Taiwan society during the Japanese colonial period. The courses provided for teacher education and the study periods changed according to policy development and were flexibly adjusted according to time and location. Figure 1.3 shows the development of Japanese schools and normal schools and course types.

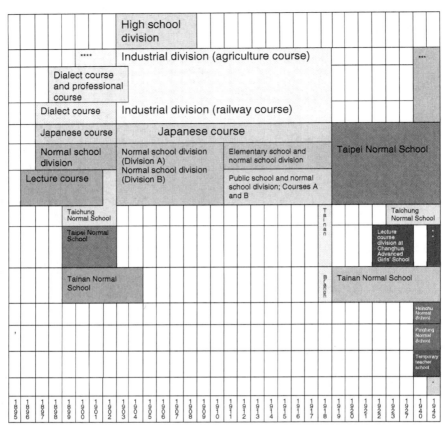

**** Railway course and telecommunications course
*** Taipei Second Normal School
** Changhua Normal School
* Youth Normal School

Figure 1.3 History of Japanese schools and normal schools

According to Figure 1.3, Japan required professionals in various fields and teachers for communicating, followed by the need to popularise the Japanese language and implement ideological education to rapidly develop Taiwan. The Japanese school system cultivated professionals in various fields and the normal-school system cultivated teachers. At the beginning of the Japanese colonial period in Taiwan, the Japanese school system was the main system and the normal school system was supplementary, the two systems coexisting. To respond to social demand for talented people, the Japanese school system provided courses to prospective teachers in various fields (e.g. lecture courses, dialect courses, agriculture courses and railway courses). Gradually, the normal school system for cultivating teachers became the main system and the Japanese school system the supplementary. In 1919, because of social demand for talented people, the two systems were integrated into one teacher education system that met the requirements of the colonised region. In 1922 (the 11th year of the Taisho period), the Taiwan Education Act and Normal School Rules were modified and the differential education institutions for Taiwanese and Japanese people were integrated into one education system (Kondo, 1994, p. 191). The teacher education system in Taiwan was completely developed and approximately 2,500 prospective teachers were trained (Lee, 1981, p. 2236). In 1933, the Taiwan Education Act and Normal School Rules were largely modified, and the study period for teacher education was prolonged by a year. In addition, in the first chapter of the Normal School Regulation, a regulation stipulated that the objective of normal schools was to cultivate loyal and righteous teachers (Taiwan Education Association, 1939, pp. 671–4).

In 1937, the Sino-Japanese War began. From 1937, military personnel resumed serving as the Governor General of Taiwan. To respond to the requirements of the national defence and economic systems, the National Mobilisation Law was enacted in 1938 (the 13th year of the Showa period) to control and use human and material resources and to achieve military goals. This law also applied to Taiwan. As the war escalated, the strategic position of Taiwan became increasingly crucial. To increase Taiwanese loyalty to Japan and their willingness to sacrifice themselves for Japan, Japanese rulers promoted Japanisation (Kominka) education (Wang, 2005, pp. 100–1); in the 1940s, Japan integrated public and national schools for this purpose. Euphemistically, Japan treated Taiwanese and Japanese people equally and provided imperial elementary education to both Taiwanese and Japanese people; in reality, Japan needed Taiwanese labour for the war (Yamamoto, 1999, p. 7).

In response to the demands of various schools for teachers, the Youth Normal School and temporary teacher schools were established to cultivate teachers required for the expansion of secondary education. In addition, Japan provided government grants to prospective teachers and adopted a job assignment system, thus efficiently assimilating Taiwanese people through the provision of Japanese ideological education (Lee, 1997, pp. 18–19; Yamamoto, 1999, p. 6).

Conclusion

In the modern history of Taiwan, the Dutch occupied Taiwan for 38 years (1624–62) while the Spanish occupied Northern Taiwan for 16 years (1626–42). The Dutch and Spanish occupation of Taiwan was called the Dutch and Spanish Era (1624–62). In addition, Taiwan was ruled by the Zheng dynasty (i.e. the Kingdom of Tungning) from 1662 to 1684 (23 years in total), the Qing dynasty (1684–1895) and the Japanese (1895–1945). The Republic of China (ROC) government regained control of Taiwan in 1945. Table 1.3 shows the 320-year development of the teacher education system in Taiwan.

Table 1.3 Development of the teacher education system in Taiwan and education policies

Period	Time	Teacher education institution	Education policies
Dutch occupation of Taiwan	1624–62	Church/aboriginal teacher schools (concept)	Missionary
Spanish occupation of Taiwan	1626–42	Church schools	Missionary
Zheng dynasty	1662–83	Academies	Cultivating talented people
Qing dynasty	1683–1895	Imperial examination system	National control
Japanese colonial period	1895–1945	Japanese schools/normal schools/temporary teacher schools	National control

During the Dutch and Spanish occupation, both the Dutch and Spanish attempted to use Taiwan as a base for evangelical and trading operations. Thus both the Dutch and Spanish educated Taiwanese people through evangelism. In addition, the Dutch and Spanish adopted a management strategy that unified religion and education to control the thoughts and actions of Taiwanese people through evangelism. Most schools were affiliated with churches. Churches not only undertook missionary work, but also implemented education practices. In the early stages, school teachers were missionaries and administrative staff did not belong to a specialised agency but rather were associated with religion. Education was provided by churches.

During the Dutch and Spanish occupation of Taiwan, a variety of classics were translated and used as textbooks to teach aboriginal people in Taiwan. Aboriginal people were taught to use Roman letters to write their languages. The documents written in Roman letters were called the Sinckan Manuscripts, in which aboriginal people in Taiwan used written words for the first time. In 1642, the Dutch designated 50 aboriginal people, who were literate and knowledgeable about Christianity, as teachers to educate indigenous tribes. In addition, to train high-quality aboriginal teachers, the Dutch founded missionary schools at Sinckan and Soulangh and used parts of churches as classrooms. In 1657, an aboriginal teacher school was founded in Madou to train aboriginal teachers. The scale of this school was limited. Before the school was completely constructed, the Dutch were defeated by Koxinga and withdrew from Taiwan. The Dutch began to occupy Taiwan in 1624 and yielded to Koxinga in 1662. During the 26-year occupation of Taiwan, the Dutch mainly undertook missionary work and operated business. Today, several cotemporaneous documents written in the Roman alphabet can still be located.

In 1662, Koxinga defeated the Dutch and commenced the Kingdom of Tungning, which lasted 23 years (1662–84). Koxinga was a Confucian and an intellectual, and had concern regarding education. He established the Chuxianguan in the 11th year of Emperor Shunzhi to cultivate talented people.

Koxinga died before founding any schools. His son, Zheng Jing, commissioned Chen Yonghua to erect a temple and school, and to educate talented people. The education system in the Kingdom of Tungning likely originated from the education system of the Ming dynasty. Education administration agencies and various levels of educational institutions were established. In the early stages, a teacher education system was not completely established and scholars from mainland China or retired academics of the Ming dynasty and the gentry who sought refuge in Taiwan were invited to teach students. In the 23rd year of Emperor Kangxi (1684), Zheng Keshuang accepted the title granted by the Qing dynasty and the Kingdom of Tungning (1662–84) ended. Taiwan was then included in the territory of the Qing Dynasty. Subsequently, the imperial examination system was introduced into Taiwan, and was integrated with the education institutions established during the Zheng dynasty to form a modern school education system in Taiwan. Most teachers were people who had passed the various stages of the Imperial Examination. The instructional materials were mostly the Four Books and the Five Classics. No specific teacher education system existed.

After the treaty of Shimonoseki was signed on 8 May 1895, Taiwan became a colonised territory of Japan. Izawa, who emphasised the value of nationalist education for ruling a country, became the first director of the Bureau of Educational Affairs in Taiwan and actively implemented the assimilation policy in education based on the concept of nationalism. The characteristics of the teacher education system may be summarised as follows.

- Japan controlled the teacher education system, provided government grants to prospective teachers and adopted a job-assignment system.
- Japan requested Taiwanese people to be loyal and obedient to the country and the emperor, to comply with regulations and to earnestly follow national education policies. Japan also facilitated assimilation and Japanisation education.
- The Governor General of Taiwan determined the salary of teachers. Elementary education teachers were equivalent to local public servants.

The Governor General of Taiwan completely controlled the development of the normal school system and provided government grants to prospective teachers who later became educational public servants, popularised the Japanese language, and implemented Japanisation education. According to the normal school system, prospective teachers were offered government grants, were later assigned jobs and became public servants whose income and life were secure. These advantages of the normal school system became incentives for talented people to receive teacher education and the normal school system efficiently cultivated policy executors who were loyal to national ideology. By implementing the normal school system, Japan cultivated numerous local education bureaucrats during a short period of time who loyally implemented assimilation and Japanisation education, thus effectively controlling Taiwanese people and their self-identification.

Overall, during the Japanese occupation of Taiwan (from 1895 to the end of the Second World War), elementary school attendance in Taiwan increased from 5 per cent to over 70 per cent. The normal school system for teacher education implemented by Japan was a critical factor in this phenomenon.

References

Chen, H. W. (2008) "A Historical Research on the Formation of Official Language Studies in Taiwan Under the Japanese Rule and the Editing of the Textbooks". Doctoral dissertation, Tohoku University, Sendai, Japan (in Japanese).

Cheng, D. S. (ed.) (2000) *Developmental History of Taiwan*. Taipei: Jong Wen Books (in Chinese).

Chong, Q. H. (1993) *History of Education in Taiwan Under the Japanese rule*. Tokyo: Taga Shuppan (in Japanese).

Compilation Committee for history of Education (1941) *Evolution of the Education System After the Meiji Period*, 11. Tokyo: Ryu Gin Sha (in Japanese).

Hosoya, T., Okuta, S., Kouno, S. and Konno, Y. (eds) (1990) *New Pedagogy Encyclopedia 3*. Tokyo: Dai-ichi Hoki (in Japanese).

Kaminuma, H. (1974) "History of education in Taiwan", in Satoru Umene (ed.), *Compendium of Global Educational History 2: The History of Education in Japan*, II. Tokyo: Kodansha, pp. 258–359 (in Japanese).

Kann, R. (2001) *Formosa Inspection Report*, trans. S. D. Cheng. Taipei: Institute of Taiwan History, Academia Sinica (in Chinese).

Kobayashi, F. (1994) *Higher Education in Japan Colonial Taipei Imperial University: Construction and Characteristics*, Grants-in-Aid for Scientific Research in 1992–1993, Research Results Report. Tokyo: MEXT, pp. 227–34 (in Japanese).

Komagome, T. (1994) *Comprehensive Research Before World War II Colonial Education Policy in Japan*, Comprehensive Research Before World War II Colonial Education Policy in Japan, Grants-in-Aid for Scientific Research in 1992–1993, Research Results Report. Tokyo: MEXT, pp. 297–314 (in Japanese).

Kondo, J. (1994) *The Coeducational System and Japanese Education: Study on the Japanese Language Education in the Colonial Taiwan*, Comprehensive Research Before World War II Colonial Education Policy in Japan, Grants-in-Aid for Scientific Research in 1992–1993, Research Results Report. Tokyo: MEXT, pp. 191–208 (in Japanese).

Lee, R. H. (1970) *Taiwan Provincial Annals, 5: Education*. Nantou: Taiwan Provincial Historical Documents Archive Committee (in Chinese).

Lee, Y. H. (1981) *A Study of Primary Education in Taiwan Under the Rule of Japan*. Taichung: Rui He Tang (in Japanese).

Lee, Y. H. (1997) *Teacher Training in Taiwan During the Japanese Colonial Period*. Taipei: SMC Publishing (in Chinese).

Lin, H. D. (ed.) (1977) *History of Taiwan*. Nantou: Taiwan Provincial Historical Documents Archive Committee (in Chinese).

Nakamura, T. (2001) *History of Dutch Formosa, Last Volume: Society and Culture*. Taipei: Daw Shiang Publishing (in Japanese).

k uchi, K., Kaigo, M. and Hatano, K. (1973) *Collected Works in Education (3): History of Modern Education*. Tokyo: Syougakukan (in Japanese).

Taiwan Education Association (ed.) (1939) *History of Education in Taiwan*. Tokyo: Koduka Honten (in Japanese).

Tsau, Y. H. (2010) *Studies into the Early History of Taiwan, Updated*. Taipei: Linking Publishing (in Chinese).

Wang, C. C. (2005) *Taiwan Civic Education and Characteristics During Japanese Occupation*. Taipei: Taiwan Shu Fang (in Chinese).

Wang, J. B. (2014) *Taipei Historical Documents Quarterly: Educational Administration, 1981–2011*. Taipei: Taipei City Archives Committee (in Chinese).

Wang, J. T. (1978) *Historical Documents on History of Education in Taiwan*, new edn. Taipei: Commercial Press (in Chinese).

Wu, H. M. (1994) *Comprehensive Research Before World War II: Colonial Education Policy in Japan*, Grants-in-Aid for Scientific Research in 1992–1993, Research Results Report. Tokyo: MEXT, pp. 65–82 (in Japanese).

Yamamoto, R. (1999) *The Girls' High School of Researchers in Colonial Taiwan*. Tokyo: Taga Shuppan (in Japanese).

Yamazaki, S. and Nogami, N. (1990) *History of Taiwan*. Taipei: Woolin Publishing (in Japanese).

2 Teacher education policy and policy direction in Taiwan

Yung-Ming Shu

Introduction

This chapter focuses on the period from the retrocession of Taiwan (i.e. the end of World War II (WWII)) to the present (1945–2014)),[1] which shows the transition from nationalization to marketization, a process involving numerous political factors. From the political perspective, the period between 1945 and 2014 can be divided into four time points. From 1945 to 1949, Taiwan was retroceded to China, but the Nationalist Government had not retreated to Taiwan. Martial Law was implemented in Taiwan in 1949 and lifted in 1987, marking the period featuring one-party dominance and severe political control. Because of the different political atmosphere, this time period can be further divided into the early and late Martial Law periods before and after 1971, respectively. Since 1987 until the present, Taiwan has undergone political openness and marketization.

This chapter proceeds along two axes. Because policies related to teacher education were typically legislated after changes in political circumstances, the primary axis of this paper consists of time periods identified based on political circumstances. For each period, the political background is first detailed, followed by a description of the measures regarding teacher education, which are assessed based on nationalization and marketization. The nationalization referred to in this paper can be regarded as the re-Chinalization of Taiwan after colonization by the Netherlands, Spain, China during the Qing dynasty and Japan. By contrast, the power of marketization did not become the dominant trend in Taiwan until 1994.

From Taiwan's retrocession to the Nationalist Government's retreat (1945–49)

Political background and educational environment

Changes caused by the shift in rulers may be imagined. From the cultural perspective, the changes that occurred between 1945 and 1949 involved de-Japanization and re-Chinalization (Huang, 2007). Because the transfer of sovereignty was governed by officials from mainland China, the expectations of the *benshengren* (i.e. local Taiwanese people whose ancestors arrived in Taiwan before the Japanese colonization, as distinct from the *waishengren*, who came to Taiwan from mainland China after WWII) of the new government were destroyed. Conflicts frequently occurred between the *benshengren* and *waishengren*, eventually resulting in the 228 Incident in 1947, during which a *benshengren* was arrested for selling contraband cigarettes, which led to public protests and attacks against *waishengren*. Subsequently, the then central government increased its armed forces. Numerous *benshengren* elites were arrested, sentenced or disappeared without proper trial procedures. The 228 Incident, despite causing the estrangement of and division between the *benshengren* and *waishengren* in the following decades, had increased the stringency of state control.

Primary measures for normal education

Decolonization and re-Chinalization

During this period, the Japanese education system was replaced with the Chinese system. In the Japanese colonial era, an academic year commenced on 1 April and comprised three terms. After Taiwan's retrocession, the academic year was modified to comprise two semesters with the first semester commencing on 1 September. In addition, the language medium in schools was altered, and Japanese teachers were replaced. Regarding the language medium, the Taiwan Provincial Mandarin Promotion Council, headed by Chien-Kung Wei, was established in 1946. The council established 19 Mandarin promotion centres in counties and cities and assigned Mandarin promotion commissioners (Huang, 2007). In addition, the Taiwan Provincial Translation and Compilation Centre and Taiwan Culture Association were established. Thus Mandarin promotion has remained the primary task and objective in Taiwan's education. Before Martial Law was lifted, people were allowed to speak only Mandarin in schools; other dialects were prohibited.

Increase in normal schools

With regard to education for elementary school teachers, four normal schools located in Taipei, Taichung, Tainan and Changhua were retained from the Japanese colonial era. In particular, the Changhua Youth Normal School was built to realize Japanization in the colonial era. During the period from 1945 to 1949, these normal schools continued to adopt the Teachers College Regulation Amendment announced in 1942 and the Elementary School Teacher Certification Regulation announced in 1944. Because of the demand for teachers, eight normal schools were established by 1948 (i.e. Taipei, Taipei Female, Hsinchu, Taichung, Tainan, Pingtung, Hualien and Taitung Normal Schools – see the website of the History of the Ministry of Education). Japanese governors raised the student entry requirement to junior college level in 1943, but it was lowered to high school level by the Taiwan Provincial Government. Students who studied at normal schools were financed by the government and were assigned job placements after graduation as civil servants. Thus teaching was considered to be an "iron rice bowl" meaning a secure job (Shen, 2004).

In 1946, the Taiwan Provincial Education Division established the Teacher Selection Committee for selecting high school and elementary school teachers. The Taiwan Provincial Teachers College, established in 1946, is located at the preparatory department of Taihoku Imperial University (currently National Taiwan University).

Certification and recruitment of teachers

Despite the increase in normal schools, the high number of teacher vacancies which resulted after the Japanese teachers had left could not be filled instantly because several years of teacher education were required. Thus training programmes were opened for recruitment. According to *Taiwan Education over Ten Years* published by the Taiwan Provincial Government in 1955, the programmes included a teacher training programme (one year), preparatory college (one year), accelerated teacher education class (two years), accelerated teacher education programme (four years), training course for aboriginals (one year), general teacher education and pre-school teacher education for music, physical education and art (three years), and special teacher education (one year) (Shen, 2004, p. 60). All of these programmes had various entry criteria and the graduates were assigned to various regions. Nonetheless, these were only temporary and short-term measures.

In 1945, the Regulation for National School Teacher Certification was announced. Certification was the fastest approach to recruiting teachers. More than 5,000 elementary school teachers were hired within four years through certification.

On average, 70 per cent of applicants were qualified to be elementary school teachers, a percentage considered to be high. However, this approach was a method the government had to resort to during the post-war period.

Table 2.1 Number of applicants and qualified elementary school teachers

Year	Number of applicants	Formal teachers	Substitute teachers	Total
		Number of qualified teachers		
1945	1,901	1,251 (66%)	169 (9%)	1,421 (75%)
1946	7,958	4,392 (55%)	1,439 (18%)	5,821 (73%)
1947	8,134	2,177 (27%)	3,418 (52%)	5,595 (79%)
1948	1,367	317 (23%)	557 (41%)	874 (64%)
Total	19,360	8,138 (42%)	5,583 (29%)	13,721 (71%)

Source: Shen (2004).

The orientation of nationalization and marketization

The trend of nationalization, which focused on eliminating the influence of Japanese colonial rule on Taiwan, was inevitable in this period. At the time, the Taiwan Provincial Government perceived Japan as the enemy country during WWII and the suzerain of Taiwan. Therefore, the task of nationalization was considerably arduous and was a process equivalent to re-Chinalizing the citizens of Taiwan, a nation that has sustained 50 years of colonial rule. Language was the basic target. Japanese was shifted to Chinese, but the term *Guoyu* (national language) was retained in the school curriculum. At that time, approximately six million people populated Taiwan, among whom 70 per cent of the residents spoke Japanese. Thus the task of national language promotion was allocated to elementary and secondary schools to achieve the goal of eliminating Japanese culture and indoctrinating the Chinese consciousness (Huang, 2007, p. 224).

Marketization continued to exert some influence despite playing only a limited role during this period. To recruit a sufficient number of teachers from the labor market, the salary for government-funded students and teachers had to be competitive in order to surpass the attractiveness from the market. Therefore the salary and welfare of teachers were equal to those of civil servants, which acquired the market advantage at the time when mainland China remained mired in the turmoil of civil war.

Early Martial Law period (1949–71)

Political background and educational environment

The political environment between 1949 and 1971 was rather severe. The Nationalist Government of the Republic of China (led by the Kuomintang (KMT)) lost mainland China and retreated to Taiwan, resulting in Taiwan shifting from a province to a state, where the central government is located. In political terms, the early martial law period was a time of an anti-communist and anti-Soviet Union position. The major enemy of the Nationalist Government was the communist regime in mainland China. When the Cultural Revolution (1966–76) occurred, Chiang Kai-Shek established the Chinese Cultural Renaissance Committee in 1966 to promote the Chinese cultural renaissance movement (see the website of the History of the Ministry of Education). When reflecting on the reasons for losing mainland China, Chiang regarded the failure in education as a crucial factor. Therefore, strengthening control on education was considered to be a necessary measure. In a speech on the relationship between revolution and nation-building in 1951, Chiang stated:

> To transform education, the first step is restoring teachers' morality and obligation, and the second task is establishing model teachers of exemplary virtue. The effects of education lie in the change in disposition and the cultivation of moral character. Therefore, teachers should encourage and cultivate students

based on state righteousness and national interests. Thus, students can have the aspiration of loving and saving their country to achieve the missions of combating communists and the Soviet Union and saving and building the nation.

(Chang, 1968, p. 1800)

Thus military education was implemented in 1951, beginning in normal schools and afterwards extending to junior colleges and universities. At that time, military training instructors had substantially high authority. This measure still exists in universities; however, the authority of such instructors has gradually decreased after the abolition of Martial Law.

The control of the ruling KMT was realised in all school levels. The Security Maintenance Secretary was established in secondary and elementary schools. In addition, the KMT created the Intellectual Youth Party, targeting university students. Every student at a normal school was asked to join the party by military training instructors. In addition, the China Youth Corps[2] established brigades in normal schools, designating principals as the leaders. Therefore students collectively joined the organization in the orientation (Shen, 2004). During the early Martial Law period, enhancing the national spirit was a focus in education, aiming to reinforce the anti-communist intentions of the people and to condemn the communists for the destruction they imposed on the Chinese culture.

Primary measures for normal education

Positioning of the education system

The education system implemented in normal schools was altered during the early Martial Law period. From 1960, the Taipei, Taichung and Tainan Normal Schools were transformed into three-year Taiwan provincial junior teacher colleges for graduates from senior high schools or equivalents. They were further reformed into five-year junior teacher colleges in 1963 for junior high school graduates, and the remaining normal schools were subsequently transformed into five-year colleges until 1967. In 1963, the Ministry of Education announced the Normal School Curriculum Standard, and the textbooks for several subjects were unified (see website of the History of the Ministry of Education).

Taiwan Provincial Normal University for secondary school teachers was redefined as National Taiwan Normal University in 1967. In the same year, Kaohsiung Female Normal School was renamed Taiwan Provincial Kaohsiung Teachers' College. Moreover, the Taiwan Provincial College of Education (currently the National Changhua University of Education) was founded in 1971 in Changhua, Taiwan and enrolled self- and government-funded students. These changes were in preparation for extending national education from six to nine years in 1968 (see the website of the History of the Ministry of Education). The education for secondary school teachers was similar to that in universities; therefore, boarding and management systems were less rigid than those in junior teacher colleges.

Student management in normal schools

Paramilitary management was applied to education in normal schools and junior teacher colleges. All students were required to live on campus and abide by strict rules. They would wake up at the same time in the mornings, perform sports activities, consume meals together and attend self-study sessions at night. Students were strictly forbidden to leave school premises without permission. Living education was emphasised, dress codes and the appearance of students were stringently regulated. In other words, military standards were enforced in all aspects of life, including eating, clothing, housing, movement, education and entertainment (Shen, 2004). Military training instructors were the executors.

Based on military standards, school activities consisted of a high level of spiritual training (i.e. ideological guidance). For example, reading mottos and delivering motivational speeches were indispensable procedures during the flag raising ceremony. Class activities focused on enhancing national spirit, singing military and patriotic songs and analysing political affairs, and had to be integrated with activities of the China Youth Corps. Subjects such as Chinese, history, geography, Chinese culture, music and art particularly emphasised patriotism and national spirit, all of which were the focus of student competitions, such as speeches, posters, calligraphy, general knowledge tests and debates (Shen, 2004).

Teacher supply and demand

Because of the gap in the salary of teachers and that offered for other jobs as well as the capacity of normal schools and the conservative prediction of demand for teachers, the proportion of qualified teachers remained low. Several programmes and regulations were therefore implemented, such as the Quality Improvement Project for School Teachers in 1955, the Quality Improvement Project for Secondary School Teachers in 1955, the Regulation for the Registration and Certification of Secondary School Teachers in 1958, the Regulation for the Registration and Certification of Elementary School Teachers in 1958 and the normal school curriculum standards and relevant regulations (see the website of the History of the Ministry of Education). Consequently, the certification system was constructed, serving as the basis for advanced studies and certificate conversion.

However, the extension of national education from six to nine years induced teacher shortage in secondary schools. According to Chen-Chiu Pan, who was the then Education Commissioner, the decision for national education extension was partly triggered by the six-day war between Israel and Egypt in 1967. The KMT government believed that Israel's victory was attributed to the high quality of its citizens. Thus the government announced in 1967 that the extension of national education was to be implemented within the following year (Pan, 2004), implying that secondary schools had only one year to recruit a sufficient number of teachers. An expedient approach was therefore adopted in which all graduates who had a degree higher than junior college level could become teachers. They were merely required to take courses during the summer vacation to compensate

Table 2.2 Number of secondary school teachers who took pre-service training courses and their educational degrees

Academic year	1968	1969	1970	1971	Total
Degree	Number of teachers				
University	487 (23.5%)	538 (23.2%)	613 (17.2%)	497 (18.9%)	2,135 (20.1%)
College	510 (24.6%)	816 (35.0%)	1,483 (41.4%)	855 (32.5%)	3,664 (34.6%)
Junior college	1,010 (48.8%)	820 (35.2%)	1,228 (34.5%)	1,097 (41.8%)	4,155 (39.2%)
Military school	34 (1.6%)	27 (1.2%)	177 (4.9%)	63 (2.4%)	301 (2.9%)
Other	30 (1.5%)	128 (5.4%)	70 (1.9%)	116 (4.4%)	344 (3.2%)
Total	2,071	2,329	3,571	2,628	10,599

Source: Lee (1985).

for academic credits. Table 2.2 shows the number of teachers who took courses for academic credits and their degrees.

Although this type of expedient training course was actually held annually, the number of teachers during these years was the largest. For example, secondary school teachers were required to have a Bachelor's degree. However, at that time, only 54.7 per cent of secondary school teachers who did not have academic credits had a Bachelor's or college degree, and the remaining teachers had no academic credits or the required degree. Table 2.3 presents the distribution of educational degrees of junior high school teachers in 1975, six years after nine-year national education was implemented.

In Table 2.3, only (1) and (3) are teachers who received formal secondary school teacher education; however, they accounted for only less than 20 per cent

Table 2.3 Educational degrees of provincial junior high school teachers in Taiwan

(1)	(2)	(3)	(4)	(5)	(6)	(7)
Graduated from domestic or overseas normal universities, teacher colleges, universities or education department of universities	Graduated from graduate schools of domestic or overseas, public or private universities	Graduated from the special training courses at normal universities, those at teacher colleges or junior teacher colleges	Graduated from domestic or overseas, public or private universities or colleges	Graduated from public or private junior colleges	Graduated from public or private senior high schools, vocational high schools or normal schools	Others
3,198	39	1,541	11,161	7,338	2,153	898
12.15%	0.15%	5.85%	42.39%	27.87%	8.18%	3.41%

Source: Lee (1985).

of the total junior high school teachers. This may be related to the inability of universities that specialize in secondary school education, including National Taiwan Normal University, Taiwan Provincial Kaohsiung Teachers' College (restructured and established in 1967) and Taiwan Provincial College of Education (founded in 1971) to expand their scopes within a short timeframe.

The orientation of nationalization and marketization

The trend of nationalization was prominent during the early Martial Law period. For the KMT government, the goal of nationalization was to survive and reflect on their defeat in losing mainland China, as Taiwan was its last shelter. Thus the degree of nationalization in this period exceeded that in the previous period, and the focus of nationalization changed from de-Japanization to re-Chinalization. The military education and the education of the three principles of the people and national spirit indicated that education had become a type of spiritual defence, which was the reason that secondary and elementary school teachers were exempted from paying income tax. This exemption policy continued until 2012.[3] From current perspectives, the nationalization policy can be considered to be Chinalization, in which the local elements of Taiwan were suppressed. For example, students at all school levels were allowed to speak Mandarin only. In addition, to reinforce the national spirit, schools particularly promoted traditional Chinese elements, overlooking English education implemented in normal schools and junior teacher colleges. English was taught beginning in junior high schools and not in elementary schools.

Market forces were tenuous during this period. Because secondary and higher education opportunities remained limited, and students in normal schools were financed by the government, studying at normal schools was attractive and even became the only option for middle- and lower-class students. In addition, this was related to the occupational prestige of teachers. According to Ho and Liao (1969), who ranked 18 occupations, "[t]he occupational class of secondary and elementary school teachers was higher than that of lawyers, bank staff, general civil servants, and journalists" (cited in Chen, 2008, p. 266). Lin (1971) conducted similar research in 1971 determining that the "occupation of secondary school teachers was ranked 14, higher than that for lawyers. The occupation of elementary school teachers was ranked 16, higher than that for district court judges, pilots, journalists, and county/city councillors". At that time, the economy of Taiwan began to surge, and market factors were insignificant; thus teachers had high prestige because of the traditional literati and officialdom concept that education and qualification are essential for life and the notion that people should respect teachers and their teaching. Teachers were therefore highly respected, particularly in rural areas.

Late Martial Law period (1971–87)

Political background and educational environment

The nationalization policy was loosened in the late Martial Law period because the Republic of China withdrew from the United Nations in 1971 and the aim to retake mainland China was hopeless. Politically, the force of Taiwanization emerged, requesting Taiwan's identity and going against the China-oriented policies. Because forming political parties was banned under Martial Law, government opponents formed the Tangwai movement (comprising people outside of and opposed to the KMT) and asked for additional space for political participation. They protested against the permanent National Assembly (criticized as the "10-thousand-year Congress") and the continuous re-election of Chiang Kai-Shek as the president. In addition, they criticized the allocation of legislator seats by the central government based on the configuration adopted in mainland China and the allocation of civil servants based on the distinction between *benshengren* and *waishengren*. These demands for political democracy resulted in the abolition of Martial Law in 1987 and the subsequent realization of democracy. From an educational perspective, because of the nine-year national education, the general public was enlightened, exhibiting favorable expectations from political democratisation.

In the late Martial Law period, the government began to develop Taiwan economically, leading to the rise in market forces. In 1971, the gross domestic product (GDP) per capita was US$447 and the economic growth rate 12.45 per cent. In 1987, the year of the abolition of Martial Law, the GDP per capita had increased to US$5,265 yielding an economic growth rate of 10.68 per cent (National Statistics, 2014). This economic development was called the Taiwan economic miracle. Economic development enabled the government to provide additional educational opportunities, increasing public expectations and the requirement for education.

Primary measures for normal education

Normal Education Law 1979

Junior teacher colleges originally conformed to the Junior College Act. However, considering the specific characteristic of teacher education, the government recognized the necessity of enacting a specific regulation. Thus the 1979 Normal Education Law was sanctioned to legitimize all existing measures as follows (Chen, 1998, pp. 173–4):

1. Normal education should be implemented by government-established normal universities and colleges and other public educational colleges (Article 2).
2. Normal universities and colleges should focus on the cultivation of national spirit, moral character, professionalism and teaching of literacy (Article 13).
3. Normal university and college students are exempt from paying tuition fees and are funded by the government (Article 15).
4. Normal university and college students who received government grants and completed their studies with passing grades are assigned practicum and job placements by the educational administration; within the prescribed

period, they cannot engage in work domains other than education or continue further studying (Articles 16 and 17).
5. Normal universities and colleges and departments of education may enrol university graduates and provide them with one-year educational training (Article 5).
6. Normal universities and colleges shall cooperate with education administrations to facilitate teaching in secondary and elementary schools and kindergartens (Article 14).
7. Teacher in-service training shall be enhanced (Articles 6, 19 and 20).

Article 5 particularly targeted subjects that few students studied. This measure was similar to the Postgraduate Certificate in Education system implemented in Britain. Previously, students could become qualified teachers by graduating only from normal schools. Certification and registration were not required for subsequent job practice until 1980, when the Regulation for Registration and Certification of Secondary and Elementary School Teachers was announced, which served as the basis for teachers to convert their certificates by undertaking advanced studies. Correspondingly, the Teacher In-Service Training Regulation was announced in 1985, although planning in this regard remained inadequate.

Junior teacher colleges were elevated to university level

The economic development and improved quality of life led to an increase in the standard level of requirement for the teaching profession. Because the teaching profession requires a teacher to be highly knowledgeable, raising the educational qualification of a teacher to one that requires a Bachelor's degree became an inevitable trend. Thus, in 1987, nine junior teacher colleges were transformed into normal universities for senior high school graduates. In addition, these normal universities encompassed various departments similar to those in general universities. In 1991, eight teacher colleges were transformed into national universities. In 1989, the Taiwan Provincial Kaohsiung Teachers' College was designated the National Kaohsiung Normal University and the National Taiwan College of Education was renamed the National Changhua University of Education. Concerning the improvement of professional competence, from 1984, eight provincial junior teacher colleges in Taiwan adopted competency-oriented normal education, strengthening the competence of teachers in practical teaching (see the website of the History of the Ministry of Education).

The orientation of nationalization and marketization

In the late martial law period, nationalization was challenged and the local force of Taiwanization intensified. Following Taiwan's withdrawal from the United Nations, disputes pertaining to national identity had surfaced. Intense political protests and incidents of bloodshed occurred before the abolition of martial law, such as the Zhongli Incident in 1977 (in which a charge of election fraud by the ruling party in Taoyuan prefecture caused a riot). Various types of control lost their legitimacy but were gradually lifted. Although Martial Law had not been abolished, because of the substantial economic growth, people's demands increased considerably and the Martial Law system was constantly being confronted. Thus the ruling party and its assertion that Taiwan should unify with China were challenged publicly, and the voice advocating Taiwanese independence gradually emerged. People who supported unification and those who supported independence differed in political identity and visualised different national images. Thus nationalisation was perceived as an approach to achieving the goal of a ruling political party.

Regarding marketization, economic growth rendered government sponsorship in normal universities and teacher colleges unattractive. In addition, the society held high expectations for the teaching profession. Consequently, elementary school teachers were required to possess a Bachelor's degree. However, in subsequent university entrance examinations, teacher colleges were still ranked lower than the national universities and even several private universities, revealing the rank of elementary school teachers in the job market.

After the abolition of Martial Law (1987–present)

Political background and educational environment

Political revolution

The political changes after 1987 were more substantial than those in previous periods. After Martial Law was lifted, because of the death of Chiang Ching-Kuo, political power was gradually held by Li Ting-Hui, who was later elected as the first *benshengren* president. The permanent National Assembly was suspended after a series of constitutional amendments. In 1996, the first direct presidential election was held. In 2000, the party that had ruled since the Second World War was replaced by the Democratic Progressive Party (DPP). The second change of political party occurred in 2008, when the KMT again held governmental power up to the present day. Such alterations equalized the strength of both unified and independent powers, leading to a political confrontation. However, the economy in recent years has stagnated, with the GDP per capita varying between 1990 and 2013 as follows: US$8,124 (1990), US$14,704 (2000), US$18,503 (2010), US$20,057 (2011), US$20,423 (2012) and US$20,952 (2013) (National Statistics, 2014). The economic stagnation indirectly resulted in people's dissatisfaction with education and their demand for educational reform.

Changes in the educational environment

After Martial Law was abolished, old systems were constantly challenged. In 1988, Li Ting-Hui succeeded Chiang Ching-Kuo as the president, marking the point in time when governmental power was officially transferred to the *benshengren*. The political environment focused on eliminating the past and challenging the existing systems was legitimized. On 10 April 1994, the 410 Education Reform Association took to the streets to call for educational reform, appealing for the government to establish small classes and small schools, build more senior high schools and universities, promote education modernization and formulate the Educational Fundamental Act. On 28 July of the same year, the Executive Yuan passed the Establishment Guidelines for the Council on Education Reform, which was established on 21 September. The committee reformed the existing educational system based on the principle of deregulation, including the following measures (Committee on Education Reform, 1996, pp. A6–A8):

- adjusting the central educational administration system;
- modifying the educational administration and teaching in secondary and elementary school;
- protecting the professional autonomy of teachers;
- facilitating the deregulation of secondary and elementary school education
- facilitating the deregulation of higher education;
- facilitating the deregulation of establishing schools by the private sector;
- facilitating the deregulation of social concepts.

The professional autonomy of teachers is explained in the subsequent section.

Primary measures for normal education

Teacher Education Act 1994

The 1994 Teacher Education Act was produced incidentally because the government initially planned to amend only the 1979 Normal Education Law. The 1994 Teacher Education Act actualized four major reforms in teacher education presented as follows (Chen, 1998, pp. 174–5):

- *Channels for cultivating teachers were diversified.* Previously, teachers of senior high schools and below were educated at normal universities, teacher colleges or colleges of education. The 1994 Teacher Education Act enabled general universities to establish teacher education programmes and thereby participate in cultivating teachers.
- *Participation in teacher education involves a self-funding system.* Previously, students at normal schools were funded by the government, but following the enactment of the 1994 Teacher Education Act, students must pay for their own tuition fees. Government funds were granted only to departments with insufficient numbers of students studying teaching-related subjects or those willing to teach in remote areas after graduation.
- *Acquisition of teacher qualification is based on a certification system.* Before the 1994 Teacher Education Act was implemented, graduates at normal universities or teacher colleges were assigned to secondary or elementary schools for a one-year practicum, after which they could be registered as

qualified teachers. After 1994, students were required to complete pre-service teacher education courses and then pass a first-stage certification test, one-year practicum and second-stage certification test before acquiring qualification.

- *A fully funded system was adopted for teacher education.* Previously, teacher education was government-funded to achieve a supply-demand balance. After the 1994 Teacher Education Act was effected, a fully self-funded system was implemented to adjust the teacher supply and demand according to the market mechanism.

Thus the 1994 Teacher Education Act disrupted the monopoly of normal universities and teacher colleges on teacher education. Specifically, general universities were allowed to provide teacher education for secondary school and pre-school teachers, while teacher colleges still focused on teacher education for elementary school, pre-school and special education teachers, exhibiting no change. However, because of an excessive number of teachers and limited quotas, not all students could attend the teacher education courses. Moreover, teacher education was opened to Master's and PhD students (Article 9). In addition, normal universities and teacher colleges subsequently provided postgraduate teacher education courses, resulting in competition among normal universities and teacher colleges and general universities. Concurrently, the Teacher Education Review Committee was established by the Ministry of Education to manage relevant affairs, including setting curriculum standards.

Furthermore, according to Article 13, previous government-funded students in teacher education became self-funded and government funds and scholarships became supplementary. Graduates were no longer assigned job placements; instead, secondary and elementary schools were permitted to hire teachers independently. This new policy substantially affected local governments, engendering confusion over whether teachers should be recruited by local governments or by individual schools. After several years of negotiation, two approaches were formulated and it was decided that individual schools were to remain the power-holders. Schools can opt to hire teachers independently or by commissioning the local government.

Final Consultation Report on Education Reform published by the Council on Education Reform in 1996

Based on the idea of reform, the Consultation Report on Education Reform describes the professional autonomy of teachers as follows:

> Although the professional autonomy of teachers is not a basic human right, teachers are required to use their discretion according to their professional knowledge to fulfil duties. Teacher groups should participate in the selection and formulation of curricula, instructional materials, teaching methods, and assessments. The professional autonomy of teachers loses its value if it cannot generate a positive effect, impeding the development of learners. Therefore, although the professional autonomy of teachers is protected,

the self-discipline within teacher groups should be emphasised, prompting individual teachers to comply with regulations pertaining to professional groups. [...] The professionalism of teachers should focus on cultivating the ability of using technological knowledge and methods and underscore the standpoint of valuing local culture to develop an international perspective.

(Committee on Education Reform, 1996, p. A4)

The idea of reform was aimed at eliminating the previously formed ideological elements in teaching through the professional autonomy of teachers. The report suggested several practical approaches as follows:

To enhance the professional quality of teachers, the government should encourage universities and colleges to provide characteristic teacher education courses, and the Ministry of Education should respect the courses offered in these institutions and afford sufficient incentives for them to improve the systems of teaching, practicum and advanced studying. To enhance the practicum system, the Ministry of Education should facilitate the coordination and cooperation among teacher education institutions, internship schools, and local institutions for teacher in-service training and provide sufficient administrative and financial support. The teacher certification approaches, content, and criteria should be adequately formulated to ensure high teacher quality. An advanced-study system should be constructed using diverse channels to assist teachers in their career development. In addition, the Ministry of Education should provide necessary support and encouragement for the integration or transformation of normal universities and teacher colleges. In addition, the government should quickly formulate measures to manage incompetent or unqualified teachers (e.g., those demonstrating poor tutor code of conduct), and the measures should be enforced by individual schools.

(Committee on Education Reform, 1996, p. A14)

Although these recommendations were implemented to a certain extent, the effects were not necessarily as expected. For example, teacher education courses offered in individual schools were still required to comply with a universal regulation and any reform had to be sanctioned by the Advisory Committee of Teacher Education. Since 2005, teacher certification tests have been held for teachers of senior high schools and below and kindergartens.

Enhancement Programme for Teacher Education Quality and Enhancement Programme for Elementary and Secondary School Teachers' Quality

From 2007 to 2009, the Ministry of Education implemented the Teacher Quality Improvement Project which comprised five dimensions and nine schemes (see Table 2.4). This section details each scheme as well as the results of its implementation and the corresponding policy changes.

Table 2.4 Enhancement Programme for Teacher Education Quality

Dimensions	Action schemes
Teacher development	Scheme 1: To establish a standard teacher education policy
	Scheme 2: To facilitate the transformation and development of normal universities or universities of education
	Scheme 3: To regulate the systems of performance evaluation and withdrawal mechanisms for teacher education universities
Education practicum	Scheme 4: To enhance the effectiveness of education practicum
Eligibility certification	Scheme 5: To refine the teacher eligibility certification system
Teacher recruitment	Scheme 6: To construct a database system for teacher supply and demand and a supervision mechanism
Educational profession development	Scheme 7: To increase the educational degree of teachers in senior high schools and lower
	Scheme 8: To strengthen the professional competence of teachers
	Scheme 9: To operate the mechanism of recognizing extraordinary teachers and dismissing incompetent teachers

Source: Ministry of Education (2006).

SCHEME 1: TO ESTABLISH A STANDARD TEACHER EDUCATION POLICY

The term *standard* refers to the abilities that a qualified teacher should demonstrate. The standards of professional performance are available for kindergarten, elementary school, junior high school, senior high school, vocational school and special education teachers. These standards are continually being developed. The White Paper of Teacher Education in the ROC in 2012 advocates using these standards and the ideal image of teachers (i.e. "teachers who exhibit conditional love, expertise, and decisiveness") to develop professional standards for teachers (Ministry of Education, 2013, pp. 12–13; Huang, 2013, p. 162).

SCHEME 2: TO FACILITATE THE TRANSFORMATION AND DEVELOPMENT OF NORMAL UNIVERSITIES AND UNIVERSITIES OF EDUCATION

In 2005, the original teachers colleges were upgraded to universities of education, namely the National Taipei University of Education, the National Hsinchu University of Education, the National Taichung University of Education, the National Pingtung University of Education, the National Hualien University of Education and the Taipei Municipal University of Education. Another three teacher colleges were consolidated into comprehensive universities. Because of the substantial decrease in quotas, which were insufficient to accommodate the size of normal universities and teachers colleges, this scheme has only been implemented in three ways as follows (see the website of the History of the Ministry of Education):

- *Upgraded to comprehensive universities.* The National Taiwan Normal University, the National Kaohsiung Normal University and the National Changhua University of Education have been transformed into comprehensive universities. The National Tainan Teachers College and the National Taitung Teachers College were transformed into the National University of Tainan and the National Taitung University.

- *Consolidated with neighbouring universities to become comprehensive universities.* The National Chiayi Teachers College and the National Chiayi Institute of Technology were consolidated to become the National Chiayi University. The National Hualien University of Education was merged with the National Dong Hwa University and became the Huashih College of Education. The Taipei Municipal University of Education was merged with the Taipei Physical Education College to form the University of Taipei. The National Pingtung University was formed by merging the National Pingtung University of Education with the National Pingtung Institute of Commerce.
- Those independently developed into universities of education but still seeking consolidation included the National Taipei University of Education, the National Hsinchu University of Education and the National Taichung University of Education. Moreover, in 2013, the teacher education authority under the Ministry of Education was changed from the Department of Secondary Education to the Department of Teacher and Art Education.

SCHEME 3: TO REGULATE THE SYSTEMS OF PERFORMANCE EVALUATION AND WITHDRAWAL MECHANISMS FOR TEACHER EDUCATION UNIVERSITIES

Visits to teacher education departments of all universities began after the 1994 Teacher Education Act was enforced. Subsequently, relevant regulations were established such as Regulations for Establishment of Teacher Education Centres in Universities in 2002, Regulations for the Evaluation of Teacher Education Centres in Universities in 2004 and Regulations for the Evaluation of Universities with Teacher Education in 2006 and 2007, which was amended in 2011. Since 2012, a new evaluation system has been implemented and was integrated with the withdrawal mechanisms, forming an evaluation system that assesses six items, each of which is evaluated as pass, conditional pass or fail. The evaluation criteria and results are shown in Table 2.5.

- In the first semester of 2012, 12 universities and 26 education departments were evaluated, among which 19 departments passed (73.08 per cent), seven passed conditionally (26.92 per cent) and none failed.

Table 2.5 Evaluation criteria and results for teacher education evaluation

Evaluation results	Criteria
Pass	More than four items are passed and no item is failed.
Conditional pass	Only one item is failed.
Fail	More than two items are failed.

Source: Higher Education Evaluation & Accreditation Council of Taiwan (2014).

- In the second semester of 2012, 13 universities and 22 education departments were evaluated, among which 18 departments passed (81.8 per cent), four passed conditionally (18.2 per cent) and none failed.
- In the first semester of 2013, one university and four education departments were evaluated, all of which passed the evaluation (100 per cent) and none passed conditionally or failed. In the second semester of 2013, five universities and six education departments were evaluated, among which four departments passed the evaluation (100 per cent) and none passed conditionally or failed.

(Data source: Higher Education Evaluation & Accreditation Council, 2014)

Universities and departments that only passed the evaluation conditionally are requested to reduce their student enrolment by 30 per cent and those that failed are closed down. Some universities or colleges have terminated their operations because of difficulties in employing teachers and a low pass rate for the certification exam.

SCHEME 4: TO ENHANCE THE EFFECTIVENESS OF THE EDUCATION PRACTICUM

This scheme is implemented to strengthen three relationships involved in education practicum, namely the advisor–advisee relationship, the partner relationship between teacher education universities and practicum institutions and the mentor–mentee relationship. Before the enforcement of the 1994 Teacher Education Act, students in the practicum programme could act as substitute teachers, a role equivalent to that of a formal teacher. Currently, the practicum has been reduced to six months and commences after graduation. In other words, the previous process of practicum before certification has been reformed to certification before the practicum, an approach that is believed to improve the quality of practicum students.

SCHEME 5: TO REFINE THE TEACHER CERTIFICATION SYSTEM

This scheme serves to refine the certification test that has been implemented since 2005 and includes establishing a responsible authority as well as formulating examination-related measures. In addition, the certification test is a crucial mechanism for achieving standard teacher education.

SCHEME 6: TO CONSTRUCT A DATABASE OF TEACHER SUPPLY
AND DEMAND AND SUPERVISION MECHANISM

If teacher education follows a market mechanism to the letter, only information on demand and supply would be required. However, factors such as birth rate and the resignation and retirement of current teachers must be considered in estimating teacher supply and demand because the gap between being a student and becoming a teacher can range from three to five years (depending on whether the student is a postgraduate or undergraduate student). Thus the estimate may be inaccurate. In 2006, when this scheme was announced, approximately 5 per cent of qualified teachers failed to secure a formal teaching job, suggesting the necessity for an accurate estimation.

SCHEME 7: TO RAISE THE EDUCATIONAL DEGREE OF TEACHERS
IN SENIOR HIGH SCHOOLS AND BELOW

Up to 2012, the percentages of elementary school, junior high school and senior high school teachers who possessed Master's degrees or higher were 37.45 per cent, 37.77 per cent and 56.88 per cent, respectively (Ministry of Education, 2012). These percentages are still far from the goal that all teachers should hold Master's degrees. The 1984 Teacher Education Act has regulated that Master's and PhD students are required to attend teacher education programmes. However, only the Postgraduate Teacher Profession Programme offered by the National Taichung University of Education in 2012 is specifically for Master's students. Interestingly, applicants for this programme must have a teacher certificate, indicating that they have completed teacher education courses. This programme targets graduates who have acquired a teacher certificate but have yet to find a job and grants them government funds. After finishing the programme, they are assigned job placements. In other words, this programme ensures job opportunities for graduates and therefore attracts numerous job-seeking teachers (National Taichung University of Education, 2014).

SCHEME 8: TO STRENGTHEN THE PROFESSIONAL COMPETENCE OF TEACHERS

According to Scheme 8, the professional competence of teachers should be enhanced through advanced studies, the development of a second expertise and in-service training. However, the measure that has been adopted is the evaluation of secondary and elementary school teachers, which is closely related to the teacher profession. The Ministry of Education formulated the Regulation for the Pilot Evaluation of Teachers of Secondary Schools and below in 2003. In 2003, the Ministry of Education Pilot Plan to subsidise the implementation of teacher professional development evaluation was proposed. In addition, the Teachers' Act, which stipulates that all secondary and elementary school teachers must be evaluated, was amended in 2012 and serves as a legal base for teacher evaluation. Relevant regulations have also been sent to the Legislative Yuan (see Chapter 10, this volume).

The Enhancement Programme for Elementary and Secondary School Teachers' Quality was implemented from 2009 to 2012 (Ministry of Education, 2009). This project comprised five dimensions: (1) enhancing the teacher education system; (2) perfecting the teacher recruitment system; (3) facilitating the professional development of teachers and strengthening their professional intelligence; (4) developing an adequate teacher retirement and pension system; and (5) rewarding excellent teachers and dismissing incompetent teachers.

The Teacher Quality Improvement Project and Enhancement Programme for Elementary and Secondary School Teachers' Quality overlap; however, the scope of this former project is relatively wider.

Teacher supply and demand and relevant statistical data

During the time that students in teacher education were entirely funded by the government, the lack of qualified teachers was a persistent problem because of the conservative estimation and resignation of teachers, specifically teachers in elementary and vocational schools. Thus, in 1988, the Postgraduate Elementary School Teacher Education Programme, involving one-year professional training classes primarily held at night, was offered to university graduates. The programme was offered until 1993. From 1996 to 2004, the Postgraduate Teacher Education Programme was re-established, offering daytime classes. However, because of the new Teacher Education Act, students graduating from this programme could be qualified as trainee teachers only. To acquire a job, they had to complete the practicum before taking the teacher screening test (see website of the History of the Ministry of Education).

At the time when teacher education was liberalised, the problem of a declining birth rate had surfaced in Taiwan. The number of births was 305,312 in 2000 but declined substantially by one-third to 199,113 in 2013 (Interior Affairs Statistical Report, 2014). According to the Ministry of Education, elementary school first-grade enrolment is predicted to decrease from 203,638 in 2014 to 187,719 in 2017 (Ministry of Education, 2012).

The primary employment opportunities for prospective teachers consist of formal or substitute teachers in public schools. However, until 2012, only 46 per cent of certified teachers were formal or substitute teachers in public schools, and the demand will continue to decrease. Moreover, the cumulative number of fully funded unemployed teachers reached 61,784 by 2012 according to the *Yearbook of Teacher Education Statistics* (Ministry of Education, 2012) indicating the severe imbalance between supply and demand (see Table 2.6). Those who are eventually hired as formal teachers have typically taken numerous teacher screening tests over the years.

Project for Excellent Teacher Education Scholarship (2005–2013)

In the past, the average number of prospective elementary school teachers who received government funding annually was 2000. The number had decreased to 100 or more by 2003 and to less than 40 in 2004. In addition, after 2001, prospective teachers had difficulties in finding a teaching position in schools; therefore, the appeal to work as a teacher in the job market had diminished. However, the Ministry of Education continued to provide government scholarships, similar to government funding, to attract outstanding people. The Pilot Project for Excellent Teacher Education Scholarship has been implemented in two phases (i.e. 2005–9 and 2009–13), with 540 scholarships offered each year.

Table 2.6 Number and current employment status of certified teachers according to the Teacher Education Act 1994 (unit: number of people (%))

Year of certification	Total	Formal teachers (%)	Public school substitute teachers (%)	Fully funded unemployed teachers (%)
1997	999	787 (78.78%)	11 (1.10%)	201 (20.12%)
1998	2,631	1,881 (71.49%)	40 (1.52%)	710 (26.99%)
1999	7,220	5,261 (72.87%)	96 (1.33%)	1,863 (25.80%)
2000	11,384	9,213 (80.93%)	166 (1.46%)	2,005 (17.61%)
2001	16,483	13,479 (81.78%)	329 (2.00%)	2,675 (16.23%)
2002	15,929	11,679 (73.32%)	677 (4.25%)	3,573 (22.43%)
2003	17,693	10,999 (73.32%)	1,214 (7.20%)	5,420 (30.63%)
2004	17,362	9,520 (54.83%)	1,381 (7.95%)	6,461 (37.21%)
2005	18,726	7,942 (42.41%)	1,964 (10.49%)	8,820 (47.10%)
2006	17,561	7,731 (44.02%)	1,917 (10.92%)	7,913 (45.06%)
2007	13,319	5,062 (38.01%)	1,848 (13.87%)	6,409 (48.12%)
2008	9,677	4,176 (43.15%)	1,552 (16.04%)	3,949 (40.81%)
2009	7,390	2,648 (35.83%)	1,537 (20.80%)	3,205 (43.37%)
2010	7,038	2,207 (31.36%)	1,793 (25.48%)	3,038 (43.17%)
2011	5,731	1,586 (27.67%)	1,546 (26.98%)	2,599 (45.35%)
2012	5,660	1,131 (19.98%)	1,586 (26.02%)	2,943 (52.00%)
Total	174,803	95,302 (54.52%)	17,717 (10.14%)	61,784 (35.34%)

Source: Ministry of Education (2012).

Qualified students received NT$8,000 a month (approximately one-third of the salary of a university graduate), but they are required to fulfil various criteria such as acquiring certification for basic competences and engaging in educational services (e.g. participating in the Schweitzer Educational Service Program) (see the website of the Teacher Education Centre, National Hsinchu University of Education).

The largest difference between this scholarship and government funding is that students who received the scholarship were not compelled to work as teachers for a certain number of years. Instead, they were requested to acquire only a teacher certificate before being employed because of the limited job vacancies in the market. During the course of their study, they were required to participate in educational services and achieve excellent learning performance, but these are essentially different from the requirements in the past, such as living on campus. This scholarship project aimed to encourage outstanding people to devote their efforts to education, implicating the significance of marketisation. However, according to the employment survey of the first-phase scholarships for prospective teachers, the total number of prospective teachers who received the scholarship in the first phase was 754, among whom 321 (42.57 per cent) prospective teachers worked as teachers. The number of prospective teachers who worked as teachers and can be contacted was 257 (34.08 per cent). In addition, 147 (19.5 per cent) prospective teachers took advanced studies. Information on 286 (37.93 per cent) prospective teachers was missing. Overall, the economic benefit of the education scholarship system for cultivating outstanding students who aspired to become teachers was limited (Huang, 2014, p. 38)

In other words, less than half of the students who received a government scholarship (similar to the government-funded students) actually worked as teachers. Thus, Huang (2014) regarded the benefit as limited. Regardless of this limitation, the additional requirements of the scholarship for prospective teachers can enhance their teaching effectiveness (Ministry of Education, 2014).

The orientation of nationalization and marketization

Nationalization in the post-Martial Law period became a contested field for unification and independence. The 1994 Teacher Education Act applied the open-door policy. Initially, this may seem to be the victory of market forces; however, the policy still involved political factors in that the teacher education system was regarded as KMT's ideological apparatus and therefore must be destroyed. By contrast, the Democratic Progressive Party, when in power, emphasised local Taiwanese culture and attempted to exclude the Chinese culture. Moreover, since Martial Law was lifted, universities have acquired a high level of academic freedom. Particularly, after the change of ruling party, any political party cannot easily control the teacher education system. The power of nationalization was therefore substantially weakened and neutral terms, such as teaching profession, were used. However, this does not imply that state control no longer exists; it still resides within the education system, in which the ruling political party tries to intervene but is counter-balanced by the opposition parties.

As the power of nationalization weakened, the role and mission of government-funded students changed. The Excellent Exceptional Teacher Education Scholarship is a disguised government fund without employment guarantee. Scholarship receivers did not have much obligation but were expected to seek a teaching position on their own. Basically, this can be considered to be a realisation of marketization; in other words, these students were expected to be highly competitive in the labour market. By contrast, the government-funded students of normal schools and junior teacher colleges were previously required to live on campus, a requirement that comprised a high degree of ideological control and is also involved with disciplinary aspects such as education for moral living, which is in a way beneficial for students and thus should be regarded as a part of the profession (Peng, 2009).

Although nationalization and marketization are not entirely opposite powers in the labour market, they are related in terms of competition. When nationalization is emphasised, the government offers favourable conditions to attract people from the labour market. A teaching position in Taiwan can attract talented people because teachers receive benefits superior to those of civil servants. When nationalization was implemented, the government planned a teacher education system in which teachers were protected in terms of job placement, qualification screening and retirement. Thus teaching is an attractive job in the current era in which seeking a job is difficult. Currently, the government offers funding to a few students and ensures their future employment on condition that they work in remote areas or on outlying islands. This indicates that government-funded students assumed different missions at various time periods.

The trend of marketization means that teacher education is open to free competition instead of being monopolized by normal universities and teacher colleges. However, since teacher certification was implemented, the number of unemployed but fully funded teachers has exceeded 60,000, a shockingly high number that may be viewed as a disaster. This phenomenon discourages interested students and negatively influences normal universities and teacher colleges. After all, market demand can be estimated, and the quota of students in teacher education has been controlled by the government. Thus the gap between supply and demand cannot be attributed to only market factors, such as a low birth rate. No solution is available for this problem – perhaps the only solution is to encourage certified teachers to change their career path.

The White Paper of Teacher Education, ROC in 2013 (Ministry of Education, 2013) is the first white paper relevant to teacher education, consisting of four dimensions and 28 action schemes. The four dimensions are pre-service teacher education, teacher certification, teacher professional development and a teacher education support system. The white paper focused on improving the technical aspects of a teaching profession, neglecting the current problems. In addition, the white paper failed to consider factors related to nationalization and marketization. Teacher education on an ideal situation instead of the existing social context was considered. Thus whether idealized measures can be implemented is questionable.

Structural contradiction and chaos

The nationalization and marketization of teacher education, seemingly distinct from each other, are in fact two strategies derived from different political systems. In the *Social Origins of Educational Systems* (1997 and 2013 issues) written by British sociologist, Margaret Archer, two political systems exist, namely centralized and decentralized systems (Shu, 2014).

The nationalization discussed in this chapter is derived from the centralized system, featuring the control of the state apparatus over most of the resources. Regarding teacher education, teachers are civil servants with minimal autonomy. All procedures from training, recruitment and certification are state-controlled. Teacher groups are formed late and exert a minimal influence; they are merely government-affiliated organizations and therefore cannot influence policies easily (Archer, 1979). By contrast, in countries that embrace the decentralized system, all professional groups endeavour to seize authority from the government and escape from state control. Therefore, they form unions early to protect their professional interests. For example, in the United Kingdom, the National Union of Teachers strove for the rights of teacher recruitment and dismissal in 1949 and collaborated with other teachers' unions (approximately ten teachers' unions currently exist in the UK) to form the General Teaching Council in 1960. This Council, similar to the General Medical Council, was established to manage professional affairs. Moreover, in England, the General Teaching Council of England was founded in the middle of 2000 but was dissolved by the Conservative and Liberal Democrat coalition government in 2010. The General Teaching Council of England controlled the issuance of teacher certificates, requesting all teachers to pay a registration fee to become teachers (Shu, 2003). Because the state cannot control the issuance of professional certificates, teachers can hold a high level of autonomy.

Based on the aforementioned structure, teacher education in Taiwan has evolved from centralization to decentralization, despite the mixture of the two at present. Currently, the salary system for teachers is the same as that for civil servants, affording a high degree of protection. During the Martial Law period, although the Taiwan Provincial Education Association was formed in 1946, it differed from a teachers' union (see the Taiwan Provincial Education Association website). Archer (1979) asserted that members of this type of organisation must comply with the political stance of the ruling authorities. After Martial Law was lifted, teachers' associations and unions could be established in secondary and elementary schools to stand against the government. The current contradiction is that teachers possess simultaneously the civil servant's job protection and the labourer's rights and benefits. In addition, whereas the government structure is based on the centralized system, teacher education employs numerous decentralized measures, and when this contradiction will actually be resolved is unknown.

Conclusion

This chapter briefly discusses the teacher education policies in Taiwan implemented since the end of WWII to the present day from the perspectives of nationalization and marketization. The policy evolution process was divided into four periods, namely the period from the retrocession of Taiwan to the Nationalist Government's retreat, the early Martial Law period, the late Martial Law period and the post-martial law period from 1987 to the present. Clearly, teacher education in Taiwan has evolved from being a closed, nation-oriented system to an open market-oriented system after the 1994 Teacher Education Act was enacted, enabling all universities to cultivate teachers. This change is highly associated with political openness. However, because of improper planning and other factors (e.g. low birth rate), the number of teachers was excessively high, a problem that warrants immediate attention. In recent years, although the Ministry of Education has dedicated its efforts to improving the quality of teacher education, no immediate effects have been observed. In addition to the problem concerning an exceedingly high number of teachers, the adoption of market-oriented teacher education measures in the current centralized political structure has resulted in conflicts and confrontations between the government and professional teacher groups vying for governance.

Notes

1. In response to uncertainty regarding the term "Taiwan retrocession", the Taiwan History Association held the Forum for the Identification of the Historic Role of October 25 in 1995 (Wang, 2002), which adopted the perspective of Taiwan independence. However, because appropriate terms have yet to be developed, Taiwan retrocession is used in this paper.
2. The China Youth Corps is an organisation founded by Chiang Ching-Kuo, the son of Chiang Kai-Shek. This organisation provided various group activities inside and outside of campuses for students from secondary school to university, primarily focusing on recreational activities. The China Youth Corps still exists at present, but the content of activities has transformed.
3. The policy that exempted elementary school teachers from paying income tax was enforced in 1914 because of their low wages and to improve morale. This policy was retained in the Income Tax Act enacted in 1947. In 1968, the policy was reviewed but was again retained because education was regarded as a spiritual defence.

References

Archer, M. (1979) *Social Origins of Educational Systems*. London: Sage.
Archer, M. (2013) *Social Origins of Educational Systems*. London: Routledge.
Chang, Q. Y. (1968) *On President Chiang Kai-shek*, 2 vols, ed. National Chung-Shan Institute of Science and Technology. Taipei: Zhong Hua Da Dian Publishing House (in Chinese).
Chen, K. X. (1998) "Analysis of institutional changes in Taiwan's teacher education", *Journal of Educational Resources*, 23: 171–96 (in Chinese).
Chen, K. X. (2008) *Educational Sociology*. Taipei: San Min Books (in Chinese).
Committee on Education Reform, Executive Yuan (1996) *General Consultation Report or Education Reform*. Taipei: Commission on Education Reform, Executive Yuan (in Chinese).
Higher Education Evaluation & Accreditation Council of Taiwan (2014) *Information for the Evaluation of Teacher Education at Colleges, Universities and Graduate Institutions*. Retrieved from: http://tece.heeact.edu.tw/main.php?mtype=sumrepo%EF%BC%89 (in Chinese).
Huang, J. L. (2013) *The Idea and Practice of Standards-based Teacher Education*. Taipei: National Taiwan Normal University Press (in Chinese).
Huang, J. L. (2014) *Final Report on the 'Graduation Aspirations and Satisfaction Survey of Excellent Teacher Education Scholarship Students'*. Taipei: Department of Teacher Education and Arts Education, MOE (in Chinese).
Huang, Y. Z. (2007) *'De-Japanification' and 'Re-Chinafication': Rebuilding Taiwanese Culture After the War (1945–1947)*. Taipei: Rye Field Publishing (in Chinese).
Lee, Y. H. (1985) *Research on the Nine-year National Education Policy*. Taipei: Win Join Publishing (in Chinese).
Lin, Q. J. (1971) "A comparative study of the role of teachers and reform in teacher education", *Bulletin of Graduate Institute of Education Taiwan Normal University*, 13: 45–176 (in Chinese).
Ministry of Education (2006) *Enhancement Programme for Teacher Education Quality*. Taipei: MOE. Retrieved from: http://www.rootlaw.com.tw/LawArticle.aspx?LawID=A040080061003000-0950 (in Chinese).
Ministry of Education (2009) *Enhancement Programme for Elementary and Secondary School Teachers' Quality*. Taipei: MOE. Retrieved from: http://www.edu.tw/userfiles/ (15 August 2014) (in Chinese).

Ministry of Education (2012) *Statistical Yearbook of Teacher Education, Republic of China, 2012*. Retrieved from: http://www1.inservice.edu.tw/Download/Edu-paper101.pdf (in Chinese).

Ministry of Education (2013) *White Paper of Teacher Education in ROC: Promoting the Teaching Profession to Cultivate Future Talent*. Taipei: MOE (in Chinese).

National Statistics, ROC (2014) *National Income Summary*. Retrieved from: http://ebas1.ebas.gov.tw/pxweb/Dialog/varval.asp?ma=NA0101A1A&ti=國民所得統計常用資料-年&path=/PXfile/NationalIncome/&lang=9&strList=L (in Chinese).

National Taichung University of Education (2014) *Enrolment Information*. Retrieved from: http://home.ntcu.edu.tw/~OAA/RS/admiss/recruit.php?Sn=240.

Pan, Z. Q. (2004) *Interview with Mr. Zhen-qiu Pan*. New Taipei City: Academia Sinica (in Chinese).

Peng, H. S. (2009) "The disappearance of Taiwan teacher education: a turn for the better or a brewing crisis?", in H. S. Peng (ed.), *History of Education in Taiwan*. Kaohsiung, Taiwan: Liwen Publishing Group, pp. 383–414 (in Chinese).

Shen, C. L. (2004) *History of Taiwan Elementary School Teacher Training*. Taipei: Wunan (in Chinese).

Shu, Y. M. (2003) "England's General Teaching Council", in S. K. Yang (ed.), *Teacher Organizations in Different Nations and the Development of Their Professional Rights*. Taipei: Higher Education Publishing, pp. 1–23 (in Chinese).

Shu, Y. M. (2014) "The effect and interpretation of Archer's morphogenesis approach on the educational systems of different nations", in S. K. Yang, Q. R. Wang and F. J. Lee (eds), *Comparative and International Education*, 3rd edn. Taipei: Higher Education Publishing, pp. 755–82 (in Chinese).

Teacher Education Center, National Hsinchu University of Education (2014) *Laws and Regulations Regarding Excellent Teacher Training Scholarships*. Retrieved from: http://doce.web2.nhcue.edu.tw/files/11-1008-67.php (in Chinese).

Wang, Q. J. (2002) *Fifty Years of Taiwan History: Heritage, Methodology and Trends*. Taipei: Rye Field Publishing (in Chinese).

Websites

Website of the History of the Ministry of Education. Retrieved from: http://history.moe.gov.tw/milestone.asp.

Website of Taiwan Provincial Education Association. Retrieved from: http://www.tpea.org.tw/.

3 Ideologies and theories influencing the development of teacher education in Taiwan

Shen-Keng Yang

Introduction

Since ancient times it has been almost universally agreed that teachers and their education and training play a vital role not only in forming individual sound personality but also in fostering social, economic and political development, eventually leading to world peace. In ancient China, a statesman had also to be a teacher and guardian of the people. According to *The Shoo King* (*The Book of Historical Document*, J. Legge, trans.), when Keun-Chin (君陳) was appointed to be in charge of the eastern capital (1042–1021 BC) was enjoined the model the teachings of governing of the Duke of Chow who was lofty in virtue and high in prestige and acted as teachers and guardians of the people (*The Shoo King*, Book XXI-1, pp. 535–6, trans. Legge). An ideal sovereign in ancient China must act as the model to the people in the way that a teacher does to his students. In Hellenistic Greece, Plutarch (AD 46–120) (1927) asserted in his *Moralia* that people education is the source of all goodness. To provide children with proper education, teachers must be carefully selected. Teachers should not have scandals, be unimpeachable in their manners, and possess ideal experience (διδασκάλους γὰρ ζητητέον τοῖ ς τέκυοις, οἳ καὶ τοῖς βίοις εἰσὶν ἀδιάβλητοι καὶ τοῖ ς ῥόποις ἀνεπίληπτοι καὶ τοῖ ς ἐμπειρίαις ἄριστοι).

In view of the crucial role that teachers play in the cultivation of virtuous people and in the promotion of cultural and socioeconomic development and world peace, institutes for teacher education and training have been established since the seventeenth century. The first *École Normale* (normal school) was established in 1684 by Jean Baptiste de La Salle (1651–1719), who was born to a rich family and donated all his wealth to the community for feeding and educating the poor. The *École Normale* was established with the intention of providing basic training in teaching skills, leadership, and religious matters to those who taught in primary schools for the poor in the parish (Hermans, 2013; Leo, 1921, pp. 60–6; Maximin, 1922). In Germany, the first teacher training institute, the *Seminarium Praecetorum*, affiliated with Halle University (est. 1694), was established by A. H. Francke (1663–1727) in 1696. The institute was intended to provide necessary studies to students in the theology faculty of the university who wished to teach in the *Orphanage House* (Guthmann, 1964,

p. 5). The first teacher education institutes in seventeenth-century Europe were primarily religious.

After the Renaissance and the Enlightenment, the church authority was gradually replaced by the state authority, following the secularization trends and the emphasis on human development and social progress. From 1648, state absolutism was generally accepted, especially under Louis XIV of France, and extended to almost all European countries except England. In Germany, although absolutism of the whole empire could not be actualized, the rulers of the Prince States had absolute power in their territories. The rulers led the states through unification of all governmental functions under their rule. The state ceased to depend on the church, and it was a logically consistent policy that the church served as a unit of the state. The foundation of a state was based on its necessity. The establishment of a culture state manifested as the full assertion of the ruler's power, and a national education system needed compulsory schools for educating moral and competent citizens (Vogelhuber, 1949, p. 75). It was under such a historical occasion that Friedrich Wilhelm I (1683–1704) issued the first *Edict of School Attendance for All Children* (*Das Edikt zur Allgemeinen Schulpflicht*) in 1717. The Edict stipulated that children from 5 to 12 years old should attend school until they can read and write and have memorized the Catechism (Walz, 1988, p. 63), a lofty ideal for the first stage of forming a cultural state. However, problems arose; in addition to a financial deficit, qualified teachers remained lacking for the instruction of children.

To address these problems, Friedrich der Große (1712–86) (Friedrich the Great) promulgated the Royal Prussian General State School Regulation (*Königlich-Preußischen General-Landschul-Reglement*) in 1763. The Regulation stipulated that parents of the state were obligated to send their children to school and were not allowed any excuse to have their children help earn their living. The tuition paid to the teachers was also increased. The most crucial policy in the *Regulation* was that teachers must be trained in the teaching methods and must pass probation in the *Küster- und Schulmeister Seminarium für die Kurmark* before their recruitment. The *Seminarium* was established by J. J. Heckter (1707–68) in 1763 (Walz, 1988, p. 70). This was the first formal state-mandated teacher training institute in the world. In 1794, the French National Convention (1794–5) reached the decision to establish in Paris an *école normale* where citizens of the republic who were instructed in useful science would be taught to teach. This was the first law in France to stipulate the basic requirement of a teacher. All teachers should be trained in the state-mandated *école normale* before their employment (Edwards, 1991, pp. 238–9). Both in Germany and France, the state strengthened its control over teacher training from the eighteenth century.

Spranger (1971, pp. 52–3) contended that the state should use drastic measures to cope with the increasing financial demand of school construction and maintenance after the enactment of compulsory school attendance laws or edicts. The enforcement of the compulsory school attendance laws or edicts in the German Empire during the transition from the nineteenth to the twentieth century was not intended to achieve educational equality but mainly to unify all people under the sovereign's will (Paulsen, 1912, p. 85). The primary motive for the compulsory school attendance law of the German Empire was to win in the struggles between states, especially in the military competition at that time. Germany's victory in the 1870–1 Prussian–French war was attributed by many historians to the success of the German enforcement of compulsory school attendance. The success of compulsory school attendance was largely due to the state-mandated teacher education in Germany. On the *Bayrische Lehrerzeitung* of 14 March 1873, German teachers were applauded as the main cause of the victory in the war. Henceforth, the state strengthened its power over the control of teacher education. Many European countries such as France, Belgium, and England followed Germany and strengthened their state power in controlling teacher education.

The state power in the management of teacher education substantially increased during the two World Wars in European countries after the emergence of many new nation states and nationalism. In the twentieth century, as Boli and Ramirez (1987) mentioned, state education systems became indispensable components of modern nation states and were widely institutionalized. The state brought all people under its aegis as members of the national policy through the enactment of universal compulsory education. The enhancement of people's basic competency through universal school attendance mandated by the state was the prerequisite for strengthening the state's external powers. Hence, education became not only a duty but also a right (Soysal and Strang, 1989). According to Bendix (1964) and Weber (1976), the establishment of the education system, including the teacher education system, was often core to the formation of state nations. The most notable example is the German Weimar Constitution in 1919, which authorized the state to supervise the national school system (Art. 2, Sect. 1 of GG.) According to Reuter (2003, p. 29), central to the state's supervision of education is the protection of the full development rights of children and youths and the compliance of the policies for the welfare state. Accordingly, the state is obliged to maintain an education system providing all people with equal development opportunity without any discrimination. The state's power to control compulsory education was substantially increased in the Compulsory Education Law of the Reich (*Reichsschulpflichtgesetz*), dated 6 July 1938. It stipulated that pupils could be forced by police action into instruction and that legal guardians could be punished with monetary fines and imprisonment if they did not ensure education for their children.

Thomas Schirrmacher (2012) mentioned that the 1938 Compulsory Education Law was based on National Socialism. It was unfortunately adopted by the federal states and not rolled back, and was applied in the federal states in an unchanged form for a long time.

In France, the state control of teacher education can be traced to its origin in 1764 when Louis-René de la Chalotais (1764) published his *Essay on National Education*. La Chalotais argued that it is the state, not the church, that should hold the reign of educational power and that those who hold the state as the highest authority, not God, should be entrusted with the youth. After the Revolution in 1789, the state power in controlling education was further strengthened by the establishment of the *National Convention* (1792–5). On 30 October 1794, it proposed to establish an *école normale* for those who taught useful sciences. The 1808 decree of Napoleon the First (*Le décret du 17 mars 1808 de Napoleon 1er*) further strengthened the state's power to control national education affairs. The centralized power of the state was weakened after the enactment of *La loi du 2 mai 1982 dans le cadre de la décentralisation* and *La loi du 22 juillet 1983 relative à la repatrition des compétences entre les communes, les départements, les régions et l'État*. However, teacher education remains under state regulation. The 1989 Education Orientation Law (*La loi d'orientation sur l'éducation du juillet 1989*) stipulates that every department shall establish one teacher education institute (*institut universitaire de formation des maîtres* (IUFM)) in substitution of the traditional *école normale superieur*. In 2012, the IUFM was replaced by *les écoles supérieures de professorat et de l'éducation* (Yang et al., 2014, pp. 303–11). Despite the institutional reorganization and curriculum changes, all prospective teachers shall take a state exam before their recruitment as civil servants. Hence, the state plays a powerful role in regulating teacher education in France.

In England, Wales and the USA, the state's power in regulating teacher education is not as strong as that in Germany and France. The state in the UK and USA has power only in accrediting teacher education programs and licensing teachers. In the UK, the Teacher Training Agency (Training and Development Agency for Schools from 2005 and the National College for Teaching and Leadership from 2013) only has responsibility for accrediting teacher education programs. In the USA, the federal government is entitled only to implement the minimum required standard framework for qualified teachers and award teaching licenses to those who have completed a recognized teacher education program. The recognition of teacher education is based on the accreditation result from the National Council For Accreditation of Teacher Education (Wissenschaftsrat, 2002, p. 57). After the No Child Left Behind Act of 2001, the federal government strengthened its power to regulate the standards of teacher education. The NCLB ACT of 2001 specified that all children deserved quality education and held schools and their teachers responsible for educating all children in America. The criteria of teaching and teacher education changed from process indicators of quality teaching to outcomes of teaching, from the number of hours of college courses to the passing of state-mandated achievement tasks (Houston, 2009, p. 20).

Concomitant to the centralized tendency of state-controlled teacher education, international moves of market-driven teacher training emerged, especially in the UK and the USA. With rapid globalization and the quick progress of science and technology, the neo-liberal state regime gradually replaced the welfare state. The neo-liberal discourses commodify education by depicting it as an economic drain linked to an unsustainable welfare state (Burchell, 1966). Education, as with other social services and products, can be traded in the marketplace (Blum and

Ullman, 2012). Schools and colleges, including teacher education programs, must be corporatized to compete for profit in the education market. In the USA, the UK, and many other countries, the proposals to deregulate teacher education to promote competition among higher education institutions, private for-profit training agencies, and school districts will, as Apple (2001) mentioned, reinvigorate teacher education and make these programs more cost-effective and efficient. Visible performance assessed in terms of the state's or professional organizations' standards gained general approval and endorsement from education, policy, and business leaders in the USA (Vallie and Rennert-Ariev, 2002).

The pendulum swinging between strict state control and free marketization in teacher education can be observed also in Taiwan, especially after the abolition of the Martial Law on 15 July 1987. However, Taiwan's convoluted history under Dutch (1624–62), Spanish (1624–83), and Japanese (1895–1945) colonialism and the rule of Zheng Chenggong and his heirs (1662–83) and the Qing dynasty (1683–1895) has complicated the education system, especially teacher education, as a tool for consolidating imperial control over the colonized territory. After the restoration of Taiwan to China in 1945, the policy of "uprooting Japan, implanting China" was adopted to extirpate the effects of Japanese colonialism in Taiwan and to establish a new national identity (Huang, 2007). The state strengthened its control over teacher education after the government of the Republic of China relocated to Taiwan following military defeat in 1949. The Grand China-oriented nationalism in teacher education was substantially emphasized after the enactment of Martial Law on 20 May 1949. After the abolition of Martial Law in 1987 and the enactment of the revised Teacher Education Law, market-driven capitalism entered education and teacher education discourses. Thus state control was replaced by market competition and pluralization in teacher education (Yang, 1998a, 2006, 2013). Furthermore, teacher education in Taiwan as influenced by Western colonialism and dominated by the hegemony of Western forms of knowledge and power has been confronted with the issues of adaptation to the American knowledge form and mindset in suitable local situations. Postcolonial critique is thus leveled against not only the Western imperialistic system of economic, political, and cultural domination but also the Eurocentric knowledge and mindset as manifested in recent teacher education reforms. This chapter provides a historical analysis of the ideologies and theories influencing the development of teacher education in Taiwan.

Teacher education under Dutch and Spanish colonialism

From the sixteenth century, the colonial imperialism of the West has extended worldwide. As Latouche (1989, p. 9) mentioned, with improving means of communication, the European powers, in fierce competition, scrambled for the last fragments of "uncontrolled" land on the planet. With the superiority of his civilization in the wake of the industrial revolution, the white man believed himself to be charged with the sacred mission to civilize the non-Western world. Education, as one of the tasks for civilizing the conquered area, was thought to be the "white man's burden". Missionaries and teachers accompanied by the military and merchants were charged with the sacred mission to civilize the so-called savage mind with Christian doctrine.

Taiwan, a small island (with an area of 36,000 km²) situated in the South-Eastern China Sea, was contacted by Western settlers early in the sixteenth century. According to Heylen (2012), the Portuguese set foot on Taiwanese soil early in 1582, although no archaeological evidence has been found that could testify to the existence of a temporary settlement resembling those of the Dutch and the Spanish. During the expansion of Western imperialism, the Dutch seized Taiwan as a crucial entrepôt in Holland's worldwide trading network in 1624. To consolidate her colonial control, Holland appointed Georgius Candidus as the Pastor of Zeelandia, today's An-Ping in Taiwan, in 1627. In his *Discourses*, Georgius Candidus recounted his missionary and educational life in Taiwan. To preach Christian doctrine to the aboriginal people, he learned the aboriginal language. With the help of Robertus Junius, the Bible was translated into the aboriginal language by using the Romantzy pronunciation system, and was called the "Sinkan Manuscript". In 1636, four young aboriginals were selected to learn the Romantzy language system to become future teachers. In 1642, 50 aboriginals with a satisfactory command of reading and writing were commissioned with the task to develop education. Schools were established and affiliated to churches to educate the prospective missionaries and teachers. Spain, another trade superpower at that time, occupied Northern Taiwan. The friars of St Dominic were also charged with the mission of preaching Christianity in Tamshui and Keelung. After the Dutch expelled the Spanish from Taiwan, they experienced a shortage of teachers for the newly occupied area. More Taiwanese people were selected to be trained as future teachers. Similar to seventeenth-century European countries, teacher education was controlled by the church in Taiwan. However, in Taiwan, teacher education also played a crucial role in subjugating the people as colonized subjects through uprooting their Taiwanese identity.

Teacher education under Japanese colonialism

Taiwanese resentment against the Dutch high-handed measure of colonialism continued until Zheng Chenggong (Koxinga) left Fukien Province and led his forces to Taiwan in 1661 after frustration in his fight against the Qing dynasty in mainland China.

In 1683, Koxinga's 12-year-old grandson surrendered to the Manchu court, and Taiwan entered the Qing Dynasty as a prefecture of Fukien Province. In 1895, Taiwan was surrendered to Japan because China (Qing dynasty) was defeated by the Japanese military invasion. During the Qing dynasty's administration from the seventeenth to the nineteenth century, the study of Confucian classics was specifically emphasized. Prefectural and district academics were supported with public taxes and revenue from lands attached to the academics. However, most hopeful and privileged youths employed private tutors or private academics to prepare for the imperial examinations and try to obtain a literati rank. A conciliatory policy was adopted to subjugate the learned people under state control.

After occupying Taiwan, Japanese colonial builders devised a system that was particularly Japanese through learning from the rich colonial experience of European mega-imperial powers (Kublin, 1959, pp. 68–9). Education was thought to be the most effective strategy to bring the people of the newly acquired territory under imperial control and impart to them the national characteristics of the ruling race (Department of Educational Affairs of the Government-General of Formosa, 1916, p.4). Six pioneer teachers under the directorship of Izawa Shuji were sent to Taiwan under the protection of the Imperial Army led by Admiral Viscount Kobayama, the first Governor General of Formosa. Izawa and his pioneer teachers established the first Japanese school, the Schizangan School, in 1895. Because of the resentment of Taiwanese people against Japanese colonialism, the pioneer teachers had substantial difficulties gathering children for the new Japanese school. On New Year's Day in 1896, six pioneer teachers were murdered in an attack by a company of rebels. Their painstaking labor in the first attempt at colonial education ended up being in vain.

As Kublin (1959, pp. 76–7) commented, in the early days of Japanese occupation, Formosa was considered to be as great a military and strategic liability as an asset. The development of Formosa was never an end in itself, but rather a means to an end. The Japanese rulers allowed no interference in or opposition to their plans to establish the desired relationship between Formosa and the mother country. Administered by a military governor backed by a strong imperial army, Formosa transformed into an "island of policemen" under Japanese rule.

Under military administration, the Imperial Ordinance was promulgated in 1896. The Ordinance put the organization of schools under direct control of the Government-General of Formosa. The Japanese language school in Tahoku (Taipei) and the language institutes in larger towns throughout the island were established. Many teachers were urgently needed.

To satisfy the large demand for teachers in the newly established language institutes, 45 Japanese men from their homeland were invited to Taiwan to be trained in the Formosan language in *ad hoc* training classes for several months. These trained men were distributed among several schools as teachers, simply to meet the pressing demand. To provide regular teachers, Normal Schools were built in 1896. However, because the urgent demand for trained teachers of native schools was too large to wait for the first graduates of Normal Schools, the government again invited licensed teachers from Japan and instructed them in the Formosan language as well as some other necessary branches of study to prepare them for teaching in Taiwan.

Wu (1983, pp. 10–22) and Tsurumi (1977, pp. 1–14) commented that the colonial government in the early period adopted a "separatist" education policy. Only Japanese children were admitted to primary school (*Shogakko*). The common school (*Kogakko*) was established for Taiwanese children. In each of the two types of schools, the aim of education was different. Mixing the two was not permitted, and the required qualifications for teachers in the two types of schools were also different. Taiwanese people who intended to teach the Japanese language were admitted to three newly established normal schools in Taipei, Taichung, and Tainan. Their three-year course included ethics, the Japanese language, composition, reading, arithmetic, book-keeping, geography, history, science, calligraphy, music, gymnastics, and pedagogy. These were all taught in contemporary Japanese normal schools.

However, the normal schools in Japan offered also English, handicrafts, and agriculture or commerce. The science curriculum in Japan was substantially better organized. Taiwanese people aged 18 to 25 who graduated from a Japanese language institute (or common school after 1899) were eligible to apply for entrance to a normal school. The entrance requirement was lower: only four completed years of Japanese schooling were required.

From mid-1918, the education changed drastically. The "assimilation" (*doka*) policy in 1922 claimed equal education opportunity between the Japanese and Taiwanese. From 1930 to 1945, the ending of Japanese colonialism, the "assimilation" policy was translated into one of militant "Japanization" or "imperialization" (*kominka*), that is transformation of all Taiwanese people into Japanese. Despite the policy rhetoric, there existed a chasm between the Japanese and Taiwanese. Only a small percentage of Taiwanese applicants were admitted to middle school and almost none to a formerly all-Japanese school. Although the normal school curriculum was amended following the example of Japan's normal school, the lower status of Taiwanese teachers remained unchanged. When Japan's normal schools became equivalents of three-year specialized colleges in 1943, the format of Taiwanese schools followed suit. However, the change meant more on paper than in fact for many students. Middle school or girls' high school graduates had to complete three-year regular normal school courses and thus their training was extended a year. However, others entered this three-year higher *kokumin gakko* (elementary school after assimilation policy) course (a two-year extension course after a regular six-year *kokumin gakko*) and then a two-year normal school preparatory course. As before, these students spent a total of 13 years in school before becoming qualified teachers; evidently, their qualifications were lower than those in Japan.

Japanization reached new heights after 1940 with a campaign that forced Taiwanese people to take Japanese surnames and penalized natives who spoke any language except Japanese. The strict policy substantially increased the chasm between the Japanese and Taiwanese. The movement of resentment against the Japanese authority intensified. Education, as the technology of the soul in the Foucauldian sense, became a governing tool of Japanese rule. The contents of teacher education were carefully checked to ensure they conveyed as much patriotism as possible, and teachers were constantly admonished to develop the national spirits of their pupils. Teacher education thus played a vital role in the dissemination of patriotic disciplinary discourses in Taiwan under Japanese colonialism.

De-Japanization and re-Sinicization of postwar cultural reconstruction

After the restoration of Taiwan to China in 1945, the urgent task of the Taiwan authority was to extirpate the effects of Japanese colonialism in Taiwan and to establish a new national identity. De-Japanization and re-Sinicization constituted the major policy of post-war cultural reconstruction (Huang, 2007). T.-R. Yang (1994) mentioned that cultural reconstruction during the early period of postwar Taiwan (1945–7) was quite different from the national formation process of European nation-states. Instead, it was an artificial construct imposed by the government to form a Sinica-centric national consciousness and identity. To uproot the influences of the Japanization policy under Japanese colonialism, strict measures were adopted to prohibit the use of the Japanese language and Japanese school textbooks. Before the Japanese surrendered, the Taiwan Investigation Committee (台灣調查委員會) was established on 17 April 1944 under the supervision of the Central Design Bureau (中央設計局), the highest administrative organization directed by Chiang Kai-che, who was charged with the mission of overall planning in military and political affairs during World War II. The first urgent task of the Committee was to draft the Scheme of Taking Over Taiwan Administration Plan (台灣接管計畫綱要), issued on 23 March 1945. Concerning cultural and educational affairs, the scheme stipulated that national consciousness should be strengthened and all Japanese language institutes should be transformed into Chinese language institutes. The prospective school teachers should be trained in the Chinese language with particular emphasis on the improvement of their teaching and disciplinary competence. National consciousness and the Three Principles of People (nationalism, democracy, and livelihood) of the Nationalistic Party (Kuomintang) should be emphasized in the teacher training programs.

After Taiwan's restoration to China, the Bureau of Administration Office in Taiwan Province (台灣省行政長官公署) was established as the highest organization to unify political and military affairs. The first Head of Taiwan Administration, Chern Yi, arrived in Taiwan on 24 October 1945, and on 31 December, he announced the Outline of Administrative Work in Taiwan, proposing three main construction works: political, economic, and mental construction.

Mental construction was actually cultural reconstruction. Given the strong influence of the Japanese language and culture, the urgent task of the mental construction was to uproot Japanese culture and strengthen the Chinese cultural nationalism of the Taiwanese people. The Administrative Work required that within one year, all the students and teachers could speak Chinese and be familiar with Chinese literature and history. Chinese language, Chinese literature, the Three Principles of People, and Chinese history were mandated as required courses in the curricula of every school. The Japanese language was prohibited.

In the General Administration Report to the Provincial Assembly in Taiwan, the Committee of Promoting Chinese Language and more normal colleges and normal schools were proposed to be established to familiarize prospective teachers with the Chinese language, history, and teaching methods for increasing their competency to promote Chinese culture. De-Japanization and re-Sinicization were the primary missions of teacher education during the post-war reconstruction.

Teacher education under the Martial Law

The Grand China-oriented cultural nationalism was substantially emphasized after the government of the Republic of China relocated to Taiwan after military defeat in 1949. Under the imminent danger of military invasion and internal subversion from Communist China, student unrest as well as social conflict between the native Taiwanese and new immigrants caused an urgency to form a solid national defense force. It was under such an urgent circumstance that the Martial Law was promulgated on 20 May 1949.

Education, specifically teacher education, was considered to be the most crucial spiritual national defense force. Nationalism and Chinese culture education were emphasized in the school curriculum, especially in teacher training programs. To consolidate the spiritual national defense force, teacher training institutions were established exclusively by the government and limited to public institutions. In addition to three normal universities for training secondary school teachers, eight normal schools for primary teachers, equivalent in level to the high school, were upgraded to three-year junior normal colleges in 1960, and then to five-year normal colleges in 1963, admitting junior high school graduates to receive teacher professional preparation courses equivalent to a two-year associate degree. In 1987, following the worldwide trend of teacher professionalization, the junior normal colleges were further upgraded to four-year teachers' colleges conferring Bachelor's degrees. From the institutional perspective, teacher education was monopolized by the state, and thus played a crucial role in exerting sovereign power over docile subjects under the Martial Law.

Furthermore, to consolidate the spiritual national defense force, the caring technology of the soul in the Foucauldian sense was subtly employed in the teacher training arrangements. The students enrolled in normal universities or teachers' colleges enjoyed the waiving of tuition fees and living expenses borne by the government. The fifth-year practice teaching at an appointed school provides for payment amounts almost equivalent to the salary of a qualified teacher. Greater weight is given to the personality formation and Chinese culture education of prospective teachers. Thus *Sun Yat-sen's Thought*, *Four Books*, *Gymnastics*, and *Military Drill* were included in the teacher training curriculum in addition to the courses of teaching subjects and pedagogy (Chen, 1998, p. 173; Fwu and Wang, 2002, p. 157; Yang, 1998b, p. 150).

Teacher education as a crucial spiritual national defense force must be controlled by the state by establishing clear-cut criteria or standards as a policy instrument of strict state mandate. Competency-based teacher education satisfies this requirement of the state's tight control over the people through disciplining teachers. The concept of competency can be traced to its origin in the legal field, in which it was applied primarily to legal proceedings of the limit, sphere, or area of jurisdiction. From the end of the seventeenth century, this term referred to abilities from knowledge and experience (Hébrard, 2013). This meaning of the concept of competency is consistent with the notion of what contemporary competency-based education denotes.

In the USA, the effort to reform teacher education and training in the 1960s commenced with the adoption of the model of competency-based education, which particularly emphasizes measurable behavioral objectives and a systematic institutional design and curriculum (Ford, 2014). Following America, Taiwan initiated competency-based teacher education reform in the early 1980s. Teams of investigation led by presidents of junior teacher colleges in Taiwan were sent to the USA to examine the theories and practices of competency-based teacher training (Lin, 1984). The Education Department of Taiwan Provincial Government, ROC, issued Essential Points for Enacting Competency-based Education in Junior Teacher Colleges (Draft) in 1982. Competency-based education, as a soft technology of state control over the people's soul in the Foucauldian sense, was a favorite strategy of governance during the last few years of martial law in Taiwan.

Teacher education as proposed in the 1984 scheme of reforming the school system

Concomitant with the education reform efforts of *A Nation at Risk* released by President Ronald Reagan's government in the USA in 1983, the Taiwan education authority launched a reform of the school system in 1984. Ideologies underlying the American education reform were the awareness of educational mediocrity and its unfortunate consequence of losing international competitiveness in the global economy. Following his election in 1980, President Reagan appointed Terrel H. Bell as the Secretary of Education who created the National Commission on Excellence in Education to carefully examine American education problems and to spur a Sputnik-like reform. In 1983, the Commission on Excellence in Education released its report *A Nation at Risk: The Imperative for Educational Reform*.

The report identified the weakness of the curriculum and teaching that led to students' low performance. According to the report, American students were too often taking "general studies" tracks that left them without adequate mathematical skills, without sufficient time in the classroom, and with a general lack of study skills. Concerning the defect in the quality of teachers and teacher education, the report asserted that too many teachers came from the bottom quarter of high schools and colleges; teachers received poor training and their salary was too low to attract competent students to pursue teaching jobs. The report suggested an increase in teaching standards and advocated that teachers should receive more education while teachers' salaries should be market driven, competitive, and performance-based.

The Taiwan education authority modeled its educational reforms after the American example and launched its reform of the school system in 1984.

On 22 April 1983, the first meeting of the Research Group of Reforming School System was held under the chairmanship of the Minister of Education, Professor Huei-Sen Zhu, and Professor Liu Jen was elected as the leader of the group at the meeting. After one year of study, the group recommended the Scheme of Reforming School System, which was approved by the Ministry of Education in 1984. In the suggested reorganization of the school system, two proposals for reforming teacher education were recommended. Proposal I suggested that both primary and junior high-school teachers should be educated in five-year teacher colleges, that is a four-year BEd program plus one year of practicum, whereas teachers of senior high school and vocational school should be educated in normal universities. Proposal II recommended that the teachers at various school levels should all be educated in normal universities. The minimum requirement for qualified teachers in primary and junior high school was a BEd degree, whereas for teachers in senior high school it was at least an MEd degree. In response to the reform initiative of the Ministry of Education, the Chinese Comparative Education Society – Taipei (1984) held a conference on school reform on 24 December 1983; the resulting recommendations to the ministry were published in 1984. However, both the proposals by the research group and by the Comparative Education Society have never been put into practice.

Market-stricken logic in the 1994 Revised Teacher Education Act

Since 1980, high-tech industries have developed rapidly in Taiwan. To promote economic development, the logical efficiency of capitalism was introduced in Taiwan and gradually became the dominant ideology governing social and cultural developments. The rapid economic growth and political stability gave the government confidence that the Martial Law was no longer necessary; hence, it was abolished on 15 July 1987. Two opposition parties, the Democratic Progress Party and the New Party, were also established to compete against the Nationalist Party (Kuomintang) (nowadays, the People First Party and the Taiwan Solidarity Union are the opposition parties). Complete democratization was achieved in the Taiwanese political arena.

With rapid political democratization, technological progress, and economic flourishing, social forces emerged to press for education liberalization and open access to teacher training. On 10 April 1994, an organization composed mainly of middle-class citizens staged a mass demonstration demanding education reform. The movement, later called "The 410 Demonstration for Education Reform", marked one crucial milestone in the Taiwanese history of education reform. Its main appeal was to demand the removal of all unreasonable controls and restrictions imposed on education by the authoritarian government and to return the right to education to citizens, parents, students, teachers, and schools.

Under the pressures of various social forces, the newly revised Teacher Education Act was promulgated on 7 February 1994 to meet the demand for "pluralizing and diversifying teacher education" (Yang, 1998b, pp. 484–5).

Notably, not only did the Chinese nomenclature of the Teacher Education Act change from *shih fan jiau yü fa* (*shih fan* means teacher as a model person for the people) to *shi tzu pei yü fa* (*shih tzu* means teacher as one of the work force) but also the underlying ideology of teacher education completely shifted from "personality education" to the "cultivation of competent teaching forces". The formation of the teacher's professional ethos was not as crucial as before. As indicated earlier in this chapter, the formation of the "model person" was deemed critical in teacher education during the period of Martial Law because the "model person" played a crucial role in strengthening the nation's spiritual defense. However, the "formation of the model person" was severely criticized for its militaristic tone by liberal scholars and the statesmen of the Democratic Progressive Party. The liberals contended that the "formation of the model person" would become a political instrument to tacitly impose the political ideology of the governing party on the people through teacher education. The liberals and opposition parties strongly demanded that market-driven logic should replace the planned "model-person formation" in teacher training.

With market-driven logic integrated into the newly revised Teacher Education Act, the Regulations of the Establishment and the Academic Faculty of Teacher Education Programs Offered by Universities and Colleges promulgated on 26 June 1995 encouraged the universities to establish teacher training programs with distinct features. To succeed in the highly competitive market for teaching jobs, almost all qualified universities set up a specifically characteristic teacher education program to attract students. Accordingly, not only the criteria of selecting students but also the arrangements and contents of teacher training programs varied from university to university. Teacher education was completely marketized and diversified.

Neo-liberal "deregulation" in the 1996 Final Consultation Report on Education Reform

The market-based education reform was further strengthened by the gradual implementation of the recommendations proposed in the 1996 Final Consultation Report on Education Reform. The report responds to the urgency for the liberalization of education demanded by middle-class citizens in Taiwan and also reflects the international trends of neo-liberal policies of education reform in many countries (Cochran-Smith *et al.*, 2013; Furlong, 2013; Guerrero and Farruggio, 2012).

Internationally, neo-liberal discourses have become hegemonic in education decision-making and program formation in international organizations and in many developing and developed countries in the last three decades. The Organisation for Economic Cooperation and Development (OECD) and the World Bank are, as Mahon (2010) indicated, often associated with the diffusion of ideas and practices founded upon neo-liberalism. The recent reports of the OECD concentrate, as Lynch (2006) mentioned, strongly on the role of education in servicing the economy to the neglect of its social and developmental responsibilities; under the neo-liberal market-driven logic, education has been commercialized as simply a saleable commodity. Three main principles have been accordingly employed in restructuring the education system, including teacher education: deregulation, competitiveness, and privatization. Deregulation refers to the removal of the substantive role of the state in controlling teacher education, except as a guarantor of education rights and the minimal requirement of teaching forces. Competitiveness is the justification for the dismantling of procedural state bureaucracies and the releasing of governmental sponsorship for education to public and private agencies that compete for it. Privatization describes the sale of governmental service, including education, to profit-oriented stakeholders. These three ideas and principles have been universally deployed in the mandate of education rearrangement, retribution, and relocation of education resources, and in education governance systems in international organizations and in many countries. The education indicator systems of the OECD are primarily focused on elements of education that are seen as developing "human capital" and thus leading to economic growth. The intentions of the Programme for International Student Assessment launched by the OECD since 2000 focus on the improvement of education systems in participant countries. However, its policy recommendations are led by the principle of increasing school efficiency, an approach to national education based on neo-liberal economics (Froese-Germain, 2010).

In the European Union, neo-liberal discourse has also dominated the projects of European education reform and knowledge production. The European Higher Education Area, the Vienna-Budapest Declaration 2010, and the European Research Area (European Commission, 2000), as two constituent pillars of the "Europe of Knowledge", rely heavily on a market-driven economic rationale which favors the liberation of markets, in tandem with regulations from the World Trade Organization and the General Agreement on Trade in Services for education services, rather than reinforce education as a public good. Under market-driven logic, reduction of the public education budget for private investment in education is the major policy strategy with the serious consequences of school closures, larger class sizes, and the diminishing of learning opportunities culminating in the removal of whole education disciplines or specialties in some counties. The Resolution on the Impact of Neo-liberal Policies on Education, reached by the European Region of Education International 2014 Special Conference, criticizes the neo-liberal policies implemented by many European countries as "promoting market values of entrepreneurship and competitiveness in the education sector at the expense of universal human values" and as "promoting fragmented knowledge and skills at the expense of broader education and the pedagogy which should be shaping the democratic citizens of the future".

Not only in international agencies such as the OECD and EU, but also in many countries such as the UK and the USA, market-driven mechanisms are adopted in recent education reforms. The UK 2002 Education Act allows schools to become mini companies and to take over other schools, evidently privatizing education services as mandated by neo-liberalism. In the USA, the

Obama administration with Arne Duncan as the education secretary has aggressively promoted an education program with three main elements: calibrating teacher salaries to student tests, shutting down and "reconstituting" schools deemed to be failing, and expanding privately-run, mostly non-union charter schools. Accountability, privatization, and competitiveness characterize the Obama administration's agenda for education reform.

Following the aforementioned worldwide neo-liberal ideology in education reform, Taiwan also adopted economic deregulation, international competitiveness, and teacher education reforms. Deregulation, a concept borrowed evidently from the neo-liberal economic circle, is the motto integrated throughout the *Final Consultation Report for Education Reform* released by the cabinet-level task force, the Consultation Committee on Education Reform, in 1996. Under the motto "deregulation", education is considered as a free-flowing commodity. The values of education are dependent on the marketized principle of supply and demand. Any governmental control on the ideological constraint must satisfy the requirement of the education market.

The Report (Consultation Committee on Education Reform, 1996, p. 92) criticized the planned teacher education monopolized exclusively by national teacher's colleges and normal universities for being insensitive to the market-demand and lacking competitiveness and aspiration for learning of teacher-students. Accordingly, professionalism cannot be cultivated; the ideal teacher quality cannot be reached. Paradoxically, the Report equates market competitiveness with professionalism in teacher education.

The market-driven mechanism of teacher education was actualized in the 2002 Amended Teacher Education Act promulgated on 24 July 2002. The amended Act stipulated that the internship of a beginning teacher be shortened from one year to six months and that the payment for internship be waived, evidently from the perspective of complete economic consideration. Moreover, the licensure examination replaced the old accreditation process for selecting qualified teachers. The state plays a role in ensuring the quality of teacher education.

Ideologies underlying recent standards-based teacher education reform

The aforementioned analysis showed that even in the neo-liberal agenda of a free market in teacher education, the state still plays a vital role in controlling the minimum requirement of a qualified teacher. For ensuring teacher quality, teacher appraisal has been adopted in many countries either by the state or by state-mandated agencies. Various sets of standards have been set up as criteria of teacher appraisal to achieve different purposes of evaluation in numerous countries.

In the USA, early in 1992, the Interstate New Teacher Assessment and Support Consortium (1992) issued a set of core teaching standards as part of a systematic reform to articulate and align high standards for teachers and students.

The National Board for Professional Teaching Standards was founded in 1987 to define "what teachers should know and be able to do" and to "support the creation of rigorous, valid assessments to see that certified teachers do meet those standards". Standards for 24 certificate areas have been developed to identify specific knowledge, skills, and attitudes that support accomplished teaching practice. In 1997, the American Association of Colleges for Teacher Education initiated the Standards-based Teacher Education Project to strengthen the preparation of new teachers and, since then, has worked with more than 45 teacher education programs in seven states. The project focuses on aligning the programs with national and state academic content standards and professional teaching standards. According to Hursh's (2001) estimation in 2001, State Education Departments in 49 states have development standards in subject areas and a majority of the states have implemented high-stakes standardized tests that students are required to pass to graduate from a particular grade or high school. With the imposition of standards and tests, State Education Departments and school district administrators can assess teachers' performance and put teachers under the state's surveillance.

In addition to the USA, many countries worldwide have enthusiastically launched a teacher appraisal policy. The Australian Institutes for Teaching and School Leadership issued the *National Professional Standards for Teachers* with the aim to "promote excellence". The standards have crucial implications for teacher accreditation and reaccreditation, and therefore for the teacher education curriculum (Santoro *et al.*, 2012). The First Global Teacher Education Summit held in 2011 in Beijing discussed issues on the professional standards for teachers of the 28 countries included in the OECD survey *Review on Evaluation and Assessment Frameworks for Improving School Outcomes*. A total of 22 countries reported having policy frameworks (national or state laws or regulations) in place to regulate one or more types of teacher appraisal. To achieve fair and reliable teacher appraisal, it is imperative to establish different sets of professional standards for various kinds of teacher evaluation (OECD, 2013).

Embracing this international trend in standards-based teacher education reforms, Taiwan also launched a series of policy schemes of standards-based teacher education innovation. The Ministry of Education commissioned the Chinese Teacher Education Society – Taipei (2005) to conduct a research project on teacher education reform in 2005. In addition to the recommendations for the improvements of five dimensions of teacher education, the resulting policy document *Proposal for Improving Teacher Education, ROC* proposed that teacher education policy be based on professional standards. This recommendation was then included in the 2006 Enhancement Program for Teacher Education Quality. One of the nine policy schemes proposed to initiate a standards-based teacher education policy, Scheme 8 of the program recommends strengthening teachers' professional competence. The main policies on teachers' professional standards and competencies were incorporated into the *White Book of Teacher Education in ROC* issued by the Minister of Education in 2012. Standards-based teacher education has become the most crucial policy instrument to improve teacher quality. Governments and professional associations are confronted with the issues of how standards should be defined and what scope and extent should be applied. Furthermore, under clearly defined professional standards, although teacher quality can be controlled, the state might also impose surreptitiously its favored ideology on prospective teachers by using well-designed standard teacher education programs.

References

Apple, M. (2001) "Markets, standards, teaching and teacher education," *Journal of Teacher Education*, 52 (3): 182–96.

Bendix, R. (1964) *Nation-Building and Citizenship*. New York: John Wiley & Sons.

Blum, D. and Ulman, C. (2012) "The globalization and corporatization of education: the limits and liminality of the market mantra," *International Journal of Qualitative Studies in Education*, 25 (4): 367–73.

Boli, J. and Ramirez, F. R. (1987) "The political construction of mass schooling: European origins and worldwide institutionalization (with J. Boli)," *Sociology of Education*, 60 (1): 2–17.

Burchell, G. (1996) "Liberal government and the techniques of the self," in A. Barry, T. Osbourse, and N. Rose (eds), *Foucault and Political Reason: Liberalism, Neoliberalism and Rationalities of Government*. Chicago: University of Chicago Press.

Chen, K.-H. (1998) "The transition of teacher education in Taiwan," *Journal of Educational Resources*, 23: 171–95 (in Chinese).

Chinese Comparative Education Society – Taipei (1984) *School System Reform: Policy and Perspective*. Taipei: Wen Ching Book Co. (in Chinese).

Chinese Teacher Education Society (2005) *Proposal for Improving Teacher Education*. Taipei: Chinese Teacher Education Society (in Chinese).

Cochran-Smith, M., Piazza, P., and Power, C. (2013) "The politics of accountability. Assessing teacher education in the United States," *Educational Forum*, 77 (1): 6–7.

Commission on Excellence in Education (1983) *A National at Risk: The Imperative for Educational Reform*. Washington, DC: GPO.

Committee on Education Reform, Executive Yuan (1996) *General Consultation Report for Education Reform*. Taipei: Commission on Education Reform, Executive Yuan (in Chinese).

Department of Educational Affairs of the Government-General of Formosa (1916) *A Review of Educational Work in Formosa*. Taipei: Department of Educational Affairs of the Government-General Formosa.

Edwards, R. (1991) "Theory, history, and practice of education: fin de siècle and a new beginning," *McGill Journal of Education*, 26 (3): 238–9.

ETUCE (2014) *The Future of the Teaching Profession Background Document*. Paper presented at the Regional Special Conference of Education International Meeting, Vienna, November.

European Commission (2000) *Communication from the Commission: A Strategy for Smart, Sustainable and Inclusive Growth*. Brussels: European Commission.

European Higher Education (2010) *Budapest-Vienna Declaration on the European Higher Education Area, Budapest-Vienna*. Retrieved from: http://www.ehea.info/.

Ford, K. (2014) *Competency-based Education: History, Opportunities, and Challenges*. Adelphi, MD: UMUC Center for Innovation in Learning and Students Success.

Froese-Germain, B. (2010) *The OECD, PISA and the Impacts on Educational Policy*. Canada: Canadian Teachers' Federation.

Furlong, J. (2013) "Globalisation, neoliberalism, and the reform of teacher education in England," *Educational Reform*, 77 (1): 28–50.

Fwu, B. J. and Wang, H. H. (2002) "From uniformity to diversification: transformation of teacher education in pursuit of teacher quality in Taiwan from 1949 to 2000," *International Journal of Educational Research*, 22 (2): 155–67 (in Chinese).

Guerrero, M. and Farruggio, P. (2012) Neoliberal teacher preparation: conceptualising a response in the US borderlands," *Education Inquiry*, 3 (4): 553–68.

Guthmann, J. (1964) *Über die Entwicklung des Studiums der Pädagogik*. Bühl/Baden: Konkordia AG.

Hébrard, P. (2013) "Ambiguities and paradoxes in a competence-based approach to vocational education and training in France," *European Journal for Research on the Education and Learning of Adults*, 4 (2): 111–27.

Hermans, M. A. (2013) "John Baptist de la Salle and the first brothers: Christian educators for the society of their time," *Journal of Lasallian Higher Education*, 4 (2): 1–21.

Heylen, A. (2012) "Taiwan's historical relations with Europe: perspective on the past and the present," in J. Damm and P. Lim (eds), *European Perspectives on Taiwan*. Germany: Springer Verlag, pp. 28–45.

Houston, W. R. (2009) 'Teachers in history," in L. J. Saha and A. G. Dworkin (eds), *International Handbook of Research on Teachers and Teaching*. New York: Springer US, pp. 15–23.

Huang, Y. Z. (2007) *"De-Japanification" and "Re-Chinafication": Rebuilding Taiwanese Culture After the War (1945–1947)*. Taipei: Rye Field Publishing (in Chinese).

Hursh, D. (2001) "Neoliberalism and the control of teachers, students, and learning: the rise of standards, standardization, and accountability," *Cultural Logic*, 4 (1): 1–7.

Interstate New Teacher Assessment and Support Consortium (1992) *Model Standards for Beginning Teacher Licensing, Assessment and Development: A Resource for State Dialogue*. Retrieved from: http://programs.ccsso.org/content/pdfs/corestrd.pdf.

Kublin, H. (1959) "The evolution of Japanese colonialism," *Comparative Studies in Society and History*, 1 (2): 67–84.

Latouche, S. (1989/1996) *The Westernization of the World: The Significance, Scope and Limits of the Drive Towards Global Uniformity*, trans. Rosemary Morris. Cambridge: Polity Press.

Legge, J. (trans.) (1994) *The Chinese Classics*, Vol. 3: *The Shoo King*. Taipei: SMC Publishing.

Leo, B. (1921) *The Story of St. John Baptist de la Salle*. New York: P. J. Kennedy & Sons.

Lin, M. T. (1984) "The fundamental ideas of competency-based teacher education," *Research in Education and Psychology*, 9: 191–214 (in Chinese).

Lynch, K. (2006) "Neo-liberalism and marketisation: the implications for higher education', *European Educational Research Journal*, 5 (1): 1–7.

Mahon, R. (2010) "After neo-liberalism? The OECD, the World Bank and the child," *Global Social Policy*, 10 (2): 172–92.

Maximin, F. (1922) *Les Ecoles normales de Saint Jean-Baptiste de la Salle – Étude historique et critique*. Procure Générale EFC.

Ministry of Education (2006) *Enhancement Programme for Teacher Education Quality*. Taipei: MOE. Retrieved from: http://www.root--law.com.tw/LawArticle.aspz?LawID=A040080061003000-0950 (in Chinese).

Ministry of Education (2009) *Enhancement Programme for Elementary and Secondary School Teachers' Quality*. Taipei: MOE. Retrieved from: http://www.edu.tw/userfiles/ (in Chinese).

Ministry of Education (2012) *White Paper of Teacher Education in ROC: Promoting the Teaching Profession to Cultivate Future Talent.* Taipei: MOE (in Chinese).

OECD (2013) *Teachers for the 21st Century: Using Evaluation to Improve Teaching.* Paris: OECD Publishing.

Paulsen, F. (1912) *Das deutsche Bildungswesen in seiner geschichtlichen Entwicklung.* Leipzig: Teubner.

Pierre, H. (2013) "Ambiguities and paradoxes in a competence-based approach to vocational education and training in France," *European Journal for Research on the Education and Learning of Adults*, 4 (2): 111–27.

Reuter, L. R. (2003) "Erziehung- und Bildungsziele aus rechtlicher Sicht," in H. P. Füssel and P. M. Roeder (eds), *Recht-Erziehung-Staat.* Weinhem & Basel: Beltz, pp. 28–48.

Santoro, N., Reid, J. A., Mayer D. and Singh, M. (2012) "Producing 'quality' teachers: the role of teacher professional standards," *Asia-Pacific Journal of Teacher Education*, 40 (1): 1–3.

Schirrmacher, T. (2012) *25th IVR World Congress Law Science and Technology* (No. 110). Frankfurt am Main: Goethe universität.

Soysal, Y. N. and Strang, D. (1989) "Construction of the first mass education systems in nineteenth-century Europe," *Sociology of Education*, 62 (4): 277–88.

Spranger, E. (1971) *Zur Geschichte der deutschen Volksschule.* Heidelberg: Quelle & Meyer.

Tsurumi, E. P. (1977) *Japanese Colonial Education in Taiwan.* Cambridge, MA: Harvard University Press.

Valli, L. and Rennert-Ariev, P. (2002) "New standards and assessments? Curriculum transformation in teacher education," *Journal of Curriculum Studies*, 34 (2): 201–25.

Vogelhuber, O. (1949) *Geschichte der neueren Pädagogik.* München: Franz Ehrenwirth Verlag.

Walz, U. (1988) *Eselsarbeit für Zeisigfutter. Die Geschichte des Lehrers.* Germany: Athenäum Verlag.

Weber, E. (1976) *Peasants into Frenchmen: The Modernization of Rural France, 1870–1914.* Stanford, CA: Stanford University Press.

Wissenschaftsrat (2002) *Empfehlungen zur Reform der staatlichen Abschlüsse.* Saarbrücken: Geschaftsstelle Drs. 5460/02.

Wu, C. T., and Huang, S. C. (2002) "The development of teacher education policy in Taiwan (1945–2001)," in Chinese Teacher Education Society (ed.), *Retrospect and Prospect of Teacher Education Policy in Taiwan.* Taipei: Pro-Ed Publishing, pp. 1–28 (in Chinese).

Wu, W. H. (1983) *A Study on Teacher Education in Taiwan Under the Japanese Occupation (1895–1945).* Taipei: Taiwan Normal University (in Chinese).

Yang, S. K. (1998a) "Teacher EDUCATION REFORM in the USA and Taiwan – a comparative analysis and proposed research agenda," in Y. T. Lin (ed.), *Educational Changes During the Turn of 20th-21th Century.* Taipei: Wen Jen (in Chinese).

Yang, S. K. (1998a) *Comparison, Understanding and Teacher Education in International Perspective.* Frankfurt am Main: Peter Lang.

Yang, S. K. (1998b) "Teacher education reform in the USA and Taiwan," in Y. T. Lin (ed.), *The Evolution of Education During the Turn of the Millennium.* Taipei: Wen Jein (in Chinese).

Yang, S. K. (2006) "From colonization to professionalization: historical construction of teacher professionalism in Taiwan," in W. D. Wu and T. H. Kao (eds), *Quality, Innovation and Prospective.* Taipei, TWN: Hsiye Fu, pp. 625–52 (in Chinese).

Yang, S. K. (2013) *Educational Development from Colonialism to Post-colonialism in Taiwan*. Symposium paper presented at the meeting of the First Africa for Research in Comparative Education Society, Africa, Cameroon, March.

Yang, S. K., Wang, C. R., and Hsu, H. J. (2014) "Education system in France," in S. K. Yang, C. R. Wang, and Eric F. J. Lee (eds), *Comparative and International Education*. Taipei: Higher Education Press, pp. 259–334 (in Chinese).

Yang, T.-R. (1994) "Nationalization and indigenization – ethnic identity movements and their educational impact in Taiwan," *Education Journal of the Chinese University of Hong Kong*, 21 (2): 127–37.

4 The ideology, implications, and application of teacher profession standards

Jia-Li Huang

Introduction

Taiwan's revised Teacher Education Act, approved in 1994, transformed education in Taiwan from a state-planned, sponsored, and assigned teacher education system under the Normal Education Law into a competitive, self-sponsored, and independent job-seeking model. Under the Normal Education Law, only institutions within the official Normal Education System, including twelve normal universities and teacher colleges (often referred to as the "normal education system" in Taiwan) and the Education Department at the National Chengchi University were allowed to educate prospective teachers to support elementary and secondary school education. After the revised Teacher Education Act of 1994 was promulgated, however, any university in Taiwan was permitted to educate prospective teachers to support elementary and secondary school education as long as approval was granted by the Teacher Education Review Committee under the Ministry of Education. At one point, there were a total of 74 universities providing teacher education, including nine under the normal education system, 64 universities that offered education programs, and two universities in which School, College, and Department of Education were founded. By the end of 2004, the number of people who had secured a teaching license was up to 17,362, and this amount subsequently increased to 18,726 by the end of 2005, setting new records since restrictions governing the teacher education market were relaxed (Ministry of Education, 2007, p. 111). Taiwan's birth rate, however, began to decline in 1983. By 2011, the average couple in Taiwan gave birth to less than one child (0.895); in fact, Taiwan now has one of the lowest birth rates in the world. By 2013, the birth rate was 1.265 (Ministry of the Interior, 2013). The low birth rate in Taiwan has had a dramatic impact on the number of school-aged children. Population estimate statistics provided by the Department of Household Registration of the Ministry of the Interior show that the overall number of first graders in Taiwan and Fujian Province steadily declined from 291,267 in the 2006 academic year to 281,296 in 2007, to 247,263 in 2008, to 234,328 in 2009, to 219,400 in 2010, to 213,255 in 2011, and to 193,074 in 2012 (Ministry of Education, 2013, pp. 8–9).

Despite the declining birth rate in Taiwan, universities with teacher education have continued cultivating a large number of teachers to support elementary and secondary school education under the operational logic of free competition on the teacher education market since 1994. A large number of prospective students qualified to take teacher education programs were recruited in the very beginning but had to subsequently undergo preliminary screening and secondary screening due to increasingly strict requirements. The number of students recruited for teacher education programs peaked in 2005. A total of 174,803 prospective teachers completed programs between 1994 and 2012. Since only around 4,800 in-service teachers retire each year from public schools on average, as many as 61,784 graduates obtained their teaching license but were unable to obtain a teaching position in schools between 1994 and 2012. Table 4.1 reveals a total of 61,784 people had a teaching license but were not employed in a teaching position as of 2012.

With prospective teachers being cultivated in great quantities, the originally planned preliminary screening and secondary screening system, which only required submission of documents without specific evidence of performance, appears to have only been a superficial solution; it did not effectively control the quality of teachers. The desire to relax the market of teacher education and select outstanding teachers under the competitive logic did not seem to yield the effects expected as a result of the transforming social environment. In other words, the marketized teacher education practice could not address the problems of the increasing number of teachers and compromised quality of teachers. As a result, in addition to dealing with the "overly prepared" nature of teacher education and the inability to control the quality of teachers purely through competitive market forces, the Ministry of Education began tracking the total number of teachers while aiming to increase the quality of teachers at the same time. This is why the Plan for Teacher Education Quantity was

Table 4.1 Prioritized specialty and employment of people with a teaching license issued by the revised Teacher Education Act of 1994

Specialty	Number of people	Educated and licensed	In-service	Acting or substitute teachers in public schools	Yet to secure a teaching position
Kindergarten and pre-K	14,593	4,990	1,092		8,511
Elementary school	67,983	32,324	8,223		27,436
High school - general subject	68,081	43,859	6,398		17,824
High school – specialized subject	12,754	6,219	782		5,753
Special education	11,392	7,910	1,222		2,260
Total	174,803	95,302	17,717		61,784

Source: Ministry of Education (2013, p. 46).

Table 4.2 Number of new teachers developed between 2008 and 2012 in Taiwan

Year	Actual recruitment	Education practicum	Successful completion of teacher qualifying test/acquisition of teaching license
2008	8,866	10,690	8,315
2009	8,245	8,740	6,932
2010	8,615	8,333	6,853
2011	8,493	6,218	5,641
2012	8,131	6,907	5,608

implemented in 2004. Strategies such as implementing a teacher qualifications exam, restructuring "normal/teacher universities", and teacher education evaluation were adopted to hopefully reduce the number of teachers developed within the next five years by 50 per cent. This goal was fulfilled in 2009 (Lee, 2008). Statistical yearbooks of teacher education of 2008 through 2012 are shown in Table 4.2.

As is indicated in Table 4.2, the expected number of teachers developed each year in Taiwan currently remains at around 8,500. The number of people having actually acquired the teaching license is kept at 5,600 and the number of teacher education institutions also dropped from the peak of 74 to 52 in 2014.

While controlling the number of teachers, Taiwan also initiated the four-year Enhancement Program for Teacher Education Quality in 2006 in order to create benchmark-like role models and fulfill the goal of "adequate quantity and exquisite quality" and "retaining the good and eliminating the bad". In the *White Paper of Teacher Education* released in 2012, Taiwan declared again that it would adopt the standards-based teacher education (SBTE) policy. The hope was to cultivate highly qualified teachers under the marketized teacher education model where standards were adopted to control the quality of teachers during their education process and to keep marketization and control in balance to accordingly maintain existing marketized orientation of teacher education on the one hand and ensure a certain level of quality on the other.

Not everyone, however, understands what a SBTE policy is. At the very least, there are currently no state-level teacher profession standards (TPSs) in Taiwan. Despite this absence, there are currently three versions of standards that are the most well known, including the Teacher Profession Standards for School Teachers of Different Education Stages developed by the Republic of China Teachers Education Society in 2006 (the "Society Version"), the Index Version released by the Ministry of Education to facilitate teacher professional development evaluation in 2007 (the "Index Version"), and the version prepared by the Ministry of Education in 2014 in order to facilitate the development and release of state-level professional standards for teachers (the "Draft Version"). These three versions are analyzed herein. The government does not officially sanction the Society Version. It comprises the collected results of research and development projects conducted by the Teachers Education

Society upon authorization by the Ministry of Education and is meant to ensure the quality of teachers. In addition, it laid the initial groundwork for the SBTE policy in Taiwan. It has not, however, been fully implemented due to political contention over Taiwan's education policy (Huang, 2010). The Index Version was developed to facilitate professional development evaluation of teachers in Taiwan and be defined as the basis for formative and summary evaluation. To reflect the diverse needs of schools at different levels, however, they can choose and adjust the standards required and the contents involved. As such, the Index Version varies from school to school. The Draft Version is the latest collection of TPSs in Taiwan. It meets development requirements of both Taiwan and the international community. However, it has yet to be released. All of this shows that Taiwan is gradually familiarizing itself with the concept and practice of TPSs. A consensus has not yet been reached with regard to the specific content of TPSs; however, it has resulted in Taiwan becoming held up at the construction stage of standards despite the fact that SBTE policies are already an international trend (Sun, 2009). Only when Taiwan's society reaches a desirable level of consensus on TPSs will they actually be enforced. This article aims to explore the development history of SBTE in Taiwan, the idea of SBTE and comparison of the various versions, and the application of TPSs in Taiwan. The results of this analysis may serve as a reference for relevant research and policy-making.

Standards-based teacher education

Policy development background

Taiwan is known for its Confucian cultural background that traditionally holds teachers in very high esteem. As such, the reputation and social status of teachers in the past were never considered to be inferior to those of other professions. The state had direct and strict control over teacher education institutions, the number of prospective teachers graduating from the normal education system, and the qualifying process for teachers. This, according to the social closure idea introduced in the class consciousness of the new Weberian theory, is conducive to the protection of teachers' professional standing, reputation, and authority (Huang, 2008). Teachers' professional standing and occupational reputation brought about by social closure are built on the professionalism of teachers. When the quality of teachers reaches the required professional level and there is additional strict control by the state over teachers' qualification, it helps shape social closure. In order for the phenomenon of social closure to exercise the function of protecting teachers' professional standing, strict control by the state is required. The public will then recognize teachers' professional standing and occupational reputation.

Since the Teacher Education Act of 1994 was implemented in Taiwan, however, a large number of prospective teachers have been cultivated under a diversified teacher education model. The low birth rate, however, has resulted in those holding a teaching license to be unable to land a teaching job. This has accordingly led to a depreciation of the value of a teaching license and reduced the efficacy of preventing non-professionals from acquiring such a license. In addition, with the implementation of the Educational Fundamental Act of 1999, the use of corporal punishment on students was banned, and teachers had to demonstrate professionalism while educating their students. As a result, the traditional authority of teachers has since gradually waned, and the professional standing of teachers has likewise undergone gradual changes given the social context. Changes to the internal and external environments for teacher education have made teachers' professional standing and occupational reputation no longer comparable to those in the past. As a result, in addition to state control, teachers were subsequently required to demonstrate professionalism. Enhancing teachers' professional standing hence came to the attention of the government once again.

In light of international trends in teacher education, the marketized education model and the strategy of having the state control the quality of teachers have become similar goals that Taiwan aims to pursue in its teacher education. The Enhancement Program for Teacher Education Quality of 2006, where the standards-based policy was declared, for example, was based on the Teacher Education Policy Proposal of Teachers Education Society of ROC (Wu, 2005). In the Teacher Education Policy Proposal, experiences in other countries such as the US, Canada, the UK, New Zealand, Australia, Germany, France, Japan, and China, for example, were analyzed and summarized into five aspects, namely pre-service preparation, education practicum, teacher qualification exams, teacher screening, and professional development of teachers. The Proposal also described eight comprehensive action plans, including establishing an SBTE policy, assisting with the restructuring and development of normal/teacher universities, strengthening performance evaluation for universities with teacher education, creating the teacher qualification system, configuring the review mechanism for the supply and demand of teachers, and a teachers database system to serve as a reference for policy ideas and system design (Teachers Education Society of ROC, 2005). Because most of the contents of the Teacher Education Policy Proposal were integrated into the policy implementation under the Enhancement Program for Teacher Education Quality and the 2012 *White Paper of Teacher Education* reiterated the SBTE policy direction, it helped finalize the SBTE policy. After it was finalized, the creation of TPSs became a top priority for the government. Other goals, such as how newly created professional standards would be utilized to control the quality of teachers, what specific timing would be adopted during the professionalization process, which evaluation method should be utilized, and who would carry out such an evaluation must also be incorporated into the plan.

As far as Taiwan is concerned, international experiences are an important reference. The rise of SBTE in the international community, however, pertains to the trend of marketized education reforms. In the late 1970s, in particular, the "great debates" in the UK revealed that ineffective school education led people to question teachers' professional knowledge. This shows that the history of transforming teacher education is closely intertwined with school education reform. In the 1980s, the tenets of neo-liberalism became increasingly popular and accepted in the UK and the US. At that time, neo-liberals believed that adoption of free market principles and pursuing the principle of "freedom to choose" could help bring about competitive advantages and greater quality (Apple, 2006, p. 11). Under this market-oriented trend of thought, the rights of consumers were protected and budget subsidies became the incentive to support those meeting national requirements in order to make qualified people more competitive. The same concepts also resulted in the application of market competition logic in the area of teacher education policy. Neo-liberals support diversified teacher education; teachers therefore can be developed in different universities so that schools have a variety of options and can select best the teachers based on the logic of a competitive market in order to better ensure quality. Relatively speaking, in the assertion of enhancing quality of teacher education through the market under neo-liberalism, the substantial performance of the standardization movement has become the optimal mechanism for the state to control and enhance quality (Zeichner, 2003, p. 502). Although the history of education reform in Taiwan is unique and the diversified marketized teacher education model was adopted to coincide with international trends, it is worth considering whether a mandatory SBTE policy taken by the government also has to fully match international trends. Performance and control over the quality of teachers should be the supporting values of policy-making. Standardization is a strategy that a state can adopt to control quality in the midst of market competition. On the one hand, competitive advantages can be enhanced through the market competition logic. On the other hand, the standard mechanism enables the state to manage and re-define the quality of teachers. Standards are useful not only for safeguarding teacher quality but also for maintaining state control. By examining the contents and application of standards, it becomes clearer how a nation can define expectations for the quality of teachers and management principles.

Content of standards-based teacher education

Definition and connotations of standard

A standard can mean two things. The term was first used in a military sense referring to a flag or banner around which an outstanding emperor or commander could gather together troops when declaring defeat or victory in battle. Given this definition, a standard represents a type of action with a specific direction. It is a commitment to a certain action and exercises the effect of leading toward that specific direction (Stephenson, 1999, p. 249). Under the second definition, a standard is a model to ensure consistency of measurements or weights. In this case, standard implies measurement as a tool for measuring or determining something (Ingvarson and Rowe, 2008, p. 10).

Sykes and Plastrik define a standard as "a tool for rendering appropriate and precise judgments and decisions in the context of shared meanings and values" (1993, p. 4). Under this definition, standards must possess the following traits (Sykes and Plastrik, 1993):

1. Standards are tools to fulfill a purpose; they are useful and practical.
2. The rigidity of judgements and decisions will depend on the contents of the standards and the aspects involved.
3. Standards are helpful in terms of making judgements and decisions which accordingly affect the implementation results.
4. Standards encompass particular significance and value resulting from their authoritative source (e.g. experts, scholars, bureaucracy, etc.).
5. The process to create common standards is both political and technical.

As far as their contents are concerned, standards not only comprise directed action but also evaluation or measuring tools that can be used to determine the degree of such an action. The term "standard" implies, at the very least, the path to the destination or a requirement or eligibility. It can also be the basis or tool to determine different levels of expression. Since the measurement of a standard focuses on a degree of evaluation and encompasses different levels, reaching a consensus in society on standards becomes relatively important (Sykes and Plastrik, 1993, p. 3). From these distinct properties, the purpose of establishing a standard or the measurement of its contents is always policy-based. This allows a standard to fulfill a particular ideal and achieve specific results desired by a government. In order to accomplish such a desirable outcome, certain people will take part in the process of setting up the measuring criteria and accomplish the desired goal of the government in accordance with the specified concept and benchmarking methods. This argument, to a certain degree, shows the role of the government in establishing TPSs and defining teachers' professional standing. It is similar to the challenge Whitty (2002, p. 23) posed: "Who has the legal authority to define the 'professionalism' of teachers?" The intermediation of the state in teachers' qualification is particularly necessary in order to protect students and ensure the quality of teachers. By spearheading the screening and education of teachers, the government is influential in coding teachers' professional knowledge and in selecting and educating qualified teachers (Larson, 1977). Under the marketization model of teacher education, the government does not guarantee a teaching position at schools. Teachers must compete with one another and find their own teaching job. The government, however, can exercise its power in defining TPSs and engage in coding knowledge to keep track of teachers' professional knowledge and skills. The general public and parents can also determine teachers' capabilities by standards set by the government (Strain, 1995, p. 41). Therefore the government's ideology is hidden in the contents and the implications, while the application of standards directly affects the capabilities of teachers and defines their level of professionalism.

Implications of standards-based teacher education

As far as the definition of "standard" is concerned, SBTE theoretically implies guidance for action and can be used to measure and determine a degree. Historically, however, SBTE can be traced back to the competence-based teacher education in the 1960s that emphasized objective evaluation to ensure quality of teacher education based on a specific goal and performance-based teacher education to understand how a teacher performs and demonstrates the desirable knowledge, attitude, and technique, etc. in the context (Lindsey, 1973).

As far as the history of competence-based and performance-based teacher education is concerned, SBTE represents a legacy of the tradition of seeking out social efficiency. In the 1990s, when equal emphasis was placed on performance and substantial results during the education reform, it was emphasized that teacher education had to be determined through a set of qualifications underlying teachers' professional knowledge, and skills that were explored through performance-based evaluation and evaluation results were used subsequently (Zeichner, 2003, p. 498) to acquire or renew the teaching license, for example. Contemporary SBTE emphasizes the measurement of substantial performance so that standards are adopted as the basis for determining the substantial performance of implementers. As such, it can be referred to as performance-standards based teacher education (Valli and Rennert-Ariev, 2002). Examples include the US Interstate New Teacher Assessment and Support Consortium (INTASC) (renamed as the Interstate Teacher Assessment and Support Consortium, InTASC) and the National Board for Professional Teaching Standards (NBPTS), both of which adopt performance-based setting of standards, use the same set of standards, and evaluate performance and issue certificates accordingly. In summary, by the definition and the development history, SBTE means the creation of an ideal teacher image, and requirements of implied expectations in society on the basis of teachers' professional knowledge, in order to make ideal teachers a reality and to guide teachers while they plan their professional development. In addition, it encompasses the use of performance evaluations to keep track of teacher profession knowledge and the skills of teachers and gauge the extent to which teachers' mindsets comply with the ideal image and requirements as the subsequent basis for conferring or denying a license (Huang, 2013).

In order to put the SBTE policy into practice, nationwide TPSs established by the state have become the core policy document. Nationwide TPSs further empower the government in the extent of intervention it has with teachers' competences. It is not difficult for the state to create an ideal teacher's image or come up with a slogan for the SBTE policy. It is, however, difficult for the state to implement in reality and for it to exercise its intermediary influence by making the standards acceptable to people at respective stages. It concerns how the state creates a control mechanism for the market-oriented teacher education system that has been designed and strikes a balance between marketization and state control accordingly to fulfill the purpose of cultivating qualified teachers.

A comparison of different versions of teacher profession standards in Taiwan and their respective underlying ideologies

As TPSs are transformed from policy to real-world practice, the underlying beliefs and the contents are issues that the relevant stakeholders, including teacher education institutions, in-service teachers, teachers' associations, and parents' organizations, deeply care about. According to the defined policy, an SBTE is implemented at the national level. The state should create an ideal teacher's image to guide the performance requirements and level for teachers before service, during the induction period, and during in-service. Examples include the new teacher professionalism in the UK (McCulloch, 2001), "what teachers should know and be able to do" in the US (Hirsch et al., 1998), and the new value, skills, and knowledge (V3SK) of teachers for the twenty-first century in Singapore. Taiwan also defines a teacher's image in the *White Paper of Teacher Education* (2012) as someone with "love for education, competence, and power to achieve". In other words:

> A teacher should focus on caring for his/her students and feel the needs of students in the new era, respond to the changing society, and take the contemporary challenge for the cause of education. In addition, when faced with a diversified society and educational environment, a teacher must be capable of thinking critically in order to understand the relationship between education and politics, economy, and society and reflect on their different roles and contents of work in different times as it helps demonstrate education as a profession. A teacher should also collaborate with peers and schooling assistants in seeking innovation, proactively fulfill their mission to teach students the fundamental relationship between oneself and society, the knowledge and skills to live in society, and to help students answer questions in the learning process, assist in exploring the diversified potentials of each student, and help students build the ability to criticize, reflect upon themselves, and the right attitude so that each student is likely to realize self-fulfillment.
> (Ministry of Education, 2012, p. 12)

From a comparison between the characteristics of teachers in the UK, the US, Singapore, and Taiwan, showed that teachers are equipped with the same characteristics of required knowledge, skills, and attitude, including professional identity and attitude toward students, teaching, peers, parents, and the community and professional knowledge and skills toward the curriculum, teaching, class management, and counseling. What is different is that Taiwan places higher emphasis on the virtues of teachers, that is the professional standing and authority of teachers in society that help them provide a role model for the general public (Ministry of Education, 2012, p. 16).

A further review reveals that despite the yet-to-be-released professional standards for teachers at the national level in Taiwan, there are at least three versions of the said standards available on the market at present (that is the Society Version, the Index Version, and the Draft Version), including the Index Version that is already adopted by and implemented in schools to help with professional development of in-service teachers. A comparison of the three versions of the TPSs is shown in Table 4.3.

As shown in Table 4.3, the substantial contents reflect the identical depiction of an ideal teacher by the government despite the different versions of the TPSs. A teacher must possess teacher profession knowledge and skills, including familiarity with education beliefs, curricular development and design, teaching practice, evaluation, counseling, and creating a favorable environment for learning. In addition, a teacher must possess the right attitude toward his/her profession, including constantly growing and advancing him/herself, complying with requirements for teachers, and exploring/collaborating on instructional issues.

In terms of the formality, the three versions differ in their wording. As stated by Ingvarson and Rowe (2008, p. 16), standards have to be able to guide readers clearly through the ideas behind the tasks, demonstrate contents or items that teachers should know and be able to carry out in order to facilitate quality opportunities for students to learn, confirm the unique characteristics that teachers should know and be able to demonstrate, and describe how teachers can make the best of their profession and the measurability. The Society and Index Versions are unable to include tasks that teachers are expected to perform to the desired level of accomplishment as those described in the Draft Version.

As far as Taiwan's experience of putting professional development evaluation indicators for teachers into practice is concerned, the Index Version empowers school teachers to establish their own professional development indicators in light of the fact that evaluation of teachers has yet to form a culture in Taiwan (Huang and Chang, 2014) despite the trial operation of professional development evaluation for teachers starting in 2006. This was intended to emphasize the importance of professional development for teachers and to let teachers accept the application of teacher evaluations as a way to urge them to pursue professional development. The Index Version, which is rooted in the concept of school-based indices, allows teachers to develop their own indicators according to their own needs for professional teacher development. As a result, professional development indicators for teachers differ from place to place. This stands in contrast to other countries where performance standards are in place at each respective stage for teachers.

The application of teacher profession standards

Underlying concept

According to an analysis by Sykes and Plastrik (1993) and Darling-Hammond (1990, 2001), focusing on the professionalization process of teaching under the professional model is preferred in terms of application scope and approach to

Table 4.3 Comparison of contents of the three types of teacher profession standards in Taiwan

Version	Society version	Index version	Draft version
Academic year	2007	2014	2014
Underlying concept	1. Student-centered 2. Including diversified professional requirements for teachers	1. Self-reflective 2. Professional interaction with peers	1. Student-centered 2. Fulfillment of teachers' responsibilities as the premise
Total number of standard dimensions	5 dimensions	4 dimensions	3 dimensions
Standard dimension/ evaluation content	[Evaluation Dimension] 1. Basic professional attainments of teachers 2. Competence and attitude 3. Curricular design and teaching 4. Class management and counseling 5. Research development and advancement	[Evaluation Content] 1. Curricular design and teaching 2. Class management and counseling 3. Research development and advancement 4. Competence and attitude	[Evaluation Dimension] 1. Professional knowledge and skills 2. Professional practice 3. Professional devotion
Standard items	1. Curricular design 2. Teaching practice 3. Knowledge of subject 4. Teaching evaluation 5. Class management 6. Counseling knowledge and skills 7. Advancement and growth 8. Research and innovation 9. Competence 10. Attitude 11. Basic professional attainments	1. Curricular planning 2. Lesson plan 3. Presentation 4. Teaching skills 5. Learning evaluation 6. Class management 7. Resources management 8. Course evaluation 9. Teaching evaluation 10. Professional growth 11. Self-development 12. Professional attitude	1. Professional knowledge and awareness of important education issues 2. Knowledge of the subject field and related teaching knowledge and skills 3. Curricular and instructional design capabilities 4. Teaching strategies for enhanced efficacy 5. Adequate approach to learning evaluation 6. Class management efficacy 7. Supportive learning environment and awareness of differences among students 8. Fulfillment of professional responsibilities as educator by providing needed counseling 9. Devotion to enhancing professionalism as teacher 10. Coordination capability and leadership

standards, including accreditation of institutions, teaching license by the government, and advanced certification of specific capabilities or compliant performance behavior. With the professionalization process of teachers as the scope, standards are applied to licensing, certification, and evaluation substantially. In other words, the scope of application of TPSs covers the licensing, certification, and evaluation of teachers during the professionalization process, including screening, induction, evaluation during the pre-service period, continuing development of professional culture and formation of regulations. Application of TPSs focuses on the professionalization process and is meant to keep configurations for respective stages under check. *Teachers' Standards* in the UK (Department for Education, 2014), for example, define the ideal scope of application as follows.

Acquisition of qualified teacher status

Since TPSs imply expectations from the government and the public and are based on the professional knowledge of teachers, the government has to take advantage of the contents of the standards while reviewing applicants for the teaching license to make sure that they meet the eligibility requirements before a license is issued. For those wishing to obtain the eligible teacher status nowadays in Taiwan, in addition to completing education programs, they must finish a six-month education practicum and successfully pass the teacher qualification exam. As long as the teacher licensing process remains unchanged, TPSs can be applied to review teacher education status in each participating university. Universities with teacher education shall comply with TPSs while establishing eligibility requirements for students of teacher education programs and review them regularly.

Evaluation of qualification during induction

The induction is the period of time in which teachers first enter schools as teachers to experience school life together with students. In the United Kingdom, in particular, the teacher licensing system consists of two stages. Applicants have to meet the requirements set forth in the Teachers' Standards while being evaluated during the induction period before being eligible to receive a teaching license. In Taiwan's case, the induction period begins with a six-month education practicum and an initial period of beginning to work as a teacher in a school is also part of the induction period. As the teacher profession standards in the UK are used in the induction period, the standards of Taiwan are used in the education practicum period as well so that interns know the professional knowledge, skills, and disposition they must acquire in a school setting, while universities with teacher education and education practicum can understand the level of professionalism expected of interns in their performance. Professional standards in this sense can be used as a screening tool for accomplishments during the education practicum and subsequently serve as the basis for interns to obtain their teaching license.

Professional development and annual evaluation for beginning teachers

The UK experience shows that Teachers' Standards help individual teachers that have a teaching license and are currently teaching in schools review their own teaching performance and plan their future professional development, including observing, preparing for, and reflecting upon instructions, etc. Letting in-service teachers examine their own performance and plan professional development is also applicable given the context in Taiwan. In-service teachers can take advantage of TPSs. The standards can serve as a tool that helps reflection upon the teaching process and the planning of professional development in the future. In addition to professional development, the standards can also be utilized in the annual evaluation of teachers' performance, the so-called teacher evaluation. In Taiwan, however, teachers' associations neither support teacher evaluation nor believe in the fairness of teacher evaluation design. Further negotiations are required to make TPSs a basis for the annual evaluation of teachers' performance. In addition, TPSs can be used during the professional development process and serve as the basis for teachers to renew or update their teaching license. Of course, it relies on planning with regard to how the renewal or update of the teaching license can integrate with the teacher evaluation system given the context in Taiwan in the future.

Promotion of teachers

In addition to enabling in-service teachers plan their professional development and work together with other teachers, TPSs can also be applied to the promotion of teachers. With TPSs that define the different levels of performance, in particular, the government can use them to recognize teachers of outstanding performance. Aside from honoring additional salaries, different roles in the professional division of labor are given. This will inspire teachers to expand their different professional competences. In Taiwan, however, the teacher evaluation system is resisted, and the teacher career ladder system featuring spontaneous application by teachers and professional division of labor is not supported either. There will be opportunity in the future for substantial discussions to facilitate the planning of the teacher promotion system so that TPSs can also exercise the function of demonstrating the role of teachers in the professional division of labor, and praising teachers.

Management of inappropriate behavior of teachers

In the UK, Teachers' Standards are used to evaluate teachers with behavioral performance falling short of expectation and serve as the basis for adequate counseling or discontinued employment. In Taiwan, however, the time required for the management of inappropriate behavior of teachers tends to drag on and it often ends up going to court. Therefore, there is space for applying the standards to the misconduct of teachers.

Certification of institutions by teacher education evaluation

For the control over the quality of teacher education, there are generally two approaches adopted by governments in different countries. One is evaluation as in the UK and the other is accreditation as in the US, for example. Although the two approaches differ in conceptualization and actual operation (ENQA, 2006; Huang, 2012), they exercise the same effect in terms of quality assurance. In the UK and the US, TPSs are interlinked with teacher education evaluation and are meant to review whether teacher education institutions are capable of cultivating talent meeting established professional requirements. They are able to adequately evaluate the performance of graduates from teacher education programs. Despite the existence of teacher education evaluation in Taiwan, the yet-to-be-announced TPSs have made it difficult for teacher education evaluation to be linked with TPSs.

As far as the developmental context in Taiwan is concerned, the unique teacher education process is equipped with a mechanism for controlling the quality of teachers such as the qualification exam and teacher education evaluation, despite the absence of state-level TPSs. The system to consolidate teacher evaluation, replacement of the teaching license, advancement, and professional division of labor, however, is yet to become a reality. If TPSs are announced in Taiwan to be an important reference document for the teacher education process, the government has to have convincing reasons available and provide rational policy governance for the establishment of these professional standards in order to bring about results that are reasonable and meet the expectations of teachers and the general public, particularly because TPSs begin with the professionalization movement and are meant to enable the government to demonstrate substantial performance and fulfill the quality control purpose under the operation mechanism on the market.

Taiwan's experience in configuring and applying teacher profession standards

TPSs in Taiwan, regardless of whether the Society Version, Index Version, or Draft Version is adopted, appear chaotic and confusing due to a lack of integration at the central level. Taiwan lacks systematic and consistent criteria for teacher education evaluation, licensing, and professional development certification. A closer look at the underlying causes of the aforementioned issues reveals the following possible culprits.

Unique sociopolitical environment

Ever since political restrictions were lifted in 1987, Taiwan has become a relatively free society; this is also true of its education system. Numerous education organizations began organizing formal protests and lodging official complaints in 1994. The organizations demanded education reforms, including the adoption of smaller classes and smaller schools, universal access to high school and university education, "modernization" of education, and the establishment of the Educational Fundamental Act. The Executive Yuan formed the Committee on Education Reform in 1994 to take charge of planning directions and strategies to be followed in free and democratic education reforms, including breaking away from the monopolized teacher education market under the normal education system, impacting not only subsequent education reforms but also the teacher education model and system. The political system in which the winning party rules also set the prelude to political power alternation. Society in Taiwan was filled with bottom-up appeals for reforms. Democratic and free discussions gradually took shape. As a result, the government has to listen to the voices of all stakeholders with regard to various education reform issues, which also has an effect on the length of time involved in the reformation or promotion of an act.

Political influence on the consolidation of the SBTE policy

When the four-year Enhancement Program for Teacher Education Quality came into force in 2006 in Taiwan, it was based on the SBTE policy. However, the contemporary policy planner was later transferred to another position and the successor failed to precisely implement the SBTE policy, declaring only that SBTE should be consolidated by universities with teacher education in the form of administrative announcements, without any relevant strategies or making TPSs the basis for issuing a teaching license (Huang, 2010). Even though the Ministry of Education had announced the four-year Enhancement Program for Elementary and Secondary Teachers' Quality in 2009, it failed to make SBTE the mainstream policy or to expand and consolidate the various strategies to facilitate SBTE by developing evaluation, planning, and applying the scope and applicability of the professional standards, and carrying out research, for example. In effect, the transfer of the policy decision-maker impacted the consolidation of the SBTE policy and the development of TPSs, as well as the planning timeframe of other relevant institutions.

Conservative, realistic, and isolated teaching culture

As a result of Confucian culture, teaching in Taiwan is a respected and authoritative profession. As the education level of parents increases and society becomes more democratic and free, the students' right to education is gaining prominence. As such, teaching is not as well reputed as it was traditionally under Confucianism. Given this social context, teachers in Taiwan appeared to carry the traits of conservatism, individualism, and presentism of teacher culture as indicated by Lortie (1975). As a result, the professional knowledge, skills, and disposition included in the TPSs could hardly be emphasized. The promotion of professional development evaluation, the mentor teacher system, the learning community, and the professional learning network for teachers, among others over the past years in Taiwan, however, have been in favor of teachers forming a collaborative culture that will help them observe each other's classes and reflect upon themselves as well as reform their teaching approach. If the formation of a collaborative culture among teachers continues into the future, it should be helpful in terms of applying TPSs while in service.

Lack of trust in schools

Teachers and administrators in schools should basically work together to help students' learn. Under the traditional culture where teachers were considered to be civil servants in Taiwan, both the evaluation system and benefits appeared to be similar. Nowadays, although teachers are not civil servants and have autonomy over their teaching profession, the evaluation system has remained unchanged. Furthermore, the salary structure remains identical to that in the past. In light of the daunting task of revolutionizing the salary structure for teachers, rating teachers according to their actual performance and deciding the deserved salary accordingly remain difficult in the contemporary school setting. When administrators have an influence over teachers' performance or when the ability of administrators to rate teachers is challenged, in particular, teachers will find it difficult to believe the rating score. As a result, the school as a whole is not operating on the basis of trust. This will also affect the application of TPSs. It is particularly true when TPSs are the criteria in teacher evaluation and also the basis for rating teachers' performance. The lack of trust in the school culture will undermine consolidation of TPSs.

Lessons learned from Taiwan

The SBTE policy was set in Taiwan because there were too many teachers pending placement and marketized teacher education was unable to keep track of the quality of teachers. It also rationalized and legitimatized government intervention. Although it follows a similar trend in the international community, the unique context in Taiwan makes it inevitable that issues in society will be addressed while promoting the SBTE policy. If Taiwan's experiences are used as a reference, the contextual issues in Taiwan should become fairly discernible, including the following.

Belief underlying the formation of the SBTE policy

Implementing the SBTE policy is to ensure the efficacy of teacher education and also to control the quality of teachers under the marketized teacher education model. The government establishes TPSs in order to guide teacher education and serve as the criteria for evaluating teachers. Furthermore, to help the general public and teachers in Taiwan understand the rationale of the policy is a mission to be fulfilled by the government before the latter promotes the SBTE policy in order to form a consensus on the policy.

Gradually advancing scope of application and target of TPSs

TPSs encompass the expectations of the state and the public for teachers and also for the foundation of teachers' professional knowledge and skills; this means that those who have secured a teaching license are qualified teachers in accordance with the standards. They help lay the groundwork for teachers' professional standing and reputation in society. Meanwhile, for in-service teachers, professional standards help them with self-reflection and facilitate collaboration among teachers. TPSs are also criteria by which teacher education institutions are evaluated. As such, their applicability reaches out to people and institutions. Given the context of Taiwan, the application of TPSs must consider the short term, mid term, and long term. In the short term, TPSs such as teacher education evaluation and the professional development of in-service teachers are to be integrated into the existing system in Taiwan. In the mid term systems implemented over the past few years – teachers' licensing and the confirmation of eligibility during the induction period – are something that can be planned for the time being and implemented accordingly in Taiwan. The long term, on the other hand, requires a greater amount of time in terms of communication and planning. The implementation of teacher evaluations, promotions, and management of inappropriate behavior, among other issues, are entirely reliant on government intervention. In other words, with Taiwan's experience as an example, the underlying ideology and application of TPSs should be planned and implemented sequentially.

Understanding the maturity of the application context for TPSs

With regard to the scope of application of TPSs, there are contextual factors to be considered while consolidating SBTE. Such contextual factors can include the teaching culture, the campus culture, the direction of education reform, teachers' associations, policy promoters, and an effective system. These contextual factors are also important in terms of their influence on the teacher education policy in Taiwan. They can affect where the SBTE policy is headed, too. In particular, the voice of the people is highly valued in the sociopolitical environment of Taiwan. With input from all related stakeholders, communication takes a long time in the promotion of any policy and is heavily reliant on the wisdom of the policy-maker in question. Therefore, to promote the SBTE policy in any state, it is necessary to understand the maturity of the local sociopolitical context, whether there is an effective system to facilitate the application of TPSs, and whether or not to support the underlying concept of TPSs. All of these must be clarified before any policy can be promoted.

Designing a system to smoothly implement TPSs

After a government announces its SBTE policy directions and establishes state-level TPSs, the next step should be to design related systems applying the standards.

To apply TPSs to different stages, in particular, it is necessary to adjust the contents of the standards in order to internalize them and respond to the varying degrees during the professionalization process. In addition to adjusting the contents of TPSs, the question of how different stages and different aspects are evaluated should also be accounted for in the design in order to better measure true performance. Performance indicators corresponding to TPSs should be used to determine the extent of compliance and serve as the basis for subsequent results to be utilized. After the government establishes its TPSs, subsequent systems including performance measures of the professional standards, levels of performance and evaluation methods for different stages, determination criteria, and application of results, among others, must be designed together, too, in order to implement the SBTE policy.

Recognizing the potential effects and impacts of applying TPSs

As previously discussed, when a state defines its SBTE policy directions and establishes TPSs, it is necessary to define the conceptual underpinning and framework of the policy. Taiwan is faced with the dilemma of whether it should follow the international trend by adopting marketized teacher education in order to demonstrate teacher education performance, to control the quality of teachers, and to enhance teachers' professional standing and occupational reputation. On the other hand, there is no denying that it is questionable whether such an SBTE policy is the only way to enhance teachers' professional standing and occupational reputation. As such, a variety of possible impacts and resistance is inevitable. Therefore, knowledge of the underlying differences among TPSs should not be ignored during the process of implementing TPSs. Examples abound of other nations, such as Finland, which have not adopted TPSs and yet retain a relatively respected professional standing and occupational reputation in the international community. In summary, when the government applies TPSs, core values, namely "standardization" and "respecting teachers as professionals", must be strictly adhered to in order to respond to the effects of adopting professional standards during the implementation process as well as to fulfill the purpose of reiterating both the professionalism and quality of teachers.

References

Apple, M. W. (2006) *Educating the "Right" Way: Markets, Standards, God, and Inequality*, 2nd edn. New York: Routledge.

Darling-Hammond, L. (1990) "Teacher professionalism: why and how?' in A. Lieberman (ed.), *Schools as Collaborative Cultures: Creating the Future Now*. Philadelphia, PA: Falmer, pp. 25–50.

Darling-Hammond, L. (2001) "Teacher testing and the improvement of practice," *Teaching Education*, 12 (1): 1–24.

Department for Education (UK) (2014) *Teachers' Standards: How Should They Be Used?* Retrieved from: https://www.gov.uk/government/uploads/system/uploads/attachment_data/file/283567/Teachers_standards_how_should_they_be_used.pdf.

ENQA (2006) *Mapping External Quality Assurance in Central and Eastern Europe: A Comparative Survey by the CEE Network.* Retrieved from: http://www.enqa.net/pubs. lasso.

Hirsch, E., Koppich, J. E., and Knapp, M. S. (1998) *What States Are Doing to Improve the Quality of Teaching.* Seattle, WA: Center for the Study of Teaching and Policy, ERIC Document Reproduction Service No. ED 427007.

Huang, J. L. (2008) "A sociological analysis on institutions of teacher profession," *Journal of National Taiwan Normal University: Education*, 53 (3): 125–51 (in Chinese).

Huang, J. L. (2010) *Standard-based Teacher Education Reform in the Context of Globalization: The Case in Taiwan.* Paper presented at the International Academic Forum hosted, the Asian Conference on Education 2010: Internationalization or Globalization? 2–5 December 2010, Ramada Osaka, Japan.

Huang, J. L. (2012) "Comparative framework and theories on teacher education accreditation systems in different countries," in S. K. Yang, Q. R. Wang, and F. J. Lee (eds), *Comparison of Teacher Education Accreditation Systems in Different Countries.* Taipei: Higher Education (in Chinese), pp. 17–40.

Huang, J. L. (2013) *The Idea and Practice of Standards-based Teacher Education.* Taipei: National Taiwan Normal University Press (in Chinese).

Huang, J. L. and Chang, M. W. (2014) "Comparing and thinking about issues concerning the design of systems inspiring teachers in Taiwan from international perspective," in C. J. Wu and J. L. Huang (eds), *Challenges of Teacher Education in Face of 12-Year Basic Education.* Taipei: Teachers Education Society of ROC, pp. 195–256.

Ingvarson, L. and Rowe, K. (2008) "Conceptualizing and evaluating teacher quality: substantive and methodological issues," *Australian Journal of Education*, 52 (1): 5–35.

Larson, M. S. (1977) *The Rise of Professionalism: A Sociological Analysis.* Berkeley, CA: University of California Press.

Lee, F. J. (2008) "Teacher education," in the National Institute of Educational Resources and Research (ed.), *Education Yearbook of Republic of China, 2007.* Taipei: National Institute of Educational Resources and Research, pp. 225–74 (in Chinese).

Lindsey, M. (1973) "Performance-based teacher education: examination of a slogan," *Journal for Teacher Education*, 24 (3): 180–6.

Lortie, D. C. (1975) *School-teacher: A Sociological Study.* Chicago: University of Chicago Press.

McCulloch, G. (2001) "The reinvention of teacher professionalism," in R. Phillips and J. Furlong (eds), *Education, Reform and the State.* London: Routledge, pp. 103–17.

Ministry of Education (2007) *Statistics Yearbook of Teacher Education, Republic of China, 2006.* Retrieved from: https://inservice.edu.tw/Download/Edu-paper95.pdf (in Chinese).

Ministry of Education (2012) *White Book of Teacher Education in ROC: Promoting the Teaching Profession to Cultivate Future Talent.* Taipei: MOE (in Chinese).

Ministry of Education (2013) *Statistical Yearbook of Teacher Education, Republic of China, 2012.* Retrieved from: http://www.edu.tw/FileUpload/1052-16924/Documents/101.pdf (in Chinese).

Ministry of the Interior (2013) *Fertility Rates of Childbearing Age Women.* Retrieved from: http://sowf.moi.gov.tw/stat/year/list.htm.

Stephenson, J. (1999) "Evaluation of teacher education in England and Wales," *TNTEE Publications*, 2 (2): 191–201. Retrieved from: http://tntee.umu.se/publications/v2n2/pdf/20England2.pdf.

Strain, M. (1995) "Teaching as a profession: the changing legal and social context," in J. Busher and R. Saran (eds), *Managing Teachers as Professionals in Schools*. London: Kogan, pp. 39–57.

Sun, C. L. (2009) *The Future of Teacher Education Policy and Practice*. Taipei: Pro. Ed. (in Chinese).

Sykes, G. and Plastrik, P. (1993) *Standard Setting as Educational Reform: Trends and Issues Paper No. 8*. Washington, DC: ERIC Clearinghouse on Teacher Education and American Association of Colleges for Teacher Education.

Teachers Education Society of ROC (2005) *Teacher Education Policy Proposal*. Taipei, TWN: Teachers Education Society of ROC (in Chinese).

Valli, L. and Rennert-Ariev, P. (2002) "New standards and assessments? Curriculum transformation in teacher education," *Journal of Curriculum Studies*, 34 (2): 201–25.

Whitty, G. (2002) "Teacher professionalism in new times," in W. C. Hsieh and Sophian M. L. Wen (eds), *School Management and Leadership*. Taipei: Hung Yen, pp. 1–29.

Wu, W. D. (2005) "Establishing a professional teacher education system," in Teachers Education Society of ROC (ed.), *Teacher's Educational Beliefs and Professional Standards*. Taipei: Psy. Ed., pp. 231–48 (in Chinese).

Zeichner, K. M. (2003) "The adequacies and inadequacies of three current strategies to recruit, prepare, and retain the best teachers for all students," *Teachers College Record*, 105 (3): 490–519.

Part 2
Developing teacher education

5 The development of pre-service teacher education courses

Yu-Fei Liu

Introduction

In *On Teaching*, Tang dynasty scholar Han Yu described the responsibilities of teachers, stating, "Teachers convey doctrine, impart professional knowledge, and resolve doubts". Han also emphasised the function of teachers in transferring reason and knowledge and answering questions, asserting that "people are not born with knowledge", but must study under teachers to learn. However, the modern era of rapid knowledge advancements and network technology innovations has influenced and altered student learning models. In addition, network technology has threatened to replace the functions and roles of teachers gradually. In view of this, establishing the ideal image of a teacher (encompassing the responsibilities and roles of teachers) that corresponds with the contemporary era is crucial. Cultivating prospective teachers who conform to this ideal image through pre-service teacher education (which includes designing relevant courses for enhancing the ability of prospective teachers to use information to impart knowledge and provide guidance and counselling for resolving doubts) is even more critical.

According to Article 3 of the Teacher Education Act of 1994, pre-service teacher education courses are "the various applicable courses to be taken in accordance with this Act before undergoing teacher certification". Therefore, in the teacher education system, among the three primary stages of pre-service education – internship and introduction (including certification examinations) and in-service education – pre-service teacher education lays a critical foundation for the career development of a professional teacher. In addition, the content planning and implementation of pre-service teacher education courses deeply influence the cultivation of the professional knowledge, attitudes, and teacher image of prospective teachers. On a national level, the relevance of pre-service teacher education is as described in the White Paper of Teacher Education in ROC, published by the Ministry of Education in 2012: "The key to a country's future lies in education. The quality of education is founded on excellent teachers". The human resources that are fostered through education and training are key factors in promoting social and economic development and improving international competitiveness. Teacher education is a critical project and the core of developing education quality. Therefore, according to the concept that excellent teachers drive a nation's development, the first stage of teacher education, pre-service teacher education, involves cultivating diverse professional knowledge and skills among prospective teachers. These skills, which include information integration in teaching, lifelong learning, and adaptive coaching, enable teachers to cope with the changes in the educational environment caused by globalisation and informatisation, the professional development needs of a society that engages in lifelong learning, the effect of population aging and declining birth rates, and the changes in campus and family ecology (Ministry of Education, 2012). Pre-service teacher education courses are critical to actualising the philosophy that excellent teachers drive a nation's development.

In teachers' career development, pre-service teacher education is a critical period for acquiring professional teaching knowledge. Thus governments must rely on the implementation of pre-service teacher education courses to cultivate competent teachers and implement educational reform policies and address social needs, which is crucial to establishing the position of the teaching profession in society. The framework and content of pre-service teacher education courses and the ideas behind course design are critical to the career needs of teachers and the requirements of national policy development. However, for this reason, when pre-service teacher education courses are developed, the educational philosophies and ideologies of the current generation frequently dominate the course content; thus content is repeatedly reviewed and revised following changes in education. As indicated below, in reality, the national framework formulated by a country (such as revisions to relevant laws, including the Normal Education Law of 1979 and the Teacher Education Act of 1994, changes in education philosophy, and depictions of a teacher image) frequently control and influence pre-service education, which is as critical to teacher education as a foundation is to constructing a home. Therefore, from a macroscopic historical viewpoint, we analyzed the development of pre-service teacher education courses and the philosophies and content therein. A microscopic view of trends in Taiwan's teacher education policies was then considered to analyze the architecture and categorisation of current course design. Finally, we determined the challenges and reform trends in pre-service teacher education courses and proposed relevant recommendations.

Philosophies, content, and development of pre-service teacher education courses

In Table 5.1, the development of pre-service teacher education courses in post-war Taiwan is divided into two stages according to the announcement and implementation of the Teacher Education Act in 1994: unified teacher education (1949–93) and pluralistic teacher education (1994–present). We explain these stages as follows.

Table 5.1 Development of pre-service teacher education courses in Taiwan

Stage	Unified teacher education (until 1993)	Pluralistic teacher education (since 1994)
Legal basis	Normal Education Law of 1979	Teacher Education Act of 1994
Positioning	Planned-type: Training = Demand Teaching positions available immediately after training	Reserve-type: Training > Demand No guarantee of immediate teaching positions
Type	State controlled	Marketised
Major policies or laws	• 1933–78: The Normal School Rules • 1968: Implementation of 9-Year Compulsory Education • 1979: Promulgation of the Normal Education Law	• 1994: Promulgation of the Teacher Education Act of 1994 • 2002: Amendment to the Teacher Education Act of 1994 adopted • 2006: Announcement of Enhancement Programme for Teacher Education Quality • 2006: Announcement of Regulations for Evaluation of Universities with Teacher Education • 2009: Announcement of Enhancement Program for Elementary and Secondary Teachers' Quality • 2012: Publication of the White Paper of Teacher Education in ROC • 2013: Ministry of Education establishes the Department of Teacher and Art Education • 2014: Implementation of 12-Year Basic Education
Teacher image	Excellent Teachers Drive a Nation's Development: promoting national reconstruction and revival (clergy)	Excellent Teachers Drive a Nation's Development: improving the international competitiveness of the nation (laborers, specialists)
Course philosophy	Humanist philosophy Competency-based philosophy (beginning in the 1960s) Criticism- and reflection-based philosophy (beginning in the 1980s)	Focus on practical skills
Course content	• General courses: equivalent to current general education courses. Aimed at fostering common culture and laying a broad knowledge base in preparation for specialised and professional education.	• General courses: courses that students should take in order to receive the degree. • Specialised courses: emphasis on cultivating specialized knowledge and skills in the disciplines teachers teach and the areas of expertise

(Continued)

Table 5.1 Development of pre-service teacher education courses in Taiwan (Continued)

Stage	Unified teacher education (until 1993)	Pluralistic teacher education (since 1994)
Course content	• Specialized courses: emphasis on research and academics. Aimed at improving specialized knowledge and skills. • Educational profession courses: emphasis on practicality. Cultivation of the professional knowledge and skills and the professionalism that are essential for teachers.	• Educational profession courses: education credit courses for cultivating the education knowledge and skills needed for future disciplines (a) foundational education courses (b) courses on education methods (c) teaching materials, methods, and practicums (d) elective courses
Educational institutions	Normal education system (Normal/teacher universities and colleges and universities with education departments)	Schools in the normal education system, centres for teacher education at public and private universities and colleges
Implementation methods	State-sponsored system, registration and distribution system	Primarily privately funded (public funds and grants), testing and screening
Course review approach	Administrative review	Professional review: teacher education evaluation

Unified teacher education (1949–93)

The characteristic of this stage was state control, most evident during the period of Martial Law (1949–87). Therefore the implementation and cessation of martial law can be used to divide this stage into two periods to analyze the philosophies and content of pre-service teacher education courses during each period.

Philosophies and content of teacher education courses during the Martial Law period (1949–87)

After the central government of the ROC moved to Taiwan in 1949, the principles guiding policy-making included fighting communism, resisting Soviet Russia, recovering and building the nation; these policies also formed the foundation of education (Wu, 1991). According to the unique political system of an authoritarian country and the goals of national reconstruction and revival, the government clearly expressed that national defense was the top priority, and teacher education was a critical aspect of mental defense and construction. No effort was spared in promoting teacher education. In 1950, the Ministry of Education promulgated the Implementation Outline for Education to Suppress Communist Rebellion and Build the Nation, a successor to Article 5 of the ROC Education Aims and Implementation Guidelines (1929), which stated that "teacher education is the origin of national education for implementing the

Three Principles of the People". The philosophy of pre-service teacher education courses at that time focused on national spirit, Mandarin language training, both academic and vocational education, and a balance of knowledge and skill to cultivate competent and ethical professionals capable of serving as the foundation for building the nation (Chen, 1991). In other words, the ideal image of a teacher was that of a leader capable of cultivating young minds to promote national reconstruction and revival. Therefore pre-service teacher education became a major channel through which to propagate and instill the national development ideology of the Three Principles of the People; nationalism permeated the course content and implementation of pre-service teacher education.

The promulgation of the Normal Education Law 1979 provided a legal basis for teacher education. Under national control, teaching colleges became the primary institutions for teacher education. Programmes and government grants were available to cultivate prospective teachers. The government's implementation of planned teacher education policies improved teacher qualifications and the practice of professional education subjects, and also ensured the relevance of teacher education courses (Huang, 2014). In addition, national planning unified teacher education courses at each school. The education philosophy was initially humanistic, emphasising character moulding, self-concept and the conservation of a liberal education. Beginning in the 1960s, Huang *et al.* introduced an emphasis on establishing skill targets and a competency-based philosophy of observable and concrete performance skills in teaching practice (Huang, J. L., 2013). Beginning in the 1980s, an emphasis on situational analysis and decision-making opportunities was integrated into education. This philosophy of criticism and reflection specified that teachers should be critical and research-oriented or reflection-oriented, and be able to criticise and reflect on knowledge and skills (Tang, 2007).

Philosophies and content of teacher education courses during the period following the end of Martial Law (1988–93)

After Martial Law was lifted, a heightened democratic consciousness among the people, the rise of social movements and conceptual trends in the education market resulted in questioning and criticising the unified teacher education system and the closed content of pre-service teacher education courses. With reference to Table 5.1, the primary objective of pre-service teacher education shifted to emphasise cultivating quality teachers who should teach and were able to teach. Therefore, first, educational profession courses cultivated teachers who should teach, integrating education expertise on classroom management, course design and operation of instructional media to increase the effectiveness of student learning. Second, specialised education courses cultivated teachers who were able to teach; courses were planned around the core specialised capabilities required in a discipline to ensure that teachers possessed the required skills before entering the workforce for improving the learning knowledge and skills of students. Finally, general courses and education practicums ensured that teachers possessed a foundation in cultural literacy and humanistic concern and capabilities in liberal studies; teachers expected more from themselves and were willing to undertake the mission of fostering an exceptional younger generation (Ministry of Education, 2005). A series of struggles with and demands from education reform groups forced the government to appease public opinion and incorporate some of the ideas these groups advocated (Wang, 2008). The government began to review and draft amendments to the Normal Education Law of 1979 that would gradually open education opportunities to general universities and colleges. In other words, the mechanisms of the education market would be used to select capable and willing teachers. This concept was integrated into the teacher education system and courses following major changes to the Taiwanese political system. However, overall, nationalist values and beliefs continued to direct Taiwanese teacher education policy until a pluralistic teacher education policy was established in 1994 (Preparatory Office of the National Academy for Educational Research, 2009).

Pluralistic teacher education (1994–present)

This stage was characterised by marketization, particularly from the latter half of the 1990s to the first half of the 2000s. However, because teacher education system policies were rapidly and excessively loosened in the early 1990s, the operations of teaching market mechanisms could not be adjusted immediately, resulting in imbalances in teacher supply and demand. Austerity policies began to be adopted in 2006; the change in policy guidelines for teacher education during this year can be used to divide this stage into two periods: the relaxation of unification and the tightening of diversification. The first period involved volume expansion, whereas the second period focused on quality improvement. The philosophies and content of pre-service teacher education courses during each of these periods are as follows.

Philosophies and content of pre-service teacher education courses during the opening and loosening of policies (1994–2005)

In 1994, when the government revised the original Normal Education Law of 1979, renaming it the Teacher Education Act of 1994, the teacher education system entered a stage of diversification. During the stage of unified teacher education (1949–93), teacher education courses were of the planned type, that is training fulfilled demand and teaching positions were available immediately after training completion. By contrast, during the stage of pluralistic teacher education (1994–present), teacher education courses were of the reserve type, that is the training exceeded demand, and available teaching positions were not guaranteed (Ministry of Education, 2005). The nature of course design has enhanced the opening of teacher education channels to strengthen market mechanisms with free competition, improving the fundamental literacy and professional knowledge of prospective teachers. In addition, implementation methods have shifted from government funding for prospective teachers to private funding with government grants. Therefore course philosophies are competency-based and include concrete goals, objective assessments and quality control to fulfill the requirements of market competition.

During this stage, the government has repeatedly emphasised the operations of marketization mechanisms and attempted to eliminate any hints of nationalism. However, the ideal teacher image has continued to foster the philosophy that excellent teachers drive national development, and using teaching education policy to improve international competitiveness has been emphasised. In addition, a series of regulations and policies have been used to check and control course content and review methods. In other words, the law permits teacher education institutions to autonomously develop or consider specialized and professional courses that are based on individual institution characteristics and to submit plans for these courses to the central authorities for approval before implementation. Nevertheless, in reality, the policies planned by the central government have forced teacher education institutions to implement provisions without much flexibility or independence.

Philosophies and concepts of pre-service teacher education courses during the tightening of policies (2006–present)

The opening and loosening of policies during the first period ended the monopolization of the market by normal school students, allowing young people who wished to become teachers to fulfil their dreams. In addition, these reforms were a response to societal demands at the time, including pluralism, openness and freedom, and therefore received widespread support. However, rapid and excessive liberalisation soon led to a swift increase in the supply of prospective teachers on the teaching market. Moreover, the declining birth rate shrank market demand for teachers, causing an influx of "stray teachers" (people who have teacher's certificates but are unable to find permanent teaching jobs). Because demand exceeded supply, outstanding students may have feared enrolling in teacher education programmes, resulting in concerns that teacher quality was falling and mediocre teachers were driving away talented teachers in the teaching market. Some teacher education institutions tended towards instrumental training to cultivate prospective teachers rapidly while ignoring substantive content. This led to controversies involving the addition of credits and tuition to pre-service teacher education courses (Preparatory Office of the National Academy for Educational Research, 2009). More than ten years after teacher education reform was promoted, the pluralistic and open policy direction began to be questioned (Lee *et al.*, 2011).

Facing the need to balance the quantity and quality of teacher education, the government began by controlling the quantity of teacher education (Huang, J. L., 2013). Thus the improvement strategy employed during this period shifted from loosening policies to tightening policies. The quantity of teacher education institutions was reduced, and institutional evaluation and assessment was increased to alleviate overall demand for teaching positions and prevent excessive numbers of "stray teachers". This stabilized the supply and demand imbalance in the teaching market. To guarantee the quality and professionalism of teachers, in 2006, the Ministry of Education announced the Enhancement Programme for Teacher Education Quality. This programme stressed the importance of establishing standards-based teacher education policies and strengthening the professional competence of teachers, advocating for high quality in appropriate amounts. Similarly, in 2009, the Enhancement Programme for Elementary and Secondary Teachers' Quality was established to control the quality of teacher cultivation and improve teachers' professional knowledge, a matter that all sectors of society wish that the government could improve (Ministry of Education, 2009). Regarding pre-service teacher education during the cultivation stage of teacher education, the following have been promoted: specialized curricula and credit charts for trainee teachers; reviews and revisions of professional courses for pre-service primary and secondary school teacher education; teaching evaluations for teacher education instructors; and tracking of improvement measures. In other words, the ideal teacher image shifted from labourer in the education market to expert. Thus, course philosophies included a balance of quantity and quality, relying on societal expectations and standards to balance market performance and emphasising the standards-based philosophy. Institutions of teacher education have sought to use a standards-based philosophy to design and assess education and pre-service teacher education courses; thus the performance of prospective teachers can be monitored during every aspect of the learning and teaching processes, and the degree to which prospective teachers satisfy the standards of the ideal teacher image can be verified. The specific practice of this philosophy has received gradual attention.

However, standards-based teacher education is a method of state intervention. The government clearly defines the ideal teacher image and establishes the teacher profession standards for teachers to ensure quality (Yang, 2003). Therefore, by announcing the Regulations for Evaluation of Universities with Teacher Education in 2006 and establishing the Ministry of Education's Department of Teacher and Art Education in 2013, the central authorities in the teacher education system fully displayed state control of the marketization touted by the government. In particular, the White Paper of Teacher Education in ROC (published in 2012) and the Main Points on the Implementation of Professional Curricula and Credit Charts in Pre-service Teacher Education (published in 2013) indicated that in coordination with the implementation of 12-Year Basic Education, pre-service teacher education courses must provide credits, strengthen the teaching ability of prospective teachers and enable prospective teachers to preserve the morality of the teaching profession. Thus the education market operations managed by the government still involve state control of the quality of teacher education philosophies and teacher education courses. Although nationalism was superficially abolished, an excessive emphasis on democracy and market mechanisms focused on students and societal expectations caused pre-service teacher education course reform to stress practicality and underemphasize theory, an outcome that has drawn criticism and sparked discussion among scholars. This is discussed more fully in the following section.

In summary, in every era, the philosophy of pre-service teacher education courses has made the point that excellent teachers drive a nation's development. Even pluralistic teacher education (1994–present) that has incorporated marketization has been unable to avoid state control and intervention.

Structure, type and existing regulations of pre-service teacher education courses

Structure, type and existing regulations

According to the Teacher Education Act of 1994 (revised 4 June 2014), the Enforcement Rules for the Teacher Education Act of 1994 (revised 4 January 2011), the Professional Education Curricula and Credits for Pre-service Primary and Secondary School Teacher Education Courses and the Main Points on the Implementation of Professional Curricula and Credit Charts in Pre-service Teacher Education (published 17 June 2013), pre-service teacher education courses are divided into five categories: kindergarten, elementary school, secondary school, primary and secondary school, and special education (classes). Existing provisions for their structures and types are as follows.

Structures and types of pre-service education courses

1. *General courses* – courses that students should take in order to receive the degree.
2. *Specialized courses* – courses pertaining to specialized knowledge and skills required for the disciplines taught by teachers.
3. *Educational profession courses* – credit courses on the education skills and knowledge required for each teacher type. These include common courses, Foundational Education Courses, Courses on Education Methods, Teaching Materials, Methods, and Practicums, and Elective Courses and the particular courses for each teacher type. After review by the Teacher Education Review Committee, courses are implemented following approval by the central authorities. Table 5.2 shows the educational profession courses and minimum required credits (hours) for each type of pre-service teacher education course after the revisions for the 2013 academic year.
4. *Education practicums* – these are half-year, full-time education practicums, involving teaching practice, mentoring (of a class) practice, administrative practice and professional development activities.

LENGTH OF SCHOOLING FOR PRE-SERVICE TEACHER EDUCATION

In principle, schooling for each teacher's department lasts two to four years, followed by half a year of education practicum courses.

Table 5.2 Professional education subjects and minimal required credits for pre-service teacher education classes: 2013 academic year

Structure and type	Category	Kindergarten	Elementary school	Secondary school	Primary and secondary school*	Special education
Basic teaching curriculum		4 / 14**	10		10 / 38	1. General Education Courses: 10 / number (based on number of hours stipulated for the education stage)
Foundational education courses		4 / 8	4 / 8	4 / 8	4 / 8	2. Common professional courses for special education: 10
Courses on educational methods		4 / 14	10 / 12	10 / 12	10 / 12	3. Professional courses for special education in each category: 10
Teaching materials, methods and practicums		4 / 4	10 / (20–22)	4 / (4-6)	14–18 / (24–26)	4. Elective courses for special education in each category: 10
Elective courses		32 (Professional Educate Skills and Knowledge Courses)	6 / (46-47)	8 / (46-47)	8–12 / (46-47)	
Educational profession courses (minimal total credits)		48	40	26	50	40
Field study for each teaching category***		54	72	54	90	Based on number of hours stipulated for the education stage

*In accordance with teaching requirements, beginning in 2004, institutions of teacher education may combine secondary and elementary school planning into the category of primary and secondary school teacher education. This may be implemented after approval from the central authorities.
**(Minimum required credits) / (Total credits listed)
***Minimum number of hours

PARTICIPANTS OF PRE-SERVICE TEACHER EDUCATION COURSES

In addition to students, depending on the requirements approved by the central authorities, university graduates may be recruited to take pre-service teacher education courses for a minimum of one year plus half a year of education practicums. Furthermore, those with at least undergraduate degrees from foreign universities who fulfil the standards of the pre-service teacher education courses may apply to attend half a year of education practicums after obtaining permission from the central authorities.

Scope of pre-service teacher education courses

Those who have obtained qualified teacher certificates in one category and have completed pre-service teacher education courses in another category are awarded teacher certificates in the second category by the central authorities. They need not attend education practicums and take teacher qualification tests.

Tuition for pre-service teacher education courses

Tuition is primarily paid for by the students. However, public funds and grants are available. After publicly funded students graduate, they must serve at schools in remote or special regions.

The development of the structures and types of educational profession courses

The development of the structures and types of educational profession courses in postwar Taiwan has included increases and reductions in subjects and numbers of credits. With the exception in 1972, when no courses on teaching materials and methods were offered, the four main axes of foundational education courses (education methodology courses, courses on teaching materials, methods and practicums, and electives (no electives were offered before 1971) have been adhered to. With the exception of the 16 credits in 1972, the number of total credits has consistently remained near 26 (Huang, J. J., 2013). For example, regarding secondary schools, according to the Chart of Compulsory University Courses revised and announced by the Ministry of Education in 1983, teacher colleges were required to add a total of 26 credits in educational profession courses, including 22 credits in seven common compulsory subjects. Information Education was added as an elective. A total of four credits in two out of seven subjects had to be selected (Tang, 1990).

After the beginning of the pluralistic teacher education stage (1994–present), according to the secondary school education programme provisions announced in 1995, even though the number of credits remained at 26, the compulsory subject credits were changed to 12 credits in six subjects. The following subjects underwent relatively substantial changes: among foundational education courses, Introduction to Education was changed from four compulsory credits to two elective credits, Education and Career Counselling was changed from being compulsory to being an elective, and Philosophy of Education and Sociology of Education were changed from being electives to being compulsory. Among courses on education methods, Educational Anthropology, Classroom Management, Educational Testing and Measurement, and Counseling Theory and Practice were added. Simultaneously, 26 subjects were added to the elective courses recommended by the Ministry of Education, and 14 credits were required in seven subjects. Among these subjects, Information Education was changed to Computers and Teaching. In addition, teaching methods and technology courses, including Course Design, Instructional Media, Techniques for Behavioral Change and Education Statistics, were added. The following three trends in education reform can be observed from these substantial revisions.

- *Substantial reduction of compulsory subjects and increased elective subjects.* Compared with pre-service teacher education courses before 1994, compulsory subjects were substantially reduced and elective subjects were increased. This indicates that the government aimed to afford teacher education institutions more opportunities and flexibility to establish electives. In addition, courses became more diverse, which corresponded to educational reforms trending towards liberalisation and openness.
- *Emphasis on a competency-based philosophy and criticism and reflection.* Compared with pre-service teacher education courses before 1994 that emphasized humanistic and competency-based philosophies for general education and teaching, the added compulsory and elective subjects in 1995 exhibited reform trends that emphasised the competency-based philosophies of teaching specialization. The addition of Philosophy of Education and Sociology of Education as compulsory courses also symbolized stressing a philosophy of criticism and reflection.
- *Oriented towards practical techniques.* Among the 12 credits in compulsory subjects, the ratio of theoretically oriented (foundational education courses) to practically and technically oriented (education methods courses and teaching practicums) courses was 1:2. A minimum of half of the elective courses recommended by the Ministry of Education were oriented towards practical techniques.

In 2003, compulsory credits were revised to 14–16 in seven subjects. A substantial portion of these changes pertained to the foundational education courses. Introduction to Education was reverted to a compulsory course, indicating a renewed emphasis on overall and comprehensive understanding. Educational Anthropology was changed from being a compulsory course to being an elective course. Among courses on education methods, the elective Course Design and Instructional Media courses were transformed into Course Development and Design and Instructional Media and Operations. In addition, the system was changed so that three out of six course selections were compulsory. This change indicates that in accordance with the 9-Year Compulsory Education implementation and rapid technological development, improvements to comprehensive course competency and the ability of prospective teachers to use technological media were emphasised to increase teaching effectiveness (Huang, J. J., 2013). Although the number of elective subjects increased to 30, the credits were reduced to 12 in six subjects. Subjects on relevant contemporary social issues, such as Multicultural Education, Life Education, Gender Education and Human Rights Education, were added and the fields included expanded gradually. The following two education reform trends can be derived from these revisions.

- *Slight increase in compulsory courses and decrease in elective courses.* Compared with the 1995 pre-service teacher education courses, compulsory courses were increased slightly and elective courses were reduced slightly, indicating that the government became aware of the supply and demand imbalances in the teaching market and intended to adopt reform trends including diverse austerity measures.
- *Emphasis on practical techniques.* Among the 14–16 compulsory credit subjects, the ratio of theoretically oriented (foundational education courses) to practically and technically oriented (education methods courses and teaching practicums) courses was 1:2.5 (1:3). Among the 30 elective courses recommended by the Ministry of Education, subjects pertaining to relevant contemporary social issues were added. A total of at least 18 subjects were practically and technically oriented, indicating that the reform trend towards practical and technical subjects became stronger.

In 2013, the number of compulsory subject credits was revised to 18 credits in nine subjects. Compared with 2003, a relatively substantial portion of the changes were in the education methods courses. In accordance with the implementation of 12-Year Basic Education, the original Educational Testing and Measurement course was changed to Learning Assessment. Course Development and Design and Instructional Media and Application were added, comprising five subjects selected out of six. On the other hand, although the total number of electives was reduced to eight credits from among 23 subjects, Topics in Education (2 credits) was newly added as a "required" elective subject in response to the practical requirements of educational institutions to ensure that teachers understood relevant contemporary topics of interest to all fields. The so-called "required" elective subject refers to the need for prospective teachers to select this elective subject and acquire the credits in spite of its elective property. In addition, Education Service Learning was listed as an essential course and then Secondary School Field Study was fixed at a minimum of 54 hours. Furthermore, Teachers' Professional Development (including Teachers' Professional Ethics) was also added to cultivate the ethics of prospective teachers and enable them to understand the responsibilities and professional development of teachers. In accordance with the implemented 12-Year Basic Education, Remedial Teaching and Adaptive Teaching (including Forming Cooperative Learning Groups and Differentiated Teaching) were added as elective subjects to strengthen the adaptive and diverse teaching abilities of prospective teachers. In regard to major reforms in other categories, in accordance with pre-school integration, the number of credits required for prospective kindergarten teachers was increased from 26 to 48. Overall, the Ministry of Education reformed teacher education courses to strengthen prospective teachers' capabilities in practical teaching, adaptive counselling, differentiated teaching and diverse assessment. Cultivation and pragmatism were integrated to train teachers who were passionate about education and possessed professional and executive capabilities (Department of Teacher and Art Education, 2013). The following three education reform trends can be observed from these revisions.

- *Increased compulsory courses and decreased elective courses.* Compared with the 2003 pre-service teacher education courses, the increased compulsory courses were relatively substantial. These revisions were intended to strengthen the core competencies of novice teachers and enable them to enhance the physical and mental development of their students, as well as be competent in counseling, communication and classroom management. Therefore, courses on education methods were revised to a minimum of ten credits in five subjects. In other words, reform trends emphasizing strengthening teachers' professional competence and diverse austerity measures according to state control became even more apparent.
- *Emphasis on practical techniques.* Among the 18 credits in compulsory subjects, the ratio of theoretically oriented (foundational education courses) to practically and technically oriented (education methods courses and teaching practicums) courses was 1:3.5. Among the 23 elective subjects recommended by the Ministry of Education, such as the "required" elective subject of Topics in Education, Education Service Learning, Teachers' Professional Development (including Teachers' Professional Ethics), Remedial Teaching and Adaptive Teaching (including Forming Cooperative Learning Groups and Differentiated Teaching) were added, creating a total of 17 practically and technically oriented subjects and increasing the ratio substantially. In particular, policies were amended to strengthen the practical teaching capabilities of prospective teachers, specifying that prospective teachers should have at least 54 hours of on-site learning at primary and secondary schools (non-half-year educational practice). The purpose of these reforms was to strengthen educational profession courses for prospective teachers and incorporate specialised courses in the disciplines taught, converting these courses into competencies within the actual teaching process (Department of Teacher and Art Education, 2013). In other words, the reforms sought to improve the practical teaching capabilities of future teachers. Educational reform trends emphasizing practical techniques became more apparent and concrete.
- *Established policy purposes.* Compulsory subjects, such as Learning Assessment, Topics in Education, Remedial Teaching, and Remedial Teaching and Adaptive Teaching (including Forming Cooperative Learning Groups and Differentiated Teaching), were added in accordance with 12-Year Basic

Education. In other words, the policy purposes of designing and planning pre-service teacher education courses were to advocate and facilitate implementing national policy. Although Reading Education (formerly Reading Comprehension Education) was not a new subject, in accordance with the current trends, it was also upgraded to become one of the education subjects necessary to enhance national competitiveness.

Overall, the central education authorities must approve implementing teacher education courses in Taiwan (Yang and Huang, 2011). Even during the stage of pluralistic teacher education, the emphasis of the so-called diversification was the diversity of teacher education institutions. Among the frameworks and types of teacher education courses (including general courses, specialized courses, educational profession courses, and education practicums), with the exception of general courses and specialized courses, the decrees of the Ministry of Education standardized and controlled educational profession courses and education practicums (Huang, 2014). In particular, since the implementation of diverse austerity policies in 2003, state control of the number of credits and subject content of educational profession courses, regardless of whether they are compulsory or elective, has become increasingly apparent. Therefore, even though provisions stipulate that schools can freely establish their own elective subjects based on their prospective teachers and institution characteristics, in reality, teacher education must implement the centralized plans for teacher education courses; little space remains for designing and implementing unique courses.

In addition, the emphasis of market-oriented reform trends that focus on practical and technical skills have gradually reduced the ratio of theoretical courses. Because the number of credits is limited, fostering a theoretical foundation in students and developing theoretical perspectives is difficult. In addition, the lack of a specified ratio of theoretical and practical courses among electives may cause students to avoid difficult courses and take easier courses instead, selecting practical courses and neglecting a theoretical foundation (Wang, 1997).

Challenges and reform trends for pre-service teacher education courses

In 2012, the Ministry of Education announced the White Paper of Teacher Education in ROC: Developing the Teaching Profession, Educating a Person Takes a Lifetime. This policy White Paper clearly revealed current challenges and opportunities in pre-service teacher education courses in Taiwan. The focuses and latest reform trends are detailed as follows.

Supply and demand imbalance in the teaching market has reduced prospective teacher quality

The oversupply of teacher education directly affects the employment difficulties prospective teachers encounter upon graduation. Thus the number of people attending prospective teacher programmes has dropped, and exceptional students are less willing to join the teaching profession; prospective teacher programmes are struggling to find the most suitable candidates. This vicious circle indirectly enhances doubts about the purpose and results of pre-service teacher education courses. To improve the supply and demand imbalance in the teaching market, the government began to plan annual improvements for elementary school teacher preparation in 2012. The number of teachers per class was increased from 1.5 to 1.7 to afford ample human resources when teaching and increase teaching vacancies in each county, attracting exceptional students to the teaching profession (Ministry of Education, 2012). This created the potential to expand teacher demand gradually. In addition, to address the problem of teacher supply, the Ministry of Education presented the Deliberation Plan for Amending the Teacher Education Act of 1994, revising the stipulations in the Teacher Education Act of 1994 (amendment announced on 28 December 2005) to "certification first, practicum later". Thus public hearings were held at four sites around the country on 14 August 2014. A broad range of opinions regarding the draft of the amendment to the Teacher Education Act of 1994 was sought for reference (Ministry of Education, 2014). This amendment will cause the following two effects.

Changes to the definition and positioning of pre-service teacher education courses

According to Articles 3 and 7 of the current Teacher Education Act of 1994, pre-service teacher education courses refer to the relevant courses required before teacher certification. These courses include general courses, specialized courses, professional courses in education and education practicums. However, in the draft of the amendment, education practicums have been removed and included in teacher accreditation. In other words, prospective teachers can apply for six-month, full-time education practicums only after passing the teacher qualification exam.

This can be viewed as considering the needs of prospective teachers and education institutions, preventing wasted resources (eliminating the cost burden of practicums for students who are unclear about their goals and reducing the counseling burden for practicum institutions) and controlling the quality and quantity of practicum teachers. These steps may solve the teacher supply and peripatetic teacher problem. However, these steps exhibit the reform trend towards austerity policies of government control and intervention and gradual marketization in the teacher education stage. In addition, they may worsen the problem of "teaching for testing" in existing pre-service teacher education courses. The performance of prospective teachers on the teacher qualification exam has consistently been a major evaluation criterion for teacher education institutions. Without the buffer of a half year of education practicums, the test scores of prospective teachers are directly influenced by the pre-service teacher education courses at teacher education institutions. In short, the trend of transforming pre-service teacher education courses into cram school is problematic.

Changes in the meaning and orientation of pre-service teacher education courses

Under state control, the potential problem of teaching for testing in pre-service teacher education courses has emerged. Course content may have to include more test content and exercises to enable prospective teachers to pass the tests within a short period of time (two to four years). Semi-obligatory remedial teaching may also be required for prospective teachers who fail to achieve this objective. In addition, because pre-service teacher education courses lack the practical learning opportunities involved in the half-year, full-time education practicums, pre-service teacher education courses must include more subjects focusing on practical skills to offset the lack of actual teaching, classroom management and counseling situations. However, whether observations or trial teaching can replace the real learning situations encountered in half-year, full-time education practicums remains questionable. Consequentially, theoretically oriented courses may be compressed, potentially intensifying the problem of a bias towards practice and a lack of theory.

Professional education knowledge and skills of pre-service teacher education courses at each stage require systematic integration and holistic planning

1. Because current credit planning is limited, the practical teaching content of educational profession courses is insufficient.
2. The integration of specialized discipline knowledge and primary and secondary teaching materials is inadequate.
3. Course design for discipline teaching competency is insufficient.
4. Professional teaching competency, specialized discipline competency and discipline teaching competency have not been integrated comprehensively.
5. Teacher education courses pertaining to aspirations, ethics and morals are also lacking. Thus cultivating prospective teachers with strong moral character is difficult. After becoming teachers, teachers may struggle to encourage moral education in primary and secondary schools. Promoting "the culture of the teaching profession" (including Han's idea in *On Teaching*) is difficult and imparting knowledge and resolving doubts is challenging.
6. The teacher education process lacks experiential and reflective activities. Prospective teachers have few opportunities to participate in collective dialogue on personal growth experiences and education events or to criticize, question and reflect upon education beliefs and values.

Therefore, in response to these problems, the Ministry of Education proposed revisions in the Main Points on the Implementation of Professional Curricula and Credit Charts in Pre-service Teacher Education (issued 17 June 2013). These revisions included increasing the number of compulsory credits in courses on education methods and adding the compulsory practically and technically oriented subjects of Topics in Education, Education Service Learning, Teachers' Professional Development (including Teachers' Professional Ethics), Remedial

Teaching and Adaptive Teaching (including Forming Cooperative Learning Groups and Differentiated Teaching). Prospective teachers are also required to participate in practicums at primary and secondary schools (non-half-year education practicums) for a minimum of 54 hours. The purpose of these revisions was to enrich the practical teaching content of educational profession courses, foster the ethics and morality of prospective teachers and increase experiential and reflective activities that can improve the ability to criticise and reflect. In addition, the Deliberation Plan for Amending the Teacher Education Act of 1994 was developed to revise the content of Article 6 of the current Teacher Education Act of 1994. These substantial revisions will exert the following two effects.

- *Changes in the categories of pre-service teacher education courses: removal of the primary and secondary school teacher category.* The category of primary and secondary school teachers was created in response to implementing the 9-Year Compulsory Education. In accordance with teaching requirements, teacher education institutions could merge their planning for secondary and elementary schools into the category of primary and secondary school teachers. These plans can be implemented after approval from the central authorities; however, no teacher education institutions have applied for this merging currently. In addition, the government has determined that implementation would be challenging, partially because the development of prospective teachers for secondary schools and for elementary schools differs. These plans will therefore be eliminated (Ministry of Education, 2014).
- *Changes in the administration of pre-service teacher education courses: government reviews standards for pre-service teacher education courses.* The drafted amendment revises Article 4 of the existing Act. The object of review has been changed from "professional teacher education courses" to "the standards of pre-service teacher education courses". In addition, Article 10 has been revised to stipulate that the planning of courses in each category should be consistent with the standards of pre-service teacher education courses. Thus many planning principles for pre-service teacher education courses in each category are stipulated. For example, each teacher category should include prospective teachers with professional competency in disciplined teaching, adaptive counseling and the integration of issues into teaching. The promotion of character education and service learning activities for prospective teachers should also be strengthened to conform to the professional standards and performance indicators of each teacher category. According to pre-school integration policy, professional competency courses pertaining to teaching and nurturing required for prospective kindergarten teachers have been added. Teacher education universities have formulated these courses on the basis of the course standards provided by the central authorities and they have submitted them for approval to the central authorities (Ministry of Education, 2014). In other words, the government reviews the standards of pre-service teacher education courses. The actual practice of these courses influences whether state control is direct or indirect and the orientation of the checks on each level.

In summary, the content of the Deliberation Plan for Amending the Teacher Education Act of 1994 shows that the reform methods adopted by the government to address the current concerns in Taiwan's pre-service teacher education courses tend towards austerity measures and reinforce state control and marketization. Therefore claims that the amendments depart from the intention for diversification in the Teacher Education Act of 1994, and controversies over whether the government is revising the Act to defend unified education, have emerged in society.

Conclusion

In this chapter, we analysed the development of pre-service teacher education courses in post-war Taiwan and the course philosophies and content from a macroscopic, historical perspective. After various political systems, rapid economic development and dramatic social change, the Taiwanese pre-service teacher education system has changed substantially. The development of the philosophies and content of pre-service teacher education courses reflects the various education ideologies at each stage, emphasizing the different demands on professional competency. Nevertheless, the philosophy that excellent teachers drive a nation's development and the policy of state control have consistently remained the main axes of Taiwanese teacher education policy. Analysis on a microscopic level reveals that designing the framework and types of pre-service teacher education courses is the most direct method of implementing these philosophies and policies. Therefore state control has frequently become the subject of criticism and has been challenged by scholars and the public. Appropriately moderating and operating relaxed policies and austerity policies has also become a major difficulty and test for the government. Pluralistic teacher education has entered its twentieth year since the promulgation of the Amendments to the Teacher Education Act of 1994 and shifted from marketization towards state control, proposed in the Deliberation Plan for Amending the Teacher Education Act of 1994. This is a major turning point in the development of the teacher education system and pre-service teacher education courses. In particular, with the gradual implementation of 12-Year Basic Education, people are paying close attention to whether these revisions to teacher education policy and pre-service teacher education courses can correspond to education reform and serve as supporting measures. In the following section, we summarize the analyses and discussions from each section and present related recommendations.

Course planning: relaxing state control to establish unique courses within teacher education institutions

The government promulgated the Teacher Education Act of 1994 to fulfill the requirements of a pluralistic and open society (Ministry of Education, 2009). However, the so-called unified system mentioned in the act refers to teacher colleges, whereas the pluralistic system refers to teacher education universities

(Ministry of Education, 2005); the Act emphasises only the diversification of teacher education channels. Therefore, after the teacher education system became pluralistic and preparatory, whether teacher culture and quality truly improved remains questionable. Similar to the national planning control, despite diversification of teacher education institutions, teacher resources such as funds and equipment are inconsistent. In addition, because the state regulates the course curriculum, although courses can be changed freely, programmes adhering to similar formats must be created. Although establishing unified institutions appears neat and orderly, diversity and creativity are lost. In other words, to achieve professional competency among prospective teachers that is adequate for responding to various external situations, such as changing examinations or shifts in the supply and demand of the education market, the country's fixed foundational requirements (such as the accreditation of institutions of teacher education and requirements for course structure) are necessary.

However, the purpose and ideal of marketization should be to diversify teachers, and not merely recruit teachers from multiple sources. Diversifying teachers depends on the planning and actualization of diverse and unique courses. Although the Enforcement Rules for the Teacher Education Act of 1994 stipulate that universities and colleges can establish educational curricula according to their characteristics and teacher requirements, and implement curricula upon approval from the Ministry of Education, in reality, the courses at each school are controlled. In addition, the Main Points on the Implementation of Professional Curricula, Credit Charts in Pre-service Teacher Education and the 2014 Deliberation Plan for Amending the Teacher Education Act of 1994 complicated matters. In particular, policy requirements by the Ministry of Education to increase the number of compulsory credits have received criticism from multiple teaching universities. Teachers from the centres of teacher education at the National Chung Hsing University and the National Tsing Hua University have jointly petitioned the Ministry of Education multiple times under the name of the Teacher Education Development Association of the Republic of China, asking the government to withdraw specifications for prospective teachers, courses and curricula lengths at teacher education universities. They hope the curriculum and course design can be decided entirely by universities to maintain academic freedom and university autonomy (Chou, 2014).

In addition, Chen-Yung Lin, former head of the Office of Teacher Education and Career Services at the National Taiwan Normal University (NTNU), has called on the Ministry of Education to respect the spirit of university autonomy and allow teacher education universities to develop their own education credit schedules according to university characteristics, a move that would diversify teacher education in Taiwan in response to a pluralistic society. Therefore, in its formal teacher education courses, the NTNU has proposed an education credit schedule that differs from that of the Ministry of Education, emphasising the cultivation of disciplined teaching and practical capabilities. In addition, the NTNU has planned increased cooperation with local education bureaus and high schools to provide prospective teachers with richer practical experience, decreasing the gap between theory and practice. Former Minister of Education, Chao-Xiang Yang, has indicated that the system of the Teacher Education Act of 1994 changed substantially throughout implementation. However, teacher education universities have not varied much, failing to achieve the objective of diverse teacher education. Yang has recommended that the Ministry of Education engage in further liberalisation and deregulation. Chairman Shu-Ling Hwang of the Teacher Development Association of the Republic of China has also indicated that the Ministry of Education has considerable control over teacher education universities, which already lack room for creativity and cannot develop diverse teacher education. Hwang stressed that the Ministry of Education should reduce administrative control (NTNU, 2014). However, confusion encountered when establishing specialized subjects in teaching universities and universities in general poses a great challenge to the government's comprehensive liberalization of pre-service teacher education courses (Chou, 2014).

Scholars have continually debated whether the nation should regulate or deregulate pre-service teacher education courses and the appropriate level to which this regulation or deregulation should occur. However, as suggested by Yang, who referred to the teacher education reform in Germany, the Ministry of Education should commission professional education associations and specialized discipline associations to determine the knowledge and competency standards to which teachers of all levels should adhere. Different module combinations should be provided to guide schools or categorize teacher education subjects. Students should also be able to select course modules appropriate for their career development according to personal interests and plans. Thus schools could display the unique characteristics of their teacher education programmes and students could select the courses they require. This method is consistent with the law of market supply and demand and may prevent the current problem of teacher oversupply (Yang, 2006).

In response to the appeals and suggestions of numerous scholars, the Ministry of Education is currently reducing the gap between teacher education and practical training in accordance with the development of 12-Year Basic Education, strengthening pre-service university teacher education courses and practical course content in service education (Department of Teacher and Art Education, 2014). The Ministry of Education is preparing to promote subsidies for establishing teaching and research centres in the field of secondary education within teacher education universities. This plan can be regarded as reform involving course management. After 12-Year Basic Education was implemented, the diverse learning and counseling needs of students required responses from similarly diverse teachers. Therefore the ability levels of students in unified state-controlled pre-service teacher education courses or public and private teacher education institutions are inferior to the ability levels of students taking unique courses in specific fields planned and developed by each teacher education institution. The Ministry of Education aspires to use teaching and research centres to establish cooperation among institutions of teacher education with unique courses in similar fields. Moreover, to maintain the effective establishment of unique courses, teacher examinations and methods of state control that emphasize accreditation based on the examination pass rates of students should be loosened and revised. An emphasis on a unified national standard for examination pass rates should be avoided. Such a focus can lead to teaching for testing (university teachers teach only the content to be tested) or test-guided learning (students study only the content tested on the examinations). These trends impede the development of unique courses.

Course proportions: a balance of theoretical courses and practical and technical courses

In recent years, a continuous wave of reforms has affected teacher education. In particular, with the implementation of 12-Year Basic Education and philosophies emphasizing individualization and adaptation, the teaching and counseling roles and capabilities of teachers have received considerable attention. Responses and improvements to the teacher education system are critical. The public has scrutinized and questioned the appropriateness and comprehensiveness of pre-service teacher education course content and frameworks. People want future teachers to possess the knowledge and skills required for their new jobs before they enter schools (Chou, 2014). Thus the Professional Curricula and Credit Charts in Secondary School Pre-service Teacher Education have emerged. However, as mentioned above, although these reforms reflect and cater to the demands of the education market, they also exacerbate the emphasis on practice and technique in pre-service teacher education courses. The requirement for 26 credits limits the space for electives pertaining to foundational education theory. As a result, prospective teachers may engage in selective avoidance behaviour, avoiding difficult classes in favour of easy classes. Macroscopic historical perspectives, philosophical speculation and analysis, criticism and introspection must be developed when studying the philosophy, sociology and history of education (Chou, 2014). If this does not occur, the learning gained in practical and technical courses, such as Topics in Education, may be useful for only superficial educational topics, preventing students from observing clear causal relationships and original conditions. The opinions of the media may even control the judgements of prospective teachers, preventing them from gaining an in-depth understanding of major topics in education.

Therefore, as stated by Chou, a series of practical and technical subjects can be introduced to improve the ability of current or prospective teachers, enabling them to respond to the doubts elicited by 12-Year Basic Education without blaming the teacher education process or the pre-service teacher education courses. Whether or not the environment can allow teachers at educational institutions to display and use the course content they learned during the development stages should be considered. Thus, a learning community has been advocated. Manabu Sato, who triggered a wave of education reform in Taiwan beginning in 2011, hosted the World Association of Lesson Studies at the University of Tokyo in November 2011. Referring to experiences from overseas visits and numerous years of research and observation, Sato stated that in China, South Korea and Taiwan, because the pressures of the examination system are high, teachers struggle to depict an image of high-quality learning or to enable students and their families to comprehend learning styles involving creative, critical and exploratory thinking (Sato, 2012). The government must therefore adjust the principles guiding the current pre-service teacher education courses and adopt educational reforms that balance theoretical, practical and technical subjects.

In summary, the wave of austerity policies and reforms from the Deliberation Plan for Amending the Teacher Education Act of 1994 raised questions about the effects and influences. People are focusing on how the Taiwanese government will achieve a balance between state control and liberalization and between regulation and deregulation.

Historically, Taiwan's education system has emulated that of Japan. However, in recent years, Japan has also contended with the challenge of state control. The scholar Yasuyuki Iwata compared and analyzed the teacher education systems of various countries in East Asia, including those in Japan, Taiwan, China and South Korea. Iwata determined that all have adopted open and pluralistic systems. However, Japan differs dramatically from the other countries, which generally emphasize state control of the particulars of the entrance to and completion of teacher education. The Japanese government did not enforce total control; instead, it established an accreditation system for teacher education courses to guarantee teacher quality (Iwata, 2013). Thus, because unified national control is lacking, teacher quality varies greatly and teachers lack a sense of mission. In addition, the application of the accreditation system for teacher education courses has tended towards explicit indicators, including gradual interference with and regulation of the content of pre-service education courses (including specialized education subjects and professional education subjects). This harms the autonomous development of universities and is questionable in its ability to improve the quality of teacher education.

In addition, in 2000, Japan began to revise the Enforcement Regulations of the School Education Law, eliminating the existing appointment provisions for school principals (elementary to high school). A system of "principals (and assistant principals) without educational profession background" was introduced, opening principal posts to those without teaching certificates or even teaching experience, who possess experience in private enterprises (Liu, 2013). Businesspeople who had never taken pre-service teacher education courses and did not possess teaching licenses were allowed to serve as principals, introducing market-oriented management concepts. Although this scheme involved risk and controversy, it was effective, creating an atmosphere of innovation and course reform. This system challenged the existence and importance of the teacher education system and pre-service teacher education courses. Recently, student suicides caused by bullying and corporal punishment have occurred frequently. The notion that "school common sense lacks social common sense" (Shogakukan, 2003) renewed criticism that was aimed at school education and teachers. Therefore, local governments in Japan developed numerous reform strategies for hiring faculty, including Principals Introduce the Values of the Outside World and the 2014 Academic Year Appointed Principals Shall Employ Outside Talent. In other words, the importance of principals reflecting the values of civil society was emphasised. Moreover, to enhance teacher skills and renew trust in teachers, the Japanese government reverted to reviewing pre-service teacher education course content affecting the teacher development stages at teacher education universities (Central Council for Education, 2014). In addition, the government stressed that teacher education universities should cooperate with local boards of education and reflect board opinions in pre-service education courses to develop a cognitive balance between "school common sense" and "social common sense" among prospective teachers. Japanese scholars have asserted that during the functional development of teachers, teacher education universities should foster the skill of continuous learning, including introspection, in pre-service teachers and create a teacher image involving continuous learning (Yada, 2014). In short, Japan's successes and failures indicate that market mechanisms cannot be used solely to control the total quantity of teacher education or to regulate the content of pre-service teacher education courses. Appropriate state control of quality and quantity remains necessary. The philosophy that excellent teachers drive a nation's development is advocated by numerous countries around the world. However, excellent teachers are not necessarily homogeneous. Maintaining a balance between state control and marketization through the certification of teacher education institutions and teacher certification systems is a common transnational issue.

The professional education process comprises three continuous, inseparable and mutually influential stages of development: pre-service education, practicum and introduction (including examinations) and service education. Pre-service teacher education courses are controlled easily by the direct influence of the demands of practicums and introductions (particularly examinations). In addition, they are indirectly influenced by the professional growth requirements of the service education stage. Thus Yen (1990, p. 15) indicated "the teacher education courses established by teacher colleges or universities are only the starting points and not the ending points of teacher education". These three stages must be planned comprehensively. Revisions to education practicums according to the Deliberation Plan for Amending the Teacher Education Act of 1994 must be cautious and supporting measures must be planned to prevent pre-service teacher education courses from becoming short-term credit courses or accelerated cram schools that focus only on enabling students to pass the teacher qualification exam. Planning would enable these courses to truly cultivate a foundation of professional education knowledge and lifelong learning, allowing pre-service teachers to develop and expand their potential abilities continually in the second and third stages. As in Sato's "learning community", the role of the state is to support and build mutually beneficial relationships, not to exert control. Consistent and continuous planning, development and implementation of these three stages requires consensus, cooperation and effort from prospective teachers, education colleagues, local residents and governments.

References

Central Council for Education (2014) *About the Nature of School as a Team and Faculty's Responsibilities for the School Education in the Future (Advisory)*. Retrieved from: http://www.mext.go.jp/b_menu/shingi/chukyo/chukyo0/toushin/1350537.htm (in Japanese).

Chen, B. J. (1991) "The reflection and review of four decades of the development of compulsory education in Taiwan", in J. H. Lai and C. C. Huang (eds), *Taiwan's Development Experience Since the Restoration*. Taipei: Research Center for Humanities and Social Sciences of Academia Sinica, pp. 271–203 (in Chinese).

Chou, Y. W. (2014) "Challenges in teacher education after the implementation of 12-Year Basic Education', in C. J. Wu and J. L. Huang (eds), *Challenges of Teacher Education in Face of 12-Year Basic Education*. Taipei: Teacher Education Society of ROC, pp. 23–43 (in Chinese).

Department of Teacher and Art Education (2013) *The Ministry of Education Made Amendments to the Professional Curriculum of Pre-service Teacher Education for Strengthening Teacher Candidates' Professional Competence*. Retrieved from: http://epaper.edu.tw/news.aspx?news_sn=20309 (in Chinese).

Department of Teacher and Art Education (2014) *The Plan of Establishing Secondary Education Field-teaching and Research Center at Teacher Training Colleges/Universities*. Retrieved from: http://www.edu.tw/treasure/filedown.aspx?Node=1123&Index=2&WID=1112353c-88d0-4bdb-914a-77a4952aa893 (in Chinese).

Huang, J. J. (2013) "A Comparative Study in the Professional Curriculum of Pre-service Teachers' Teacher Education Program in Secondary Schools Between Taiwan and Japan". Unpublished Master's thesis. National Changhua University of Education, Changhua (in Chinese).

Huang, J. L. (2013) *The Idea and Practice of Standards-based Teacher Education*. Taipei: National Taiwan Normal University Press (in Chinese).

Huang, J. L. (2014) "The institution of obtaining teacher qualification since 1949 in Taiwan: perspective from historical institutionalism", *Chung Cheng Educational Studies*, 13 (1): 1–43 (in Chinese).

Iwata, Y. (2013) "On Japanese style teacher education reform: considering about the issues on quality development under the 'open system'", *Japan Society for the Study of Education*, 80 (4): 414–26 (in Japanese).

Lee, Y. F., Chiang, F. S. and Hsieh, I. C. (2011) "The importance of context analysis in educational borrowing: a study of social context for teacher education in America and its implication for Taiwan", *Journal of Educational Research and Development*, 7 (1): 35–52 (in Chinese).

Liu, Y. F. (2013) "The meaning of the system of 'principles without educational profession background' to the educational reforms about leadership for learning in Japan", *Journal of Education Research*, 229: 129–44 (n Chinese).

Ministry of Education (2005) *Education Categories: Teacher Cultivation*. Retrieved from: http://140.111.1.127/ct.asp?xItem=7120&ctNode=818&mp=1 (in Chinese).

Ministry of Education (2009) *Enhancement Program of Elementary and Secondary Teachers' Quality*. Retrieved from: http://www.edu.tw/pages/detail.aspx?Node=1169&Page=9001&Index=2&WID=1112353c-88d0-4bdb-914a-77a4952aa893 (in Chinese).

Ministry of Education (2012) *White Book of Teacher Education in ROC: Promoting the Teaching Profession to Cultivate Future Talent*. Taipei: MOE (in Chinese).

Ministry of Education (2014) *The Public Hearing Agenda of 2014 Program of the Amendment of Teacher Education Act 1994*. Taipei: MOE (in Chinese).

National Taiwan Normal University (2014) *Emphasizing on Teacher Education and Taking into Consideration of Theory and Practice*. Retrieved from: http://pr.ntnu.edu.tw/news/index.php?mode=data&id=13770 (in Chinese).

Preparatory Office of the National Academy for Educational Research (2009) *Final Report of the Review and Prospective of Teacher Education Policy*. Retrieved from: http://workshop.naer.edu.tw/9/study/link5_2.pdf (in Chinese).

Sato, M. (2012) *School Memoirs: The Practice of Learning Community*. Tokyo: Shogakukan (in Japanese).

Shogakukan (2003) *Latest Basic Education Terms*. Tokyo: Shogakukan (in Japanese).

Tang, W. L. (1990) "A Study in the Professional Curriculum of Teacher Education Programs in Secondary Schools in Taiwan". Unpublished Master's thesis, National Taiwan Normal University, Taipei (in Chinese).

Tang, W. L. (2007) "The dialogue between the philosophy and practice of the teacher education: a research of the professional curriculum', in S. C. Chou and L. H. Chen (eds), *The Challenges and Reflection of Educational Reforms*. Kaohsiung: Liwen Publisher, pp. 3–26 (in Chinese).

Wang, C. R. (1997) *The Construction of Teacher Education Programs in Junior High Schools in Taiwan*. Taipei: Shi Ta Books (in Chinese).

Wang, J. H. (2008) "The status of teacher education in Taiwan: a reaction to change in demographic structure", *NTTU Educational Research Journal*, 19 (2): 143–82 (in Chinese).

Wu, C. T. (1991) *The Outline of Educational Implementation for Counter-insurgency and the Founding of the Nation*. Retrieved from: http://terms.naer.edu.tw/detail/1312129/?index=1 (in Chinese).

Yada, S. (2014) "Prospects of reform in teacher education in Japan: concentrating on some policies by the Ministry of Education after the publication of the Report by the Central Council for Education in August, 2012", *Bulletin of Tokai Gakuen University, Human Science*, 19: 137–50 (in Japanese).

Yang, S. K. (2003) *Examination of Taiwan's Teacher Education Policy and System Through Comparative Education Theory*. Paper presented at the "Review and Prospects of Taiwan's Primary School Teacher Education" Symposium held at the National Taiwan Normal University's Department of Elementary Education, Taichung (in Chinese).

Yang, S. K. (2006) "State steering, market mechanisms and recent teacher education reform in Germany", *Journal of Educational Research and Development*, 2 (1): 119–44 (in Chinese).

Yang, S. K. and Huang, J. L. (2011) "Comparative analysis of the teacher education systems and teacher quality in different nations'", in S. K. Yang and J. L. Huang (eds), *International Comparison on Teacher Education System and the Status of Teacher Quality*. Taipei: MOE, pp. 353–401 (in Chinese).

Yen, F. P. (1990) 'Teacher education policies in social change'", in Teacher Education Society of ROC (eds), *Teacher Education Policies and Issues*. Taipei: Shi Ta Books, pp. 1–19 (in Chinese).

6 The education practicum from the development of teacher education in Taiwan

Wei-Ling Tang

Introduction

Since the pluralistic and open policy was adopted in 1994 in accordance with the Teacher Education Act, teacher education in Taiwan has been transformed from a planned system into a market-oriented model. The market-oriented teacher preparation became the main reform of teacher education policy. The policy enacted a double track, separating teachers preparation with job placements. The universities with teacher education became mainly responsible for preparation and the subsequent practicum stage. The Ministry of Education would verify or hold the qualification reviews for teachers and then local education administrative departments would hold the teachers' screening tests. Reserve teachers, as long as they completed the tests successfully, could enter the job market and become school teachers. This is the "cultivation and placement separated" system that separates teacher education from placement. Under this teacher education system, prospective teachers would complete teacher education courses as required by the Ministry of Education, obtain eligibility for the preliminary review as soon as they graduated from the teacher education program, and then start the practicum as interns at an elementary or secondary school. The practicum lasted for a year and they would receive allowances from the government on a monthly basis during this period. As long as they had a pass score for the practicum and acquired teacher's status through the secondary review, they could participate in the teachers' screening tests to seek eligibility for placement and, accordingly, get a job.

Since 1994, teacher education-related laws and regulations have gone through several changes. The most important turning point that had an effect on the contents of the practicum was the amendment in 2003; the practicum duration for prospective teachers was shortened to six months and the original verification system consisting of the preliminary and secondary reviews was changed to the teacher qualification exam after completion of the practicum. The six-month education practicum policy has continued since 2003. Whether there will be any changes to it in the future or not is something to be explored in this chapter. Over the past 21 years, in particular, normal education schools have been reformed, transformed, and even merged with comprehensive universities to become new universities. Their original mission in teacher education changed, which impacted the practicum that had taken root in the traditional normal teacher education. While practicums were taking shape among normal universities, education universities, and comprehensive universities in even larger quantities, the aspects of the education practicum being impacted by this trend, whether it helps enhance practicum quality or not, are still awaiting advanced analysis.

Adopting a document analysis method, this article explores developments concerning the education practicum system in teacher education laws and regulations of Taiwan, including policies, laws, and regulations of the Ministry of Education that have to do with the rises and falls and developments of education practicums. Specifically speaking, the Teacher Education Act and its Enforcement Rules, Teacher Education Action Plan, White Paper of Teacher Education, and policies promoted by the Department of Teacher and Art Education will be analyzed. Finally, the influence of professional development schools (PDSs) for the education practicum set by qualified and quality education practicum institutions will offer systematic support for prospective teachers in the future in Taiwan.

Teacher education laws and regulations and the revolution of the education practicum system

The teacher education system and education practicum reflect a cultural ideology. In the United Kingdom, for example, the practicum system is full of apprenticeship because of its tutor system in cultural tradition. In Germany, J. Fr Herbart, a proponent of German idealism, on the other hand, believed that practicum schools did not aim at interns practicing teaching experiences that mentors were familiar with and instead focused on reflecting upon the learned education theories; it differed from the technical principle-based idea of the practicum in the United Kingdom and the United States (Yang, 1994). In fact, the education practicum in the teacher education system of Taiwan, when analyzed, has multiple goals or functions, including: validating education rationales; combining education theory and practice; realizing tasks and responsibilities of teachers; becoming familiar with teaching methods and skills as well as with class management and student guidance; developing education administrative skills; cultivating virtues and merits as a teacher; consolidating professional attainments in education; exploring real problems; and inspiring professional aspirations, etc. (Lee, 2006; Lin and Lin, 2013; Wang and Lai, 2004). Education practicums are an important part of the teacher education system.

Education practicum system in the Normal Education Law of 1979

The official inclusion of education practicums in teacher-related laws and regulations of Taiwan began with the Normal Education Law announced in November

1979. The Law looked at the normal education policy as the spiritual national defense to help define the normal education and to facilitate the comprehensive and substantial plan of normal education. It stipulated that the normal education institutions, namely normal schools, consisted of junior teachers colleges, normal universities, and other teacher development and in-service institutions established by the government. Students did not have to pay for their tuitions with state-sponsorship while studying at normal schools. For public education colleges and departments, state-sponsored openings could also be provided for secondary school teachers and other education professionals. After state-sponsored students completed their studies with passing grades, they would be assigned by the education administrative agency to attend practicums off campus that lasted for a year. Those having completed their practicum with passing grades would be qualified for graduation and could continue teaching at the original practicum school.

Articles 11 and 12 of the Law, in particular, specified that "to reinforce the teaching practicum for students graduating from normal schools, they have to attend the practicum for another year besides the required duration of studies" (Legislative Yuan, 1979a, 1979b). The Ministry of Education established the "Implementation Guidelines for Education Practicum Guidance Provided to Students Having Completed Studies" at the National Taiwan Normal University to help reinforce practicum guidance provided to the students (National Taiwan Normal University, 2014). State-sponsored students at the three normal universities and the Department of Education at the National Chengchi University that were in charge of cultivating teachers to support secondary school education, were required to take the teaching practicum course worth four credits during their studies. They would be assigned with a one-year practicum after having completed studies, that is the post-completion practicum, which was combined with the teaching practicum on campus to be the education practicum. Later the scope of application was extended to cover the nine junior teachers colleges cultivating teachers to support elementary school education (Tang, 1994). The Normal Education Law continued with the teacher education policy of the one-year off-campus practicum after completion of studies at normal universities and required that the same should apply to contemporary junior teachers' colleges in order to signify the importance of the education practicum.

Because of the state-sponsored nature, these interns providing their academic scores and willingness lists were systematically assigned by the education administrative agency and substantially took up the openings for teaching positions in secondary or elementary schools. They could continue to teach at the same school after they had achieved pass grades for the practicum. As such, interns at this time taught classes on their own without practicum guidance. They were assigned full responsibilities as a teacher, had obligations to fulfill as a teacher, and could enjoy the rights of a teacher as they were technically serving in the capacity of an official teacher. In other words, the normal universities and the department of education at the National Chengchi University that were cultivating teachers to support secondary school education during this period were faced with the dilemma that, despite their ideals, the education practicum was not valued at all. The practicum became a mere formality. Besides, there were issues such as the uncertainty about the role of interns and the insufficient professionalism of mentors, let alone their ability to help interns and provide them with various types of practicum guidance. Only nine teachers colleges were equipped with a practicum guidance office and specialists and dedicated funds for use exclusively in practicums and hence had a relatively healthy organizational structure (Yang, 1993; Yang *et al.*, 1994).

One-year education practicum in the Teacher Education Act of 1994

In response to the transformation of the social structure, the political, economic, cultural, and educational changes, and the need to develop elementary and secondary school education, the Normal Education Law was amended and the name was changed on 7 February 1994 to the Teacher Education Act. The post-change Teacher Education Act featured pluralistic teacher education channels, the creation of the teacher qualification exams, and concurrent state-sponsored and self-sponsored offers, and reinforced the education practicum and in-service education for teachers. Reinforcement of the education practicum, in particular, involved amendment of the additional one year of practicum only to students who had completed their studies at pre-service teacher education courses, were qualified in the preliminary screening review, and intended to acquire their teacher qualifications. It also required a practicum guidance office at normal schools to take charge of practicum guidance in order to consolidate the education practicum system (Legislative Yuan, 1992, 1994). Upon closer inspection, the cultivation of teachers and other education professionals at this time was under the auspices of normal schools and universities and colleges equipped with education colleges, departments, institutes, or education programs. Teacher education referred to the pre-service, practicum, and in-service stages for teachers and other education professionals to support elementary and secondary school education. Anyone having completed pre-service education courses and been qualified through the preliminary review could obtain their intern status. After the one-year education practicum, they could obtain qualified teacher status as long as they had successfully completed the practicum and been qualified through the secondary review. Teacher education at the time was mainly self-sponsored but both state sponsorship and financial aids were available.

As part of the regulations governing the education practicum system, the Regulations Governing Teacher Qualification Exams and Education Practicum for K-12 Schools by the Ministry of Education specified that an education practicum should consist of a teaching practicum, a class affairs practicum, an administrative practicum, and seminars. Interns should engage themselves in the teaching practicum under the guidance of their mentors at the education practicum institutions; the teaching hours per week may not exceed one-half of the basic number of hours taught by a school teacher and interns must participate in all education events arranged for the education practicum from start to finish. Seminars lasted for at least seven days and interns must return to their preparation schools at least once a month in order for teacher preparation institutions to strengthen the guidance provided to interns (Ministry of Education, 1995). There were no substantial and specific requirements with regard to the class affairs practicum and administrative practicum laws and regulations; the practicum system also gave rise to quite a few problems, one of which was that it was becoming "formal" (Ou, 1996; Yang, 1997; Yen et al., 1998). In light of the criticism coming from all directions, the Ministry of Education started to revise the Teacher Education Act in 2002 and embarked on major reforms of the education practicum system, including canceling practicum allowances, shortening the duration of the education practicum to six months, collecting practicum guidance fees, and organizing teacher qualification exams, etc. (Wang and Lai, 2004).

Six-month education practicum in the Teacher Education Act of 2002

The revised Teacher Education Act was announced on 20 June 2002. Articles concerning the education practicum include the following (Legislative Yuan, 2003):

- *Article 1.* Develop teachers for K-12 schools, to augment the supply of teachers and advance their professional expertise.
- *Article 2.* Teacher education shall be provided by normal schools and universities with teacher education-related departments or teacher education centers.
- *Article 5.* Establishment of teacher education centers at universities shall be approved by the central competent authority. The central competent authority shall establish regulations governing related matters, such as the establishment conditions and procedures, faculty, facilities, student recruitment, curricula, required years of study, and discontinued operation, among others.
- *Article 6.* When organizing pre-service teacher education curricula, universities with teacher education shall plan the said courses separately for teachers to teach at high schools, elementary schools, kindergartens, and special schools (classes) and submit them to the central competent authority for approval before implementation.
- *Article 7.* To meet instructional demands, the teaching subject areas for elementary and secondary school teachers may be consolidated as an elementary-secondary school teacher program. Teacher education includes pre-service teacher education and teacher qualification exams. Pre-service teacher education curricula include ordinary courses, specialized courses, professional courses in education, and education practicums.
- *Article 8.* For those taking pre-service teacher education curricula, the duration of studies including their original majors shall basically be limited to

four years in addition to another six months of education practicum. Those with outstanding performance may graduate early in compliance with the requirements of the University Act. The six months of education practicum courses, however, cannot be reduced.

- *Article 13.* Enrollees in teacher education programs shall be required primarily to pay tuition and fees, but both scholarships and grants shall be provided by governments. State-sponsored students shall serve schools in remote or special areas after graduation. The central competent authority shall establish the regulations governing the value of state sponsorship and financial aids, the number of years at maximum that state-sponsored students are entitled to state sponsorship, management of violations, and allocation.
- *Article 15.* Universities with teacher education shall be configured with a practicum and employment guidance unit to organize education practicums, help graduates find a job, and provide education assistance to local schools. The education assistance at the local level shall be handled jointly with competent authorities at all levels, in-service teacher education institutions, and schools or kindergartens.
- *Article 16.* K-12 schools shall cooperate with universities with teacher education by organizing full-time education practicums. The competent authorities shall supervise matters related to education practicums and provide the necessary budget and assistance.
- *Article 17.* Universities with teacher education may set up affiliated experiment schools, kindergartens, or special schools (classes) reflective of the types of teachers they cultivate to provide education practicums, experiments, and researches.

Education practicums under the new system began on 1 August 2003 in accordance with the abovementioned laws and regulations. This new system differs from the old in that the education practicum is included as part of pre-service teacher education for prospective teachers. The intern is identified as a student. The duration of the education practicum is shortened to six months and may not be further shortened when outstanding students graduate early. Meanwhile, practicum allowances are canceled and practicum counseling fees equivalent to four credits are collected. Teacher education centers or practicum and employment guidance units are responsible for raising the funds for the organization of related practicum activities. The competent authorities shall supervise education practicums and provide the necessary budget and assistance (Legislative Yuan, 2003; Lin *et al.*, 2007).

Contents of current education practicum laws and regulations and related administrative orders

The laws and regulations that are available at present and have an effect on the education practicum system include the Teacher Education Act, the Teacher

Education Act Enforcement Rules, the Guidelines for Universities with Teacher Education to Organize Education Practicum, and the Implementation Guidelines for Ministry of Education to Subsidize Universities with Teacher Education in Consolidating Education Practicum Guidance.

Teacher Education Act and Teacher Education Act Enforcement Rules

The Teacher Education Act announced on 7 February 1994 specifically stipulated that the purpose of teacher education was to "develop teachers for schools at the senior high and lower levels, as well as kindergartens, to augment the supply of teachers and advance their professional expertise". The latest amendment involved Article 24 which was revised on 6 June 2014 and came into force on 1 February 2015 (Ministry of Education, 2014a, 2014b). The Teacher Education Act Enforcement Rules were established and promulgated by the Ministry of Education on 22 February 1995. It went through a partial amendment on 4 January 2001 followed by amendment to all 14 articles on 11 August 2003. Although Articles 4, 6, and 8 were released on 4 January 2011 after they were revised, the changes made in 2003 continued to be the most crucial. The following are the contents relating education practicums separated out from the Teacher Education Act and its Enforcement Rules (Ministry of Education, 2012a, 2014a, 2014b).

It is defined in the Teacher Education Act that teacher education includes pre-service education and the teacher qualification exams. Pre-service education curricula for teachers, on the other hand, include general courses, specialized courses, professional courses in education, and an education practicum. Normal schools and universities with teacher education-related departments or teacher education centers are in charge of providing pre-service teacher education curricula. Those who can take pre-service teacher education curricula include sophomores and undergraduates in the higher year of study; they shall complete the studies by the end of four years and take an education practicum over a period of six months. Those with outstanding performance, however, may graduate early in accordance with the University Act but the six-month education practicum may not be reduced. Universities with teacher education centers may also recruit current graduate students of master's or doctoral programs wishing to take pre-service teacher education curricula to be school teachers in future. Students that have completed the required pre-service teacher education curricula with passing grades will receive a Certificate of Successful Completion of Pre-service Teacher Education issued by the universities with teacher education. Those who have acquired the Certificate of Successful Completion of Pre-service Teacher Education and passed the teacher qualification exams will receive a teaching license issued by the MOE. For teachers who have already obtained a teaching license for a certain category and have completed general courses, specialized courses, and professional courses in education as part of pre-service teacher education for another category and acquired the certificate later, the government shall issue a teaching license for the subsequent category. These teachers do not have to take the education practicum or the teacher qualification exams.

The Teacher Education Act also specifies the functions of universities with teacher education in practicum guidance. They shall be configured with a practicum and employment guidance unit to organize education practicums, help graduates find a job, and provide education assistance at the local level. As far as the institutions involved in the implementation of education practicums are concerned, besides original universities with teacher education, schools at K-12 schools or special schools (classes) shall all cooperate with universities with teacher education by organizing full-time education practicums. The government, on the other hand, shall supervise the organization of education practicums and related matters and provide the necessary budget and assistance. The education assistance at the local level as indicated in the preceding paragraph shall be handled jointly with competent authorities at all levels, in-service teacher institutions, and schools or kindergartens. The most symbolic and historical tradition of the education practicum is that universities with teacher education may set up affiliated experiment schools, kindergartens, or special schools (classes) reflective of the types of teachers they cultivate to provide education practicums, experiments, and research.

In accordance with the University Act, both graduates from universities who have completed general courses, specialized courses, and professional courses in education and current graduate students of master's and doctoral programs who are holders of a bachelor's degree and have completed ordinary courses, specialized courses, professional courses in education, and also the credits required in order for them to get a master's or a doctor's degree, must take part in a six-month full-time education practicum. The practicum usually begins in August each year and ends in January of the following year or begins in February and ends in July. To facilitate education practicums, universities with teacher education shall screen schools at K-12 schools or special schools (classes) to be education practicum institutions and sign a practicum contract with all of them to facilitate the organization of full-time education practicums. Universities with teacher education must establish; applicable requirements for the implementation of education practicums, including principles for the selection of supervisors at the universities and mentors at the education practicum institutions; how practicum counseling is done; the guidance provided or the number of interns to be counseled; the contents of the education practicum; education practicum matters; practicum evaluation items and methods, and practicum time; weekly hours of teaching for interns, their rights and obligations; and the practicum contract, and the management of failing education practicum grades. Universities with teacher education may collect education practicum guidance fees equivalent to four credits from interns participating in the six-month practicum. The contents of the education practicum include the teaching practicum, the class affairs practicum, the administrative practicum, and seminars. Ratings provided by the university with teacher education and the education practicum institution shall account for 50 per cent of the total score, respectively.

Guidelines for Universities with Teacher Education to Organize Education Practicum

In order to improve the quality of the education practicum and boost the efficacy of guidance, the Guidelines for Universities with Teacher Education to Organize Education Practicum were established in 2005 in accordance with the requirement of Article 16 of the Teacher Education Act. Some of the articles were revised later in 2012 and 2014. The following summarizes the contents of the articles (Ministry of Education, 2005, 2012b, 2014c). The Guidelines specify that the aims of the education practicum are to enhance the following four skills: to understand a teaching scenario in a class and exercise teaching skills; to understand education targets and exercise class management skills; to observe and participate in school administration and understand how a school operates; to understand the responsibilities and roles of teachers and develop professionalism. It clearly defined: a university with teacher education as a normal school and a university with a teacher education-related department or teacher education center; an education practicum institution as a school at K-12 or a special school (class) screened by the university with teacher education to provide education practicums; a supervisor as a professor at the university with teacher education hired to provide interns with guidance; and a mentor as a teacher at the education practicum institution recommended by the institution to the university with teacher education to provide interns with guidance.

Universities with teacher education shall form an education practicum deliberation group headed by the president, vice president, or the highest-ranking supervisor at the university in order to deliberate on education practicum-related issues; staff operations shall be under the charge of the education practicum unit. Members include related administrative representatives and heads of related departments/colleges/institutes; representatives from the competent authority and the education practicum institution may be convened when it is considered necessary. The university with teacher education shall decide the date that interns shall report to the education practicum institution. Interns applying for the education practicum may submit their application to the original university with teacher education or other universities that offer teacher education for the same category; the practicum will last for six months. Universities with teacher education shall establish requirements for interns to use related resources on campus during the practicum period.

The Guidelines for Universities with Teacher Education to Organize Education Practicum revised by the Ministry of Education on 20 April 2012 stipulate that grades for education practicum interns are jointly given by the university with teacher education and the education practicum institution; a score of 60 is a pass grade. Ratings provided by the supervisor at the university with teacher education account for 50 per cent while those by the education practicum institution account for the other 50 per cent (Ministry of Education, 2012b). Items to be rated on by the university with teacher education and the education practicum institution and their ratios include courses under the teaching practicum, the class affairs practicum, the administrative practicum, and seminars, primarily teaching and class affairs practicums and secondarily the administrative practicum and seminars. In principle, the teaching practicum (including at least one demonstration) grade accounts for 45 per cent of the total practicum score, the class affairs practicum for 30 per cent, the administrative practicum 15 per cent, and seminars 10 per cent.

The Ministry of Education released a partial amendment to the Guidelines for Universities with Teacher Education to Organize Education Practicum on 15 September 2014 that provide indicators of education practicum performance for different categories, and offer universities with teacher education the discretion to make adjustments according to their development characteristics. The following describes the contents of the official letter in detail (Ministry of Education, 2014c). In order to organize education practicums, universities with teacher education must establish their own implementation details, including contents of the education practicum to be planned, assessment items and methods, the compilation and printing of education practicum handbooks, the organization of education practicum workshops, descriptions of the rights and obligations, among other matters, of supervisors, mentors, and interns, eligibility requirements for education practicum applicants, and the management mechanism for failure to engage in the education practicum, etc. The practicum guidance may be provided:

- *On-site visits.* Supervisors will visit education practicum institutions to provide guidance and interview the head, mentors, and interns at the education practicum institutions.
- *Through seminars.* Universities shall organize workshops or seminars on campus basically once a month.
- *Through correspondence.* Universities shall compile education practicum guidance publications and send them out to interns for their reference.
- *Through counseling.* Universities shall set up direct lines and online access to provide interns with consultation services.
- *Through results sharing.* Universities shall organize events for interns to release their accomplishments in the education practicum and share their thoughts.

The Partial Amendment to the Guidelines for Universities with Teacher Education to Organize Education Practicum (Ministry of Education, 2014c) specifies that universities with teacher education shall screen supervisors who are capable of instructing interns and are willing to do so; those with at least one year of teaching experience in a K-12 or a special school (class) or any other educational institution will be prioritized in the screening. Universities with teacher education shall also organize related seminars that help supervisors and mentors grow their professionalism and enhance the quality of the education practicum. Supervisors at universities with teacher education shall provide guidance to 12 interns at maximum and the guidance may count for one to three hours of teaching. When it is considered necessary in reality, supervisors specializing in education and respective subjects may provide joint guidance. Supervisors shall visit education practicum institutions for the provision of guidance. The Guidelines also require that the local education authorities (LEAs) publish a list of K-12 schools suitable for organizing education practicums and which are also willing to provide practicum opportunities on the Educational Internship Information website by 30 September each year. For the screening of education practicum institutions by universities with teacher education, the Guidelines also include five criteria:

- The geographical accessibility of a university with teacher education to provide guidance is taken into consideration.
- A sound administrative structure, a sufficient number of qualified teachers, and complete software and hardware facilities to support a sufficient education practicum environment will be provided.
- Institutions having been accredited by the competent authority to be excellent or having passed the fundamental accreditation will be prioritized.
- Institutions spontaneously referred by the universities with teacher education will be necessary.
- Institutions without major violations for which improvements were demanded by the local education authorities yet were not done in the past three years.

Meanwhile, how unqualified interns will be handled by education practicum institutions is clearly addressed. For interns who are unfit for a practicum before they apply for the education practicum or fail to abide by the requirements while taking education practicum courses – whose performance is undesirable for example – their application to take part in the education practicum may be rejected or they may be required to discontinue the education practicum while their case is deliberated and approved in the meeting of the education practicum deliberation group called for by the education practicum institutions and the universities with teacher education. Before they receive assistance and make improvements, they may be barred from submitting an application for another education practicum or restoring their participation status in the education practicum. Education practicum institutions are specifically asked to inform universities with teacher education of the leave of absence of their interns. The universities with teacher education can organize education practicum performance rating and follow-up guidance accordingly.

It is especially worth noting that performance indicators of education practicums for respective categories of interns are established to serve as a reference for universities with teacher education. The performance indicators of the education practicum for elementary school teachers, for example, include four major items, namely planning teaching and learning for students; developing adequate teaching and assessment; creating a positive and proactive learning environment; and developing a professional attitude as a teacher. Under each item are three to six performance indicators and sub-indicators under two to five indicators (Ministry of Education, 2014c). These indicators can serve as a substantial reference for universities with teacher education while they conduct performance-based education practicums.

Implementation Guidelines for the Ministry of Education to Subsidize Universities with Teacher Education in Consolidating Education Practicum Guidance

To help universities with teacher education organize education practicum guidance, the Ministry of Education announced the Implementation Guidelines for the Ministry of Education to Subsidize Universities with Teacher Education in Consolidating Education Practicum Guidance on 14 March 2002 in accordance with the Teacher Education Act. The Guidelines were later amended four times (on 13 February 2004, 28 July 2009, 9 June 2010, and 23 March 2012 respectively). The latest Guidelines were released on 3 March 2015 (Ministry of Education, 2015a). The hope is to strengthen the tripartite relationship among universities with teacher education, education practicum institutions, and interns, through the Executive Order and consolidate education practicum guidance (Ministry of Education, 2012c, 2015b). The Guidelines consist of two types of subsidies, basic and quality, to help with the basic operation of education practicums, encourage practicum institutions, and assist universities with teacher education in screening quality education practicum institutions for the ultimate goal of constructing a sound education practicum environment.

In accordance with these Guidelines, the Ministry of Education provides NT$50,000 to NT$250,000 based on the total number of interns. Practicum schools receiving the subsidies must print practicum handbooks and briefing publications, and organize seminars and consultations for interns; hold activities such as visiting schools, observing teaching on site, and serving disadvantaged students in elementary and secondary schools; pay for hours of teaching and provide economically disadvantaged interns with financial aids, etc. Specifically, supervisor handbooks, mentor handbooks, and intern handbooks for different categories (secondary schools, elementary schools, special schools, and kindergartens) shall be printed and published. Brief messages, correspondence or publications on education practicum guidance shall be compiled and printed. Induction workshops and workshops on campus (at least once a month), seminars or symposiums (with topics covering various teaching skills), and consultation services shall be organized for interns. Visits and observation tours to education practicum-related institutions will be organized. Various events will be organized on campus for interns to serve disadvantaged elementary or secondary school students. Various events will also be organized to inspire interns on campus. Meanwhile, hourly pay will be provided to supervisors and financial aid will be provided to economically disadvantaged interns reviewed and approved by the local education authorities where the intern's household is registered as a low-income earner or low and middle-income earner, among other actions taken to help improve the quality of the education practicum.

For quality education practicum institutions selected by universities with teacher education, one to five of them may be subsidized in accordance with the total number of interns upon application. They may be subsidized for two consecutive years, with each to receive up to NT$250,000. NT$50,000 of it will be used to purchase related teaching and administrative software and hardware for the practicum guidance. Those having passed in the evaluation of the following year will receive a subsidy of NT$150,000 to help with education practicum-related matters, allowances, hourly pay, workshops on practicum guidance skills, training sessions for qualified mentors, and engagements in improving quality of interns. Education practicum institutions, however, may only be referred by a university with teacher education and the Ministry of Education subsidies shall occur only once.

The Ministry of Education's budget for "outstanding education practicum institutions" is expected to last for two consecutive years. Respective institutions shall implement corresponding plans and submit annual reports covering the overall implementation and benefit assessment to the Ministry of Education for review. When it is considered necessary, the Ministry of Education will form a review group to inspect on site the eligibility of quality education practicum institutions to receive the sponsorship.

The above summarizes the contents and related requirements of laws and regulations concerning education practicums. Jia-Li Huang *et al.* analyzed issues of education practicums at respective institutions and areas for improvement (Huang *et al.*, 2013). They found that all institutions tend to be conservative and abide by the Guidelines for Universities with Teacher Education to Organize Education Practicum announced by the Ministry of Education; they only regulated the ratios of the teaching practicum, the class affairs practicum, the administrative practicum, and seminars without providing specific guidance, substantial contents in all respects, and assessment criteria of education practicums. In other words, there is still room for improvement.

Measures to enhance quality of education practicums

Enhancement Program for Teacher Education Quality of 2006 and Enhancement Program for Elementary and Secondary Teachers' Quality of 2009

The Ministry of Education announced the four-year Enhancement Program for Teacher Education Quality in 2006 (Lin *et al.*, 2007). Solution 4 deals with the education practicum and emphasizes the implementation of teacher education-related laws and regulations, such as the Teacher Education Act and the Guidelines for Universities with Teacher Education to Organize Education Practicum. The hope is to strengthen the tripartite relationship (instruction, partnership, guidance) in education practicums, the mentor teacher system, and the teacher careers ladder system to reinforce the skills of mentors and reward outstanding mentors, supervisors, and interns through the "three teachers, three rewards" system. Meanwhile, education practicum resources can be integrated and distributed, the utilization of the education practicum budget can be reflected upon, and professional development schools can be promoted in order to establish a quality education practicum institution system (Huang et al., 2013).

The Ministry of Education's Enhancement Program for Elementary and Secondary Teachers' Quality of 2009 continued with the strategies such as the consolidation of laws and regulations, the reinforcement of a certification and reward system for mentors, and incentives for high-performing practicum institutions and staff from 2006. At dimension 1 "advancing teacher education" of the Program of 2009, comprehensive consideration was given to the education practicum system implementation strategies, including changing teacher qualification exams to take place before the education practicum, and the change was included in the amendment to the Teacher Education Act, the education practicum screening was organized, and the guidance list of practicum institutions was created. This is something relatively unique in the education practicum system (Huang et al., 2013).

Report on Education in the ROC and White Paper of Teacher Education

The emphasis on education practicums was substantially demonstrated in the Report on Education in the ROC released in 2011. The Report recommends that qualification of supervisors and education practicum institutions should be reinforced. Meanwhile, establishment of a certification system for mentors and reinforcement professional development schools are also the directions to improve practicum quality (Ministry of Education, 2011; Huang et al., 2013).

The White Paper of Teacher Education provided by the Ministry of Education in December 2012 (Ministry of Education, 2012d) emphasizes the core values of "teaching assets, responsibility, exquisiteness, and sustainability" and consists of nine development strategies and 28 action plans based on the four dimensions, namely "pre-service teacher education", "induction", "in-service professional development", and "support system for teacher education". It creates a professional standards-based teacher education system with the underlying idea of education and placement and depicts the blueprint of teacher education for the next ten years. In Action Plan 7, Perfecting Professional Competences of Teachers of the White Paper, it is advised that teacher qualification exams can take place before a practicum. The possibility of extending the duration of the education practicum and the contents of the teaching practicum, the class affairs practicum, the administrative practicum, and seminars may be defined in order to further refine the existing education practicum system. For the education practicum and regulation of the weights of individual practicums, intern support, alert, and elimination mechanism will be established. Universities with teacher education shall collaborate with one another in the establishment of a regional practicum alliance center to integrate guidance provided to interns in their area, reasonably share costs of practicum guidance, and establish applicable laws and regulations.

Action Plan 8 of Advancing Skills of Mentors and Supervisors' Qualification aims at improving quality of guidance provided in the education practicum setting, and involves the augmentation of current requirements for supervisors, providing an incentive and support system, enhancing the skills of supervisors, and ensuring the quality of practicum guidance provided. As far as mentors are concerned, it is advised to enhance their guidance quality through a certification mechanism, which will help ensure that they are equipped with practicum guidance skills and facilitate professional developments for mentors. Action Plan 9 of Establishing the Professional Development School (PDS) system focuses on the creation of a partnership between a university with teacher education and K-12 schools to facilitate educational researches, experiments, and practicums, to make a joint effort in the cultivation of outstanding prospective teachers, to promote teacher professional development, and to exercise the functions of a tripartite relationship in the education practicum and enhance the quality of school education. After reorganization, the Ministry of Education also set up the Department of Teacher and Art Education in 2013 to take charge of teacher education planning and promote teacher education-related operations (Ministry of Education, 2012d).

Program for Universities with Teacher Education to Develop Outstanding Teacher Education

The Ministry of Education adopted competitive incentives in 2007 and organized the Program for Universities with Teacher Education to Develop Outstanding Teacher Education to hopefully focus resources and prioritize budget investment in teacher education at selected universities (Department of Secondary Education, Ministry of Education, 2012a). By 2010, respective teacher education institutions had demonstrated unique characteristics in their development, such as: innovation and creative teaching; integration of important education issues into curricula; professional certification for outstanding teachers; internationalization of teacher education; integration and adjustment of resources available at teacher education institutions; teacher downsizing for exquisite education; education and guidance provided to prospective teachers; and implementation of quality of education practicums in order for the Ministry of Education to subsidize universities in improving the overall quality of teacher education and providing prospective teachers with a sounder learning environment. The Ministry of Education again revised the plan entitled Program for Universities with Teacher Education to Develop Outstanding Teacher Education in accordance with the suggestions brought forth in the Eighth National Conference on Education in 2011 to augment the subsidies and encourage universities with teacher education to examine themselves while trying to advance their effort in and features of teacher education, such as prospective teachers, teacher education curricula, professionalism of the faculty, clinical teachers, and talent teams to support teaching materials and methods of subjects. In order to put into practice the program on refining quality of teacher education introduced in the Report on Education in the ROC of 2011, substantial strategies were established to support the development of exquisite universities with teacher education and encourage universities to develop their characteristics. Meanwhile, to go with the planning introduced in the Report on Education, the Program was further revised to be the Guidelines for Universities with Teacher Education in Developing Exquisite Characteristic Development Subsidization Project (Ministry of Education, 2014d). The sponsorship was group-based to more specifically define and augment tasks associated with teacher education, distinguish outstanding development of teacher education in all aspects, and take care of issues associated with 12-year Basic Education, elementary and secondary school courses, and characteristics of teacher education at individual schools, and encourage universities with teacher education to take care of both prospective teachers needed by the state. Respective universities submitted their plans and allocated the required resources on campus to promote professional development schools, creating a win-win situation for universities with teacher education and elementary and secondary schools. The Program of the Ministry of Education has been very fruitful.

Establishment Alliance for Elementary School Teacher Education

Teacher education is the cornerstone of education. Only outstanding teachers can contribute to outstanding education (Ministry of Education, 2012e). To cultivate outstanding teachers, the Ministry of Education places equal emphases on pre-service education and in-service professional development by linking universities with teacher education, elementary schools where teaching takes place, and administrative units for education to jointly cultivate qualified teachers who are capable of teaching and willing to teach. The Establishment Alliance for Elementary School Teacher Education was promoted in June 2011 to create a collaboration pattern for universities, the central government, local government, and elementary schools. These were linked to form a close teacher education partnership and a sound teacher education policy implementation network that served as a model in teacher education in order to enhance the quality of teaching. The alliance was established in order to link important elements of theory and practice by introducing a practicum as part of teacher education and to strengthen the tripartite relationship in an education practicum, that is the instruction-based relationship between supervisors and interns, the partnership relationship between universities with teacher education and education practicum institutions, and the guidance relationship between mentors and interns, to accordingly strengthen teaching skills and knowledge in the students learning and realize the quality education practicum (Department of Secondary Education, Ministry of Education, 2012b).

Universities with teacher education in charge of the education for elementary school teachers, including teaching knowledge and skills, in the past were the educational universities or comprehensive universities known for their education programs at the state or city level, nine in total, transformed from traditional teachers colleges or normal education institutions. These universities continued to develop and be integrated. This gave rise to the teacher education and utilization alliance program for elementary schools. The program consisted of three stages, namely the preparation period in 2011, the configuration period in 2012, and the promotion period in 2013, and features progressive implementation and development for maximum efficacy. The collaboration cycle mechanism consisting of education and placement was activated to streamline the three parts of teacher education, namely pre-service teacher education, induction education as part of the practicum, and teacher professional development. Among the education universities assisted by the Ministry of Education in their transformation were those separately upgraded to be comprehensive universities, namely the National Tainan University and the National Taitung University, and those merged with other comprehensive universities such as the National Dong Hwa University or other academies to become new comprehensive universities like the University of Taipei and National Pingtung University. There are three retained education universities at present, namely the National Taipei University of Education, the National Hsinchu University of Education, and the National Taichung University of Education. These unique universities from the normal education system are responsible for cultivating teachers to support primary, preschool, and special education. Through collaboration among universities with a teacher preparation and application alliance center (including a teaching center in the field of study), elementary schools, education administrative institutions, and compulsory education guidance group and joint efforts from specialists in education theory and practice, the teaching and learning results of teacher education can be enhanced. In addition, teachers participating in the practicum are given a "clinical" opportunity to combine theory and practice; it shortens the distance between faculty in universities with teacher education and teachers at elementary schools (Electronic News Division, Department of Secondary Education, Ministry of Education, 2012b).

Ministry of Education Outstanding Education Practicum Performance Award and Incentive Guidelines

Certification and incentive measures for practicum schools and mentors were both emphasized in the Ministry of Education's Enhancement Program for Teacher Education Quality of 2006 and Enhancement Program for Elementary and Secondary Teachers' Quality of 2009. The "three teachers, three rewards" is an example of a reward system according to the Ministry of Education

Outstanding Education Practicum Performance Award and Incentive Guidelines (Ministry of Education, 2015b). The effort of the Ministry of Education is to encourage supervisors at universities with teacher education, interns participating in an education practicum, and mentors at education practicum institutions to proactively take part in the education practicum and help the interns put professional standards and theories they have learned into action by rewarding their contributions to the education practicum. It is meant to boost the efficacy of education practicums and enhance the quality of teacher education through the outstanding performance award provided. It is, however, pending further assessment to determine whether certification or incentive measures can help enhance the overall capabilities of a practicum institution to cultivate teachers and boost the capabilities of the mentors or not (Huang *et al.*, 2013).

Conclusion

While the education practicum system was taking shape in Taiwan, many systematic and practical issues had to be addressed. Examples include: education practicums falling short of exercising substantial effects; insufficient collaboration between teacher preparation institutions and education practicum institutions; disagreement on whether education practicums should last for six months or a year; convergence in the contents of education practicums as a result of the laws and regulations of the Ministry of Education while practicum quality differs from school to school without substantial indicators; interns turning into human resources during practicum; deviations in practicum programs; or the inability to determine actual competences as a teacher through teacher qualification exams. The Ministry of Education, local education authorities, individual teacher preparation institutions, and practicum schools, however, are jointly dealing with issues facing the practicum system and considering solutions through different ways of communication or collaboration, which may be encouragement, incentive, supervision, inspection, or accreditation in the revision of teacher education-related laws and regulations, organization of nationwide educational conferences, and release of various reports and education administrative proposals.

This chapter analyzes the history of laws and regulations such as the Normal Education Law and Teacher Education Act and provides insights relating to the current education practicum system in accordance with the Teacher Education Act Enforcement Rules, the Guidelines for Universities with Teacher Education to Organize Education Practicum, and Implementation Guidelines for Ministry of Education to Subsidize Universities with Teacher Education in Consolidating Education Practicum Guidance. Further elaborations are made possible through reports and various measures of the Ministry of Education with regard to its education practicum quality policy such as the five types of documents, solutions, reports, or protocols, namely: the Enhancement Program for Teacher Education Quality; the Enhancement Program for Elementary and Secondary Teachers' Quality; the Report on Education in the ROC and White Paper of Teacher Education; the Outstanding Teacher Education Program and Guidelines in

Developing Exquisite Characteristic Development Subsidization Project; the Establishment Alliance for Elementary School Teacher Education; and the Ministry of Education Outstanding Education Practicum Performance Award and Incentive Guidelines. Particular attention should be paid to the practicum mentor certification and training program, the three awards for outstanding education practicum performance (for the mentor, the instructor, and the intern), and the certification system for education practicum institutions to become professional development schools in the Ministry of Education's Enhancement Program for Teacher Education Quality of 2006. The Ministry of Education Outstanding Education Practicum Performance Award and Incentive Guidelines established in 2014 are still ongoing at present. They concern the consolidation and efficacy of education practicums and the enhancement of professional knowledge and skills in interns. Whether or not it is feasible to enhance practicum efficacy through external requirements such as the certification of staff and institutions or incentives for outstanding performance, however, is pending further observations and comprehensive assessments. The 2012 Guidelines for Universities with Teacher Education to Organize Education Practicum, on the other hand, already had relatively detailed regulations with regard to practicum contents and their weights in the score. In 2014, the Ministry of Education suggested that individual universities with teacher education should revise their assessment indicators for interns and implement them accordingly, indicating that the establishment of professional standards for teachers had progressed from implementation and development among in-service teachers to interns with standard professional knowledge and skills established for interns. Whether or not individual teacher preparation institutions will substantially implement practicum knowledge and skill indicators, however, is pending examination over time.

As far as policies are concerned, the Report on Education released by the Ministry of Education in 2011 focused the development on creating a professional and quality teacher education policy system featuring the promotion of education universities in Taiwan, the establishment of an exemplary model for teacher education, implementation of professional standards for teachers, consolidation of the prospective teacher trait assessment and guidance mechanism, advancement of teacher education programs, education practicums, and teacher qualification exams. It also stipulates that mentors should have certain years of experience in teaching and working at elementary or secondary schools, proactively promotes the certification system for education practicum institutions and practicum mentors, shapes professional development schools, and reinforces the close combination among the three parties, that is universities with teacher education, education practicum institutions, and interns, to substantially realize professional development schools. Education practicums can go beyond the pre-service stage to include the in-service stage (Tang, 2012). The 2012 White Paper of Teacher Education continued to establish a teacher preparation system emphasizing both professional standards and teacher education and placement, and introduced more substantial development goals – to precisely evaluate the knowledge and skills of interns, to ensure quality of practicum mentors, and to establish professional development schools to realize the three-way practicum relationship, for example. With regard to the future development of education practicums in Taiwan, the Ministry of Education is currently revising the Teacher Education Act; one of the possible major changes is "exam before practicum", the purpose of the change being to help the interns focus on the practicum if they can take the teacher qualification exam first before the practicum and then enter the job market. The performance and quality-based teacher education practicum system in Taiwan is developing toward professionalism, standardization, and excellence of teachers through teacher preparation institutions with a "cooperative and competitive" relationship in addition to supervision, accreditation, and incentives for outstanding performance from administrative education institutions.

Acknowledgement

This study was the partial result of "Research on the Accreditation of Professional Development Schools" supported by the National Pingtung University of Taiwan. I would like to thank the colleagues who contributed to the PDS project, anonymous reviewers, and the editors for their comments.

References

Department of Secondary Education, Ministry of Education (2012a) *Outstanding Teacher Education Program Helps Cultivate Outstanding Teachers-to-be*. Retrieved from: http://epaper.edu.tw/topical.aspx?topical_sn=667 (in Chinese).

Department of Secondary Education, Ministry of Education (2012b) *Pre-service Teacher Education and Placement Alliance for Elementary Schools Leads by Example in Teacher Education Collaboration*. Retrieved from: http://epaper.edu.tw/print.aspx?print_type=topical&print_sn=696&print_num=5 (in Chinese).

Huang, J. L., Sung, Y. T., Lin, P. J., Hu, S. T., Lin, W. J., and Yang, C. S. (2013) *Final Report of Planning Contents of Six-month Full-time Education Practicum and Performance Assessment*. Taipei: Department of Teacher and Art Education, Ministry of Education. (in Chinese).

Lee, C. F. (2006) "Practicum for teachers and issues of qualification exam," in Chinese Education Society, Chinese Comparative Education Society, and Teacher Education Society of ROC (eds), *Challenges and Prospects of Teacher Education*. Taipei, TWN: Shi Ta Books, pp. 91–123 (in Chinese).

Legislative Yuan (1979a) *Legislative Yuan Agenda Related Documents*. Retrieved from: http://lis.ly.gov.tw/lgcgi/lgmeetimage?cfcec9cccfcccfcfc5c7d2cec6 (in Chinese).

Legislative Yuan (1979b) *Normal Education Law* (in Chinese).

Legislative Yuan (1992) *Legislative Yuan Agenda Related Documents*. Retrieved from: http://lis.ly.gov.tw/lgcgi/lgmeetimage?cfcec7c6cecccfcec5cac8ced2cac6cb (in Chinese).

Legislative Yuan (1994) *Teacher Education Act* (in Chinese).

Legislative Yuan (2003) *Teacher Education Act* (in Chinese).

Lin, C. T. and Lin, S. H. (2013) *Theory and Practice of Education Practicum: Becoming a Qualified Teacher*. Taipei: Wunan (in Chinese).

Lin, H. F., Wang, H. L., and Teng, P. H. (2007) "The current situation, policy and prospect of elementary and secondary teacher education in Taiwan," *Journal of Educational Research and Development*, 3 (1): 57–79 (in Chinese).

Ministry of Education (1995) *Regulations Governing Teacher Qualification Exams and Education Practicum for K-12 Schools* (in Chinese).

Ministry of Education (2005) *Guidelines for Universities with Teacher Education to Organize Education Practicum* (in Chinese).

Ministry of Education (2010) *Eighth National Conference on Education*. Taipei: MOE (in Chinese).

Ministry of Education (2011) *Report on Education in the ROC*. Retrieved from: http://www.edu.tw (in Chinese).

Ministry of Education (2012a) *Enforcement Rules of the Teacher Education Act*. Retrieved from: http://law.moj.gov.tw/LawClass/LawHistory.aspx?PCode=H0050001 (in Chinese).

Ministry of Education (2012b) *Guidelines for Universities with Teacher Education to Organize Education Practicum*. Retrieved from: http://tece.heeact.edu.tw/upload_file/laws/10/13940863615.pdf (in Chinese).

Ministry of Education (2012c) *Implementation Guidelines for Ministry of Education to Subsidize Universities with Teacher Education in Consolidating Education Practicum Guidance*. Retrieved from: http://www.edu.tw/pages/detail.aspx?Node=1389&Page=9045&Index=8&WID=1112353c-88d0-4bdb-914a-77a4952aa893 (in Chinese).

Ministry of Education (2012d) *Keynote Report of Pre-service Teacher Education and Placement Alliance for Elementary Schools*. Retrieved from: http://epaper.edu.tw/print.aspx?print_type=topical&print_sn=695&print_num=517 (in Chinese).

Ministry of Education (2012e) *White Paper of Teacher Education in ROC*. Retrieved from: http://www.edu.tw/userfiles/url/20130115115257/%E4%B8%AD%E8%8F%AF%E6%B0%91%E5%9C%8B%E5%B8%AB%E8%B3%87%E5%9F%B9%E8%82%B2%E7%99%BD%E7%9A%AE%E6%9B%B8.pdf (in Chinese).

Ministry of Education (2014a) *Teacher Education Act*. Retrieved from: http://law.moj.gov.tw/LawClass/LawOldVer_Vaild.aspx?PCODE=H0050001 (in Chinese).

Ministry of Education (2014b) *Historical articles of the Teacher Education Act*. Retrieved from: http://law.moj.gov.tw/LawClass/LawHistory.aspx?PCode=H0050001 (in Chinese).

Ministry of Education (2014c) *Operating Guidelines for Universities with Teacher Education to Organize Education Practicum* (in Chinese).

Ministry of Education (2014d) *Guidelines for Universities with Teacher Education in Developing Exquisite Characteristic Development Subsidization Project*. Retrieved from: http://edu.law.moe.gov.tw/PrintLawContentDetails.aspx?id=FL024842 (in Chinese).

Ministry of Education (2015a) *Implementation Guidelines for Ministry of Education to Subsidize Universities with Teacher Education in Consolidating Education Practicum Guidance*. Retrieved from: http://edu.law.moe.gov.tw/PrintLawContentDetails.aspx?id=FL029754 (in Chinese).

Ministry of Education (2015b) *Ministry of Education Outstanding Education Practicum Performance Award and Incentive Guidelines*. Retrieved from: http://edu.law.moe.gov.tw/PrintLawContentDetails.aspx?id=GL000510 (in Chinese).

National Taiwan Normal University (2014) *Education Practicum Guidance Workshop: Making Education in Taiwan Better and Better*. Retrieved from: http://pr.ntnu.edu.tw/news/index.php?mode=data&id=14369 (in Chinese).

Ou, Y. S. (1996) "Blind spots and breakthroughs of new education practicum system," in Chinese Education Society (ed.), *New Courses under Teacher Education System*. Taipei: Shi Ta Books, pp. 103–16 (in Chinese).

Tang, W. L. (1994) "Current practicum system for teachers in Taiwan," in S. K. Yang, Y. S. Ou, C. R. Wang, and W. L. Tang (eds), *Comparison of Practicum Systems for Teachers in Different Countries*. Taipei: Shi Ta Books, pp. 11–25 (in Chinese).

Tang, W. L. (2012) "Analysis of teaching practicum cases in professional development schools," compiled by the Teacher Preparation Center and Department of Education, *Practical Teacher Education Reforms*. Pingtung: National Pingtung University of Education, pp. 199–208 (in Chinese).

Wang, S. Y. and Lai, K. J. (2004) "Conceptual analysis of education practicum: education practicum system and reforms in Taiwan," *Journal of the National Institute for Compilation and Translation*, 32 (1): 48–59 (in Chinese).

Yang, H. C. (1997) "Ideals and reality of education practicum system," in Teacher Education Society of ROC (ed.), *Teaching Profession and Teacher Education*. Taipei: Shi Ta Books, p. 227–67 (in Chinese).

Yang, S. K. (1994) "Cultural ideology and development backgrounds of practicum systems for teachers in different countries," in S. K. Yang, Y. S. Ou, C. R. Wang, and W. L. Tang (eds), *Comparison of Practicum Systems for Teachers in Different Countries*. Taipei: Shi Ta Books, pp. 1–10 (in Chinese).

Yang, S. K., Ou, Y. S., Wang, C. R, and Tang, W. L. (1994) *Comparison of Practicum Systems for Teachers in Different Countries*. Taipei: Shi Ta Books (in Chinese).

Yang, Y. H. (1993) *Study on Tasks and Troubling Issues in Life for Students Having Completed Studies at Teachers Colleges and Attending in Practicum*. Taipei: Shi Ta Books (in Chinese).

Yen, C. H., Tang, W. L., and Wang, Y. H. (1998) *Current Situation and Issues of Mentors under New Practicum System in Taiwan*. Paper presented at the Symposium of the Theory and Practice of Guidance Provided at Contract Practicum Schools. Hualien: National Hualien Teachers College (in Chinese).

7 Teacher professional development in Taiwan

Bo-Ruey Huang

Introduction

This chapter aims to describe the situation of teacher professional development in Taiwan. With the diversity of teacher education systems and institutions, Taiwan teacher professional development represents a gradual shift in governance from the model of centralized and state regulation to new professionalism and marketization.

The TALIS survey (OECD, 2009) defined teacher professional development as "activities that develop an individual's skills, knowledge, expertise and other characteristics as a teacher". Meanwhile teacher professional development is defined by the European Commission (2010) as "the body of systematic activities to prepare teachers for their job, including initial training, induction courses, in-service training, and continuous professional development within school settings". In the White Paper of Teacher Education in ROC, the definition of teacher professional development is: "By independent, cooperative, formal or informal learning or training activities and through the process of self-reflection, teachers enhance professional knowledge, skills and improve their professional image. Teacher professional development aims to improve the quality of school education and reach the target of school education effectively".

In the definitions of teacher professional development mentioned above, the first two mainly focus on the activities of teacher professional development, while the latter further points out the purpose of teacher professional development. The range of the definition from the European Commission is wider, including initial teacher training. Because that aspect has been described in other chapters of the book, this chapter will not discuss it further.

Traditionally, the concept of teacher professional development in Taiwan is mainly based on teacher in-service training and learning. In the 1990s, the movements of educational reform in Taiwan led to changes in the ideas of the teacher education system and teacher professional development. The framework of teacher professional development gradually attempts to build up a teacher career ladder and construct a consortium system of teacher professional development.

The second section of this chapter will explain the historical evolution of Taiwan teacher professional development while the third section will describe the current framework and important connotations of Taiwanese teacher professional development. The fourth section will analyze the trends and significance of the Taiwanese teacher professional development and the final section is our conclusion.

Historical evolution

The historical evolution of teacher professional development in Taiwan can be divided into three stages. The first stage is from the colonial period to 1978. At this stage, whether under the colonial ruling or the Kuomintang government, related measures to enhance the ability or quality of teachers belong to the initial establishment phase. The second stage is from 1979 to 1993. In this stage, the laws clearly regulate the institutions of and approaches to teacher in-service training and education. The third stage is from 1994 to the present. Along with the diversification of the teacher education system, teacher professional development policies had been heading towards a new professionalism and market orientation, in an attempt to establish a more comprehensive framework.

Stage of system construction (in the early twentieth century to 1978)

During the Japanese colonial rule in Taiwan, six normal schools were set up and equipped with a Short-term Training Department. The Normal School Rules of 1943 stipulated that those qualified to attend Short-term Training were those who "possess the Taiwan National Primary School quasi-discipline teacher certificate, or equivalent degree or above, with two years of a fixed number of studies". After the restoration in Taiwan, normal schools originally subordinate to the Governor General changed to being subordinate to the Provincial Normal Teachers School. The Taitung Normal School, Hualien Normal School, Kaohsiung Woman Normal School, and Chiayi Normal School were set up. These normal schools not only took charge of the task of teacher education, but also gave guidance to the local National Education.

In the early years after Taiwanese restoration, due to the lack of teachers, a large number of substitute teachers entered schools. In order to improve the quality of teachers, the government actively promoted the work of teacher in-service training. The main methods included: in-service training classes, advanced studies for outstanding teachers, and workshops and seminars held during the summer vacation. For primary school teacher in-service training, a "Teacher Training Center" was founded in 1956 in Banciao. From 1963 to 1967, nine teacher three-year colleges were restructured into five-year teacher colleges in succession. They also conducted two-year teacher qualification classes for in-service school teachers with a high school degree. In addition, the Taiwan Provincial Government set up Teacher Advance Classes for in-service teachers, directors, and principals without normal education background under the age of 45 to learn voluntarily.

With regard to secondary school teacher in-service training, the first such training was held at Taiwan Provincial Normal University in 1958. In 1959, a Center of In-service Training was organized in the Taiwan Provincial Normal University. In 1968, compulsory education was extended to nine years; therefore, the quality of secondary school teachers became imperative. The Provincial Taiwan Secondary School Teacher In-service Training Center set in Changhua was the first institution to provide training for secondary school teachers in Taiwan. The institution was restructured into the Taiwan Provincial Education College in 1971, the original in-service training center being restructured into an affiliated in-service training department (Lee, 2001).

Relevant laws and regulations of this period include the following. The Regulations of Appointment and Safeguard In-service Training for Compulsory School Teachers was promulgated in 1946. Article XIV of the regulations states:

> School staff should always pay attention to the promotion of the knowledge of teaching, moral cultivation, physical exercise, as well as other academic research, and participate in various research studies held by the following apparatus: 1. Holiday classes held by educational authorities; 2. Workshops for different levels of compulsory school teachers; 3. In-service training and correspondence schools affiliated to normal schools.

In 1950, the Regulations of Rewards for Elementary and Secondary School Teachers Academic Research was promulgated, which governs the scope of academic research and approach to rewards. The regulations were repealed in 1997.

Stage of Regulations (1979–93)

The activities in teacher professional development at this stage, however, still focus on in-service training while the approaches and institutions of teacher professional development began to be regulated in law. In 1979, the government considered that the content of the original Normal School Rules had been unable to adapt to the needs of the times, and announced the Normal Education Law to establish the teacher education system. Article VI states: "Normal University, Normal College, College of Education, Teachers College, and the university which is affiliated to a Department or institute of Education are able to set up night or summer departments and conduct teacher in-service training". Article 19 states: "The content of teacher in-service training should be related to the knowledge and skills of teaching". Since that time, there have been clear regulations for teacher in-service training. However, it was not until 1985 that there were promulgated more specific regulations for teacher in-service training (Lee, 2001).

Thus, in 1985, the Ministry of Education promulgated Regulations of In-service Training and Research for Elementary and Secondary School Teachers, which regulates the approaches, organization and time periods of teacher in-service training. Article 8 in the regulation states: "Teachers who participate in in-service training and get credit, degrees or certificates, are eligible to be rewarded". Article 9 states: "Teachers who participate in in-service training, internships, and other studies, who achieve good results, will be recommended to the competent educational authority and be rewarded". In the Regulations of In-service Training and Research for Elementary and Secondary School Teachers, the approach to improving teacher quality relies not only on in-service training but also on research. In-service training refers to short-term training, seminars, internships, etc., while research refers to credits, degrees, or certain qualifications.

During this stage, the basic teacher qualification had changed from a specialist college diploma to a university degree. Therefore, to obtain credits or degrees became the mainstream in teacher in-service training activity. Junior teacher colleges educating elementary teachers were upgraded to Normal Colleges in 1987. In doing so, the government intended to upgrade the teachers' educational degree to a Bachelor's degree. In 1991 they were renamed as Teachers Colleges. All nine Teachers Colleges were affiliated with the Department of In-service Training for School Teachers to obtain Bachelor degrees.

As for secondary school teachers, the government renamed the Taiwan Provincial Normal University the National Taiwan Normal University in 1967, while the other two normal universities were renamed in 1989. Three normal universities were affiliated with the Department of In-service Training, serving teachers and administrative staff with in-service Bachelor's degree classes, education credit classes or institutes of education.

However, at this stage, the situation of teacher training and research remained unclear. Article XIX of the Normal Education Act states, "The content of teacher in-service training should be related to the knowledge and skills of teaching", where "should" seems to imply an obligation; however, teachers "must" study or research. By contrast, the Regulations of In-service Training and Research for Secondary and Primary School Teachers states, "Teachers who participate in in-service training and get credits, degrees, or certificates are eligible for rewards". In other words, because teacher education is obligated by law, teachers engaged in studies or research may be rewarded. However, many studies have found that obtaining a degree was becoming the priority for teacher in-service training activities. Moreover, the process of obtaining advanced degrees may induce such negative effects as competition among school teachers in achieving the requisite qualifications, thus influencing teaching and school administration and having an effect on teaching quality and students' learning interests (Chen *et al.*, 1996; Su, 2001; Tzai, 1996).

Before the 1980s, the features and purpose of teacher in-service training and education focused mainly on two aspects: one was to obtain appropriate teacher qualifications, the other was to obtain the required university degree for teachers. The former refers to the rapid expansion of primary and secondary education, because of the urgent need for large numbers of teachers, which led to a great number of teachers entering schools without appropriate qualifications. Therefore teacher in-service training and education were an approach to obtain teacher qualifications. The latter is due to the response of the world trend. The government upgraded the school teacher degree to Bachelor's level, and teachers in the workplace had to return to the teacher education institutions to obtain higher degrees.

Stage of multi-systems (1994–2014 to the present)

In 1994, the Normal Education Law was amended to the Teacher Education Act. The teacher education system in Taiwan had been transformed from a one-dimensional, regulated, distributional system into a diverse-dimensional, reserve-type, selection system. Through the diverse selection mechanism, the purpose of the system is to improve the quality and professionalism of teachers. The Teacher Education Act expressly regulates the scope of the in-service training for teacher education, and also regulates the in-service training agency, of which Article XII (in the 1994 vision) states: "Normal teacher education university shall engage in the cultivation of teachers, and educational academic research of professional staff, as well as establish units responsible exclusively for in-service teacher training".

The Teacher Education Act was amended in 2002. Article 19 states:

> The competent authority may provide in-service training for teachers of schools at the senior high school level and below and kindergarten teachers by the following methods: 1. To establish teacher in-service training institutions individually or jointly; 2. To coordinate with or engage teacher education universities to establish various kinds of in-service training courses for teachers; and 3. To have social education institutions or legal entities approved by the competent authority hold various kinds of in-service teacher training courses.

That is to say, the organizations providing in-service training could be universities with teacher education or social education institutions and non-government organizations.

The Teacher Education Act mainly regulates the organization of teacher in-service training. As regards the right to and obligation to provide teacher in-service training, this is provided for in the Teachers' Act. Promulgated in 1995, the Teachers' Act clearly states that in-service teacher training, research, and academic activities are not only a right but also an obligation. Article 16 states: "After a teacher accepts employment, s/he enjoys the right to participate in in-service education, research, and academic exchange activities in accordance with the relevant laws and school rules and regulations". Article 17 states: "Other than fulfilling their employment responsibilities in accordance with the law, teachers have the obligation to engage in teaching-related research and further studies". And Article 22 states: "Teachers of all levels, when in service, shall be actively engaged in further studies and research on knowledge related to teaching".

The Teacher Education Act established a diversified basis of teacher in-service training while the Teachers' Act is rooted in both the right and obligatory nature of teacher in-service training. The Regulations for Senior High Schools and Lower Levels Teachers In-service Training, promulgated in 1996, further governs the approaches, institutions, credits, degrees, training time, and rewards. The objects of the Regulations apply not only for primary and secondary school teachers, but also for teachers in kindergartens and special schools. Article 3 states: "The content of teacher in-service training must be relevant to his/her own work or professional development". Article 9 governs: "Teachers, when in service, have to engage in in-service training at least eighteen hours or a credit each school year, or cumulate ninety hours or five credits in five years". The Regulations clearly regulate the basic in-service training hours. Meanwhile, the Regulations are beginning to encourage school-based in-service training. That is to say, schools could conduct in-service training activities.

The Regulations for Senior High Schools and Lower Levels Teachers In-service Training were abolished in 2003. Currently, the Regulations for Teacher In-service, Research and Rewards, amended in 2004, govern the qualification of in-service training teachers. Teachers who intend to participate in-service training should do so based on the following conditions: teaching requirement, improvement in teaching quality, school development needs, personnel deployment status, years of service at school and so on. Teachers participating in-service training or research should sign a contract with the school to define their rights and responsibilities.

In the past decade, besides the existing regulations and the teacher in-service training system, a more comprehensive teacher professional development mechanism has been in plan. Firstly, in 2005, "regional teacher in-service training centers" were set up in twelve teacher education universities to provide regional in-service training courses (Chang and Lee, 2006). Secondly, "compulsory education advisory groups", since 2005, have been set up to build curriculum and teaching counseling teams of teachers from central to local counties, providing counseling services on teaching. Thirdly, the College for Teacher Professional Development and Continuing Education was planned to be set up in 2006. Finally, a 2006 pilot for the evaluation of teacher professional development was officially implemented in 2009 and was continued for eight years up to 2013 (Lee, 2006, 2009, 2010).

Teacher professional development framework

The Ministry of Education announced the Enhancement Program for Elementary and Secondary Teachers' Quality in 2009 for achieving the goals of quality, professional development and sophisticated effectiveness of teachers. There are five levels in the content of the program:

- Level 1 is to advance the teacher education system.
- Level 2 is to complete the teacher recruitment system.
- Level 3 is to enforce teacher professional development and promote teacher professional knowledge and skills.

- Level 4 is to rationalize the teacher retirement and bereavement compensation system.
- Level 5 is to reward outstanding teachers and eliminate incompetent teachers.

Level 3 in the Enhancement Program for Elementary and Secondary Teachers' Quality, concentrating on teacher professional development, contains two focal points. The first is the Teacher In-service Training and Advanced Education, and the second is the Establishment of Teacher Professional Development Evaluation System. The former, focusing on teacher professional development and advanced training, includes four implementation strategies:

1. To construct an integrative system of teacher in-service training among central, local, and school levels.
2. To promote the professional competence of principals and teachers.
3. To build pluralistic teacher in-service training and education systems.
4. To established a teacher career ladder system. The latter, the establishment of an evaluation system of teacher professional development, enforces "Elementary and Secondary School Teachers' Professional Development Evaluation" as the main strategy. The impetus duration of Enhancement Program for Elementary and Secondary Teachers' Quality is a four-year term, from 2009 to 2012.

(Ministry of Education, 2009)

In 2013, along with the transformation of government organizations, the Ministry of Education integrated the business of teacher education and art education, reorganized the Department of Teacher and Art Education, and meanwhile announced the White Paper of Teacher Education in ROC. There are four dimensions in the White Paper with nine development strategies and 28 action programs. The four dimensions are:

1. Teacher education and preparation
2. Teacher induction and consultation
3. Teacher professional development
4. Teacher education supporting systems.

The third dimension – "Teacher professional development" – includes six action programs:

1. Program for in-service training system
2. Program for practice-based teacher learning
3. Program for teacher support and consultation
4. Program for incentives for teacher professional development
5. Program for teacher evaluation system
6. Program for incompetent teacher consultation and treatment.

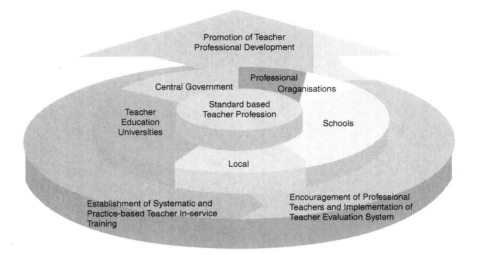

Figure 7.1 Promotion strategies of teacher professional development
Source: MOE (2012).

Specifically speaking, the strategies about teacher professional development in the White Paper also focus on the "in-service training" and "teacher evaluation". Figure 7.1 is the strategy illustration regarding teacher professional development represented in the White Paper. In short, both in the Enhancement Program for Elementary and Secondary Teachers' Quality and the White Paper of Teacher Education in ROC, there are two focal points regarding teacher professional development. One is to build a teacher in-service training system, the other is to implement the evaluation of teacher professional development (Ministry of Education, 2012).

Teacher in-service training

The traditional approach to teachers' professional growth is mainly based on in-service training. However, there is a huge gray zone existing in the methods, institutions, positions, and functions of teacher in-service training. Chen *et al.* (1996) analyzed the situation of elementary and secondary teacher in-service training. They found that it was ambiguous whether the nature of teacher in-service training belongs to duty or welfare either in law or in practice. Teacher in-service training was mainly provided by the official workshops that dominated. Professors from universities gave lectures for workshops which were generally too theoretical to meet practical needs. These workshops were usually not well-scheduled. Schools were usually informed to join the workshop at short notice and thus it interfered with the schools' daily operations. What is more, some activities combined teacher in-service training and pre-service teacher education. It confounded these two functions, leading to the ineffectiveness of training and education.

In the other research, Tzai (1996) found that the motivation for teacher in-service training tended to follow utilitarian aims. The purpose of teachers on in-service training was to attain a degree or obtain credits in order to get promotion and qualify for a raise in salary. The institution of teacher in-service training was formalized; the place of teacher in-service training was limited within specific organizations. The refresher courses and pre-vocational education was not very different, so there was no help in enhancing the professional knowledge of in-service teacher training. In-service training activities were mainly held in teacher normal universities and colleges, and refresher courses relied more on theories as well as pre-vocational teacher education. In addition, the only means of teacher career development was to participate in administrative work. There were no other institutionalized teaching-related career development approaches. That is to say, teaching performance could not be identified or be clearly recognized in schools.

Accordingly, Tzai (1996) suggested that career development in terms of teaching stages should be established. Accompanied by the imminent implementation of the new internship system, experienced teachers could be offered more professional tasks, by reducing teaching hours and increased additional emoluments. The long-term objective was to establish a teacher career ladder system. Teachers should be offered different tasks in different career steps to elaborate their professional knowledge and skills.

Based on the suggestion mentioned above, the Ministry of Education commissioned Professor P. Z. Tsai to carry out "Studies on the Teacher Career Ladder System". In the studies, Tsai (1996) divided teacher career development into four stages, namely: Beginning Teachers stage (six years); Backbone teachers stage (five years); Professional teachers stage (five years); Experienced teachers stage. Before advancing a grade at each stage, teachers have to be examined through five aspects: merit, in-service training, professional performance, exceptional performance, and other. In-service training includes knowledge and skills of pedagogy, discipline, and administration; professional performance contains teaching, student counseling and research work behavior; exceptional performance involves participation in school activities and community activities. The teacher in-service training is regarded as one of the review aspects in the promotion. At each stage, corresponding training content and required hours are designed. Before being promoted, teachers have to participate in school, regional, county, and provincial teacher learning centers and academic organizations to attain at least 216 hours of training, which means the average number of training hours per year should be in excess of 43.

In addition, Chen *et al.* (2006) also point out that a teacher in-service training system corresponding to different teacher career development steps should be constructed. In addition, the refresher courses for teacher professional development should be designed to enable sustainable empowerment. In their research, a set of indicators according to teacher professional performance was suggested, and the weights of the teacher career development indicators should depend on each kindergarten, elementary, and secondary school level.

In the White Paper in 2012, in the teacher in-service training system emphasis was put on "systematic" and "practice-based" as two primary characteristics. Based on "teacher profession standards", there are seven categories framed in refresher courses. They are:

1. curriculum design and teaching;
2. classroom management and counseling;
3. further studies and development;
4. commitment and devotion;
5. school management and leadership;
6. emerging issues and characteristics; and
7. practical intelligence and life.

Table 7.1 represents the systematic teacher in-service training framework.

There are some characteristics in the systematic teacher in-service training framework mentioned above. Firstly, in the organizational functions, the framework vertically integrates responsibilities and resources allocation among central, teacher education universities, local schools, and professional organizations. It also combines the utility of resources from research, industry, and government to provide support for multi-oriented professional development for teachers. Secondly, a multi-adaptive learning strategy of in-service training is planned. It suggests a practice-based in-service training, and the practical implementation of the refresher courses of learning, implementation, adaptability, diversity, innovation, creativity, and other elements. Finally, the style, method, time, and approaches of in-service training should adopt principles of diversity and flexibility in order to meet the requirements of the school context (Ministry of Education, 2012).

Teacher professional development evaluation

With regard to the teacher evaluation, the Education Reform Consultant Committee Concluding Report in 1996 appealed for the need to enhance teachers' professional quality and to establish an educational evaluation system. In 2003, the Promotion of the Pilot Implementation Project for Professional Development Evaluations of Teachers Funded by the Ministry of Education was announced. Then in 2006, a pilot implementation of the evaluation of the professional development of school teachers was begun. According to the Promotion of the Pilot Implementation Project for Professional Development Evaluations of Teachers, the purpose is to assist teachers in their professional growth, to enhance the professionalism of teachers and to improve teaching quality. The purpose of the evaluation is not teacher performance appraisal, but teacher professional development, and is irrelevant to the teacher grading system. Moreover, these regulations emphasise that the evaluation is a feedback mechanism for assessing teachers' performance, which encourages teachers not only to continue developing their professional capacity but also to practice at least to the minimum professional standards in the interests of students.

Table 7.1 Systematic teacher in-service training framework

Teacher career development steps		Step of exploration and establishment (1–3 years)	Step of transformation (10 years)	Step of mature	Step of advancement
Contents of refresher courses		1. curriculum design and teaching; 2. classroom management and counseling; 3. further studies and development; 4. commitment and devotion; 5. school management and leadership; 6. emerging issues and characteristics; and 7. practical intelligence and life.			
In-service training hours	Assign	36 (hrs)	18 (hrs)	18 (hrs)	18 (hrs)
	Empowerment	18 (hrs)	36 (hrs)	36 (hrs)	36 (hrs)
Training hours per year		At least 54 (hrs)			
Supporting systems	Central level		Ministry of Education, National Academic of Educational Research, Central Compulsory Education Advisory Group, discipline centers, discipline-group centers		
	Teacher education university level		Normal teacher universities, educational universities, universities affiliated with college of education, Department of Education or Center of Teacher Education		
	Regional level		local educational authorities, bureau of inspectors, county compulsory education advisory group, county educational development centers, in-service teacher training centers		
	School level		school administrative units, curriculum development committees, grade curriculum development groups, learning field curriculum development groups, teaching research groups, professional learning communities, teaching tutors, school alliance centers		
	Professional organization level		teacher professional groups, parents' groups, principal professional groups, academic groups, cultural education groups, social educational institutions		

Source: MOE (2012).

In addition, the main spirit of the evaluation of teacher professional development is to encourage schools to freely apply for the pilot implementation and teachers to participate voluntarily. The evaluation encourages teachers to self-reflect and interact among peers for professional growth, and teaching and classroom management are the main contents. The expectation lies in leading the school-based orientation of school administration and inspection, enhancing students' learning performance and effectiveness.

The content of the evaluation of teacher professional development includes four dimensions:

- curriculum design and teaching;
- classroom management and counseling;
- further studies and development;
- commitment and devotion.

These four dimensions are the same as the former four categories of the "systematic teacher in-service training framework" represented in the White Paper of Teacher Education. These four dimensions are important elements from the teacher career development stages to teacher professional development standard.

On the criteria or indicators of teacher professional development evaluation, many scholars have engaged in relative research. The aim of Pan *et al.* (2004) was to construct an indicator system to evaluate elementary and junior high school teachers' professional competence. The system aimed to appraise both common and specific professional skills of teachers from different subjects. The framework of the system consisted of three layers: "domains of competence", "dimensions of competence", and "competence indicators". Based on above domains and dimensions, 35 indicators were developed. Later, Pan *et al.* (2007) provided nine standards for the teacher profession:

- knowledge of discipline, pedagogy, student development, and learning;
- curriculum and instructional activity design;
- usage of appropriate teaching strategies and resources to improve student learning;
- the ability to adjust instruction according to students' learning outcomes;
- creation of an environment conducive to learning;
- usage of resources properly for students counseling;
- reflection and professional development;
- positive interaction with school colleagues and parents;
- fulfillment of education professional responsibilities.

Chang and Kuo (2011) found that there are five trends in the "teacher professional development standards" from relative studies. First, the development of teacher professional standards is a long-term investment process with a lot of manpower involved. The major stakeholders – education scholars, experts in various disciplines, primary school teachers – should fully participate, cooperate, and seek consensus in the standards. Second, the foundation of teaching research had transmitted research into traditional teacher effectiveness research to constructivism research. Third, although the focus of the teacher professional standard is on the curriculum, teaching, and classroom management, other professional performances by teachers, such as student counseling, teaching reflection, learning communities, and professional liability, are taken as generalized teaching. Fourth, teacher professional standards used to emphasize teachers' teaching but turned into taking account of the student's learning process and results. Fifth, teacher professional standards tend first to develop common core standards of various disciplines and each learning stage, then develop teacher professional standards in specific subjects and learning phase.

To establish evaluation standards or criteria is the primary work of the professional development evaluation of teachers. However, the practice of teacher professional development evaluation allows competent educational authorities and schools the flexibility to establish evaluation criteria according to local conditions.

Schools, in promoting teacher professional development evaluation work, would choose one or several areas of evaluation to carry out every year corresponding to school development work. Table 7.2 shows the numbers of participating teachers and schools in the evaluation of teacher professional development from 2006 to 2013.

Table 7.2 shows that the number of teachers and schools participating in the evaluation of teacher professional development is increasing every year. In fact, the number of participants and their willingness to participate among all schools and teachers nationwide is relatively low, with only 1,571 schools (about 40 per cent of the total in the country) and 53,835 teachers (about 25 per cent of the total) took part in the evaluation of teacher professional development in 2013. One of the reasons for the low participation rate is that teachers and schools can join in at will. Chin *et al.* (2013) concludes that a high level of recognition of the implementation of evaluation of teacher professional development contrasts with a low willingness to participate among teachers. They also pointed out that the main factor behind the low participation rate of teachers in the program was their workload, doubt regarding the evaluation, and only partial

Table 7.2 The number of teachers and schools participating in the evaluation of teacher professional development

School year	Number of schools	Number of teachers
95 (2006)	165	3,425
96 (2007)	244	6,211
97 (2008)	302	8,848
98 (2009)	610	17,896
99 (2010)	788	23,318
100 (2011)	1,028	31,663
101 (2012)	1,221	42,913
102 (2013)	1,571	53,835

implementation of the program. Huang (2013) also found that the nature of index is different between teacher professional development evaluation and teacher license: the standard level and judgement of teacher professional development evaluation are less serious because of the freedom of choice in schools.

Yeh (2010) points out that teacher professional development evaluation merges multiple ideas of evaluation: school-based evaluation, formative evaluation, meta-evaluation, program evaluation, self-evaluation, growth-focus evaluation, and evidence-based evaluation. During policy formation, teacher professional development evaluation does not take into consideration performance appraisal, the dismissal of incompetent teachers, and the teacher grading system. It also combines different levels of resources, such as central, county, and city governments, academic institutions, national and local level educational groups, and non-profit and non-governmental organizations.

Research into teacher professional development evaluation reviews the implementation and effectiveness of the different levels or variety of stakeholders. The research of Chin et al. (2013) investigated not only teachers but also systems, local governments, funding, resources, and parents. The research by Chang (2013) investigated the problems of implementing the evaluation of teacher professional development from the level of the teacher, school, and competent educational authority. From 2006, the evaluation of teacher professional development evaluation was piloted and in 2009 was formally implemented up to 2013. Researchers concluded that the lack of laws or regulations impacted on teachers' willingness to participate and the pace of its promotion (Chang, 2009, 2013; Chin et al., 2013; Pan et al., 2010).

From state control to marketization

According to the previous two sections, the professional development of Taiwanese teachers in the twentieth century has mainly focused on in-service teacher training activities. The state plays a leading role in policy planning, the implementation of agencies, and the effectiveness of enforcement. Until the twenty-first century, a diversified and comprehensive framework for in-service teacher training and the evaluation of teacher professional development was developed. Traditionally, the governance of teacher professional development focused on state control, but now government power has gradually become decentralized to local schools or teachers.

Marketization professionalism

Yang et al. (2005), in analyzing teacher professional management mechanisms from the teacher professional theories, points out a new professionalism that has emerged. The new professionalism, also known as "commercialized professionalism" or "marketization professionalism", emphasizes the examination of professional performance using business management skills and objective accountable criteria. The trends of enterprise performance management and standards of accountability transform the teaching profession's aims of providing knowledge, service, and care into those of standard criteria, quality control, market mechanisms, and social recognition.

In this context, the teacher profession has characteristic technical features. In contrast to the traditional concept of the teaching profession, the deliberative process of teacher professional development has become an essential part of management control of teachers. Therefore, in order to meet the requirements of the management doctrines, control of the quality of teacher professional development is a key point for the recruitment of teachers, curriculum planning, teacher qualifications acquired by teacher selection, appointment, treatment, working conditions and teacher professional development. Relevant literature and research are engaged in constructing standards or indicators of teacher professionalism or capacity (Chang, 2004; Pan *et al.*, 2004; Pan *et al.*, 2010). These standards or indicators attempt to evaluate teachers' behavior more comprehensively in order to control the quality of the teaching profession.

In addition, under the policies stressed by market doctrine and performance management, new professionals must undergo basic training, meet the capacity requirements, meet the needs of consumers, and achieve the required performance standards. Under this logic of market operation, teachers have to manage personal information or daily life behavior and provide evidence of personal efficiency and quality. Lee (2009) found that the implementation of teacher professional development enabled teachers to "cultivate the habit of self-reflection on teaching" and "arrange teaching files". Chang *et al.* (2010) found that the effects of schools conducting teacher evaluation were: (1) to stimulate teaching reflection; (2) to improve teachers' confidence; (3) to promote teachers' discussions and sharing with each other; and (4) to produce relevant teaching information as evidence of school evaluation. On the other hand, the investigation of Chin *et al.* (2013) pointed out that in the evaluation of teacher professional development, paperwork and file management are emphasized too much.

In short, in the context of marketization professionalism, teachers are seen as objects the quality of which must be controlled. Consequently, in in-service teacher training, the learning content is clearly divided into seven areas that must be carried out separately. Meanwhile, teachers are also proscribed to complete a minimum number of hours per year. Besides, in the evaluation of teacher professional development, teachers' professional performance was separated into aspects of teaching, classroom management, in-service training and attitude. Teachers have to provide evidence to prove individual professionalism and quality.

New social actors

The management mechanism of teacher professional development in Taiwan displays marketization features. This management mechanism emphasizes the establishment of specific standards for and quality control of the teaching profession on the one hand, and aims to achieve social recognition and to respond to consumer demand on the other. Teacher professionalism is considered to be a public service dependent on the needs of the society. But, in defining the implications of teacher professional standards or in the process of the implementation of the evaluation of teacher professional development, the power of government is gradually shrinking, and various social actors will play relatively important parts within it.

The relevant literature mentioned in the third section shows that in-service teacher training in the earlier stages mainly focuses on official training activities. After the framework of teacher professional development in the White Paper is published, systematic practice-based in-service teacher training encompasses not only a growing number of private and unofficial institutions sponsoring teacher training activities, but also the teacher professional development support systems which are characteristic of a more comprehensive coverage of the central teacher education universities, local government agencies, schools, and various professional organizations at different levels.

In terms of the evaluation of teacher professional development, research and reviews not only analyze the connotations of implementation issues, but also examine the evaluation from the perspectives of multiple stakeholders. In the evaluation of teacher professional development, the system is divided into school-based inspection and evaluation, teacher self-reflection, and peer professional interaction. In the article "Prospects of teacher evaluation for professional development in Taiwan: view from the perspective of practice-based teacher learning", Chang (2013) reviewed the problems and issues regarding the implementation of the evaluation of teacher professional development from the aspects of teachers, schools, and educational authorities, etc. In the article "A study of the effectiveness of teacher evaluation for professional development", Chin et al. (2013) also investigated and analyzed the evaluation from different sources, such as teachers, schools, county and city governments, parents, experts, and academics.

In-service teacher training and the evaluation of teacher professional development are two axes of teacher professional development in Taiwan. Various social actors and multiple stakeholders play increasingly important roles in the governance of teacher professional development and, in relation to this, the state or government no longer has the sole or principal position. In short, the in-service training activities and teacher evaluation of teacher professional development represent decentralization. It empowers teachers, schools, parents, local governments, and private organizations to participate in the field of teacher professional development policies.

After decentralization

The characteristics of the in-service training support system, including practice-based teacher learning, free participation in teacher evaluation, the professional development community, and other interactive activities, show that the government is just one of many actors in the governance of teacher professional development. The government, in the process of decentralization, is linked with many other actors in policy-making and implementation. But that does not mean that the government has reduced actual impact on the relevant policies; on the contrary, the state and various social actors across the whole system of the management of teacher professional development are combined together.

By combining government and various social actors, the implementation and promotion of teacher professional development policy is actually associated with more power than the state on its own. Apparently, the state seems to have abdicated in the process of policy implementation, but in fact stakeholders and social actors are absorbed in rejoining the governance of teacher professional development. In other words, in the idea of marketization, the management mechanism of open government has been directed to expand the role of social actors' participation and represented a decentralized pattern of governance.

However, in the decentralization process of the governance of teacher professional development, there have also been some problems. With regard to the in-service teacher training system, although the relevant laws and regulations clearly defined "Teachers who intend to participate in in-service training should focus on the needs of the teaching requirement, improve teaching quality and school development", and the basic in-service training hours were regulated in the Teacher In-service Training Framework, they failed to explicitly regulate that the results of in-service training or research should meet the needs of teaching and classroom or how to present specific contributions or actual effectiveness of teacher in-service training. It means the discrepancy between "teachers have the right to self-education" and "results and effectiveness of in-service training" still exists.

On the other hand, the expectation from the evaluation of teacher professional development is that it will enhance students' learning performance and effectiveness through leading the instructional leadership of school administration and school-based evaluation. However, because of the voluntary nature of the program, the outcomes are insignificant, not only in terms of its popularity and contribution to the teaching profession but also in terms of student learning. Relative research also points out the same issue: "In the study of teacher professional development evaluation effectiveness, the focal points mainly remain on teacher professional development and improving the quality of teaching. There is lack of direct concern in enhancing the effectiveness of student learning. So the impact on student learning from teacher professional development evaluation should be studied further" (Chang, 2013).

Conclusion

This article describes the situation of teacher professional development in Taiwan. With the diversity of the teacher education system and institutions, Taiwanese teacher professional development represents a gradual shift in governance from the model of centralization and state regulation to a new professionalism and marketization.

Traditionally, the concept of teacher professional development in Taiwan has been mainly based on teacher in-service training and learning. In the 1990s, the movement for educational reform in Taiwan led to changes in ideas about the teacher education system and professional development. The framework of teacher professional development has gradually attempted to build toward a teacher career ladder and construct a consortium system of teacher professional development.

The historical evolution of teacher professional development in Taiwan can be divided into three stages. The first stage is from the colonial period to 1978. During this stage, whether under colonial rule or the Kuomintang government, related measures to enhance the ability or quality of teachers belong to the initial establishment phase. The second stage is from 1979 to 1993. In this stage, legislation clearly regulates the institutions and approaches of teacher in-service training and education. The third stage is from 1994 to the present, bringing in the diversification of the teacher education system, teacher professional development policies towards a new professionalism, and market orientation, in order to try to establish a more comprehensive framework.

Before the 1980s, the features and purpose of in-service teacher training and education mainly focused on obtaining the necessary teacher qualifications or the required university degree. The former refers to the rapid expansion of primary and secondary education in the process, because of the urgent need for large number of teachers, which led to many teachers entering schools without the necessary qualifications. Thus, in-service training and education were set up to obtain teacher qualifications. This latter is due to teachers' response to the world trend in which the government upgraded the requirement for school teachers to have a Bachelor's degree. Teachers in the workplace had to return to the teacher education institutions to obtain the degree.

Under the formation of the privileged professionalism discourse in the 1980s and 1990s, teacher professional development represented a shift in governance and diversity in Taiwan. Since the 2000s, teacher learning is seen as an active and constructive process that is problem-oriented, grounded in social settings and circumstances, and taking place throughout teachers' lives. As a consequence, researchers have emphasized the notion of ongoing and lifelong professional learning embedded in schools as a natural and expected component of teachers' professional activities and a key component of school improvement. Both in the Enhancement Program for Elementary and Secondary Teachers' Quality (2009) and White Paper of Teacher Education in ROC (2012), there are two focal points concerning teacher professional development. One is to build an in-service teacher training system, the other to implement the evaluation of teacher professional development.

Approaches to teacher professional development in Taiwan represented a shift of governance. The power of state control is gradually being decentralized to local schools and teachers. New ways of conceptualizing teacher professional development in Taiwan are emerging.

First, there has been a gradual shift from input control towards outcomes and output control. In the production and delivery of public services, institutional forms have become more important than efficiency and productivity. Under the principle of commercialized professionalism, the features of teacher professional development in Taiwan include teacher professional standards and quality control. Not only have professional standards or criteria for teachers been regulated, but also the evaluation of experimental teacher professional development has been taking place since 2006.

Second, there has been a shift in perspective with regard to state–society relations and dependencies. The state has nearly always been engaged in some type of negotiation with other significant structures in society. The state evolved as an actor that remains in control of a number of unique power bases in society; at the same time, however, the state has become increasingly dependent on other societal actors. There is a triple-level system – central–regional–school. The in-service education system for teachers, regional education consultant areas and teacher education universities are coordinated. The national teacher in-service network, Internet-assessed learning, and municipal in-service training centers are providing teacher training resources and an excellent training environment.

References

Chang, D. R. (2004) "The plan and strategy of profession-based teacher evaluation," *Bulletin of National Institute of Education Resources and Research*, 29: 170–83 (in Chinese).

Chang, D. R. (2009) "The problem and solving strategies of teacher evaluation for professional development in elementary and secondary schools," *In-service Education Bulletin*, 26 (5): 17–24 (in Chinese).

Chang, D. R. (2013) "Prospects of teacher evaluation for professional development in Taiwan: view from the perspective of practice based teacher learning," *Educational Information and Research*, 108: 1–30 (in Chinese).

Chang, D. R. and Kuo, S. F. (2011) "Problems and prospects of the practice and research of teacher professional development in Taiwan", *Journal of Teacher Education and Teacher Professional Development*, 4 (2): 21–44 (in Chinese).

Chang, D. R. and Lee, J. D. (2006) "Teacher education," in National Institute of Educational Resources and Research (ed.), *Education Yearbook of the Republic of China, 2002*. Taipei: National Institute of Educational Resources and Research, pp. 241–64 (in Chinese).

Chang, D. R., Li, C. T., and Chou, L. H. (2012) "A case research of the practicing progress and influencing factors on formative teacher evaluation in a junior high school," *Journal of Education Practice and Research*, 23 (2): 65–93 (in Chinese).

Chen, M. J., Chiou, S. Y., and Chen, H. C. (2006) "The study of steps of teacher career development for Taiwan secondary school, primary school and kindergarten," *Educational Information and Research*, 72: 17–32 (in Chinese).

Chen, S. F., Ding, G. Z., and Hong, L. Y. (1996) *Examinations of Teacher Education and In-service Training Systems*. Taipei: Committee on Education Reform, Executive Yuan (in Chinese).

Chin, M. C., Chen, C. H., Wu, C. T., and Guo, C. Y. (2013) "A study of the effectiveness of teacher evaluation for professional development," *Educational Information and Research*, 108: 57–84 (in Chinese).

European Commission (2010) *Teachers' Professional Development – Europe in International Comparison*. Luxembourg: Office for Official Publications of the European Union.

Huang, J. L. (2013) *The Idea and Practice of Standards-based Teacher Education*. Taipei: National Taiwan Normal University Press (in Chinese).

Lee, C. L. (2009) "A Study of Advancing and Evaluating Teachers' Professional Development in Elementary Schools in Taichung City." Unpublished Master's thesis, Department of Education, National Taichung University of Education, Taichung, Taiwan (in Chinese).

Lee, F. J. (2006) "Teacher education," in National Institute of Educational Resources and Research (ed.), *Education Yearbook of the Republic of China, 2007*. Taipei: National Institute of Educational Resources and Research, pp. 225–74 (in Chinese).

Lee, F. J. (2009) 'Teacher education," in National Institute of Educational Resources and Research (ed.), *Education Yearbook of the Republic of China, 2007*. Taipei: National Institute of Educational Resources and Research, pp. 241–88 (in Chinese).

Lee, F. J. (2010) "Teacher education," in National Institute of Educational Resources and Research (ed.), *Education Yearbook of the Republic of China, 2009*. Taipei: National Institute of Educational Resources and Research, pp. 263–302 (in Chinese).

Lee, Y. H. (2001) *History of Taiwan Normal Education*. Taipei: Nan Tian (in Chinese).

Ministry of Education (2006) *Enhancement Program for Elementary and Secondary Teachers' Quality*. Taipei: MOE (in Chinese).

Ministry of Education (2012) *White Book of Teacher Education in ROC: Promoting the Teaching Profession to Cultivate Future Talent*. Taipei: MOE (in Chinese).

OECD (2009) *Teaching and Learning International Survey (TALIS)*. Paris: OECD.

Pan, H. L., Chang, D. R., and Chang, S. J. (2007) *The Construction of Teacher Evaluation Standards: A Delphi Analysis*. Eastern Asian Education Evaluation Forum.

Pan, H. L., Wang, L. Y., Chien, M. F., Sun, Z. L., Chang, S. J., Chang, S. S., Chen, S. H., Cen, S. M., and Tsai, B. Z. (2004) "Developing a profession competence indicator system for teachers of elementary and secondary schools," *Educational Research and Information*, 12 (4): 129–68 (in Chinese).

Pan, H. L., Wang, L. Y., Chang, S. C., Wu, C. H., and Cheng, S. H. (2010) "A Program Evaluation about the Pilot Program of Teacher Evaluation for Professional Development in Junior High and Elementary Schools," Thematic Research Report Commissioned by the Ministry of Education. Unpublished (in Chinese).

Su, S. W. (2001) "The development of secondary and elementary school teacher in-service training in Taiwan," in S. K. Yang (ed.), *International Comparison on In-service Teacher Education*. Taipei: Yangchi Culture, pp. 221–78 (in Chinese).

Teacher Professional Development Evaluation (2014) *The Participating School Number of Teacher Professional Development Evaluation in 95 Academic Year to 102 Academic Year*. Retrieved from: http://tepd.moe.gov.tw/chinese/05_download/01_list.php?fy=34 (in Chinese).

Tsai, P. Z. (1996) "Basic framework of teacher career ladder system in Taiwan elementary and secondary schools," in P. Z. Tsai (ed.), *Teacher Career and Ladder System*. Kaohsiung: Liwen Culture, pp. 155–90 (in Chinese).

Tzai, C. H. (1996) "Problems and solutions of currently elementary and secondary school teacher professional development," in B. H. Huang and K. S. Chen (eds), *Investigation on Important Issues of Teachers at the Senior High School Level and Below*. Taipei: Committee on Education Reform, Executive Yuan, pp. 37–50 (in Chinese).

Yang, S. K., Huang, J. L., Huang, S. L., and Yang, C. S. (2005) "On teacher professional management mechanism from the viewpoint of teacher professional theories," in Teacher Education Society of ROC (ed.), *Teacher's Educational Belief and Professional Standards*. Taipei: Shinli, pp. 55–88 (in Chinese).

Yeh, L. C. (2010) "The viewpoints and implementations of teacher professional developmental evaluation for 1–12 schools," *School Administration*, 69: 159–85 (in Chinese).

Part 3
Improving teachers' professional performance

8 Development of teacher education institutions in Taiwan

Chou-Sung Yang

Introduction

The quality of a country's education is dependent on the quality of the teachers. Therefore countries around the world continue to actively reform their teacher education systems to train capable teachers and reinforce national competitiveness. In the United States, the Teaching and Higher Education Act of 1998, the Educational Excellence for All Children Act of 1999 and the No Child Left Behind Act of 2001 were introduced to emphasize the importance of competent teachers. In addition, the US government formulated and implemented numerous policies to improve teacher education (Peng, 2002). According to the 2002 annual report proposed by the US Department of Education (US DoE, 2002), which addressed the topic "Meeting the highly qualified teachers challenge", the DOE proposed a streamlined teacher qualification method with high standards for verbal ability and content knowledge as an alternative channel to conventional teacher education programmes to train highly qualified teachers. In 2011, the topic "Building a high-quality teaching profession" was further addressed and discussed at the International Summit on the Teaching Profession, an event collaboratively organized by the US DoE and the Organisation of Economic Cooperation and Development (OECD). *The Importance of Teaching: The Schools White Paper 2010*, published by the UK Department for Education (DfE), also emphasized that "no education system can be better than the quality of its teachers". This publication essentially focused on enhancing education standards and advocated that teacher quality and teacher education are the key policies for future educational reform (DfE, 2012). In Taiwan, the Ministry of Education (Ministry of Education, 2012a) published the *White Paper of Teacher Education* in 2012, which contained policies for reform and future development and showed the value that the MOE placed on teacher education reform.

The development of teacher education in Taiwan can be divided into two periods, specifically before and after the amendment of the Teacher Education Act made by the Legislative Yuan in 1994. Prior to this amendment, the standards for teacher education were based on the Normal Education Law of 1979, which focused on promoting a uniform, closed, restricted and publicly funded teacher education system. By contrast, the 1994 amendment introduced numerous policies for changing teacher education into a diverse, open, free and self-funded system (Wu, 2003). The amended Teacher Education Act permitted higher education institutions other than normal universities and teacher training colleges to apply and establish teacher education departments or offer teacher education programmes, inviting them to join previously established institutions in the training of future high school, secondary school, elementary school and pre-school teachers. The amended act eliminated the exclusive rights of normal universities and teacher training colleges to the teacher education market and forced these schools to compete against comprehensive universities in the acquisition of limited market resources. According to the *White Paper of Teacher Education in ROC* published by the MOE in 2012, the amendments to the Teacher Education Act caused the following changes in the teacher education system in Taiwan: (1) increased pluralistic outlook on teacher education institutions; (2) increased diversity in the campus culture and ecology of secondary schools, elementary schools and pre-schools; and (c) implementation of the teaching qualification examination to ensure the quality of teachers.

In actuality, the transition from the Normal Education Law of 1979 (uniform teacher education) to the amended Teacher Education Act of 1994 (diverse teacher education) not only broadened and diversified relevant education institutions and pathways, but also shifted the paradigm and ideology concerning whether the teacher education system in Taiwan was controlled by the government or by free-market mechanisms. During the period of uniform teacher education, education was considered the basis of economic growth, and therefore teachers were highly valued. The goal of teacher education was not only to train high-quality teachers, but also to educate and promote national defence ideology, indicating strong government intervention during this period. Consequently, the implementation of the amended Teacher Education Act in 1994, which introduced the concept of a diverse, open, free and self-funded teacher education system, loosened the regulatory power of the government over teacher education and market mechanisms became the decisive factors for the supply and demand of teachers.

The implementation of market-oriented teacher education policies after 1994 stimulated diverse qualitative and quantitative changes in teacher education institutions, which resulted in a quantitative increase in teacher education students and a qualitative decrease in the performance of teacher education students. The present study attempted to examine the underlying influences of the government and market mechanics in the discourse of teacher education. This chapter first consists of a brief review on the history of teacher education in Taiwan to understand the transition of teacher education policies and the evolution of teacher education institutions. The development of teacher education is then interpreted in relevant and non-relevant contexts. Finally, the chapter investigates the influences of government and market mechanisms on teacher education institutions as the government reluctantly gives away its control to elucidate the problems and difficulties experienced by these institutions.

Development of teacher education institutions in Taiwan

Chinese traditions and the remnants of Japanese colonisation are two major historical and cultural influences on the development of the teacher education system in Taiwan (Yang, 2003). Regarding Chinese traditions, Taiwan in essence inherited the traditional privatised education system of the Kingdom of Tungning and the Qing dynasty, during which scholars who failed the imperial examination were typically responsible for education. This system lacked a systematic teacher education system and failed to offer contemporary learning theories and teaching methods. Teacher education did not become part of the education system until the introduction of Western education systems during the modernisation movement towards the end of the Qing dynasty. The establishment of the Shanghai Public Normal Academy in 1897 became the prologue of teacher education in contemporary China (Wu and Huang, 2002), followed by the passing of the Statutes for Intermediate Teacher Education and the Statutes for Advanced Teacher Education in 1904. The content presented in these statutes was extremely detailed and complete, outlining motivations and objectives, disciplinary measures, entrance examination procedures, postgraduate obligations, accommodation, books, instruments, faculty and administrators. However, these regulations were abolished shortly after the founding of the Republic of China (Wu, 2003). Subsequently, several regulations were introduced to promote teacher education, including the Regulations for Teacher Training Schools in 1912 and the Regulations for Higher Teacher Training School in 1913. The Taiwanese government then introduced the Normal School Rules and the Statutes for Teacher Training Schools in 1932 and 1933 in an attempt to stimulate teacher education development. During the second Sino-Japanese war (1937–45), the Taiwanese government introduced the Teacher Colleges Regulations and the Teacher Education Facilities Confirmation Programme to maintain the continued growth of teacher education in Taiwan (Wu and Huang, 2002).

However, China ceded Taiwan to Japan after signing the Treaty of Shimonoseki in 1895 and Taiwan remained under Japanese rule until 1945. Thus the teacher education system in Taiwan was influenced by neither the late Qing dynasty nor the early republic era prior to its retrocession in 1945; rather, the system was primarily influenced by Japanese colonisation and rule. The Teacher Education Division of the Kokugo Gakkou (Japanese school) established during the Japanese colonial period in 1896 was the predecessor for formal teacher education in Taiwan (Lin, 1993). Japan believed that assimilation was the best method of ruling Taiwan. Therefore the Teacher Education Division of the Kokugo Gakkou only admitted Japanese students, who were then trained to be elementary school teachers to assist Japan in promoting colonisation (Wu and Huang, 2002). In 1899, the Sotokufu established the Taipei Teachers College in Taipei, the Taichung Teachers College in Chunghua and the Tainan Teachers College in Tainan. These colleges were the earliest independent teacher education colleges in Taiwan and were the first to admit Taiwanese students.

Furthermore, the Rescript on Taiwanese Education was introduced in 1919, appointing the three teachers colleges as the recognised institutions for teacher education (Lin, 1993).

After assuming control of Taiwan in 1945, the Nationalist government invited numerous Chinese scholars and experts specialising in teacher education to Taiwan to receive teacher education. The Taiwanese teacher education system established in the late Qing Dynasty was greatly influenced by Japan and thus exhibited considerable similarities with the Japanese teacher education system during the Japanese colonial period; only minor adjustments were required to converge with the teacher education system during the early retrocession of Taiwan (Wu and Huang, 2002). After 1945, the development of teacher education in Taiwan was based on the Normal School Rules decreed by the Nationalist government in 1932, the Regulations for Normal Universities and Teacher Training Colleges of 1938, the University Act of 1948 and other relevant legislation. However, these laws and regulations failed to create a complete teacher education system. The most influential law for teacher education was the Normal Education Law of 1979, which identified the primary objectives of teacher education to be the "training of sound teachers and other professional staff and researching education disciplines" (Article 11) and "supporting local high schools, secondary schools, elementary schools and pre-schools" (Article 14). In addition, the former Teacher Education Act defined teacher education institutions as "government-funded universities, normal colleges and normal technical institutes" (Article 2, Item 1), which ensured a uniform teacher education system.

Regulated by the Normal Education Law, a uniform teacher education system was enforced in Taiwan for a decade. However, this system was challenged by the freedom, openness and diversity movements in Taiwan that preceded the lifting of Martial Law and anticipation for an open teacher education increased. In 1994, the amended Teacher Education Act passed the third reading, replacing the uniform, closed, restricted and publicly funded teacher education system with a system that emphasised diversity, openness, freedom and self-funding. The primary differences between the original Teacher Education Act and the amended Teacher Education Act of 1994 were as follows: (1) the transition from a uniform to a diversified teacher education system; (2) the shift from government-funded to self-funded studies; (3) the change from government job allocation to individual job selection after graduation; (4) the addition of primary and secondary evaluation procedures; and (5) the conversion from a planning-type to a reserve-type education method (Yang, 2002). However, numerous issues emerged following the introduction of the amended Teacher Education Act in 1994. The amended Teacher Education Act underwent numerous revisions, including a major revision in 2002, to produce the current version of the Teacher Education Act. At present, the establishment and operation of teacher education institutions are regulated by the amended Teacher Education Act of 2002 (Ministry of Education, 2002).

Current status of normal universities and teacher training colleges in Taiwan

The Normal Education Law only recognised normal universities and teacher training colleges as teacher education institutions (the Education Department of the National Chengchi University was the only exception, where the number of government- and self-funded students were roughly equal and the identity, rights and obligations of government-funded students were similar to those of teacher education students). The amended Teacher Education Act of 1994 provided a legal foundation for comprehensive universities and colleges to train secondary and elementary school teachers. This amendment transformed the uniform teacher education system into a diversified system, in which comprehensive universities could establish relevant departments to train secondary and elementary school teachers, in addition to teacher education institutions. Article 5 of the amended Teacher Education Act stated that, "teacher education shall be conducted by teacher training colleges, normal universities, and universities with teacher education departments or teacher education centres". Therefore, teacher education institutions can be characterized into three types: normal universities and teacher training colleges, comprehensive universities with teacher education departments and comprehensive normal universities with teacher education centres. Detailed descriptions of the three types of institution are provided in the following sections.

Normal universities and teacher training colleges

Normal universities and teacher training colleges refer to teacher education-based universities and universities of education. The earliest universities of education were three-year teacher training schools that recruited elementary school graduates. In 1957, a total of nine teacher training schools were established throughout Taiwan, and were located in Taipei (two schools), Hsinchu, Taichung, Chiayi, Tainan, Pingtung, Hualien and Taitung. Each school was responsible for the training of public school teachers in that area. In 1967, teacher training schools were restructured into five-year technical colleges that recruited secondary school graduates. In 1987, these colleges were further restructured into normal universities and teacher training colleges and were placed under the jurisdiction of Taiwan Province or Taipei City (Taipei Municipal Teachers College). With the exception of the Taipei Municipal Teachers College, which remained within the jurisdiction of Taipei City, the remaining eight institutions were appropriated to the Ministry of Education in 1991 and promoted to national teachers colleges. Subsequently, the popularity of consolidating higher education institutions in Taiwan caused the restructuring or consolidation of several teacher training colleges, for example:

- the National Chiayi Institute of Technology and the National Chiayi Teachers College were consolidated into the National Chiayi University in 2002;
- the National Taitung Teachers College was restructured in 2003 and renamed the National Taitung University;

- the National Tainan Teachers College was reorganised in 2004 and renamed the National Tainan University;
- the Taipei Municipal, Hsinchu, Taichung, Pingtung, Hualien and Taipei Teachers Colleges were all restructured and renamed universities of education in 2005;
- the National Hualien University of Education was combined with the Donghua University in 2005 and renamed the Hua-Shih College of Education;
- the Taipei Municipal University of Education and the Taipei Physical Education College were merged in 2013 and renamed the University of Taipei; and
- the National Pingtung University of Education and the National Pingtung Institute of Commerce were combined in 2014 and renamed the National Pingtung University.

Based on this evolutionary discourse, the normal universities and universities of education currently operating in Taiwan include the National Taiwan Normal University, the National Chunghua University of Education, the National Kaohsiung Normal University, the National Taipei University of Education, the National Hsinchu University of Education and the National Taichung University of Education. However, these teacher education institutions are also being converted into comprehensive universities because of the decrease in teacher education students and the transformation of normal universities and teacher training colleges. Numerous teacher education departments in these institutions have already converted into non-teacher-education departments or have reduced the number of students in the department. Among these institutions, three primarily offer secondary school teacher training programmes (National Kaohsiung Normal University offers admissions to its elementary school teacher programs once every two years) and three offer elementary and pre-school teacher training programmes (the National Taipei University of Education previously offered secondary school teacher programmes but closed admissions in 2007). In addition, a number of these institutions have established dedicated units, such as teacher education centres (the National Kaohsiung Normal University and the National Chunghua University of Education) or teacher education and career service offices (National Taiwan Normal University), to manage teacher education affairs. For example, the Office of Teacher Education and Career Services established by the National Taiwan Normal University is the primary unit responsible for teacher education and the head of office is a full-time teacher. The National Taiwan Normal University offers secondary school teacher education programmes, including secondary school teacher training programmes and special school teacher training programmes (Ministry of Education, 2012b).

Comprehensive universities with teacher education departments

Currently, comprehensive universities with teacher education departments include the National Taiwan University, the National Pingtung University, the National Chiayi University, the National Tainan University, the National Taitung

University, the National Chengchi University, the National Chi Nan University, the National Donghua University, the Chong Yuan Christian University, the Chinese Culture University, the Asia University, and the Taiwan Shoufu University. Several of these universities have also established dedicated units, such as teacher education centres, for managing teacher education affairs. For universities without teacher education centres, education departments are typically responsible for teacher education. For example, at the Asia University and the Taiwan Shoufu University, the early childhood education departments are responsible for early childhood teacher education programmes (Ministry of Education, 2012b).

In addition to the number of students per teacher studying in the teacher education centre, the primary difference between universities with teacher education departments and those with teacher education centres is that departments are permitted to admit additional students who can obtain the qualification of prospective teacher within the department. However, these departments typically forfeit teacher training status or reduce the number of teacher students studying in the department to compensate for the constantly diminishing amount of teacher resources. For example, the National Chi Nan University established a teacher education centre for training secondary school teachers. In addition, the university offered other programmes for training secondary school teachers, such as the International Culture and Comparative Education Graduate Programme, the Educational Policy and Administration Master's Programme, the Adult and Continued Education Research Programme and the Guidance and Counseling Research Programme. However, these programmes were eventually discontinued because of the strict teacher education evaluation criteria established by the MOE. In 2012, the National Chi Nan University discontinued all secondary school teacher education programmes and was removed from the list of universities with teacher education departments.

Comprehensive universities with teacher education centres

Apart from the aforementioned two categories, universities that wish to offer teacher education are required to establish teacher education centres. Currently, a total of 35 universities, including the National Sun Yat-Sen University, belong to this category (Ministry of Education, 2012b). The MOE requested that universities clearly define the status of their teacher education centres in their organisation statutes to ensure that the rights of the teachers and students in these centres are appropriately maintained. Based on specific conditions, universities may list their teacher education centres and directors of these centres as primary units (e.g. the National Nan Chi University) or as under the jurisdiction of the academic affairs departments (e.g. the National Taiwan University).

Based on the Regulations of the Establishment and the Academic Faculty of Teacher Education Programmes Offered by Universities and Colleges introduced in 1995, an appropriate number of units can be established under the teacher education centre to assist in administration. For example, the National

Chi Nan University established an administration unit, a teaching unit, an advanced learning unit, and a training and counselling unit under the teacher education centre. The head of each unit is appointed from among full-time teachers teaching in the centre and is designated a secondary supervisor.

Influences of government and market mechanisms on the development of teacher education institutions

Influence of government on the development of teacher education institutions

Approval from the Ministry of Education is required to establish new teacher education institutions

According to Article 5 of the Teacher Education Act:

> Teacher education shall be conducted by teacher training colleges, normal universities, universities with teacher education departments or teacher education centres. The relevant central authority shall identify the departments named in the preceding paragraph. Universities establishing teacher education centres shall require approval from the relevant central authority. Regulations governing the conditions and procedures for the establishment of such centres, as well as teacher qualifications, facilities, student recruitment, curricula, term of study and discontinuation thereof shall be determined by the relevant central authority.

Based on prior regulations, three types of education institution are permitted to provide teacher education: normal universities and teacher training colleges, comprehensive universities with teacher education departments and comprehensive universities with teacher education centres. Among these institutions, normal universities, teacher training colleges and universities with teacher education departments provided teacher education long before the introduction of the Teacher Education Act. However, the teacher education offered at these institutions is essentially regulated by the MOE. Therefore, permitting universities to establish teacher education centres to offer teacher education programmes to their students was the actual source for promoting teacher education diversification. According to Article 2 of the Regulations for Establishing of Teacher Education Centres in Universities:

> Based on individual developmental features and teacher education requirements, eligible universities that wish to establish a teacher education centre must submit an application and relevant documentation to the relevant central authority. The teacher education centre can be established once the application is reviewed and approved by the Teacher Education Review Committee. (a) A minimum of five full-time teachers from various disciplines

must be appointed. The university must currently employ these teachers. (b) A minimum of 1,000 types of education material and 20 types of education journals must be available. In addition, all instruments and equipment required for teaching and research must be acquired. (c) The planning and provision of various teaching curricula and programmes must comply with the provisions listed in Article 3.

Moreover, the number of admissions and the disciplines offered are also regulated by the MOE. According to Article 6 of the Teacher Education Act:

> Teacher education universities offering pre-service teacher education courses shall determine the course plans in accordance with teaching subject areas for secondary schools, elementary schools, kindergarten, and special education schools (or classes), and submit the plans to the relevant central authority for approval before implementation. To meet instructional demands, the teaching subject areas for secondary schools and elementary schools may be planned in combination as joint elementary-secondary school teaching subject areas according to the procedures outlined in the preceding paragraph.

According to Article 7 of the Regulations for Establishment of Teacher Education Centres in Universities:

> Universities with teacher education centres must submit the desired number of admissions for various disciplines to the relevant central authorities for approval. In principle, each class should comprise no more than 50 students. The student list and relevant documents much be appropriately archived within the school.

Based on the previous discussion, the MOE controls the establishment of teacher education centres in various universities. Although the goal of teacher education was originally to promote free competition in the teacher education market, the aforementioned provisions were formulated to control teacher surplus following the saturation of the teacher workforce. In actuality, these revisions were primarily introduced by the MOE in 2006 to control the expansion of teacher education.

Curricula and programmes offered by teachers must be submitted to and approved by the Ministry of Education

According to Article 7 of the Teacher Education Act:

> Teacher education includes pre-service teacher education and teacher certification. Pre-service teacher education curricula comprise ordinary courses, specialized courses, professional courses in education and seminars. Teacher education universities shall draft plans for the specialized courses referred to

in the preceding paragraph and submit them to the relevant central authority for approval. The professional courses in education referred to in paragraph 2 include a shared curriculum that crosses teaching subject boundaries and courses in specific teaching subject areas. Such courses shall be reviewed by both the teacher education review committee and the relevant central authority prior to implementation.

According to Article 3 of the Regulations for Establishment of Teacher Education Centres in Universities:

Teacher education programmes for various disciplines must include the following content: (a) Secondary school teacher education courses must include fundamental education, education methodology, teaching material and techniques, teacher training, or education training (6 months). (b) Elementary school, pre-school, and combined elementary-secondary teacher programmes must include fundamental education, education methodology, teaching materials and techniques, teacher training and education training (6 months). (c) Special education teacher programmes (or classes) must include general education in specific disciplines, special education in general disciplines, special education in specific disciplines, and education training (6 months).

Article 5 further states:

The required credits for admission into teacher education programmes at universities with teacher education centres are as follows: (a) A minimum of 26 credits for secondary school programmes. (b) A minimum of 40 credits for elementary school programmes. (c) A minimum of 48 credits for pre-school programmes (including 32 credits from courses on professional competency for education and health). (d) A minimum of 40 credits for special school (or class) programmes. (e) A minimum of 50 credits for combined elementary-secondary school programmes. Admissions into various teacher education programmes must be based on the standards listed in Article 7, Paragraph 4. The maximal credits and course periods for the various teacher education courses must be listed by individual schools and submitted to the relevant central authority for approval.

Moreover, the MOE introduced the Implementation of the Pre-service Teacher Education Courses and Credits Table, for which Article 2 states:

The pre-service teacher education courses formulated by teacher education universities must be based on the Pre-service Teacher Education Courses and Credits Table and the highlighted provisions, and be submitted to the relevant central authority for approval. Additions and revisions to pre-service teacher education courses must be submitted for reapproval.

In other words, teacher education institutions were unable to plan curricula and courses based on their education ideologies or the features of their schools. Aspects such as course type and number of credits were regulated by the MOE, and plans for compulsory subjects were required to be approved by the relevant central authority. Schools typically abided by the regulations of the MOE to successfully obtain approval. Moreover, following the transformation of education policies, the MOE requested that schools submit curricula and courses for reapproval. This situation can be clearly observed during the implementation of the 12-Year Basic Education Policy in 2014, suggesting that the MOE remained the decisive authority for teacher education programmes.

Influence of market mechanisms on the development of normal universities and teacher training colleges

Transition of teacher education goals to meet market demands

According to Article 1 of the Teacher Education Act introduced in 1979: "Based on Article 185 of the Constitution of the Republic of China (Taiwan), this Act is specifically enacted to develop competent teachers and other education professionals, and to research teacher education". The Teacher Education Act was amended in 1994, revising Article 1 to read: "This Act is specifically enacted to develop competent teachers and other education professionals, and to research teacher education". From the initial introduction of the Teacher Education Act in 1979 to the amendment in 1994, the objective of teacher education was to "develop teachers for schools at the senior high school level and below, as well as kindergartens" and "advance [the teachers'] professional expertise", illustrating the emphasis placed on teacher quality and professional expertise in previous teacher education policies. Subsequently, the Teacher Education Act was heavily revised in 2002, the revision to Article 1 stating that: "This Act is specifically enacted to develop teachers for schools at the senior high school level and below, as well as kindergartens, to augment the supply of teachers and advance their professional expertise". In this revision, the phrases "to develop competent teachers" and "to research teacher education" were omitted and replaced with "to develop teachers for schools" being a new policy objective. These revisions evidently suggested the employment of a market-oriented logic and the change in emphasis from a planning-type to a reserve-type education method. These revisions guided teacher education to meet the demands of the job market.

Market mechanisms determined the development of teacher education institutions

Following the amendment of the Teacher Education Act, numerous universities and colleges actively expressed their interest in offering teacher education programmes. The MOE approved the majority of applications to promote teacher education diversity and free market mechanisms. A total of 25 schools were approved in the first year, collectively recruiting 2,359 students. This success prompted numerous other schools to engage in teacher education. Between 2005 and 2012, a total of 60 schools were approved, collectively offering 88 teacher education programs to 35,490 students. Among these programs, 50 were secondary education programs, 22 were elementary education programs, 13 were pre-school programs and three were special school programs (Huang, 2008, p. 246). According to the *Statistics Yearbook of Teacher Education (Republic of China)*, the peak for teacher education occurred in 2004, with a total of 24,805 students studying in related programs. However, factors such as market saturation and a reduced number of classes in schools as a result of low birth rates negatively influenced the teacher workforce, elevating the unemployment rate of teacher graduates, and increasing the number of "stray teachers". Consequently, numerous teacher education programs and teacher education centres were discontinued. From 2006 to 2011, 20 schools discontinued teacher education programs, reducing the 75 schools which originally offered teacher education to 55 (Ministry of Education, 2009, 2010, 2011, 2012b). In 2012, a total of 54 MOE-approved teacher education institutions remained, comprising three normal universities, five universities of education, ten universities with teacher education-related departments and 36 universities with teacher education centres. This number was further reduced to 52 in 2014, which is the current number of teacher education institutions in Taiwan, because the Taipei Municipal University of Education and Taipei Physical Education College were consolidated and renamed the University of Taipei, and the National Pingtung University of Education and the National Pingtung Institute of Commerce were consolidated and renamed the National Pingtung University in 2014. The number of admissions to teacher education courses each year is approximately 8,131, comprising 943 pre-school education students, 2,207 elementary education students, 4,211 secondary education students and 770 special education students (Ministry of Education, 2014).

Based on the teacher education mentality discussed in previous sections, teacher education transitioned into a free, diverse and open mechanism for market competitiveness, in which institutions self-adjusted to meet market supply and demand. In actuality, numerous schools foresaw the demand and profitability of teacher education at the initiation of the teacher education market. The establishment of teacher education facilities within schools produced positive effects, regardless of the intentions (e.g. to attract students or promote employment), which promoted the active development of teacher education institutions. Subsequently, factors such as an increased unemployment rate in the teacher workforce and excessive operating costs for education units caused numerous schools and students to withdraw from teacher education programs. This withdrawal was typically caused by market-based logic, which naturally restores the balance of supply and demand without the requirement of government intervention.

Influences of government-regulated market mechanisms on the development of teacher education institutions

According to the mentality of the Teacher Education Act mentioned in previous sections, teacher education is a market-based mechanism that adjusts autonomously according to the concept of "replacing control with competition", eliminating the requirement for government intervention. In actuality, the discourse of government intervention to adjust and ensure teacher quality could be clearly observed in the United States and England after 1980. For example, during the revision of higher education legislation in the United States in 1998, the government determined teacher quality based on the teacher certification pass rate for teacher education graduates. The government provided subsidies as an incentive to guide teacher education towards a teacher education system of accountability.

Regarding the demand for teachers in Taiwan, currently employed teachers are at risk of becoming "stray teachers" because of class reductions or school consolidation as a result of the low birth rate. Since 2007, the number of qualified teachers has remained at approximately 8,600. However, the overall employment rate of public elementary and secondary schools in 2006 was roughly 3 per cent and 10 per cent, respectively. The overall employment rate at public schools in 2011 was only 7.79 per cent, which differed considerably from the 50 per cent employment rate recorded in 2004. The difficulty of employment negatively and significantly influenced the overall development of teacher education in Taiwan (Ministry of Education, 2012a). Consequently, the MOE employed various methods for promoting the development of teacher education institutions, as listed in the following section.

Using policy tools to aid in the transitioning and development of teacher education institutions

Normal universities and teacher training colleges were the first to experience the negative impacts of a low birth rate population structure and the imbalance between supply and demand. The MOE used the incentives of personnel authority and subsidisation as policy tools to guide normal universities and teacher training colleges in restructuring or reducing the number of teacher education students. The transition models of normal universities and teacher training colleges comprised (Yang, 2002):

- transitioning into comprehensive universities (e.g. the transition of Tainan Teachers College and Taitung Teachers College into comprehensive universities);
- consolidating into comprehensive universities (e.g. the consolidation of the National Chiayi Institute of Technology and the National Chiayi Teachers College into the National Chiayi University); and
- transitioning into universities of education (e.g. the Taipei, Hsinchu and Taichung Universities of Education).

Formulating competition-based plans and requesting teacher education institutions to comply with major education policies

Together with the implementation of the 12-Year Basic Education Policy in 2014, the MOE introduced the *Guidelines for Improving the Quality of University Teachers Subsidisation Project* to reinforce teacher quality and encourage normal universities to improve the quality of prospective students (Ministry of Education, 2012c). Since 2013, the MOE has granted subsidies to normal universities in groups, aiding them in the implementation of teacher quality improvement projects. Subsidised courses include those aiming to enhance the quality of prospective teachers in their respective disciplines. For example, pre-service teacher education courses (and on-site training) were provided to enhance the concepts and strategies related to basic 12-year education, such as effective teaching, group collaboration and practice, differential teaching, discipline (field and branch) teaching, class management, parent–teacher communication, diversified evaluation, remedial teaching and adaptive counseling. This evidently demonstrated that the MOE intended to grant subsidies for competition-based plans, thus encouraging teacher education institutions to comply with major education policies. The MOE also promulgated the following standard of review in the Guidelines for Improving the Quality of University Teachers Subsidization Project: "Provide subsidy for the promotion of teacher education policies (15%), which comprise the promotion of local education and counseling (2%), promotion of teacher education research (3%), and other policies formulated by the school (10%)". This regulation also encouraged teacher education institutions to comply with major education policies.

Using teacher education evaluations to intervene in market mechanisms

Based on the market-based ideology presented in Article 1 of the Teacher Education Act and market operating logic, the continuation or discontinuation of teacher education should be determined by each normal university or teacher training college without government intervention. However, the balance between the supply of teachers in teacher education institutions and market demands changed considerably after 1994, gradually becoming a social problem. To correct this imbalance, the MOE advocated the "retaining superiority, eliminating inferiority" policy. In addition to employing various policy tools, the MOE implemented various evaluation methods to assist underperforming teacher education institutions in discontinuing teacher education programmes. Moreover, the Regulations for Evaluation of Universities with Teacher Education were amended and issued in 2006, expanding the scope of evaluation and establishing performance standards and assessment methods at each level. Evaluation items included (1) education objectives and development features; (2) administrative organisation, position and operation; (3) student admission and consultation; (4) use of resources, such as books, equipment, funds and space; (5) staffing, teacher quality and research and development outcomes; (6) planning and implementation of curricula and teaching methods; (7) education training and employment consultation; and (8) the promotion of local education counseling or job training. According to Item 7 of the Guidelines for Evaluating Teacher Education at Normal Universities and Teacher Training Colleges:

> Evaluation results must first be reviewed by a field assessment team comprising teacher and discipline evaluation committee members. Evaluation outcomes are then determined by an evaluation approval committee comprising teacher and discipline evaluation committee members. Evaluation outcomes can be characterized into the following three types: (a) pass (a minimum of four items passed and none failed); (b) conditional pass (only one item failed); and (c) fail (two items or more items failed).

According to Item 8:

> Based on the regulations established in Article 8 of the University Evaluation Regulation, the extent of teacher education at various education institutions must be approved or adjusted, accordingly: (a) Teacher disciplines that have passed evaluation may retain the number of admissions originally approved. (b) Teacher disciplines that have conditionally passed evaluation must reduce the number of admissions for these disciplines by 30%. (c) Teacher disciplines that have failed evaluation must be discontinued. Outcomes are subject to change based on current conditions following the approval of the review committee. Although the second-cycle teacher education evaluation system has already been implemented, the attempt to control performance based on evaluation results remains unchanged.

These guidelines suggest that the MOE has regained control of the number of admissions permitted for teacher education programmes by evaluating teacher education institutions. However, for these institutions, maintaining the number of admissions is crucial for sustaining operation. An insufficient number of students may result in increased cost per student and reduced lecture time for teachers, which negatively impacts the school's willingness to support teacher education, eventually causing the school's withdrawal. Therefore, teacher education evaluations have become a major challenge for teacher education institutions, and have necessitated the development and operation of these institutions to abide by relevant evaluation indicators. In addition, these evaluations conform to the various policy requirements instated by the MOE, and are therefore an alternative strategy for government control.

Controlling the number of formal teachers and reducing the number of reserve teachers in teacher education institutions

The number of reserve teachers increased following the implementation of diversified teacher education policies, and the demand for teachers decreased because of the decrease in birth rates in contemporary societies, consequently creating major problems for previously promulgated secondary and elementary school teacher education policies. Therefore, the MOE has actively implemented a series of teacher education reform policies in recent years to effectively improve the quality and quantity of teacher education and fulfill the objectives of "appropriate quality" and "retaining superiority, eliminating inferiority". In 2004, the MOE introduced the Plan for Teacher Education Quantity, and expressed the expectation of reducing the quantity of teacher education by 51.3 per cent in 2007 and 60.92 per cent in 2012, which equals to 8,521 candidates. In addition, to enhance promotion of the objective of "appropriate quality", the MOE introduced the Plan for Teacher Education Quantity (Stage 2) in 2012 to compensate for the reducing number of students in each grade and maintain the quality of high school, secondary school, elementary school and pre-school teachers (Ministry of Education, 2013).

According to the Plan for Teacher Education Quantity, normal universities must reduce the number of admissions into their teacher education undergraduate departments by at least 50 per cent within three years, beginning in 2014. The number of students to be reduced should be based on the number of admissions approved by the MOE in 2014. Universities that offer teacher education programs must submit the number of intended admissions to the MOE for approval each year. The universities are then evaluated based on the Guidelines for Evaluating Teacher Education at Normal Universities and Teacher Training Colleges. Universities that pass evaluation are permitted to retain the proposed number of admissions; those that conditionally pass evaluation may retain 80 per cent of the proposed number of admissions; and those that fail evaluation must discontinue the teacher education programs and reduce the number of admissions by 50 per cent within three years. Subsequently, the Quantitative Teacher Education Plan (Stage 2) established the threshold for the minimum overall number of teacher education admissions, which was twice the average number of teachers in employment (i.e. an average of 2,790 teachers employed between 2008 and 2012), and prevented teacher shortages by referencing the staffing and retirement conditions of teachers each year and considering the demands of various disciplines. The plan also proposed annual adjustments to the number of admissions for teacher education programmes from 2013 to 2017 based on teacher type, birth rate conditions, teacher education quality and the quality of universities offering teacher education programmes.

In summary, although the teacher education system in Taiwan retains the reserve-type mentality promoted by the Teacher Education Act, this mentality subsequently presents the policy ideology of a "planned reserve-type system". In other words, government control remains apparent in the teacher education system in Taiwan, suggesting that although the teacher education model in Taiwan is called a market-based model, teacher education is still influenced by the government.

Conclusion

Prior to the introduction of the amended Teacher Education Act in 1994, the government primarily controlled the development of teacher education institutions in Taiwan. During the Japanese colonial period, the early retrocession period and prior to the lifting of Martial Law, the government solely controlled the teacher education system in Taiwan. Therefore teacher education institutions during those periods were responsible for not only training high-quality teachers, but also promoting the hegemonic ideology of the rulers of those periods. At that time, teacher education institutions comprised only teacher training colleges, which operated under a uniform, planned, closed and controlled system. The teacher education institutions at that time were completely controlled by the government.

Following the introduction of the amended Teacher Education Act in 1994, which opened teacher education institutions, universities were permitted to submit proposals to establish teacher education programs in various disciplines based on individual features and requirements. During this time, teacher education institutions operated under a diverse, reserve, open and relaxed market-based system, and prosperity was consistent with market supply and demand. In addition, market-based logic was advantageous during this time, and government control of teacher education institutions was relaxed or non-existent. However, control of teacher education, including establishment of institutions, number of admissions, curricula and teaching methods, returned to the government following amendment of the Teacher Education Act in 2002. The MOE resumed control of teacher education institutions by employing various policies, competition plans, evaluations of institutions and administrative commands to resolve the teacher market problem. Thus, market mechanisms never substantially influenced the teacher education system in Taiwan.

In summary, the development of teacher education institutions in Taiwan appeared to alternate between the forces of the government and market mechanisms; in actuality, government control remains prevalent. Teacher education institutions in Taiwan remain restricted by the government and have yet to become completely governed by market mechanisms.

References

DfE (2012) *Schools to Get More Freedom to Manage Teacher Performance*. London: DfE.
Huang, J. L. (2008) "Elementary and secondary school teacher education revolution from the post-authoritarian of politics in Taiwan", in Y. M. Shu and Y. C. Fang (eds), *Inspiring the Education Revolution of Post-authoritarian Taiwan*. Taipei: Pro-Ed Publishing, pp. 241–73 (in Chinese).
Lin, Y. F. (1993) "The history of Taiwan's normal education", in N. H. Sui (ed.), *The History of Taiwan Education*. Taipei: Shi Ta Books, pp. 35–8 (in Chinese).
Ministry of Education (1979) *Normal Education Law*. Taipei: MOE (in Chinese).
Ministry of Education (2002) *Revising Teacher Education Act*. Taipei: MOE (in Chinese).

Ministry of Education (2009) *Statistical Yearbook of Teacher Education, Republic of China, 2008*. Taipei: MOE.

Ministry of Education (2010) *Statistical Yearbook of Teacher Education, Republic of China, 2009*. Taipei: MOE.

Ministry of Education (2011) *Statistical Yearbook of Teacher Education, Republic of China, 2010*. Taipei: MOE.

Ministry of Education (2012a) *White Book of Teacher Education in ROC: Promoting the Teaching Profession to Cultivate Future Talent*. Taipei: MOE (in Chinese).

Ministry of Education (2012b) *Statistical Yearbook of Teacher Education, Republic of China, 2011*. Taipei: MOE.

Ministry of Education (2012c) *Guidelines for Improving the Quality of University Teachers Subsidisation Project*. Taipei: MOE.

Ministry of Education (2013) *Plan for Teacher Education Quantity*. Taipei: MOE.

Ministry of Education (2014) *Statistical Yearbook of Teacher Education, Republic of China, 2013*. Taipei: MOE.

Peng, S. M. (2002) "Teacher education of USA and its implications in Taiwan", in Teacher Education Society of ROC (ed.), *The Policy and Review of Taiwan's Teacher Education*. Taipei: Pro-Ed Publishing, pp. 1–29 (in Chinese).

US Department of Education (2002) *Meeting the Highly Qualified Teachers Challenge: The Secretary's Annual Report on Teacher Quality*. Washington DC: US Department of Education.

Wu, C. S. (2003) "Teacher Education Act: past, current and future", *Journal of Education Research*, 105: 27–43 (in Chinese).

Wu, Z. T. and Huang, S. C. (2002) "Development of Taiwan's normal education policy (1945–2001)", in Teacher Education Society of ROC (ed.), *The Policy and Review of Taiwan's Teacher Education*. Taipei: Pro-Ed Publishing, pp. 1–29 (in Chinese).

Yang, C. S. (2003) "The analysis of the 'Teacher Education Act' in Taiwan", *Journal of Culture and Society*, 16: 23–41 (in Chinese).

Yang, T. S. (2002) "Teacher education as the capstone of education", *National Policy Foundation*, 2 (1): 155–9 (in Chinese).

9 Evaluation of the professional development of school teachers

Feng-Jihu Lee

Introduction

Teacher evaluation is critical to success in education. Various countries worldwide have considered teacher professional development as a crucial education policy (Furlong, 2001). This evaluation aims to ensure the quality of teacher professionalism and professional knowledge to maintain optimal professional service quality throughout the decades of teaching careers and provide teachers with a high sense of achievement. Students are effectively well educated due to the continuous improvement of their teachers and overall national competitiveness is continuously enhanced because of an unceasing supply of outstanding professionals. Therefore, evaluating the professional development and performance of teachers is inevitable. School teachers must prepare for a future of teacher evaluation.

Since 1990, the global political economy has undergone a dramatic change. People's lives are affected by postmodern thought, neo-liberalism and market economy. In addition, national education policies and reforms are immersed in empowerment, efficiency, the market, competition, accountability, school-based performance management, parental choices, multiculturalism, and the knowledge-based economy. The teaching profession has been influenced by this progression. Teachers are facing various unprecedented challenges, including the impact of postmodernism, breakthroughs in novel information technology, substantial changes in the global political economy, and the opposition between the concept of a global village and the awareness of localization (Yang, 2000).

In encountering a transition that has not occurred in a thousand years, teachers cannot rely on the experiences gained while in school or the concepts and methods they learned in pre-service teacher education programs to respond to long-term and continuously evolving demands regarding their profession (Furlong *et al.*, 2000). Teachers must constantly pursue professional development and occasionally reassess their existing knowledge. Continuous development enables teachers to withstand ever-growing requirements by students and parents, changes in curricula and teaching materials, transformations in teaching methods and strategy, and radically evolving school and social environments.

In brief, the teaching profession is transitioning under scrutiny in an environment replete with continuously changing definitions of the teaching profession. Developing a new professional culture is necessary, and teachers should not be content with improving only traditional social positions or technical abilities.

The teacher evaluation system is the foundation for managing the improvement and maintenance of high teacher quality. This scheme could stimulate teachers to engage in professional development, assist teacher growth, and strive for teaching excellence, and may serve as the drive that increases student learning performances. European countries and the United States have conducted evaluations of school teachers for many years. Similarly, Taiwan has promoted the planning and implementation of multiple relevant measures to guarantee the right to learn of each student and to respond to external pressure caused by improving the quality of the teacher profession. These measures involve programs for advancing teaching skills and trial evaluations of the professional development of school teachers. Educational researchers must establish a reasonable and feasible evaluation mechanism regarding teacher professional development to advance along with the trend of teacher evaluation in postmodern new professionalism.

Although Taiwan actively evaluates the performances of school teachers, the scheme is ineffectively implemented. Teacher quality cannot be maintained because the evaluation items are vague and teachers are not required to receive evaluations regularly. In 1971, the Ministry of Education instituted the Regulations for Performance Evaluation of the Faculty and Staff of Public Schools to assess the performance of teachers in public schools. In addition, the public and parent associations have initiated growing demands regarding teachers' professional quality. People are increasingly demanding that the professional abilities of teachers be evaluated. Numerous decisions were formulated by the central educational authorities. In addition, several cities and counties have independently promoted evaluations of primary school and junior high school teachers. Moreover, several schools implemented teacher evaluations based on academic research recommendations or directed by leading principals. Three periods (inception, planning, and preparation) were specified in this study to describe the development process of teacher evaluation regarding professional development in Taiwan.

The inception period for teacher evaluation: 1995–2000

Since 1990, professional development for teachers has been emphasized in educational reform in various countries. This subject has also influenced educational reform policies in Taiwan. The sixth chapter in the *First Period Consulting Report*, which was published by the Committee on Education Reform, Executive Yuan, in 1995, advocates that schools establish teacher consultation committees to manage teacher employment, assessment, and evaluation. The items of assessment and evaluation contained in-service education results and teaching performance. To maintain the quality of teachers, it was recommended that the evaluation results be combined with salary, discharges, classifications, and certificate renewals (Committee on Education Reform, 1995). This chapter indicated that teacher evaluations had been a reformation goal for the government. In addition, the Ministry of Education executed a third implementation strategy in the *New Student Guidance System: The Experimental Integrated Program of Instruction, Discipline, and Guidance*, in 1998. This strategy was called the "Implementation of Instructional Supervision and Teacher Evaluations". This was the first time central education administration authorities had included teacher evaluations in the items regarding educational promotion. However, this integrated project was a trial project, and the focus was not on implementing teacher evaluations. The project ended in 2004.

When reviewing educational practices in Taiwan, pilot projects regarding teacher evaluations were found in Kaohsiung City, Taipei City, and Taipei County. On 21 February 2000, the Education Bureau of the Kaohsiung City Government published the *Pilot Project Direction of Professional Evaluations for Teachers Teaching Grades Below the High School Level in Kaohsiung City*. The program began in the 2000–1 school year. This was an important milestone regarding the initiation of a systematic and large-scale professional evaluation system for teachers. In addition, in 1998, the Education Bureau of the Taipei City Government commissioned Taipei Daqiao Primary School to form a research team to conduct a planning study on teacher evaluations. Based on an experimental teacher evaluation system, this team proposed a teaching supervision system that aimed to promote the professional development of teachers through teaching mentoring. In 2002, Taipei City began a trial teacher mentoring system, which remains in effect. Moreover, the Education Bureau of Taipei County asked 15 primary schools and junior high schools to initiate a trial evaluation program of the teaching profession. These three cities were pioneers in Taiwan's promotion of professional evaluations for teachers. Primary cities and counties have since successively initiated trial programs regarding professionally evaluating teachers. The concept of evaluating teacher performances evolved gradually, and has gained public attention. In April 2003, at the 15th meeting of the Taskforce group of the Ministry of Education, the following resolution was presented: "The planning of a professional evaluation system should refer to the implementation of the teacher mentor system of Taipei City and the practical experience of Kaohsiung City when conducting a pilot project regarding the professional evaluation of teachers".

The planning period for teacher evaluation: 2001–5

In 2001, Taiwan adopted a Grade 1–9 Curriculum. Course evaluations were performed as required by the curricula guidelines. Several evaluation indicators considered teaching performance. Evaluations became a crucial measure for ensuring teaching quality as opposed to reform measures deregulating the curricula of schools. Responding to public requests asking for educational reform, the Ministry of Education convened a Review and Improvement Meeting. Discussions were held to consider establishing a teacher evaluation mechanism and improving teacher performances in teaching, to improve the current rating system for school teachers and to enhance the professional performance of teachers. Consequently, critical conclusions were reached regarding the planning of a teacher evaluation system and improving the professional growth of teachers. In November 2001, the Ministry of Education invited representatives from the National Teachers' Association and National Education Reform Association to discuss preparations for a meeting regarding the reformation of the performance appraisal and rating assessment system of public senior high school teachers and lower grades.

In July 2002, the Ministry of Education negotiated with the National Teachers' Association regarding the guidelines for drawing up contracts with teachers. In addition, the Pilot Project of Teacher Evaluations for Public Senior High Schools and Lower Grades was discussed. In September, the Improvements of Teacher Ratings, Professional Evaluations, and the Performance Bonus System for Public Senior High Schools and Lower Grades taskforce convened to reach a consensus regarding whether professional evaluations would replace the current performance appraisal. Subsequently, these conclusions were again discussed in a national meeting of Education Bureau Directors. In the meeting, a preliminary consensus was reached regarding the planning of an appraisal and evaluation system for teachers. Subsequently, the Ministry of Education established a taskforce regarding the drafting of a system of professional evaluations for teachers of public schools to respond to social expectations of teacher evaluations. The taskforce was established in 2002, and incorporated scholars, experts, teacher groups, parent groups, education administrative staff, and school administrative staff. The taskforce began to discuss a system of professional and performance evaluations for teachers immediately. In November 2002, during the first meeting, the taskforce made the following resolution: "The planning shall combine summative assessments and formative assessments. Current formative appraisal standards in Taiwan as well as international data on teacher evaluations should be reviewed". In December 2002, during the taskforce's second meeting, the following resolution was passed: "Professional evaluations and performance appraisal of teachers are two concepts. Professional evaluations assist teachers with improving their instructional quality and thus should not be related to promotions or bonuses".

In February 2003, during its ninth meeting, the taskforce formed the following resolution: "Professional evaluations, primarily based on formative evaluations, assist teachers in improving their teaching quality. Evaluation procedures should involve using self-evaluations, peer evaluations, and the establishment of teaching work files. These procedures would enable teachers to understand which areas require improvement. Over time, the number of incompetent teachers can be reduced. However, this system "should not be related to the procedures for removing inadequate and incompetent teachers". During the taskforce's 15th meeting in April, the following resolution was passed: "The elimination of incompetent teachers should be separated from teacher professional evaluations". In subsequent resolutions, the taskforce consistently restated that teacher evaluation results would not be related to teacher classifications, performance accountability, or contract terminations. In 2010, Article 5 of the Implementation Directions again stated the following concern: "The evaluations in these directions are formative evaluations. These evaluations should not be used as references when assessing teacher performances, in procedures for managing incompetent teachers, and in the teacher advancement (classification) system".

On 5 August 2003, in the 22nd meeting, the taskforce invited the principal of Taipei American School to introduce how professional evaluations for teachers were implemented in that school. In addition, the taskforce determined that "The pilot project regarding professional evaluations for teachers will reference the methods of Taipei American School and the opinions of the school principal". On 29 August 2003, in the 25th meeting of the taskforce, the group decided that the temporary title of the draft would be as follows: *Directions for the Pilot Project Regarding Professional Evaluations of Teachers in Senior High Schools and Lower Grades*.

In September 2003, the National Educational Development Conference reached the following conclusion:

> Directions for the Pilot Implementation Project of the Professional Evaluation of Teachers, funded by the Ministry of Education, should be established to assist with the professional growth of teachers. The pilot project taskforce will collaborate for 1 year before a review and evaluation of the taskforce performance is conducted. The results will then serve as a reference in the complete implementation of professional evaluations for teachers in the future.

From February to June 2004, the Ministry of Education convened the *Directions for the Pilot Project of Professional Evaluations of Teachers in Senior High Schools and Lower Grades* conference on a monthly basis. Five conferences were held, and representatives from the National Teachers' Association and parent groups were invited to discuss and determine the type, content, standards, methods, procedures and other related affairs of the project.

In July 2004, as indicated by the Minister of Education, implementation of the pilot project regarding professional evaluations of teachers was deferred until the revised draft of the Teacher Act was passed. This was due to contradictory opinions regarding the professional evaluation of teachers among members of the National Teachers' Association and the National Alliance of Parents Organization. In 2005, the Regulations for Teacher Performance Appraisals in Public Senior High Schools and Lower Grades were announced; however, the evaluation items were vague and teachers were not required to undergo evaluations regularly. Consequently, the professional quality of teachers and the educational achievement of students did not improve effectively.

In September 2005, the newly appointed Minister of Education decided that teacher professional evaluations should be reconsidered. A sixth conference was convened, in which the following decisions were reached:

- The implementation should focus on teachers' professional growth. The evaluation standards should be general. In addition, data related to the evaluation standards should be collected to provide a reference for future pilots.
- The implementation of external evaluations was granted, which would consider volunteer teaching applicants only. The trial duration was extended from one year to 2–3 years.
- The project contents should reinforce a guidance and service system to effectively facilitate the teachers' professional growth.

On 4 October 2005, the Ministry of Education, in an internally coordinated meeting, reached the decision that the pilot project would be allowed to proceed for the 2006–7 school year. On 25 October 2005, the ninth conference of the Professional Evaluation for Teachers of Senior High Schools and Lower Grades taskforce reached the decision that the revision project would now be called the Pilot Implementation Project for Professional Development Evaluations of Teachers Funded by the Ministry of Education, in which professional evaluations of teachers would be termed "formative teacher evaluations". The focus of the project would be the professional development of teachers. Schools would be encouraged to apply as trial schools, and teachers were asked to volunteer in the project. This was the first time that an official document emphasized "professional development evaluations" and no longer termed the evaluations as "professional evaluations". The purpose of this change was to alter school teachers' stereotypes of evaluations. The essence and method of this project was based on those of other countries, particularly the United States. The evaluation now focused on "formative" and "developmental" evaluations, rather than "summative" evaluations, to persuade teachers to accept the implementation of this project. To understand the experiences of local teachers regarding professional evaluations, the Ministry of Education encouraged schools and teachers to volunteer to receive professional development evaluations. Teachers and schools were told that participating in the evaluation would increase the professional literacy and teaching quality of teachers and the learning achievements of students. Since the 2006–7 school year, the Ministry of Education has adopted an approach of offering encouragement and asking for volunteers in implementing this Ministry policy because this approach was determined to be both gradual and effective. The project was steadily promoted for a duration spanning 2–3 years.

The preparation period for teacher evaluation: 2006 to the present

Promotion of the Pilot Implementation Project for Professional Development Evaluations of Teachers Funded by the Ministry of Education coincided with a national political election. Therefore, to avoid teacher evaluations becoming a topic of political debate, the project was deferred until March 2006. In May 2006, volunteer schools were allowed to apply for the trial program (Ministry of Education, 2006) and professional development evaluations for school teachers began. The performance of the trial project was reviewed annually. Moreover, the purpose of this project was to gradually intensify local teacher experiences with the professional development evaluations to construct a feasible, effective, and professional evaluation system for teachers.

In February 2006, the Ministry of Education established a taskforce for the Promotion of Professional Development Evaluation of School Teachers (hereafter referred to as the promotion taskforce). The promotion taskforce consisted of five teams:

- policy planning team;
- pilot project promotion team;
- lecture and propaganda team;
- in-service training planning team; and
- evaluation and supervision team.

The taskforce was scheduled to operate until the system of professional evaluations for school teachers officially began. In the first meeting in March 2006, the taskforce formed the following resolutions:

- The proposed evaluations emphasized school teacher opinions. In addition, a mechanism should be established to facilitate teacher professional growth after receiving an evaluation.
- When the official documents regarding the pilot project were sent to city and county governments, the documents emphasized that this project was a formative evaluation that was unrelated to teacher performance appraisals, procedures for managing incompetent teachers, or the teacher advancement system.

The implementation of the pilot project of professional development evaluations for teachers was dependent on volunteers. Moreover, the aim of evaluation was to facilitate teachers' professional growth, improve teacher professional literacy, and enhance teaching quality. In January 2007, during the eighth meeting of the taskforce, "improving student learning achievements" was added as a fourth goal to the revised implementation project. The content of the teachers' professional development evaluations was now composed of four perspectives:

- curriculum design and teaching;
- classroom management and guidance;
- research development and in-service training;
- professionalism and professional attitude.

In addition, local educational authorities and schools were provisioned with the flexibility to modify the evaluation contents. The evaluating type contained a self-evaluation and intramural evaluation (external evaluation). Evaluations could be conducted using various approaches including observations of classroom teaching, review of the teacher work files, interviews with the teachers, and data collection from student or parental comments regarding the teacher's performance. Teachers who volunteered to receive the professional development evaluations would be asked to conduct the self-evaluation and receive an intramural evaluation once a year. Furthermore, related complementary measures would be established, such as creating reference criteria and reference books on the implementation of teacher evaluation, cultivating expertise in conducting teachers' professional development evaluation, establishing a mentor teacher system, and hosting workshops. In December 2007, the 15th meeting of the taskforce determined that the construction of a comprehensive system for evaluating teacher professional development required combining teaching mentoring with professional growth. In March 2007, during the 16th meeting, the following resolution was passed. The evaluation tool should emphasize its formative nature. Evaluation results should adopt words such as excellent, satisfactory, and improvement required. These words emphasize qualitative descriptions that could help teachers understand their strengths and weaknesses in teaching.

After three years of trial implementation, in October 2008, in its 18th meeting, the taskforce determined that the word "trial" would be removed beginning in the 2009–10 school year. The teacher evaluations of professional development officially began. In addition, the taskforce decided that the project title should be changed to the Implementation Project for Professional Development Evaluations of Teachers Funded by the Ministry of Education. In September 2009, the Ministry of Education announced that the Quality Enhancement for School Teachers Project would be in effect from 2009 to 2012. This project had five primary goals. The third goal specified that the purpose of the teacher evaluations was to improve teachers' professional development, enhance professional knowledge of teachers, reinforce excellent teaching quality, and increase overall teaching effects. The practical measures were as follows:

- To devise the evaluation criteria regarding professional development of school teachers.
- To enlarge the numbers of schools and teachers involved in evaluating the professional development of school teachers annually. (The number of primary schools and junior high schools increased from 320 to 810, and the number of teachers involved increased from 6,500 to 14,200.)
- To enhance the cultivation of professionals for executing teachers' professional development evaluations.

(Ministry of Education, 2009)

At the Eighth National Education Conference held in August 2010, the participants reached a high degree of consensus concerning promoting the evaluation of the professional development of school teachers. To actualize the decisions and to promote evaluating teacher professional development actively, the Ministry of Education commissioned the National Academy for Educational Research to propose an evaluation system for school teachers in September 2011 which involved evaluation methods, procedures, processing evaluation results, and standard operating procedures.

The 2010 version of the Guidelines for the Implementation of Professional Development Evaluations of Teachers Funded by the Ministry of Education (Ministry of Education, 2010) stipulates that all teachers who volunteer for the teachers' professional development evaluations must complete a self-evaluation and undergo an intramural evaluation in accordance with each school's promotional schedule (Guidelines for the Implementation, Article 5, para. 3). Before implementing the evaluations, schools must perform adequate propagation and training regarding the evaluation purposes, contents, criteria, and methods (Guidelines for the Implementation, Article 5, para. 6). After the evaluation, the evaluation team regarding teacher professional development in each school must submit the evaluation results to all evaluated teachers by mail. In addition, adequate assistance in intramural and off-campus in-service training must be provided for all teachers based on their professional growth needs (Guidelines for the Implementation, Article 5, para. 6). Furthermore, schools must assign mentor teachers to teachers who have less than two years of experience or who have difficulties in teaching. Teachers who do not meet the criteria established by the school promotion team must co-devise a professional growth plan involving adequate personnel who are designated by the evaluation promotion team within one month of the receipt of notification. An intramural evaluation (second evaluation) will be arranged after the professional growth project is completed (Guidelines for the Implementation, Article 5, para. 7).

On 11 October 2012, the Executive Yuan passed the revised draft of the Teacher Act that was proposed by the Ministry of Education. In addition to specifying the service intervals, the evaluation for professional development of teachers was the most crucial addition to the Act (Article 17-1). The Teacher Act provides a reference regarding the evaluation of school teachers, specifying that high school, vocational high school, junior high school, and primary school teachers are required to undergo evaluation. Regarding the evaluation items, contents, indicators, methods, procedures, and uses of evaluation results, the Ministry of Education would invite educational groups to discuss the implementation procedures after the Act was enacted.

Finally, the Ministry of Education published the White Paper of Teacher Education in ROC on 15 January 2013. Chapter 5 presents nine development strategies, restating the necessity to "stimulate professional teachers and promote a system of teacher evaluations". Moreover, the Paper indicates the following:

> The complete teacher evaluation system should be composed of primarily the formative teacher evaluation and secondarily the summative evaluation.

That is, the evaluation of teachers' professional development and performance appraisal will be complementary to each other in this system.

(Ministry of Education, 2013, p. 45)

According to the developmental strategies, the Paper proposed Scheme 17 – the Scheme of Planning and Promoting Teacher Evaluation System – which comprises three tasks.

- The Teacher Act will be passed as soon as possible. This act will serve as a legal reference for teacher evaluations and the construction of the entire system.
- Based on the standards established for the teaching profession, teacher evaluation criteria should be revised, evaluation tools should be drafted, and evaluation personnel cultivated.
- Teacher performance appraisal should be implemented.

To sum up, the rights and interests of teachers may be affected by the teacher evaluations, regardless of whether the evaluation was formative or summative. Regardless of the legislative procedures regarding teacher evaluations in the Legislative Yuan, in the future, evaluation for school teachers will be enforced. Regarding nations which devote increasing attention to educational quality in global competitions, the establishment and implementation of a teacher evaluation system is a key educational reform in the new century. Teachers must be mentally prepared for a new era of teacher evaluations.

Evaluation of the professional development of school teachers: the perspective from new professionalism

Wise and Leibbrand (2000) indicated in their article "Standards and teacher quality" that familiarity with academic knowledge does not guarantee effective instruction or a professional position by teachers. This article used the seven principles of new professionalism of teachers that were proposed by Hargreaves and Goodson (1996) to investigate the evolution of professional development evaluations for teachers in Taiwan since 1995.

Teachers have pursued professional recognition, increased autonomy and self-management, and improvements in work condition and salaries. According to Hargreaves and Goodson, professionalism "defines and articulates the quality and character of people's actions within that group" (1996, p. 4). They classify teachers' professionalism into "classical" professionalism, in contrast to the more flexible, practical, extended, or complex professionalism that occurs under the influence of postmodernism. Regarding teachers as professionals, these concepts of professionalism represent different ideas but frequently overlapping contents.

Classical professionalism is modeled after laws and medical science. This emphasizes the use of strategies and rhetoric to improve a profession's social status, salaries, and work conditions. Classical professionalism is characterized by "a specialized knowledge base or shared technical culture; a strong service ethic with a commitment to meeting clients' needs; and self-regulated, collegial control rather than external bureaucratic control over recruitment and training, codes of ethics and standards of practice" (Hargreaves and Goodson, 1996, p. 5). However, most scholars consider the work and social status of school teachers as lacking most of the traits emphasized in classical professionalism. Therefore, school teachers are regarded as partial professional, quasi-professional, or semi-professional.

Hargreaves and Goodson (1996, pp. 20–1) analyzed the discourse of flexible, extended, and complex professionalism, and proposed a discourse of postmodern new professionalism, which possesses the following seven traits conducive to treating teaching as a profession:

- increased opportunity and responsibility to exercise *discretionary judgement* over the issues of teaching, curriculum, and care that affect one's students;
- opportunities and expectations to engage with the *moral and social purposes* and value of what teachers teach, along with major curriculum and assessment matters in which these purposes are embedded;
- commitment to working with colleagues in a *collaborative culture* of help and support as a way of using shared expertise to solve the ongoing problems of professional practice, rather than engaging in joint work as a motivational device to implement the external mandates of others;
- occupational *heteronomy* rather than self-protective *autonomy*, whereby teachers work authoritatively, yet openly and collaboratively, with other partners in the wider community (especially parents and students themselves), who have a significant stake in students' learning;
- a commitment to active *care* and not just anodyne *service* for students – professionalism must in this sense acknowledge and embrace the emotional as well as the cognitive dimensions of teaching, and also recognize the skills and dispositions that are essential to committed and effective caring;
- a self-directed search and struggle for *continuous learning* related to one's own expertise and standards of practice, rather than compliance with the enervating obligations of *endless change* demanded by others (often under the guise of continuous learning or improvement);
- the creation and recognition of high *task complexity*, with levels of status and reward appropriate to such complexity.

Moreover, Goodson (2003) renamed new professionalism as "principled professionalism" because teaching is primarily a moral and ethical vocation, and new professionalism "will develop from clearly agreed moral and ethical principles" as the guiding principles (p. 132). The Dean of the Institute of Education, University of London, Professor Geoff Whitty (1992), specifically emphasized that teaching is a profession that requires professional literacy. In other words, in addition to effective teaching skills, teachers must be equipped with theoretical knowledge and understanding in the context of teaching to perform rapid and flexible reflections and make practical or complex decisions (Lee, 2005).

Teachers have increased opportunity and responsibility in making discretionary judgements

According to new professionalism, teacher evaluations for formative purposes increase the opportunities and responsibilities of teachers. This stimulates teachers into activities regarding teaching, the curriculum, and students' learning. The purpose of conducting evaluations is to consider teacher potentials and demands for professional growth, and to encourage teachers to establish a cooperative culture in which they and their colleagues collectively endeavor to employ professional knowledge to solve practical problems. Therefore, emphasizing formative purposes is beneficial for encouraging teachers to acquire increased professional knowledge and skills, and reinforces professional responsibilities. These benefits could involve using various knowledge and information effectively by integrating them with teaching. Thus, instructions can be more effective and the learning achievement of students improved.

In April 2003, the 15th meeting of the taskforce made the following resolution:

Evaluations must include the following purposes:

- encouraging the professional growth of teachers;
- implementing teachers' guidance of their students;
- assisting in solving teaching problems;
- improving teaching strategies and efficiency; and
- establishing cooperation and communication mechanisms for teaching groups.

These were all formative purposes. In the 2006 version of the pilot project, Article 2 explicitly specified three purposes for the evaluation of the professional development of teachers: "The purpose of evaluation is to facilitate teachers' professional growth, improve teachers' professional literacy, and enhance teaching quality". Based on the evaluation results, the Ministry of Education offered acknowledgement and feedback for teachers' teaching, and the growth demands of individual teachers were satisfied by providing adequate assistance. In addition, to satisfy the overall growth demands of teachers, in-service education was made available. In 2001, the nine-year Grade 1–9 Curriculum for primary schools and junior high schools substituted Curriculum Standards that had been adopted for more than 50 years with Curriculum Guidelines, thereby granting increased flexibility and responsibility for curriculum planning and teaching. The prospective direction of policy-making attempts was to encourage teachers to solidify their professional knowledge and skills and to enable teachers to possess the professional responsibility for forming discretionary judgements.

Teachers have opportunities and expectations to devote themselves to moral and social purposes

As stipulated by Article 5 in the 2006, 2007, and 2008 versions of the pilot project proposed by the Ministry of Education, professional development evaluations for teachers must involve four aspects:

- curriculum design and teaching;
- class management and guidance;
- research development and in-service education; and
- professionalism and professional attitudes.

The Ministry of Education emphasized that these stipulations were flexible. By allowing local educational authorities and schools to establish adapted evaluation criteria, schools were not required to evaluate each domain each year when implementing the evaluations of teacher's professional development. Alternatively, flexible measures that suited each school's focus on developmental work could be adopted, and teacher evaluations could be performed regarding one or more key aspects. As stipulated by Article 5 of the 2006 version of the pilot project, evaluation criteria could be customized by the pilot schools based on referenced evaluation criteria regarding evaluating the professional development of teachers that were provided by educational and administrative competent authorities. The revised texts of the 2007 and 2008 versions of the pilot project are as follows: "The criteria can be customized by schools by referencing the reference evaluation criteria for the professional development of teachers as stipulated by the Ministry of Education or the governments of special municipalities, counties, or cities" (Ministry of Education, 2007).

This second principle is similar to the fourth evaluation aspect, professionalism and professional attitudes, previously described. However, teachers were inclined to focus on two behavioral aspects, curriculum design and teaching and class management and guidance, when schools were not required to evaluate each aspect each year; consequently, the indicator regarding professionalism and professional attitudes was not sufficiently explicit. Purple and Shapiro (1995, p. 81) once stated that educational professionals focus specifically on the technical aspects of teaching but do not question the fundamental cultural and social structures. In addition, educational professionals do not challenge the social, cultural, moral, and economic aspects of education policy reports. Professional teachers are unable to suggest "admirable visions" in education; instead, teachers propose revising teaching techniques. Teachers use language that is not transformative, but only adaptive. This critique is a reminder that the professional development evaluations for teachers that were influenced by new professionalism must not focus specifically on an excellent curriculum design and teaching or effective class management and guidance.

Furthermore, the concept of credentialism and an exam-centered teaching framework have been rooted in Taiwan for a long period. Consequently, parents and students devote themselves to preparing for entrance examinations. Therefore, the Grade 1–9 Curriculum for primary schools and junior high schools that was announced in 2001 removed the requirement of courses related to morality, and civic, moral, and ethical courses were eliminated from the curricula of primary schools and junior high schools. Various factors might have limited teachers' expectations regarding being involved in the purposes and values of society and morality.

Teachers and their colleagues collectively endeavor to apply professional knowledge to practical teaching in a collaborative culture

New professionalism directs teachers from traditional authority and autonomy. A novel form, a more intimate and cooperative relationship, has been developed out of the relationships among colleagues, students, and parents. Roles and responsibilities are negotiated explicitly, and models and practical affairs of increasing complexity regarding professional development are created (Hargreaves, 1994). This kind of new professionalism is gradually formed out of the disorder of educational reform and international competition. Teachers feel the anxiety caused by various reforms. However, apart from that, teachers experience liberation and empowerment, which grants them increased professional esteem and confidence. Teachers are willing to share their ideals, seek assistance, and engage in joint curriculum planning (Lee, 2008).

The British Teacher Training Agency asks that teachers be observed and evaluated. In addition, a professional conversation is required between the observer and teacher. The process of this conversation must be honest and constructive, based on definite evidence, and designed by supportive and open professional exploration with the aim of reducing fear in the teachers. The observer should provide positive suggestions and display the advantages and achievements of the teacher. Moreover, the scope in which improvement and development are necessary and the corresponding actions that must be performed should be explicitly stated (TTA, 2002, pp. 13–15). A similar model of professional conversation should be adopted in the implementation process of professional development evaluations for teachers in Taiwan. This model is beneficial to the establishment and development of the professional cooperative communities composed of teachers.

Teachers must publicly cooperate with parents and the wider communities due to occupational heteronomy rather than self-protective autonomy

The stress of teaching and administrative affairs isolates teachers in their classrooms, thereby limiting their professional interactions with colleagues. Consequently, teachers are alienated from parents and communities. Since the Education Reformation Alliance protests in 1994 for the promotion of educational reformation, schools and teachers in Taiwan have begun to interact with the public outside classrooms. In addition, teachers now allow parents who care about their children's learning processes to enter campuses and classrooms. However, the four aspects regarding the evaluation of professional development of teachers did not considered the necessity of teachers publicly cooperating with parents and communities. The evaluation aspect of cooperation among teachers, parents, and the wider society must be incorporated into future policies to systematically, effectively, and structurally encourage teachers to open the doors of classrooms. Once parental and community resources are introduced and used, and when student learning obstacles are removed by cooperation, only then can learning efficiency finally be enhanced.

Teachers are responsible for caring for their students actively and enthusiastically rather than providing only services that relieve their pain

Traditionally, schools stress the instruction of knowledge, but neglect the affective development of students. One of the evaluation criteria of teacher professional development is classroom management and guidance. However, schools may provide "services that relieve students' pain" for only a minority of students and do not actively and enthusiastically care for all students. In the future, teachers have to consider both the cognitive and affective development of students so that schools can become a learning community full of respect and care.

Teachers should perform a self-directed search for unceasing learning to develop their own professional knowledge and practical capabilities

One of the four aspects of the evaluation of professional development for teachers is research development and in-service education, which is similar to this principle of new professionalism. Teachers have to self-identify their need for research development and in-service training. Studying for a higher degree must not be driven by policies or to obtain promotions and raises. The content of research development and in-service education is beneficial for increasing academic knowledge and the curriculum planning abilities of teachers. Teachers must thoroughly understand the relationship between teaching materials to comprehensively design the goals and schedules of the curriculum. The application of this knowledge in teaching provides the basis that enables all students to become successful in learning. On the other hand, student learning results and improvements need to be strictly regulated because teachers are responsible for facilitating improvements in students. One of the goals and commitments of professional development in teachers is to enable teachers to assist every student in achieving success. In addition, teachers should exert every effort to develop their professional abilities. Goals must be established so that teachers will strive to develop. Moreover, it is necessary for teachers to update their pedagogical knowledge regarding the subjects they teach.

A comprehensive and unanimous framework does not exist in the current professional development structure that was established for teachers in Taiwan. Currently, Taiwanese teachers are only required to complete an 18-hour in-service education program. Furthermore, the system of certifying and classifying teachers has been discussed extensively without gaining consensus from scholars in educational, academic, and practical fields. Educational decision-makers should consider developing a professional development learning framework for teachers to encourage them to receive structural in-service education and achieve professional development. Diverse opportunities and practical schemes for in-service education that fulfill the overall demands of schools and the individual demands of teachers must be devised. By using skills obtained through training, teachers can arrange and conduct self-directed inquiries and learning that benefit teachers in recognizing the learning and development demands of their students. Moreover, skills regarding conducting self-evaluations, observations, peer-review, and mentoring should be developed and improved. In brief, a systematic approach and objective framework should be established regarding the in-service education and professional growth of teachers. These approaches and frameworks can prepare teachers for managing the various impacts that result from a rapidly changing political, economic, social, and cultural environment.

The high task complexity of teaching should be recognized, and social status and reward corresponding to the complexity should be provided

To confirm the high task complexity involved in teaching and to provide appropriate social status and salaries, the results of the evaluation of the professional development of teachers may become integrated with their opportunities for promotion. From 2006 up to the present, the results of teacher evaluations have not been adequately utilized. An active reward (e.g. promotion) system has not been established for teachers who achieve excellent teaching performance. However, a superior salary and enhanced work conditions may be the drive and incentives that improve teaching quality. The White Paper of Teacher Education in ROC states that "the construction of a reward system is crucial regarding teacher professional development". Therefore, the Ministry of Education provides additional rewards to teachers who volunteer to apply for advanced certificates and professional services. The Ministry is attempting to steadily and cautiously support career promotion for teachers, thereby providing corresponding rewards for teachers who possess excellent teaching qualities (Ministry of Education, 2013, p. 45). Feng-Jihu Lee suggested the following:

> The prospective teacher evaluation mechanism in Taiwan could be combined with career development (e.g. promotions to group leader, directors, or principals) for teachers. In addition, whether the certificate and classification system for teachers should be implemented to stimulate their professional growth, thereby increasing their quality and status should be considered.
>
> (2006, p. 212)

Action Plan 16 in the White Paper of Teacher Education aims to plan and promote a reward scheme regarding teacher professional development. This plan provides teachers with two approaches for professional development: administrative and teaching. Teachers who have no intention of becoming administrators can be divided into four types, which are tentatively titled as "beginning teacher", "experienced teacher", "mentor teacher", and "research teacher" (Ministry of Education, 2013, p. 92). This proposed division complies with the seventh principle of new professionalism.

Conclusion

Countries worldwide have regarded the evaluation of teachers as a crucial education policy. The purpose of teacher evaluation is to ensure the quality of the teaching profession, to maintain the optimal quality of professional service, and to recognize teachers' achievement. Moreover, students will be effectively educated because of their teachers' permanent improvement and the nation's overall competitiveness will always increase because of the perpetual supply of outstanding highly talented people. Therefore, evaluating the professional development of teachers is an inevitable global trend. Teachers have to prepare for the coming of an era of teacher evaluation.

The revision of the Teacher Act was passed by the Executive Yuan in December 2012. However, teacher evaluations have not been passed by the Legislative Yuan. Therefore, the government cannot force all schools and their teachers to participate in these evaluations. The policy continues to rely on volunteers. Consequently, the teachers' professional development evaluations are currently available to volunteer schools and teachers. Subsidies are being provided to encourage county and city governments and primary schools and high schools who wish to incorporate this professional development evaluation of teachers. Thus, when relevant laws have not yet been enacted, educational and academic researchers have a responsibility to improve practical educational affairs based on established education research results. These results serve as the infrastructure for the comprehensive implementation of professional development evaluations for school teachers in Taiwan.

From the perspective of new professionalism, it is necessary to implement the professional development evaluation for teachers appropriately, because this system will benefit teachers in improving their professional growth and professionalism. In addition, teachers have to assume responsibility for lifelong learning, which should be integrated with the teaching process to produce effective and high-quality teaching that incorporates all types of knowledge and information. These teacher evaluations, which are driven by the new professionalism perspective, demonstrate a transformation of the ideals, cultures, values, and practical affairs of teachers. Teachers embrace reform and promote innovation not only because they wish to work cooperatively and increase their obligations and responsibilities to their colleagues, but also because they wish to actively care for and be enthusiastically engaged in the student learning process. The trend of new professionalism is worthy of in-depth investigation conducted by Taiwanese in educational academic fields. Subsequently, adaptive measures can be developed in the professional development evaluations for teachers that address the various challenges of the postmodern world. This thesis adopted the seven principles of new professionalism to examine the current measures regarding the professional development evaluations constructed for teachers in Taiwan. The benefits and deficiencies that require improvement were investigated to construct a reference framework for policy-making and execution.

The ideal new professionalism teacher is a lifelong learner who is committed to the professional responsibility of continuous learning, engages in self-oriented research, and wishes to learn unceasingly to develop professional knowledge and practical abilities. These teachers must respond to and integrate all types of knowledge and information into the process of teaching, thereby satisfying the demands of knowledge consumers in information networks. Moreover, teachers should cooperate and develop with other teachers or learn relevant knowledge by using information networks to achieve professional development and improve professional literacy. Teachers could become qualified to form explicit judgements on the subjects of teaching, curriculum, and student care if they engage in in-service education and professional development and encourage their colleagues to cooperate in work. Teachers should be devoted to teaching as well as to the purposes and values of society and morality. In addition, they should publicly and cooperatively work with parents and communities, which have an in-depth and long-term influence on students. To respond to the various challenges resulting from postmodern cognition, teachers must absorb educational knowledge continuously and update their teaching skills. In conclusion, teachers are instructors as well as learners. They are the transmitters and producers of knowledge. Therefore, professional growth is their right and obligation.

References

Committee on Education Reform, Executive Yuan (1995) *The First Period Consultation Report*. Taipei: CER (in Chinese).
Furlong, J. (2001) "Re-forming teacher education, re-forming teachers: accountability, professionalism and competence," in R. Phillips and J. Furlong (eds), *Education, Reform and the State: Twenty-five Years of Politics, Policy, and Practice*. London: Routledge Falmer, pp. 118–35.
Furlong, J., Barton, L., Miles, S., Whiting, C., and Whitty, G. (2000) *Teacher Education in Transition. Re-forming Professionalism?* Buckingham: Open University Press.
Goodson, I. F. (2003) *Professional Knowledge, Professional Lives: Studies in Education and Change*. Maidenhead: Open University Press.
Hargreaves, A. (1994) *Changing Teachers, Changing Times: Teachers' Work and Culture in the Postmodern Age*. London: Cassell.
Hargreaves, A. and Goodson, I. (1996) 'Teachers' professional lives: aspirations and actualities," in I. F. Goodson and A. Hargreaves (eds), *Teachers' Professional Lives*. London: Falmer, pp. 1–27.

Lee, F.-J. (2005) "A study of quality management schemes for school teachers in the United Kingdom," *Comparative Education*, 58: 135–71 (in Chinese).

Lee, F.-J. (2006) "Preliminary planning of a teacher evaluation system for school teachers in Taiwan: some implications from England and Wales," *Journal of Educational Research and Development*, 2(3): 193–216 (in Chinese).

Lee, F.-J. (2008) "A study of the quality management system for school teachers in England and Wales," in S.-K. Yang, C.-R. Wang, and F.-J. Lee (eds), *Comparison of Systems of Teacher Quality Management*. Taipei: Higher Education Publisher, pp. 17–49 (in Chinese).

Ministry of Education (2006) *The Pilot Project for Professional Development Evaluations of Teachers Funded by the Ministry of Education*. Taipei: MOE (in Chinese).

Ministry of Education (2007) *The Pilot Project for Professional Development Evaluations of Teachers Funded by the Ministry of Education*. Taipei: MOE (in Chinese).

Ministry of Education (2009) *Enhancement Program for Elementary and Secondary School Teachers' Quality*. Taipei: MOE (in Chinese).

Ministry of Education (2010) *The Guidelines for the Implementation of Professional Development Evaluations of Teachers Funded by the Ministry of Education*. Taipei: MOE (in Chinese).

Ministry of Education (2013) *White Paper of Teacher Education in ROC*. Taipei: MOE (in Chinese).

Purple, D. E. and Shapiro, S. (1995) *Liberation and Excellence: Reconstructing the Public Discourse on Education*. London: Bergin & Garvey.

Teacher Training Agency (2002) *Supporting Induction: Part 2 Support and Mentoring of the Newly Qualified Teacher*. London: TTA.

Whitty, G. (1992) "Quality control in teacher education," *British Journal of Educational Studies*, 40 (1): 38–49.

Wise, A. E. and Leibbrand, J. A. (2000) "Standards and teacher quality," *Phi Delta Kappan*, 81 (8): 612–17.

Yang, S. K. (2000) "Prospects of teacher education for the new century," in College of Education, National Chung Cheng University (ed.), *Visions of Education for the New Century*. Kaoshung: Fuwen, pp. 483–506 (in Chinese).

10 Teacher education strategic alliances in Taiwan

Sheng-Yao Cheng

Introduction

Under the huge impacts of low birth rate and heterogeneous student enrollments, teacher education in Taiwan is facing a series of struggles it has never encountered before. First of all, the most arduous conundrum is the imbalance between the demand and supply of teacher education. Along with the establishment of teacher education centers in the non-traditional teachers colleges since the late 1990s, the Taiwanese government hopes to upgrade the quality of teacher education via market forces. However, the result is totally the opposite. The dual effects of numerous roving teachers on the waiting list and fewer young children caused a lack of demand and an oversupply of teachers-to-be. Therefore the teacher education institutions began to pay more attention to both the school sites and the quality of teacher education.

Secondly, the Ministry of Education (2005) pointed out that enrollment of teacher education would decline by 50 per cent due to the low birth rate. Furthermore, the teachers' colleges need to merge with other comprehensive universities and cooperate with school teachers and administrators in order to deal with the practical issues in the age of low student enrollment and heterogeneous student background. Thirdly, under the development of localization and globalization, the curriculum and instruction of teacher education are also forced to adjust according to economic, social, and educational phenomena. That is why the input of teacher education should change to improve the quality of student teachers and to cooperate with school teachers and administrators on the issue of classroom management, curriculum design, and instruction.

In this chapter, the importance of teacher education strategic alliances between government, teacher education institutions, and school sites is highlighted to seize the real practical problems that teacher education institutions and school sites face every day, and reformulate the curriculum and instruction that teacher education programs provided to fit the real needs of schooling. To answer the questions above, the author collected and reviewed the existing literature related to teacher education strategic alliances, and juxtaposed the research methods of documentary analysis and focus group discussion to provide some suggestion on teacher education and teacher education strategic alliances.

Teacher education strategic alliance

Definition of a teacher education strategic alliance

Since the 1970s, the concept of the strategic alliance was used to emphasize a short- or long-term partnership to overcome some upcoming struggles or maintain the status quo (Black, 2001). Porter and Fuller (1986) stressed that strategic alliances amount to the long-term sharing of resources and complementary and promising relationships to achieve a win-win situation among businesses, companies, and organizations. Burton (2004) went on to state that strategic alliances are crucial management approaches to maintain the development of an organization, improve the multiple accesses to the organization, upgrade the mutual competition between organizations, and break through the difficulties.

To apply the approach of strategic alliances in the field of teacher education, Carroll (2006) pointed out the idea of joint accountability to rethink the possibilities of providing more on-site learning opportunities for student teachers. However, university faculty members were not able to spend more time teaching their students how to cooperate and become highly qualified teachers like their on-site mentors (National Commission on Teaching and America's Future, 1996).

Feiman-Nemser (1998) suggested the key concept of educative mentoring to outline the multiple roles of on-site mentors including teacher educator, reflection inspirer, teaching inspirer, and curriculum inspirer. Carroll (2006) went on to point out that joint accountability between teacher education institutions and on-site schools should take on the responsibility for helping student teachers to construct the school-based teacher education programs. He suggested that mentors need to provide more cooperative discussion and conversation on tutoring and develop skills on mentoring and tutoring.

With limited educational resources, it would be better to work together with educational institutions and other organizations in order to improve educational quality and strengthen organizational learning. According to Carroll's findings (2006) there are three types of educational strategic alliance. The first is the horizontal strategic alliance in which similar educational organizations put in similar resources, for instance, a university and library strategic alliance. The second is the vertical strategic alliance in which different background educational organizations put different resources to achieve the final goal, such as an alliance between universities and commercial companies. The third type is the quasi-vertical strategic alliance in which the relationships among different educational organizations are between the horizontal and vertical strategic alliances.

The politics of teacher education strategic alliances

Whitty (1989) used the example of the Education Reform Act in the United Kingdom to point out that so called "national" educational reforms are always influenced by the parental choice and market forces determining the shape of the school system. He continued that the marketization trends over the issue of school reform reminded us to avoid the shortage of new right forces like school choices and global academic competition. Following these threads, when we discuss the national policy regarding teacher education, will the neo-liberal and neo-conservative positions encourage the teacher education strategic alliances to transfer to market autonomy instead of government control?

Similarly, Sachs (2010) focused on the issues of professional identity of teachers in Australia, and mentioned that democratic and managerial professionalism identified and shaped the professional identity of teachers. The forces and politics among teacher education strategic alliances could also be interrelated with government control and market forces which could format the democratic managerial teacher education strategic alliance as well.

Cheng and Jacob (2005) analyzed current educational policies all over the world into four dimensions including equity, excellence, efficiency, and choice. Furthermore, in 2007, Cheng and Jacob expanded their theories into eight forces by adding neo-right, neo-left, globalization, and localization. In their articles, the researchers analyzed the politics of educational policies through the debates between equity and excellence, choice and efficiency, neo-right and neo-left, and globalization and localization (see Figure 10.1).

The Teacher Educational Strategic Alliance could be considered one of the emerging educational policies, and the politics of the alliance should be analyzed by means of the eight forces as well. Therefore, the researcher developed a questionnaire to

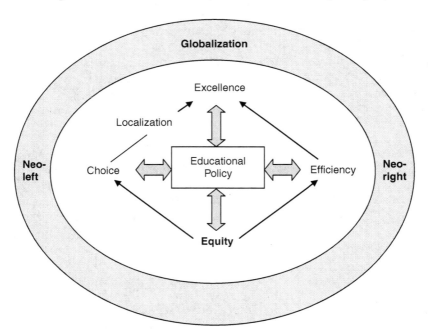

Figure 10.1 Educational policy analysis model
Source: Cheng and Jacob (2007, p. 54).

consider the equity of educational opportunity, the pursuit of educational excellence, the maintainability of efficiency, the focus of choice, the dialogue between neo-right and neo-left, and the dialectics between globalization and localization.

Global trends in teacher education strategic alliances

Since 1990, American educator John Goodlad has reminded us that universities in the United States should cooperate with elementary and high schools to create "centers of pedagogy", combining teacher education, educational research, and school reforms. Goodlad (1990) encouraged the construction of a "symbiotic partnership" to aim for "co-reform". Furthermore, Goodlad (1990) stressed that the goal of universities and elementary/high schools should be a focus on how to develop the teaching profession to rise to the demand for "good teachers". Similarly, the Holmes Group (1986) provided five major suggestions about the teaching profession including using partnerships to develop a strong intellectual base, improving the hierarchy in the teaching profession, setting up higher standards across the teaching profession, establishing the connection between teacher education institutions and K-12 schools, and encouraging schools to become the best in the field of teacher teaching and students learning.

In the Netherlands, due to the lack of school teachers, the government needed to recruit college graduates and part-time teachers to provide external teacher education to become the teacher-to-be. However, teacher education in the Netherlands needed to overcome at least three challenges (Lunenberg et al., 2000). The first was to provide a flexible curriculum for student teachers from multiple backgrounds. The second was to offer schools a learner friendly environment. Furthermore, could the faculty members and school mentors play the role of tutor to student teachers?

In order to solve these problems, the Netherlands government promoted three major teacher education strategic alliances (Lunenberg et al., 2000, pp. 255–7): competence-based curricula and assessment, teacher improvement plans, and professional standards for teacher educators. With regard to competence-based curricula and assessment, every new student teacher is provided with a portfolio of starting competencies which form the baseline of the teaching profession. Then, the teacher improvement plans referred to the responsibilities of human resources and development that teacher education should take in the Netherlands. On one hand, the mentor at the school site should provide the curricula, instruction, pedagogy, and teaching strategies while, on the other hand, faculty members in the teacher education institutions should play roles reflecting educational issues and the ability for professional development. As for the professional standards for teacher educators, the Netherlands is the first nation in Europe to set up a professional standard for teacher educators including the five abilities: agent ability, agent educational ability, organizational ability, and learning and growth abilities.

Another good example is Hong Kong. In 1998, the Hong Kong government adopted the Accelerated Schools Project set up by Professor Henry Levin of

Stanford University to establish a quality education fund to promote a three-year Quality School Project (Lee *et al.*, 2005; Levin, 2001). During these projects, universities in Hong Kong and forty K-12 schools became partners to run the systematic reforms and the holistic support of the projects to facilitate improvement efforts in both macro and micro approaches, to address the complexity of school improvement and teaching and learning. On the macro dimension (**"Big Wheel Programs"**), the team helps schools develop a self-improving process and deep-inquiry mechanism, which builds a favorable environment for school improvement. On the micro dimension (**"Small Wheel Programs"**), supports include actions and experiments to enhance the effectiveness of teaching and learning, building up teachers' professional capacity, and promoting students' growth.

To sum up the trends from the United States, the Netherlands, and Hong Kong, the teacher education strategic alliance tends to tighten the relationship between teacher education institutions and K-12 schools and improve the quality of teacher education and school reforms.

Research designs

Research methods

In this chapter, the principal investigator gathers the data via documentary analysis, focus group discussions, and questionnaire surveys (see Figure 10.2). With regard to documentary analysis, the researcher collected the research report, white book, and government documents. Furthermore, the author convened four focus group discussions in 2006 and invited educational administrators, educational researchers, and schoolteachers to think about strategies to help teacher education in Taiwan to face the low birth rate and heterogeneous students' background via a teacher education alliance. After the focus group discussions, the researcher compiled a questionnaire and conducted a survey on the issue of teacher education strategic alliances in Taiwan. The principal investigator chose three kinds of research subject, including faculty members in the teacher education institutions, educational administrators in bureaus of education, and K-12 school teachers and administrators.

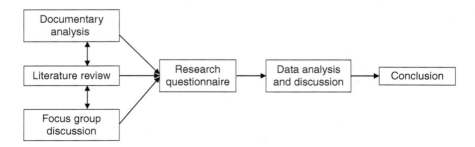

Figure 10.2 Research procedure

Table 10.1 Research subjects

Organizations	Research subject selection	Total
Teacher education institutions	One director, one faculty member and one pre-service student were selected from each institution	225
Bureaus of education	One superintendent, one director and one staff member were selected from each bureau of education	75
K-12 schools	One principal or vice principal, one teacher, one PTA member, one mentor and one student teacher from each school	1,250

Research subjects

During the questionnaire survey, the researcher gathered the research subjects into three major domains. The first comprised 75 teacher education institutions, with the director, one faculty member, and at least one pre-service teacher, making 225 subjects. The second domain involved 25 bureaus of education, each including one superintendent, one director, and one member of staff, making 75 subjects. The last domain was the K-12 schools. Each city was asked to provide one public high school, one private high school, one public vocational school, one private vocational school, one public junior high school, one private junior high school, one public elementary school, one private elementary school, one public kindergarten, and one private kindergarten. Each school needed to respond with one principal or vice principal, one teacher, one PTA member, one mentor, and one student teacher, the total being 1,250 subjects (see Table 10.1).

Questionnaire design and response

To interpret the interaction among the Teacher Education Strategic Alliance, the principal investigator highlighted that teacher education should be co-produced with the cooperation of the teacher education institutions, the bureau of education, and K-12 schools. The researcher divided teacher education into four sections, namely pre-service teacher education, student teaching, teacher certificate exam, and teacher professional development. In order to increase the validity, the researcher invited faculty members in the teacher education institutions, administrators in the bureaus of education, and K-12 school principals and teachers to form the questionnaire (see Figure 10.3). The sample size of 1,550 produced a total valid response of 966, yielding a return rate of 62.3 per cent (see Table 10.2).

Analysis and discussion

Strategies of teacher education strategic alliance in Taiwan

After the documentary analysis and focus group discussions, the principal investigator provided four dimensions of strategies for teacher education strategic

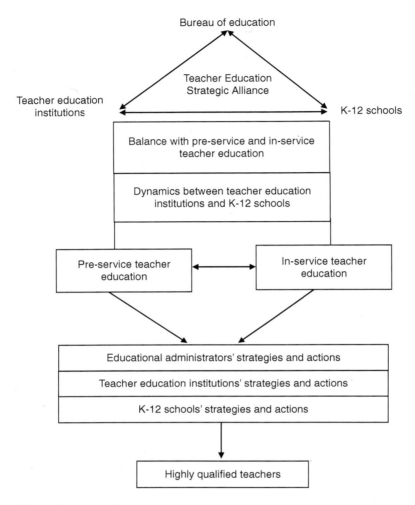

Figure 10.3 Research framework

Table 10.2 The response and return rate of the survey

Item	Bureaus of education	Teacher education institutions	K-12 school	Total
Sample size	75	225	1,250	1,550
Response	44	187	735	966
Return rate	58.7%	83.1%	58.8%	62.3%

alliance in Taiwan including pre-service teacher education, student teaching, teacher certificate exam, and in-service teacher education.

In the first domain, pre-service teacher education, the strategies covered nine approaches:

1. The bureaus of education respond to the change in population and student enrollment simultaneously and develop multiple teacher education policies.
2. Teacher education institutions respond to the change in population and student enrollment, and develop multiple curricula, instructions, and assessments.
3. Teacher education institutions cooperate with K-12 schools in order to enrich the curriculum, classroom management, and professional development of student teachers.
4. Teacher education institutions should help their faculty members to know more about the change of student enrollment and help to mentor their student teachers on the teaching profession.
5. Teacher education institutions should team-teach with K-12 teachers and administrators especially in the coursework, including curriculum and instruction, teach interns, classroom management, and counseling.
6. Teacher education institutions should provide their own school-based curriculum, like multicultural education and remedial teaching, to deal with the brand new encounter with low birth rate and heterogeneous students.
7. Teacher education institutions cooperate with K-12 schools to create best-practice teaching via the exchange of educational theories and pedagogical praxis.
8. Each teacher education institution should set up horizontal connections to encourage their students to take different programs' courses and exchange the knowledge and practical wisdom on the issues of teaching and learning.
9. Student teachers should be encouraged to establish research groups to discover the authentic problems in daily school life.

In the second domain, student teaching, there were five strategies for the teacher education strategic alliance in Taiwan:

1. Bureaus of education, teacher education institutions, and K-12 schools should set up professional development schools (PDSs) together to ensure the quality of student teaching.
2. Bureaus of education, teacher education institutions, and K-12 schools should encourage experienced school teachers to become mentors during the student teaching process.
3. Student teachers should be encouraged to serve in remote and disadvantaged schools in order to enrich the teaching profession.

4. Teacher education institutions should keep an eye on changes in student enrollment and create information centers to provide information and dialogue for faculty members, mentors, and student teachers.
5. Bureaus of education, teacher education institutions, and K-12 schools should cooperate to conduct a series of research on student teaching to strengthen the relationship among the teacher education strategic alliance.

In the third domain of the teacher education, strategic alliances, four strategies are covered:

1. Bureaus of education, teacher education institutions, and K-12 schools should help to reframe the qualified teacher exam including the teaching profession, curriculum development and instruction, classroom management, and research, along with the current social changes.
2. Bureaus of education should correspond with the student enrollment in order to increase the teacher-to-student ratio and reduce class size.
3. Bureaus of education, teacher education institutions, and K-12 schools should encourage student teachers to participate in after school teaching.
4. Bureaus of education, teacher education institutions, and K-12 schools should consider teacher recruitment and demand–supply of teacher education.

In the last domain, teacher professional development, the principal investigator included ten strategies, namely:

1. K-12 schools should encourage their teachers to expand their teaching fields and bureaus of education and teacher education institutions should create multiple teaching licenses and degree programs.
2. Teacher education institutions should provide programs related to teaching and guiding abilities in the field of low birth rate and heterogeneous student enrollment in order to renew the teachers' teaching certificates.
3. Teacher education institutions and K-12 schools should work together to discover the issues related to student learning and teacher teaching in order to upgrade teachers' ability on classroom management.
4. Teacher education and K-12 schools should cooperate to develop creative and multiple teaching methods to improve curriculum development and teaching abilities.
5. The role of teacher education institutions should transfer from pre-service teacher education only to include in-service and life-long teacher learning as well as providing Master's degree programs for the teaching and administration profession.
6. Teacher education institutions should establish multicultural consulting centers to provide teachers-to-be with advice for the upcoming teaching environment.
7. The bureaus of education, teacher education institutions, and K-12 schools should support the teacher professional evaluation system in order to praise high-quality teachers and eliminate unqualified teachers.

8. The bureaus of education, teacher education institutions, and K-12 schools should co-develop in-service teacher training programs including the teaching profession, curriculum development and instruction, and classroom management.
9. The bureaus of education, teacher education institutions, and K-12 schools should co-host educational conferences to set up on-site exchange systems and provide opportunities for teacher professional dialogue and feedback.
10. Teacher education institutions should highlight their role in helping K-12 schools to improve teachers' abilities on the teaching profession and understanding the changes of the future.

Analyses of the important indicators

Pre-service teacher education

With regard to the feedback from the bureaus of education, four important indicators for a teacher education strategic alliance are considered, namely:

1. The bureaus of education respond to the changes in population and student enrollment simultaneously and develop multiple teacher education policies.
2. Teacher education institutions respond to the changes in population and student enrollment, and develop multiple curricula, instructions, and assessments.
3. Teacher education institutions cooperate with K-12 schools in order to enrich the curriculum, classroom management, and professional development of student teachers.
4. Teacher education institutions should team-teach with K-12 teachers and administrators especially in the coursework, including curriculum and instruction, teaching interns, classroom management, and guidance.

According to the feedback from teacher education institutions, there are two important indicators for teacher education strategic alliance, namely:

1. The bureaus of education respond to the changes in population and student enrollment simultaneously and develop multiple teacher education policies.
2. Teacher education institutions should team-teach with K-12 teachers and administrators especially in coursework, including curriculum and instruction, teaching interns, classroom management, and guidance.

From the perspective of K-12 schools, there are only two important indicators, namely:

1. The bureaus of education respond to the changes in population and student enrollment simultaneously and develop multiple teacher education policies.
2. Teacher education institutions should team-teach with K-12 teachers and administrators especially in coursework, including curriculum and instruction, teaching interns, classroom management, and guidance.

Teaching interns

With regarding to the feedback from the bureaus of education, they considered two important indicators for teacher education strategic alliance during the period of teaching interns including:

1. Bureaus of education, teacher education institutions, and K-12 schools should set up professional development schools (PDSs) together to ensure the quality of student teaching.
2. Bureaus of education, teacher education institutions, and K-12 schools should encourage experienced school teachers to become mentors during the student teaching process.

According to the feedback from teacher education institutions, there are two important indicators for a teacher education strategic alliance in the period of teaching interns, namely:

1. Bureaus of education, teacher education institutions, and K-12 schools should set up professional development schools (PDSs) together to ensure the quality of student teaching.
2. Bureaus of education, teacher education institutions, and K-12 schools should encourage experienced school teachers to become mentors during the student teaching process.

From the perspective of K-12 schools, there are three important indicators, namely:

1. Bureaus of education, teacher education institutions, and K-12 schools should set up professional development schools (PDS) together to ensure the quality of student teaching.
2. Bureaus of education, teacher education institutions, and K-12 schools should encourage experienced school teachers to become mentors during the student teaching process.
3. Teacher education institutions should keep an eye on changes in student enrollment and create information centers to provide information and dialogue for faculty members, mentors, and student teachers.

Teacher certificate and recruitment

With regard to the feedback from the bureaus of education, two important indicators for a teacher education strategic alliance during the period of teacher certificate and recruitment were considered, namely:

1. Bureaus of education, teacher education institutions, and K-12 schools should help to reframe the qualified teacher exam including the teaching

profession, curriculum development and instruction, classroom management, and research along, with current social changes.
2. Bureaus of education should correspond with the student enrollment in order to increase the teacher-to-student ratio and reduce class size.

According to the feedback from teacher education institutions, there is only one important indicator for a teacher education strategic alliance in the period of teaching interns which is that bureaus of education should correspond with the student enrollment in order to increase the teacher-to-student ratio and reduce class size.

Similarly, from the perspective of K-12 schools, there is only one important indicator for teacher education strategic alliance in the period of teaching interns which is that bureaus of education should correspond with the student enrollment in order to increase the teacher-to-student ratio and reduce the class size.

In-service teacher training and teacher professional development

Regarding the feedback from the bureaus of education, two important indicators for a teacher education strategic alliance during the period of in-service teacher training and teacher professional development were considered, namely:

1. K-12 schools should encourage their teachers to expand their teaching fields and bureaus of education and teacher education institutions should create multiple teaching licenses and degree programs.
2. The bureaus of education, teacher education institutions, and K-12 schools should support the Teacher Professional Evaluation system in order to praise high-quality teachers and eliminate unqualified teachers.

According to the feedback from teacher education institutions, there are three important indicators for a teacher education strategic alliance in the period of in-service teacher training and teacher professional development, namely:

1. K-12 schools should encourage their teachers to expand their teaching fields, and bureaus of education and teacher education institutions should create multiple teaching licenses and degree programs.
2. The bureaus of education, teacher education institutions, and K-12 schools should support the teacher professional evaluation system in order to praise high-quality teachers and eliminate unqualified teachers.
3. The bureaus of education, teacher education institutions, and K-12 schools should co-develop in-service teacher training programs, including the teaching profession, curriculum development and instruction, and classroom management.

From the perspective of K-12 schools, there are three important indicators for a teacher education strategic alliance in the period of in-service teacher training and teacher professional development including:

1. Teacher education institutions and K-12 schools should work together to discover the issues related to student learning and teacher teaching in order to upgrade teachers' ability in classroom management.
2. Teacher education institutions should establish multicultural consulting centers to provide teachers-to-be with advice on the upcoming teaching environment.
3. The bureaus of education, teacher education institutions, and K-12 schools should co-develop in-service teacher training programs, including the teaching profession, curriculum development and instruction, and classroom management.

Following analysis of the unidentified findings

After reviewing the outcomes of the important indicators, the principal investigator discovers some unidentified feedbacks from the Bureaus of Education, teacher education institutions, and K-12 schools. There are four indicators that the teacher education strategic alliances have different opinions (see Table 10.3), namely:

1. Teacher education institutions should cooperate with K-12 schools to create best teaching practices via an exchange of educational theories and pedagogical praxis.
2. K-12 schools should encourage their teachers to expand their teaching fields and bureaus of education and teacher education institutions should create multiple teaching licenses and degree programs.
3. The bureaus of education, teacher education institutions, and K-12 schools should support the teacher professional evaluation system in order to praise high-quality teachers and eliminate unqualified teachers.
4. The bureaus of education, teacher education institutions, and K-12 schools should co-host educational conferences to set up on-site exchange systems and provide opportunities for teacher professional dialogue and feedback.

Analyses of the feasible indicators

Pre-service teacher education

With regard to feedback from the bureaus of education, two feasible indicators for teacher education strategic alliance were considered, namely:

1. Teacher education institutions should team-teach with K-12 teachers and administrators, especially in the coursework, including curriculum and instruction, teaching interns, classroom management, and guidance.
2. Teacher education institutions should cooperate with K-12 schools to create best teaching practices via the exchange of educational theories and pedagogical praxis.

Table 10.3 Analysis of the different opinions on important indicators

Strategies for teacher education strategic alliances	Mean (SD)	Bureaus of education	Teacher education institutions	K-12 schools	F test
Teacher education institutions cooperate with K-12 schools to create best teaching practices via the exchange of educational theories and pedagogical praxis.	3.2872 (0.64447)	3.48 (0.505)	3.38 (0.597)	3.2527 (0.65981)	4.851**
K-12 schools should encourage their teachers to expand their teaching fields and bureaus of education and teacher education institutions should create multiple teaching licenses and degree programs.	3.2784 (0.67976)	3.48 (0.590)	3.39 (0.618)	3.2380 (0.69497)	5.767**
The bureaus of education, teacher education institutions, and K-12 schools should support the teacher professional evaluation system in order to praise high-quality teachers and eliminate unqualified teachers.	3.3655 (0.63943)	3.66 (0.479)	3.42 (0.594)	3.3351 (0.65404)	6.111**
The bureaus of education, teacher education institutions and K-12 schools should co-host educational conferences to set up on-site exchange systems and provide opportunities for teacher professional dialogue and feedback.	3.2273 (0.65932)	3.41 (0.542)	3.35 (0.625)	3.1863 (0.66940)	6.145**

*$P < 0.05$; **$P < 0.01$; ***$P < 0.001$

According to the feedback from teacher education institutions, there were two feasible indicators for teacher education strategic alliance, namely:

1. Teacher education institutions should team-teach with K-12 teachers and administrators, especially in coursework, including curriculum and instruction, teaching interns, classroom management, and guidance.
2. Teacher education institutions should cooperate with K-12 schools to create best teaching practices via the exchange of educational theories and pedagogical praxis.

From the perspective of K-12 schools, there are only two feasible indicators:

1. Teacher education institutions respond to the changes in population and student enrollment, and develop multiple curricula, instructions, and assessments.
2. Teacher education institutions should team-teach with K-12 teachers and administrators, especially in coursework, including curriculum and instruction, teaching interns, classroom management, and guidance.

Teaching interns

With regard to the feedback from the bureaus of education, two feasible indicators for teacher education strategic alliance during the period of teaching interns were considered, namely:

1. Student teachers should be encouraged to serve in remote and disadvantaged schools in order to enrich their teaching.
2. Teacher education institutions should keep an eye on changes in student enrollment and create information centers to provide information and dialogue for faculty members, mentors, and student teachers.

According to the feedback from teacher education institutions, there was only one feasible indicator for teacher education strategic alliance in the period of teaching interns, namely that bureaus of education, teacher education institutions, and K-12 schools should encourage experienced school teachers to become mentors during the student teaching process.

From the perspective of K-12 schools, there was only one feasible indicator for teacher education strategic alliance in the period of teaching interns, namely that teacher education institutions should keep an eye on changes in student enrollment and create information centers to provide information and dialogue for faculty members, mentors, and student teachers.

Teacher certificate and recruitment

With regard to feedback from the bureaus of education, only one feasible indicator for teacher education strategic alliance during the period of teacher certificate and recruitment was considered, namely that bureaus of education, teacher education institutions, and K-12 schools should help to reframe the qualified teacher qualification including the teaching profession, curriculum development and instruction, classroom management, and research, along with current social changes.

According to the feedback from teacher education institutions, there is only one feasible indicator for a teacher education strategic alliance in the period of teaching interns, namely that the bureaus of education should correspond with the student enrollment in order to increase the teacher and student ratio and reduce class size.

Similarly, from the perspective of K-12 schools, there is only one feasible indicator for a teacher education strategic alliance in the period of teaching interns, namely that the Bureaus of Education should correspond with the student enrollment in order to increase the teacher-to-student ratio and reduce class size.

In-service teacher training and teacher professional development

With regard to the feedback from the bureaus of education, two feasible indicators for a teacher education strategic alliance during the period of in-service teacher training and teacher professional development were considered, namely:

1. Teacher education and K-12 schools should cooperate to develop creative and multiple teaching methods to improve curriculum development and teaching abilities.
2. The role of teacher education institutions should be transferred from pre-service teacher education only to include in-service and life-long teacher learning, and to provide Master's degree programs for teaching and administration of the profession.

According to the feedback from teacher education institutions, there were two feasible indicators for a teacher education strategic alliance in the period of in-service teacher training and teacher professional development, namely:

1. The role of teacher education institutions should be transferred from pre-service teacher education only to include in-service and life-long teacher learning, and to provide Master's degree programs for teaching and administration of the profession.
2. The bureaus of education, teacher education institutions, and K-12 schools should co-host educational conferences to set up on-site exchange systems and provide opportunities for teacher professional dialogue and feedback.

From the perspective of K-12 schools, there were two feasible indicators for teacher education strategic alliance in the period of in-service teacher training and teacher professional development, namely:

1. The role of teacher education institutions should be transferred from pre-service teacher education only to include in-service and life-long teacher learning, and to provide Master's degree programs for teaching and the administration of the profession.
2. Teacher education institutions and K-12 schools should work together to discover the issues related to student learning and teacher teaching in order to upgrade teachers' ability in classroom management.

Following analysis of the unidentified findings

After reviewing the outcomes of the feasible indicators, the principal investigator discovered some unidentified feedbacks from the bureaus of education, teacher education institutions, and K-12 schools. There were 15 indicators that the teacher education strategic alliances have different opinions. These findings represented that educational stakeholders in Taiwan still had some concerns over how to implement the new trends of teacher education strategic alliance, especially from the perspectives of bureaus of education, teacher education institutions, and K-12 schools (see Table 10.4).

Conclusions

The definition of a teacher education strategic alliance is the triangular cooperative relationship between the bureaus of education, teacher education institutions, and K-12 schools. It refers to all the teacher education processes, including pre-service teacher education, the teaching of interns, teacher certification and recruitment, and in-service teacher training and teacher professional development.

After the literature review, documentary analysis, and focus group discussions, the principal investigator proposed 28 strategies for teacher education strategic alliances in Taiwan and conducted a questionnaire survey to educational stakeholders all over the country. The return rate of the survey was 62.3 per cent, including 58.7 per cent from the bureaus of education, 83.1 per cent from the teacher education institutions, and 58.8 per cent from K-12 schools.

The major findings reveal that there are five important indicators for the upcoming teacher education strategic alliance, namely:

1. The bureaus of education respond to the changes in population and student enrollment simultaneously and develop multiple teacher education policies.
2. Teacher education institutions cooperate with K-12 schools to create best teaching practices via the exchange of educational theories and pedagogical praxis.

Table 10.4 Analysis on the different opinions on feasible indicators

Strategies for teacher education strategic alliances	Mean (SD)	Bureaus of education	Teacher education institutions	K-12 schools	F test
Teacher education institutions respond to the changes in population and student enrollment, and to develop multiple curricula, instructions, and assessments.	3.2067 (0.55716)	3.36 (0.574)	3.12 (0.610)	3.2186 (0.53983)	4.097*
Teacher education institutions cooperate with K-12 schools in order to enrich the curriculum, classroom management, and professional development of student teachers.	3.1908 (0.54455)	3.31 (0.563)	3.09 (0.558)	3.2098 (0.53740)	4.780**
Teacher education institutions should help their faculty members to know more about the changes in student enrollment and help to mentor their student teachers on the teaching profession.	3.1838 (0.59866)	3.33 (0.612)	3.10 (0.616)	3.1962 (0.59178)	3.278*
Teacher education institutions should team teach with K-12 teachers and administrators, especially in the coursework, including curriculum and instruction, teaching interns, classroom management, and guidance.	3.2453 (0.62627)	3.55 (0.504)	3.14 (0.674)	3.2534 (0.61459)	7.490**
Teacher education institutions cooperate with K-12 schools to create best teaching practices via the exchange of educational theories and pedagogical praxis.	3.1587 (0.60638)	3.42 (0.499)	3.19 (0.639)	3.1352 (0.60051)	4.799**
Each teacher education institution should set up horizontal connections to encourage their students to take different programs and courses and exchange knowledge and practical wisdom on the issues of teaching and learning.	3.0419 (0.65457)	3.26 (0.621)	2.96 (0.721)	3.0507 (0.63627)	3.952*
Student teachers should be encouraged to establish research groups to discover authentic problems in daily school life.	3.0813 (0.67436)	3.30 (0.553)	2.96 (0.729)	3.0984 (0.66258)	5.377**
Student teachers should be encouraged to serve in remote and disadvantaged schools in order to enrich their teaching profession.	2.9864 (0.72493)	3.28 (0.666)	2.79 (0.777)	3.0178 (0.70494)	11.101***
Teacher education institutions should keep an eye on changes in student enrollment and create information centers to provide information and dialogue for faculty members, mentors, and student teachers.	3.2017 (0.56952)	3.32 (0.561)	3.10 (0.608)	3.2189 (0.55761)	3.933*

(continued)

Table 10.4 Analysis on the different opinions on feasible indicators (continued)

Strategies for teacher education strategic alliances	Mean (SD)	Bureaus of education	Teacher education institutions	K-12 schools	F test
Bureaus of Education should correspond with the student enrollment in order to increase the teacher-to-student ratio and reduce class size.	3.2844 (0.71445)	2.86 (0.905)	3.25 (0.707)	3.3177 (0.69592)	8.741***
Bureaus of education, teacher education institutions, and K-12 schools should consider teacher recruitment and demand-supply of teacher education.	3.0011 (0.77609)	2.95 (0.861)	2.86 (0.815)	3.0385 (0.75781)	3.908*
K-12 schools should encourage their teachers to expand their teaching fields and bureaus of education and teacher education institutions should create multiple teaching licenses and degree programs.	3.1349 (0.66442)	3.34 (0.680)	3.18 (0.644)	3.1110 (0.66668)	3.046*
Teacher education institutions should provide programs related to teaching and guiding abilities in the field of low birth rate and heterogeneous student enrollment in order to renew the teacher's teaching certificate.	3.0211 (0.63809)	3.23 (0.527)	2.97 (0.690)	3.0221 (0.62856)	3.029*
Teacher education institutions should establish a multicultural consulting centre to provide advice to teachers-to-be for the upcoming teaching environment.	3.2264 (0.63403)	3.32 (0.639)	3.10 (0.740)	3.2514 (0.60146)	4.427*
The bureaus of education, teacher education institutions, and K-12 schools should co-host educational conferences to set up on-site exchange systems and provide opportunities for teacher professional dialogue and feedback.	3.1442 (0.59645)	3.27 (0.499)	3.23 (0.622)	3.1151 (0.59298)	3.786*

*$P < 0.05$; **$P < 0.01$; ***$P < 0.001$

3. Bureaus of education, teacher education institutions, and K-12 schools should set up professional development schools (PDSs) together to ensure the quality of student teaching.
4. Bureaus of education, teacher education institutions, and K-12 schools should encourage experienced school teachers to become mentors during the student teaching process.
5. Bureaus of education should correspond with the student enrollment in order to increase the teacher-to-student ratio and reduce class size.

Moreover, according to the feasible indicators related to teacher education strategic alliance, the researcher suggests two crucial strategies, namely:

1. Teacher education institutions should cooperate with K-12 schools in order to enrich the curriculum, classroom management, and professional development of student teachers.
2. The roles of teacher education institutions should be transferred from pre-service teacher education only to include in-service and life-long teacher learning, and to provide Master's degree programs for teaching and the administration of the profession.

Furthermore, there were seven strategies the feasibility of which the bureaus of education, teacher education institutions, and K-12 schools were worried about, namely:

1. Each teacher education institution should set up horizontal connections to encourage their students to take courses from different programs and exchange the knowledge and practical wisdom on the issues of teaching and learning.
2. Student teachers should be encouraged to establish research groups to discover the authentic problems in daily school life.
3. Student teachers should be encouraged to serve in remote and disadvantaged schools in order to enrich their teaching profession.
4. Bureaus of education, teacher education institutions, and K-12 schools should consider teacher recruitment and the demand-supply of teacher education.
5. Bureaus of education should correspond with the student enrollment in order to increase the teacher-to-student ratio and reduce class size.
6. Teacher education institutions should provide programs related to teaching and guiding abilities in the field of low birth rate and heterogeneous student enrollment in order to renew the teachers' teaching certificate.
7. The bureaus of education, teacher education institutions, and K-12 schools should support the teacher professional evaluation system in order to praise high-quality teachers and eliminate unqualified teachers.

After we reviewed the outcome of the research compared with the existing literature, we discovered that the politics of the teacher educational strategic alliance in Taiwan are still a matter of debate between governmental control and market choices (Sachs, 2010; Whitty, 1989). The teacher educational strategic alliance could be understood as a question of cooperation between the government, the schools, and the teacher education institutions. According to the research findings, the government or the Ministry of Education/Bureau of Education still wish to play a role as the gatekeepers of teacher quality, while the schools and teacher education institutions hope to keep an eye on choice and equity. Thus the current status of the teacher education strategic alliance in Taiwan could be regarded as a negotiation between the ideology of governmental control and market choice. However, if we juxtapose them with the model provided by Cheng and Jacob (2007), we will find that the debate between localization and globalization does not exist within the discussion of the teacher education strategic alliance.

References

Black, E. (2001) *IBM and the Holocaust: The Strategic Alliance Between Nazi Germany and America's Most Powerful Corporation*, 1st edn. New York: Crown.

Burton, G. (2004) *Ambivalence and the Postcolonial Subject: The Strategic Alliance of Juan Francisco Manzano and Richard Robert Madden*. New York: Peter Lang.

Carroll, D. M. (2006) "Developing joint accountability in university-school teacher education partnerships," *Action in Teacher Education*, 27 (4): 3–11.

Cheng, S. and Jacob, W. (2005) "A new approach on educational reforms: EPAM," *Educational Research Monthly*, 129: 145–54.

Cheng, S. and Jacob, W. (2007) "A comparative case study on indigenous educational policies between Taiwan and the United States," *Comparative Education Journal*, 63 (2): 40–78.

Feiman-Nemser, S. (1998) "Teachers as teacher educators," *European Journal of Teacher Education*, 21 (1): 63–74.

Goodlad, J. (1990) *Teachers for our Nation's Schools*. San Francisco: Jossey-Bass.

Goodlad, J. (1994) *Educational Renewal: Better Teachers, Better Schools*. San Francisco: Jossey-Bass.

Holmes Group (1986) *Tomorrow's Teachers: A Report of Holmes Group*. East Lansing, MI: Holmes Group.

Lee, J., Levin, H., and Soler, P. (2005) "Accelerated schools for quality education: a Hong Kong perspective," *The Urban Review*, 37 (1): 63–81.

Levin, H. (2001) *Learning from School Reforms*. Paper presented at the the International Conference on Rejuvenating Schools Through Partnership. Chinese University of Hong Kong.

Lunenberg, M., Snoek, M., and Swennen, A. (2000) "Between pragmatism and legitimacy: developments and dilemmas in teacher education in the Netherlands," *European Journal of Teacher Education*, 23 (3): 251–60.

Ministry of Education (2005) *Statistics Yearbook of Teacher Education, Republic of China, 2004*. Taipei: MOE.

National Commission on Teaching and America's Future (1996) *What Matters Most: Teaching for America's Future*. New York: National Commission on Teaching and America's Future.

Porter, M. and Fuller, M. (1986) "Coalitions and global strategy," in M. E. Porter (ed.), *Competitive in Global Industries*. Boston: Harvard Business School Press, pp. 315–43.

Sachs, J. (2010) "Teacher professional identity: competing discourses, competing outcomes," *Journal of Educational Policy*, 16 (2): 149–61.

Whitty, G. (1989) "The new right and the national curriculum: state control or market forces?" *Journal of Educational Policy*, 4 (4): 329–41.

11 The evaluation of teacher education for quality assurance in Taiwan

Jia-Li Huang

Introduction

Changes in global political and economic trends after the 1980s brought neo-liberal economic thought to the forefront of political discourse in many countries around the world. Concepts underlying the principles of market management, including accountability, consumer choice, standards, privatization, and the market mechanism, among others, manipulated politics and affected education reforms to emphasize free competition and marketization (Marginson, 2007; Roberts and Peters, 2008). Whitty *et al.*'s study (1998, pp. 39–41) showed that despite their different cultures and traditions, political regimes, and educational reforms, the United Kingdom (England and Scotland), New Zealand, Sweden, Australia, and the United States have consistently emphasized the management-based trend of thought featuring stabilizing quality with standards, consumer choice, and reflection of diversified channels on the market. Under the same line of reasoning, institutions have come to place greater emphasis on accountability, responsibility, and quality so that consumers have a greater and longer lasting sense of satisfaction with services and products. Institutions must propose specific and reliable indicators of quality on the market (Feigenbaum, 1982). In the case of schools, evaluations serve as a way to demonstrate their obligations for quality and accountability (Bok, 2003). For teacher education institutions, evaluations are also a way to demonstrate the quality of teacher education.

The term *evaluation* refers to the process by which any institution, program, or discipline determines the level of quality (Campbell and Rozsnyai, 2002, p. 23). While judging the level of quality, it is required to compare the difference against standards through the planning, collection, and information description process before making a decision with regard to the value (Ou, 2002; Stufflebeam and Shinkfield, 1985). Therefore, evaluation is to judge and make a decision over the value. It is the result after comparison and contrast with external standards. Evaluation, however, should be aimed at achieving improvement, instead of accumulating evidence, in order to show the impacts of evaluation on institutions. It is not just about comparison against specific standards. What is more important is to facilitate constant improvement and development on the part of institutions (Stufflebeam, 2000). Evaluation, according to its definition, can be accomplished in one of two ways: the bottom-line model or the organic model. The former is a preordinate or standards-based evaluation with the primary quality assurance mechanism (Guba and Linclon, 1989; Stake, 2004) while the latter is a responsive or empowerment evaluation which emphasizes a quality assurance mechanism that helps institutions constantly renew and empower themselves. Differences between the two lie in how data are collected and interpreted and the professional accomplishment of evaluators (Stake, 2004). The two types of evaluation have also appeared in the history of teacher education evaluation in Taiwan.

The Teacher Education Act, due to its focus on teacher education in Taiwan, is positioned to be special because it demonstrates not only expectations of and value placed by the state toward the quality of teacher education but also the control of the state over teacher education. In the evaluation of teacher education, Taiwan adopts a program-based stance. The program activities, features, and results are collected systematically to facilitate decision-making relating programs, improvement efficacy, and subsequent developments in the future (Patton, 2000). Because of the comparison against specific standards, it can be provided to policy-makers for subsequent management or application (Wholey, 1979). In light of the expectations from the government and the general public, external evaluations are done in accordance with a set of established standards and are meant to ensure the quality of teacher education institutions. However, it must be further clarified whether the evaluation system should be of the bottom-line or the organic model.

In light of the fact that teacher education evaluation is a mechanism used to control the quality of teacher education in Taiwan, analysis is required with regard to the development, orientation, and implementation of teacher education evaluation in order to serve as a reference to improve teacher education. Therefore, this chapter aims to analyze the development of teacher education evaluation in Taiwan and understand issues such as the design and operation of teacher education evaluation and reflections on the basis of a pluralistic market and state control, before suggestions are finally provided to support subsequent improvement.

Development of teacher education evaluation in Taiwan

Ever since the Teacher Education Act was promulgated in 1994, teacher education in Taiwan has been marketized. In order for the state to control the quality, institutions providing teacher education are evaluated. In the beginning, the evaluations were accomplished in the form of site-visits and appeared to be relatively lax. After the Regulations for Evaluation of Universities with Teacher Education was implemented in 2006 (Ministry of Education, 2006), evaluation of teacher education in Taiwan officially followed the quality control mechanism. Quality of teacher education provided at institutions was evaluated through the use of a standardized scale. The Ministry of Education used evaluation results to decide enrollment quota at specific institutions. After 2012, the system became approval-based; both good and bad results were released and the spirit of performance evaluation was continued. The following is a brief summary of the history of the development of teacher education evaluations in Taiwan.

Site visits to universities with teacher education programs (1995–2005)

Teacher education switched from a planned model to a pluralistic one as soon as the Teacher Education Act was enforced in 1994. To ensure the quality of teacher education, the Ministry of Education announced the Regulations of the Establishment and the Academic Faculty of Teacher Education Programs Offered by Universities and Colleges in 1995 (which was revised to make the Regulations for Establishment of Teacher Education Centres in Universities in 2003) after universities were allowed to set up their own teacher education centers to review the eligibility of universities. In light of the pluralistic nature of teacher education, the Ministry of Education first relaxed the policy and then tightened it. Teacher education institutions could submit applications as long as they met the establishment criteria and could start cultivating teachers once the Teacher Education Review Committee approved them. The relaxed front-end application process resulted in back-end control. The Ministry of Education started carrying out visits to universities with teacher education programs in 1996, began placing a greater emphasis on the importance of self-evaluations at institutions, and attempted to incorporate the results of evaluations into the decision-making process for increasing or decreasing the enrollment numbers for teacher education.

The practice of determining the quality of teacher education provided by universities started with the Regulations for Evaluation of Universities with Teacher Education Program announced by the Ministry of Education in 2002 that stipulated that universities with teacher education programs have to go through teacher education evaluation. The evaluation was done externally and included site evaluation and written evaluation. Written evaluation targeted institutions rated excellent or good in two evaluations in a row. When these institutions are included for the annual evaluation, the evaluation can be done in writing. As a result, when written evaluation is used for teacher education institutions, that means the specific teacher education institution has been rated excellent once (i.e. eight years have passed, given the fact that evaluations are performed at an interval of four years) or good in two evaluations in a row (12 years in total given the fact that evaluations are performed at an interval of four years). Written evaluation reports are not submitted on a yearly basis. In other words, many years will have passed in terms of controlling the quality of teacher education. According to the Regulations, evaluation results can be divided into five categories, namely excellent, good, fair, pending improvement, and undesirable. Only those rated "undesirable" must seek improvement within a limited period of time. If improvement is not made, teacher education institutions have to discontinue recruiting students for a year or discontinue the program outright. As far as the cost devoted by teacher education institutions is concerned, discontinued recruitment or discontinued programs have an effect on their personnel and administrative costs; losses are likely in the absence of a balanced return.

The Ministry of Education (2004) changed the Regulations for Evaluation of Universities with Teacher Education Programs to the Regulations for Evaluation of Universities with Teacher Education Centers in 2004 and targeted universities with teacher education centers. For normal education universities and universities with departments of teacher education, on the other hand, the Ministry of Education adopted a different plan; they are not governed by the Regulations for Evaluation of Universities with Teacher Education Centers. Those with newly established teacher education programs that are less than one year old or with a previous evaluation rating less than one year old or without evaluation for the past four years or more, or those that are determined by the Teacher Education Review Committee to require evaluation or those with self-applied for evaluation, are all subject to evaluation.

Up to this point, teacher education evaluation in Taiwan has gradually developed from relatively loose site visits to the strict utilization of evaluation results following discontinued recruitment or the discontinuation of teacher education institutions. This is used as a strategy for improving teacher education institutions. In light of the fact that cost-effectiveness associated with discontinued recruitment for a year, or discontinued operation, has an effect on the willingness of teacher education institutions to remain on the market, and on the unbalanced supply and demand, with supply more than demand in teacher education, the Ministry of Education released in 2004 the Plan for Teacher Education Quantity to have more express and purpose-oriented control over the size of teacher education; thus, the number of students recruited by normal/education universities would be reduced by 50 per cent. For universities with teacher education programs, on the other hand, the results of evaluations carried out in accordance with the Regulations for Evaluation of Universities with Teacher Education Programs are the important basis for the reduced number of students being recruited and the definition of teacher education evaluation as performance evaluation. The results of evaluations of teacher education institutions continued to be the basis for the adjustment made to the number of students to be recruited for teacher education programs up to 2013 when the Ministry of Education announced the Stage 2 Plan for Teacher Education Quantity.

Generally speaking, teacher education evaluation models at this stage already shaped the indicators, process, utilization of results, and evaluation targets and turned from visits that were more counseling-oriented to an evaluation model that placed relatively high emphasis on the attribute of performance.

First cycle of teacher education evaluation (2006–12)

The low birth rate and redundant amount of teacher education resulted in the unbalanced supply and demand in the teacher workforce in Taiwan. The Plan for Teacher Education Quantity was meant to balance exactly the enrollment numbers at institutions approved by the Ministry of Education on the results of teacher evaluation. The Enhancement Program for Teacher Education Quality announced by the Ministry of Education in 2006 reiterated the importance of teacher education evaluations to balancing the supply and demand and helping respective teacher education institutions seek improvement. To fulfill the express state-control goal, the Ministry of Education released the Regulations for Evaluation of Universities with Teacher Education in 2006; the Guidelines specified the standards for different evaluation levels, evaluation methods, and grades, and were the basis of the number of students to be recruited for teacher education on evaluation results. For Grade 1 institutions based on the evaluation results (85 per cent and above), the original enrollment numbers will be kept. For Grade 2 institutions (75–84 per cent), the enrollment numbers available for the coming academic year will be cut by 20 per cent. For Grade 3 institutions (less than 75 per cent), the program will be discontinued. The first cycle of Teacher Education Evaluation began in 2006 and ended in 2011. During this period, evaluation was outsourced and carried out by the National Academy for Educational Research between 2006 and 2008 and by the Higher Education Evaluation and Accreditation Council of Taiwan in 2009 onwards. By letting the higher education and accreditation center perform evaluations, it is symbolic of the fact that teacher education evaluation has become professionalized.

According to the Regulations for Evaluation of Universities with Teacher Education, teacher education evaluation is meant to serve as an elimination mechanism that helps discover problems, guide directions, urge improvement, and provide assistance and advice (Chang et al., 2007). Evaluations can guide teacher education institutions toward a specific education model and can help diagnose issues with teacher education institutions and determine the quality, good or bad, in order to control the quality of teacher education. In other words, teacher education evaluation has the effect of assisting institutions that require improvement or discontinuation in order to regulate the number of prospective teachers and control the quality of teacher education (Wu et al., 2011).

Teacher education evaluation is a useful mechanism to control the quality of teacher education in a state-controlled market. In 2010, the Ministry of Education called for the eighth national education meeting. With regard to teacher education and professional development, one of the top ten issues, the Ministry reiterated that evaluation of teacher education institutions would continue in order to safeguard the quality of teachers; there was already a consensus to a certain extent on teacher education evaluation as a quality assurance mechanism in Taiwan.

Second cycle of teacher education evaluation (2012–)

The Ministry of Education mentioned again in its White Paper of Teacher Education of 2012 that teacher education evaluation served as the indicator for promoting both self-study and pluralistic development of teacher education institutions in order to realize pluralistic teacher education policies that reward outperformers and eliminate underperformers, and maintain good quality and an adequate number of teachers (Ministry of Education, 2012). As far as policy goals are concerned, teacher education evaluation features self-improvement and pluralistic development of teacher education institutions; it adds the characteristic of promoting the diverse development of teacher education institutions to the existing purpose of teacher education evaluation, that is to provide assistance, guidance, and control over quality. The spirit was incorporated in the second cycle of teacher education evaluation that began in 2012.

Teacher education evaluation in Taiwan entered its second cycle in 2012. Evaluations began to be carried out by the Higher Education Evaluation and Accreditation Council of Taiwan that is considered to be professional and have the following aims:

1. To understand the administrative operation at teacher education units and the efficacy of teaching and student learning to ensure quality teacher education.
2. To guide the integration of resources available for different disciplines for the enhanced quality of education provided by respective units, reward outperformers and eliminate underperformers, and create an exit mechanism.
3. To encourage education units to develop professional characteristics and contents and enhance the quality of pluralistic teacher education to conform to professional concepts and meet actual needs in the education field.
4. To help education units analyze performance in accordance with teachers' professional attainments and create a self-improvement mechanism.
5. To understand the professional performance and core competences of prospective teachers.
6. To facilitate collaboration among teachers of pre-service education in cross-disciplinary research and make the best of the educational research capabilities of the education unit.
7. To stipulate and improve evaluation procedures and standards and provide them for education administrative institutions' reference in the future while they establish policies.

(Higher Education Evaluation and Accreditation Council of Taiwan, 2012)

With the above combined, the second cycle of teacher education evaluation features the establishment of program characteristics and keeps track of the professional performance and core competences of prospective teachers besides the existing purposes. In addition, one of the characteristics of the second cycle is the accreditation system developed for the results of evaluation to address the purpose of evaluation. Accreditation consists of three levels, namely "approved", "approved with conditions", and "not approved".

Unlike the first cycle, wherein results of the evaluation were determined by the evaluators' collegial system, evaluators took part in the evaluation meeting, and held discussions after completing their field evaluation, the second cycle involves a process flow wherein teacher education institutions have to submit the evaluation report as scheduled. Before evaluators go on a one-and-a-half-day site visit, they must first provide issues found with the evaluation report and let respective teacher education institutions respond or prepare related materials for clarification. The process flow consists of a sales presentation, inspection of the teaching environment and facilities, review of materials and related documents, interviews with teachers, administrators, students, and interns, teaching observations, evaluators' meetings, comprehensive workshops, etc. The evaluation report and preliminary judgement are submitted last.

During Stage 1, evaluators complete the evaluation feedback form and suggest accreditation results based on the actual performance of evaluation items as a whole. During Stage 2, the accreditation review committee performs substantial review of materials provided by teacher education institutions, including general descriptions, the evaluation comment form, appeal opinions, and the evaluator's replies to appeal opinions. The accreditation result and overall evaluation contents are determined at the end. In accordance with the Regulations for Evaluation of Universities with Teacher Education, the Ministry of Education adjusts the openings available for the coming year based on the evaluation results for the second cycle (see Table 11.1).

Generally speaking, the second cycle of teacher education evaluation emphasizes external evaluation. In other words, a teacher education institution must have unique programs and be equipped with a surveillance system for self-evaluation and follow-up. This will be confirmed through external evaluation (Department of Secondary Education, Ministry of Education, 2010) so that teacher education evaluation can continue to fulfill the quality assurance function and policy goal of education featuring good quality and adequate quantity of teachers.

In addition, one of the characteristics of the second cycle of teacher education evaluation is that there are two versions of evaluation to address the different natures of teacher education institutions; one is for normal/education universities and ordinary universities configured with both a teacher education center and a department of teacher education, while the other is for universities with either a teacher education center or a department of teacher education. For the second cycle, in 2012 all teacher education institutions, including normal/education universities and universities with both a teacher education center and a department of teacher education, had to take part in the evaluation.

Table 11.1 Accreditation criteria and utilization of results

Result	Criterion	Utilization
Approved	More than four items under evaluation are approved, and no single item is left unapproved.	Originally approved enrollment shall remain.
Approved with condition	Less than one item under evaluation is not approved.	30% of the originally approved enrollment.
Not approved	More than two items under evaluation are not approved.	The program shall be discontinued.

This was the first time that all teacher education institutions were included in the evaluation since 2006, when the Regulations for Evaluation of Universities with Teacher Education were announced. Despite the different evaluation indicators, consistent planning means teacher education institutions in Taiwan also have to be challenged in terms of quality assurance; there is no variation despite the different types of teacher education institutions.

An overview of the development of the teacher education evaluation system in Taiwan reveals that both a system and a consensus have been formed since its initiation in 1996. The applicability, indicators, process flow, and determination and utilization of results have all developed toward perfection. Teacher education institutions have also come to know quality assurance through evaluation in teacher education and the adjustment made to the enrollment available for their programs based on the results of evaluation. As society changes and teacher education evaluation develops toward perfection, however, teacher education institutions have also gradually shifted in their expectations of teacher education evaluation, in terms of facilitating the development of their pluralistic characteristics through teacher education evaluation. More advanced analysis is required for the teacher education evaluation system nowadays in Taiwan.

Analysis of the control feature of the teacher education evaluation system

Just like the certification and evaluation mechanisms adopted internationally, teacher education evaluation exercises a quality assurance function. The quality assurance associated with teacher education evaluation in Taiwan, however, started because of the state's effort to ensure the quality of teacher education under marketization. When evaluations are initiated by the state rather than a teacher education institution, the government can focus its control on the contents of the indicators and utilization of results. The following therefore describes the differences between the first cycle and the second cycle of teacher education evaluation in Taiwan, and discusses the contents of the evaluation indicators for the second cycle and the efficacy of utilizing the evaluation results.

Comparison of the first and second cycles of teacher education evaluation

The first cycle of teacher education evaluation in Taiwan began in 2006 and reached a conclusion by the beginning of the second cycle. Table 11.2 compares the first and second cycles of the evaluation system (Huang, 2013, p. 66).

As is shown in Table 11.2, differences between Cycle 1 and Cycle 2 not only appeared in the augmentation of evaluation purposes and merger of indicator contents but also in the decision-making process for the results of the evaluation. Results of teacher education evaluation have continued to govern recruitment at teacher education institutions, which clearly shows the idea of performance management.

Table 11.2 Comparison of the first cycle and the second cycle of the teacher education evaluation system in Taiwan

Item	Cycle 1	Cycle 2	Significance of post-change system
Undertaker	Preparations Office of National Academy for Educational Research (2006–8) Higher Education Evaluation and Accreditation Council of Taiwan (2009–)	Higher Education Evaluation and Accreditation Council of Taiwan	Handled by a professional institution
Timeframe	2006–11	2012 onward	—
Purpose of evaluation	1. To enhance teacher education performance 2. To control quality of teacher education 3. To help discover issues, provide guidance and assistance	1. To understand the efficacy of teacher education 2. To direct integration of resources available at respective institutions 3. To encourage development of professional characteristics and contents 4. To help establish a self-improvement mechanism 5. To understand the level of professional performance and core competences of prospective teachers 6. To facilitate cross-disciplinary research collaboration among teacher education instructors 7. To come up with measures that help improve the evaluation	1. To increase emphasis on professional standards and core competences of teachers 2. To help teacher education institutions establish their own improvement mechanisms 3. To facilitate integration of resources among teacher education institutions
Evaluation item	1. Education objective and development characteristic 2. Organization, positioning, and operation 3. Student screening and counseling 4. Utilization of graphics, instruments and equipment, budget, space, among other resources 5. Teacher quota, teacher quality, and research and development accomplishments	1. Target, characteristic, and self-improvement 2. Administrative organization and operation 3. Student screening and learning environment 4. Teacher quality and professional performance 5. Curricular design and instruction 6. Educational practicum and graduate performance	1. Emphasis on the establishment of a self-improvement mechanism 2. Consolidation of administrative resources and operation 3. Assistance with local education or in-service education for teachers is combined into Item 1.

Evaluation item	6. Curricular and pedagogical planning and implementation 7. Educational practicum and employment assistance 8. Assistance with local education or promotion of in-service education for teachers	—	—
Implementation	Site visit	Site visit	—
Grade	1. 85% and above 2. 75–84% 3. Less than 75%	1. *Approved*: More than four items under evaluation are approved, and no single item is left unapproved. 2. *Approved conditionally*: Less than one item under evaluation is not approved. 3. *Not approved*: More than two items under evaluation are not approved.	Express two-stage review
Result	Written evaluation reports that describe the determined grade and improvement measures for the teacher education center in the future	Strengths and weaknesses of individual evaluation items and opinions on how to improve the weaknesses	—
Evaluation decision	Evaluator collegial system	Accreditation	
Utilization of evaluation results	1. Original enrollment number available is kept. 2. The enrollment number is reduced by 20% for the coming academic year and a secondary review will be performed in the coming academic year. 3. Recruitment discontinues for the coming academic year.	1. *Approved*: Original enrollment number available is kept. 2. *Approved with condition*: Original number of enrollment available is reduced by 30%. 3. *Not approved*: The program shall be discontinued.	

Source: Huang (2013, pp. 57–84).

Indicator contents of teacher education evaluation

Teacher education institutions, when used as a mechanism of state control, not only exercise a guiding function but also help diagnose problems and determine the quality of teacher education. In this case, the fulfillment of quality control relies on the operational side of evaluation, including the contents of evaluation indicators and the utilization of evaluation results. A total of seven items appear under the contents of teacher education evaluation indicators for the first cycle, including:

- the education objective and development characteristics;
- organization, positioning, and operation;
- student screening and counseling;
- utilization of graphics, instruments and equipment, budget, and space, among other resources;
- teacher quota, teacher quality, and research and development accomplishments;
- curricular and pedagogical planning and implementation;
- educational practicum and employment assistance, assistance with local education or promotion of in-service education for teachers.

There are changes to the contents of evaluation indicators for the second cycle, including an emphasis on the establishment of a self-study mechanism, the consolidation of administrative resources and operational items, and the inclusion of assistance with local education or in-service education for teachers under Item 1 in order to address the evaluation needs of different types of teacher education institution. As described above, normal/education universities and comprehensive universities with both a teacher education center and a department of teacher education were already included in the routine teacher education evaluation for the second cycle that started in 2012. Teacher education evaluation no longer only targets institutions with teacher education centers as most of them belong to the traditional normal system or are normal/education universities consolidated as part of or transformed into comprehensive universities. These have their own the advantages in preparing teachers given the traditional teacher education model and also feature a relatively large education scale. Table 11.3 compares the evaluation indicator contents for two different types of teacher education institutions given that the teacher education evaluation process flow and utilization of results are consistent for the second cycle.

As shown in Table 11.3, among the six evaluation items, four are identical, with 66.7 per cent consistency. Under the same indicator contents and regulations, it is worth thinking whether or not there is extra space for a teacher education institution to develop diverse characteristics. In light of the fact that guidance provided under indicator contents already prevented teacher education institutions from developing their characteristics, and actual pedagogical issues associated with teacher education courses were not included for the first cycle of teacher education evaluation (Huang, 2013), it is worth observing whether or not the guidance

Table 11.3 Two different versions of indicator contents of teacher education evaluation for the second cycle

Evaluation item	Number of indicators per item		Description of difference
	Normal/education universities and comprehensive universities with both teacher education center and teacher education-related departments (A)	Teacher education center/ department in universities (B)	
Item 1 Target, characteristic, and self-improvement	5	4	(A) "Organization of assistance with professional service and in-service teacher education" is added.
Item 2 Administrative organization and operation	7	8	(B) "Administrative capabilities and beliefs of teacher education center/department director" is added.
Item 3 Student screening and learning environment	8	8	(A) and (B) are the same.
Item 4 Teacher quality and professional performance	6	6	(B) "Teacher quota at teacher education center/department" is emphasized.
Item 5 Curricular design and instruction	10	10	(A) and (B) are the same.
Item 6 Educational practicum and graduate performance	11	11	(A) The management of all indicators by the "responsible unit for organizing practicum and providing employment assistance" is emphasized.

feature of evaluation indicators for the second cycle can promote the development of characteristics in teacher education, since evaluation indicator contents for the first and second cycles are not much different from each other.

In addition, comparison shows that among the evaluation indicator contents for the second cycle the emphasis is placed on teacher education institutions within the traditional normal education system. As such, in terms of professional service and in-service teacher education as well as the operation of units that organize practicums and provide a careers service, the planning obviously targets large-scale teacher education institutions. For universities with teacher education centers, on the other hand, the administrative capabilities and beliefs of the leader and the quota of full-time (part-time) teachers are emphasized; in particular, teacher education institutions are being examined for any violation of the requirement for "assigning at least five full-time teachers specializing in the subject they teach" of the Regulations for Establishment of Teacher Education Centres in Universities. An overview of the aforementioned different indicator contents has revealed that teacher education evaluation is based on whether a teacher education institution has fulfilled or violated the related regulations. Among the teacher education institutions included in the site visit, there is obviously a different way from the five-member quota in their actual operation (Lu, 2012). The quota, however, has to be calculated in accordance with the Ministry of Education's requirements. In other words, it is pending further clarification with regard to whether evaluation indicators intended to review the operation status at teacher education institutions can help fulfill the purpose of empowering the institutions to develop pluralistic characteristics for the second cycle.

Generally speaking, whether comparing indicator contents for the first and second cycles or comparing the two different types of indicator contents for the second cycle, it has been shown that teacher education evaluation in Taiwan has been increasingly complete; nevertheless, it is expected that teacher education institutions can improve on their own and develop diverse characteristics. In terms of the different types of evaluation indicators, there is consistency. The emphasis is placed on the review of regulatory compliance and details of the actual operation level of teacher education institutions. By controlling the quality of teacher education, the state accomplishes consistent operations among teacher education institutions, which seems to leave room for strengthening the development of pluralistic characteristics under the organic model.

Utilization of the results of teacher education evaluation

The results of teacher education evaluation in Taiwan are used by the Ministry of Education to approve the enrollment numbers of the respective teacher education institutions. A reduction in the enrollment numbers for teacher education is a punishment imposed by the state based on evaluation results, and not a result of competition in the market among teacher education institutions. According to the annual statistics report on teacher education and the statistics provided on the teacher education information web for universities, after pluralistic development of prospective teachers began in 1994 in Taiwan, the number of teacher education units peaked in 2004 to reach 75. However, the number dropped to 52 by 2014, that is a total of 23 teacher education institutions backed out of the market. Among the causes for teacher education institutions to exit the preparation of the teacher workforce, as analyzed, were the following.

- The universities decided it was too costly to remain in the market.
- Devotion to the teacher workforce was not one of the incentives for students in choosing their university, with examples such as the China University of

Science and Technology (discontinued in academic year 2005), Shih Hsin University (discontinued in academic year 2006), Chang Gung University (discontinued in academic year 2007), Hsuan Chuang University (discontinued in academic year 2008), and Feng Chia University (discontinued in academic year 2009).
- Universities were merged, as occurred to a total of three universities, the National Hualien University of Education being consolidated as part of the National Dong Hwa University, the Taipei Municipal University of Education merging with the Taipei Physical Education College to become the University of Taipei, and the National Pingtung University of Education merging with the National Pingtung University of Science and Technology to become the National Pingtung University.

Only four teacher education institutions discontinued their teacher education operation as a result of unfavorable evaluation results. Table 11.4 shows the overall withdrawal of institutions from the teacher education market.

According to experience in the United States, teacher education is never a cash cow. Teacher education institutions not only spend money to acquire certification from the National Council for the Accreditation of Teacher Education (NCATE) but also have to invest resources while making efforts to seek improvement. The return, however, is relatively disproportionate (Basinger, 1998). The same situation also occurs in Taiwan. Although there is no need for teacher education institutions to spend a lot of money to take part in the evaluation, the resources involved and the value-added effect of teacher education on universities are obviously important factors for them when considering whether they should remain in the market or not. Once teacher education institutions back out of the market, however, it will be irreversible. This is particularly true in the cultivation of prospective teachers for vocational schools. With teacher education institutions backing out of the market, it can no longer be possible to cultivate outstanding prospective teachers and this accordingly makes the shortage of teachers even worse (Chou, 2012). Therefore, when the Ministry of Education consolidated the Plan for Teacher Education Quantity by basing the openings available at teacher education institutions on their teacher education evaluation results, and while the supply and demand on the market are reaching equilibrium,

Table 11.4 Overview of institutions withdrawing from the teacher education market

Academic year	Discontinued operation	Discontinued operation due to unfavorable teacher education evaluation results
2005	1	0
2006	4	2
2007	4	2
2008	8	0
2009	3	0
Total	20	4

teacher education policy-makers must think about the possibility of changing the nature of teacher education evaluation from a bottom-line model to an organic one, making the results of teacher education evaluation truly a reference for market competition without direct interference from the state (Huang, 2013). Thus evaluation results will no longer be linked to the enrollment numbers in teacher education institutions.

Exploring issues of teacher education evaluation

Since teacher education evaluation was first implemented in Taiwan in 2002, it has gone through at least two cycles. The purpose of the first cycle of evaluation was to provide guidance, diagnosis, and assistance, helping to achieve improvement which has been supported by research. Nevertheless, there were loopholes, including the absence of substantial benefits, the prevention of teacher education institutions from developing their own characteristics, and the failure of evaluation indicators to address differences in institutional attributes (Huang, 2013). In light of the fact that the second cycle of teacher education evaluation is ongoing, we would like to discuss related issues as follows.

Grading or accreditation does not help ensure the cultivation of effective teachers

In accordance with the teacher education evaluation system in Taiwan, accreditation involves a final determination based on the approval status of each evaluation item; generally speaking, it is the result of the accumulation of approved items. Whether the accumulated results of approved items ensure the quality of education provided at teacher education institutions or the quality of the teachers, however, is something to take into consideration. Applying the evaluation results, the evaluation process, and evaluation tools does not help ensure that capable teachers are being prepared (Murray, 2001). Besides, if the evidence obtained is not empirical but is the result of planning at teacher education institutions, it cannot be used to support successful pre-service teacher education. In other words, it cannot ensure the quality of teacher education or urge the institution to enhance efficacy (Graham *et al.*, 1995). According to the experience of the United States, the Teacher Education Accreditation Council (TEAC, consolidated with NCATE to become the Council for the Accreditation of Educator Preparation), established in 1993, was exactly the same product in response to a smaller teacher education scale (Bradley, 1998). The establishment of the TEAC, however, changed not only the type of teacher education institutions but also the evaluation model, from evaluation to audit. It emphasizes the differences between the self-expectations of teacher education units and the actual outcome. Self-assessment is done in an exploratory way and improvements are made (Huang, 2008; Galley, 2003).

Therefore, according to the evaluation purpose for the second cycle, teacher education evaluation should follow the organic model. This helps institutions to develop a characteristic quality assurance mechanism in response to changes to the external situation and also to learn and update themselves through the evaluation process to accomplish greater efficacy and excellence (Sanders, 2002). The design of the evaluation system includes indicator contents, the presentation of evidence, the analysis of problems, and evaluator expertise, among others, and should be carried out carefully.

The emphasis on the operation makes teacher education evaluation indicators relatively weak in terms of reflecting the learning efficacy of prospective teachers

Teacher education evaluation in Taiwan is performance-oriented with the results being the criteria used by the Ministry of Education to determine the enrollment numbers at respective teacher education institutions. As we have analyzed earlier in this article, some teacher education institutions have withdrawn from the market for a variety reasons but the number of those backing out of the market actually because of unfavorable evaluation results is relatively low. Even if self-study is included as part of the evaluation indicators for the second cycle of teacher education, the emphasis is on the improvement made by the respective education institution based on previous evaluation results or on the establishment of a self-study mechanism to review the extent of preparedness for evaluation items. Relatively speaking, the capacity of an institution to examine the learning process of prospective teachers and to discover and solve problems is ignored; as a result, it is difficult to reflect the learning efficacy of prospective teachers.

Besides, the design of evaluation indicators emphasizes whether an institution follows the laws and regulations guiding the operation, the resources invested, and curricular planning; there is little emphasis on prospective students' learning results (Chang, 2006; and Chang *et al.*, 2007; Kao, 2004; Wang and Wang, 1999). The strength of the relevance between the learning outcome of prospective teachers and the planning of its teacher education system at an institution should be reflected in the meta-evaluation, while the correlation between evaluation indicators and learning efficacy of prospective teachers should be clarified in Circle 2 of the teacher education evaluation.

Despite the different versions of evaluation indicators planned, they tend to be consistent and can hardly reflect diversity

According to Taiwan's experience, the biggest visible changes from Cycle 1 to Cycle 2 are the different teacher education evaluation indicators as a result of the different attributes of teacher education institutions. The logic underlying the train of thought is that the scale of teacher education is not necessarily identical between universities under the traditional normal education system and ordinary ones. The diversified teacher education model aims to screen outstanding teachers through market competition. It is the underlying spirit of the Teacher

Education Act of 1994. Just like the idea of the reserve-type teacher introduced in the Teacher Education Act, universities set up teacher education centers to prepare teachers after approval by the Teacher Education Review Committee. Even if graduates do not work as teachers, they have the effect of nurturing future generations. This is what is meant by a "reserve" of excellent teachers. If quality means fitness for purpose, then teacher education evaluation should also examine the extent to which the processes at teacher education institutions answer to the idea of a reserve of excellent teachers by providing diversified education, adhering to existing values and ideals, and fulfilling justice. In other words, teacher education evaluation should not only be practical but also judicious (House, 1980) so that the evaluation system can urge teacher education institutions to develop their own characteristics to truly realize diverse competition on the teacher education market.

Just as described earlier, despite the different teacher education evaluation indicators for different institutions, the contents of the indicators are highly consistent and the evaluation process is the same. As far as the reinforcement effect of evaluation indicators on the operation of teacher education institutions is concerned, despite the differences between different indicators, the processes cultivated at teacher education institutions tend to be similar. In other words, it is worth considering whether teacher education evaluation can both account for the diversified teacher education model and guarantee teacher education quality.

Despite the emphasis on the capacity of institutions to evaluate themselves, the effects of the system in terms of its operation are limited

First, teacher education evaluation values the capacity of institutions to perform self-evaluations. A self-evaluation should be a comprehensive self-study that institutions spontaneously carry out to ensure quality and a systematic process of production outcome. It relies on extensive collection and analysis of data in order to boost institutional efficacy. It is a rational decision-making model (Dean and Bowen, 1994) and also a way to control internal quality; it is something that Taiwan has been trying to reinforce for years in its teacher education evaluation.

In Taiwan's teacher education evaluation system, however, the inclusion of the self-evaluation feature as part of the evaluation indicators often only emphasizes the self-evaluation contents prior to the site visit and the supply of evaluation materials is limited only to prior to the site visit. As a result, there is insufficient momentum to drive the self-evaluations carried out by teacher education institutions. As far as the institutions are concerned, the external review focuses on the implementation of the quality control designed at institutions (Pring, 1992) in order to confirm the control of educational quality at institutions. This is totally different from the self-evaluation model within institutions. Besides, the overall design of the system does not require institutions to submit self-study status and the actual operation is reinforced under the guidance of evaluation indicators to accordingly limit the operational efficacy of self-evaluations. This becomes self-evaluation for the sake of evaluation instead of improvement.

If teacher education evaluation is organic, to reinforce the self-evaluation function, the design should be based on the overall evaluation system. Teacher education evaluation, for example, should demand that institutions submit an improvement or achievement report on a yearly basis. In terms of the design of indicator contents, on the other hand, they should facilitate a systematic review of the education process at teacher education institutions, the collection and analysis of internal process data, discovery of problems, correction of problems, and even renewal of the teacher education system.

Evaluators' subjective judgement outweighs the evaluation profession because of insufficient training

According to the experience of Taiwan, it is assumed that evaluators can evaluate teacher education institutions after they have attended the workshop in addition to the false belief that scholars specializing in education are experts in teacher education. As a result, teacher education institutions often think, "evaluators do not understand what teacher education is really about" or "evaluators are not professional enough". This is the result not only of the evaluators' lack of professional knowledge of teacher education but also of the judgement evaluators have against indicators. Therefore, power inequality results between evaluators and the institutions being evaluated or evaluators interpret indicator contents subjectively during the evaluation process and so, accordingly, have an effect on the results of the evaluation (Chang *et al.*, 2007; Kao, 2004). In other words, the specialty background of evaluators should also be emphasized in teacher education evaluation.

Conclusion

The evaluation of teacher education institutions is the mechanism through which the state controls the quality of education under marketization. As far as its efficacy is concerned, the mechanism has indeed exercised a quality monitoring effect in Taiwan. Because of the use of evaluation indicators and results, however, the value of neo-liberalism in terms of diversified teacher education, given the operational logic of market competition and performance, has come to the same effect for the preparation process adopted by teacher education institutions. States should notice whether or not the effects of the similar teacher education processes have undermined the diversified market competition logic. It is also worth thinking whether or not the excessive leadership by the state in the preparation process is in conflict with the development of diversified characteristics of teacher education institutions regarding control over quality by means of an extremely strict evaluation system. If one has to take care of both market competition, and the performance of new managerialism and the purpose of the state to control quality, the design of the teacher education evaluation system should be adjusted. Suggestions include the following.

Evaluation should be focused on the outcome of teacher education in order for institutions to develop pluralistic characteristics

Teacher education evaluation in Taiwan is based on a system that places more emphasis on the actual operations at teacher education institutions, including staff size, compliance with regulatory requirements, and curricular planning, among others, and hence is of the bottom-line model, rather than the organic model that emphasizes the reformation of systems at teacher education institutions as a result of social transformation. Although neo-liberalism emphasizes market competition and performance and encourages institutions to develop pluralistic characteristics, as far as teacher education institutions in Taiwan are concerned, the emphasis placed on the actual operation, particularly the utilization of evaluation indicator contents and results, does not leave them much space for developing pluralistic characteristics. Therefore the contents of teacher education evaluation indicators should at least be based on the outcome of teacher education, that is the quality of prospective teachers, indicator contents, and evaluation orientation should be carefully planned so it no longer focuses on the actual operation in order to promote the development of pluralistic characteristics of teacher education institutions.

Teacher education evaluation results should be utilized to reflect the spirit of diversified market competition

According to the experience of Taiwan, the state utilizes the evaluation results to determine the enrollment numbers of the respective teacher education institutions with the expectation of reaching a balance between quality and quantity with its teacher education. The underlying idea of the Teacher Education Act, however, is to cultivate teachers in large numbers to support competition on the market. While the supply and demand of teacher education are reaching equilibrium and in light of the fact that few institutions back out of the market because of unfavorable evaluation results, the utilization of teacher education evaluation results should fulfill the logic of pluralistic competition on the market and should no longer be used as the criteria for adjusting numbers for recruitment. Instead, market competition should be allowed to determine the size of teacher education at institutions. Besides, teacher education institutions have been sufficiently experienced with cultivating teachers as the evaluation system has been implemented for years. Giving consideration to actual conditions, teacher education evaluation results should not be related to how the enrollment numbers at teacher education institutions are determined. This helps realize social justice through teacher education evaluation with its goal of fitness for purpose.

Design of the teacher education evaluation system should be reinforced to facilitate self-study carried out by teacher education institutions

According to the experience of Taiwan, the promotion of self-evaluations at teacher education institutions is recommended several times in an effort to revolutionize the evaluation system. To comply with evaluator indicators and requirements, on the other hand, teacher education institutions will focus their improvement on the results of the previous evaluation and provide descriptions of how improvement has been made, which does not work well in promoting the self-study of teacher education. To promote self-study of teacher education, there should be regulations governing self-study carried out by teacher education institutions to discover problems or innovate on systems throughout the teacher education process. Teacher education evaluation should require that institutions submit improvement reports on a yearly basis and include indicators requesting that institutions describe how they discovered and addressed problems or how systems are innovated and results are reflected upon in order to fulfill the purpose of self-study carried out by teacher education institutions. The indicators of teacher education evaluation, the professional attainments of evaluators, and the evaluation process should be designed in a way to strengthen the self-study function of teacher education institutions.

Professionalism of teacher education evaluators should be enhanced to ensure the proactive effects of evaluation

According to the experience of Taiwan, evaluators play a crucial role in actual evaluations, particularly because they are providing guidance, diagnosis, assistance, and judgement to teacher education institutions. The professionalism of evaluators is demonstrated through their interpretation of how teacher education works, the evaluation evidence, their knowledge of the different operations at different institutions, familiarity with evaluation indicators, and ability to determine conformity to indicator levels, among others. The profession of evaluators is particularly important if the aim of teacher education evaluation is to help institutions develop pluralistic characteristics, as it is the only way to guide and facilitate the pluralistic development of teacher education institutions.

References

Basinger, J. (1998) "Fight intensifies over accreditation of teacher education programs," *Chronicle of Higher Education*, 45 (7): A12–13.

Bok, D. (2003) *University in the Marketplace: The Commercialization of Higher Education*. Princeton, NJ: Princeton University Press.

Bradley, A. (1998) "Alternative accrediting organization taking form with federal assistance," *Education Week*, 17 (19): 1–3.

Campbell, C. and Rozsnyai, C. (2002) *Quality Assurance and the Development of Course Programmes.* Retrieved from: http://www.cepes.ro/publications/pdf/CampbellandRozsnyai.pdf.

Chang, C. S. (2006) "An analysis of the teacher education center evaluation," *Contemporary Educational Research Quarterly*, 14 (1): 25–54 (in Chinese).

Chang, S. R., Fang, D. L., Chiu, A. L., and Lee, C. H. (2007) "The evaluation of institutions for teacher education: the evaluation system of NCATE and its implications," *Kaohsiung Normal University Journal*, 22: 1–20 (in Chinese).

Chou, Y. W. (2012) "Opinions on the establishment of minimum baseline for teacher education in Taiwan," *Taiwan Educational Review Monthly*, 1 (3): 8–10 (in Chinese).

Dean, J. W. Jr, and Bowen, D. E. (1994) "Management theory and total quality: improving research and practice through theory development," *Academy of Management Review*, 19 (3): 392–418.

Department of Middle Education, Ministry of Education (2010) *Quality Prospective Teachers at an Adequate Quantity: Announcement of Teacher Education Evaluation Results for Universities in 2009.* Retrieved from: http://www.edu.tw/news.aspx?news_sn=3140 (in Chinese).

Feigenbaum, A. V. (1982) "Quality and business growth today," *Quality Progress*, 15 (11): 22–5.

Galley, M. (2003) "Alternative accrediting body gets recognition," *Education Week*, 23 (6): 6–7.

Graham, P. A., Lyman, R. W., and Trow, M. (1995) *Accountability of College and Universities.* New York: Columbia University Press.

Guba, E. G. and Lincoln, Y. S. (1989) *Fourth Generation Evaluation.* Newbury Park, CA: Sage.

Higher Education Evaluation and Accreditation Council of Taiwan (2012) *2012 Universities Teacher Education Evaluation Plan and Implementation.* Retrieved from: http://tece.heeact.edu.tw/upload_file/news/33/fb2afb60.doc (in Chinese).

House, E. R. (1980) *Evaluating with Validity.* Beverly Hills, CA: Sage.

Huang, J. L. (2008) "An analysis on NCATE's accreditation of teacher education in the United States," *Educational Policy Forum*, 11 (3): 113–42.

Huang, J. L. (2013) "A study on teacher education evaluation in Taiwan: the perspective from quality assurance," *Journal of Educational Administration and Evaluation*, 15: 57–84.

Kao, S. F. (2004) "Reflections on teacher education evaluation: some un-examined issues," *Bulletin of Educational Resources and Research*, 29: 359–80 (in Chinese).

Kuo, S. F. (2014) "Effectiveness analysis of planning policies in the amount of teacher education in Taiwan," *Journal of Research on Measurement and Statistics*, 21: 61–86 (in Chinese).

Lu, C. C. (2012) "Issues found in the new cycle of teacher education evaluation of universities," *Taiwan Educational Review Monthly*, 1 (13): 29–31 (in Chinese).

Marginson, S. (2007) "The new higher education landscape: public and private goods, in global/national/local settings," in S. Merginson (ed.), *Prospects of Higher Education.* Rotterdam: Sense, pp. 29–77.

Ministry of Education (2002) *Regulations for Evaluation of Universities with Teacher Education Program.* Retrieved from: http://www.rootlaw.com.tw/LawContent.aspx?LawID=A040080041003600-0931223 (in Chinese).

Ministry of Education (2004) *Regulations for Evaluation of Universities with Teacher Education Center*. Retrieved from: http://www.rootlaw.com.tw/LawContent.aspx?LawID=A040080041003600-0931223 (in Chinese).

Ministry of Education (2006) *Regulations for Evaluation of Universities with Teacher Education*. Retrieved from: http://www.edu.tw/pages/detail.aspx?Node=1376andPage=9003andIndex=3andWID=112353c-88d0-4bdb-914a-77a4952aa893 (in Chinese).

Ministry of Education (2012) *White Book of Teacher Education in ROC: Promoting the Teaching Profession to Cultivate Future Talent*. Taipei: MOE (in Chinese).

Murray, F. B. (2001) "From consensus standards to evidence of claims: assessment and accreditation in the case of teacher education," *New Directions for Higher Education*, 2001 (113): 49–66.

Ou, C. H. (2002) *Education Test and Assessment*. Taipei: Psy. Ed. (in Chinese).

Patton, M. Q. (2000) "Utilization-focused evaluation," in D. L. Stufflebeam, G. F. Madaus, and T. Kellaghan (eds), *Evaluation Models: Viewpoints on Educational and Human Services Evaluation*, 2nd edn. Boston: Kluwer Academic, pp. 425–38.

Pring, R. (1992) "Standards and quality in education," *British Journal of Educational Studies*, 40 (1): 4–22.

Roberts, P. and Peters, M. A. (2008) *Neoliberalism, Higher Education and Research*. Rotterdam: Sense.

Sanders, J. R. (2002) "Presidential address: on mainstreaming evaluation," *American Journal of Evaluation*, 23 (3): 253–9.

Stake, R. E. (2004) *Standard-based and Responsive Evaluation*. Thousand Oaks, CA: Sage.

Stufflebeam, D. L. (2000) "The CIPP model for evaluation," in D. L. Stufflebeam, G. F. Madaus, and T. Kellaghan (eds), *Evaluation Models: Viewpoints on Educational and Human Services Evaluation*, 2nd edn. Boston, MA: Kluwer Academic, pp. 279–317.

Stufflebeam, D. L. and Shinkfield, A. J. (1985) *Systematic Evaluation: A Self-instruction Guide to Theory and Practice*. Boston, MA: Kluwer-Nijhoff.

Wang, B. J. and Wang, L. F. (1999) "A study on the accreditation system of NCATE and its implication for our nation's teacher education program evaluation," *Journal of Research on Elementary and Secondary Education*, 4: 1–34 (in Chinese).

Whitty, G., Power, S., and Halpin, D. (1998) *Devolution and Choice in Education: The School, the State and the Market*. Melbourne: Australian Council for Educational Research.

Wholey, J. S. (1979) *Evaluation: Promise and Performance*. Washington, DC: Urban Institute.

Wu, C. J., Huang, J. L., and Chang, M. W. (2011) "The past and future of teacher education policy in Taiwan," in National Academy of Educational Research (ed.), *The Past and Future of Hundred-year Education in Taiwan*. New Taipei City: National Academy of Educational Research, pp. 1–20 (in Chinese).

12 State control vs the market mechanism

Taiwan's experience with teacher education

Jia-Li Huang

Introduction

Historically, the territory of Taiwan has been ruled by various different powers, including the Dutch and the Japanese; later, following World War II, it fell under the administration of the Chinese Nationalist authorities. The teacher education system remained controlled by the government in the political and social climate of these eras. Teacher education was entirely under state control until 1987, when the government lifted Martial Law, and democratic ideas and the concept of market diversity blossomed and led to a multitude of changes in education policy. In terms of teacher education policy, the state's monopoly over the market is clearly embodied by the Normal Education Law of 1979, which provided a legal basis for a unified normal education system that permitted only teacher colleges and normal universities to train teachers. In addition, with Taiwan moving toward democracy politically, different voices that advocated openness and liberalization from the government and the normal education system's long-held monopoly began to emerge (Huang, 2014). A particular problem was the structural unemployment in the 1990s and with the numbers of unemployed university graduates in Taiwan increasing year after year resulted in a "highly educated but unemployed workforce" (Weng, 1996; Yang, 2002). Moreover, due to fact that the Normal Education Law was unable to sufficiently reflect the requirements of relevant interest groups and those of society (Syoug and Ji, 2012), and because of the changes in the social structure and in the political, economic, cultural, and educational landscapes, new and pluralistic values and perspectives prompted the Normal Education Law to be renamed the Teacher Education Act (Chen, 1998), implying a shift toward a market-based model for teacher education. Therefore, the Teacher Education Act of 1994 became the watershed moment for government-controlled and market-oriented teacher education in Taiwan.

On the other hand, following the promulgation of the Teacher Education Act, the number and types of teacher training institutions have proliferated. Comprehensive universities have since been permitted to join traditional teacher's colleges and normal universities in delivering teacher education curricula via the establishment of teacher education centers, thus allowing market competition mechanisms to operate in cultivating the best qualified teachers. However, the government did not immediately relinquish the quality assurance control over teacher education. It has retained the authority on areas such as defining teacher education programs, awarding teacher certificates, and evaluating the quality of teacher education programs in order to ensure teacher quality. In the country's experience of liberalizing its teacher education market, the supply and demand of teachers were factors that were not taken into proper consideration.

The balancing of quantity supplied and demanded of teachers has also been historically a crucial factor affecting teacher education in Taiwan (Chang, 2002; Huang, 2014). After teachers who were Japanese nationals withdrew from Taiwan in 1949, there was a shortage of teachers available to fill the gap left behind in schools throughout the territory, and an expedient approach for recommending and recruiting new teachers became the preferred strategy. Teacher candidates were allowed to teach in schools and later required to take professional courses in education. The system of selecting teachers first and later requiring them to participate in professional courses in education became the norm in Taiwan for the purpose of preparing qualified teachers. This allowed not-yet-qualified individuals to work as teachers, which became the government's preferred practice in filling teachers' vacancies. On the other hand, problems with teaching quality also arose with these unqualified teachers. Following the promulgation of the Teacher Education Act, however, a large number of reserve teachers were trained. This resulted in situations in which holders of a teacher's certificate were unable to hold teaching jobs. There have also been cases where certified teachers became ineffective in their teaching. All these have pointed to issues associated with the quality of teacher education following the liberalization of the teacher education market. Even though the government liberalized the market for teacher education, it did not anticipate and was not able to respond in a timely manner to the problem with under-qualified teachers as a result of the increased supply and changes in society. At the same time, this problem also revealed the fact that the existing teacher education system was poorly designed.

In 2004 the Plan for Teacher Education Quantity was introduced, allowing teacher colleges and normal universities to be transformed into comprehensive universities and at the same time reducing the number of teachers being trained, and instituting measures such as teacher education evaluation and teacher qualification examinations. This effectively reduced the number of newly trained teachers by 50 per cent within five years compared with the original plan, with the objective of stabilizing the supply of certified teachers after 2012. Once the number of teachers being trained in the system was stabilized, the design mechanism of the teacher education quality assurance system immediately sprang into action to tackle new issues for the government. In particular, with the prevailing international trends and the standards-based teacher education policy orientation announced in 2006, Teacher Profession Standards (TPSs) and related practices have become an urgent matter for the government.

After the quantity of pre-service teachers stabilized, producing core documents that specify the professional standards for teachers so as to ensure their quality became the primary task of the government. However, in a democratic society, it is necessary to take into consideration the views and interests of all stakeholders involved. A number of TPSs created at the national level have sought consensus and recognition from the widest stakeholders possible since 2006, but thus far there has yet to be a single set of national professional standards for teachers. Moreover, TPSs applied to the professional development of teachers at different stages include issuing teaching licenses, assessing beginning teachers, evaluating teachers' performance and granting advanced certificates. All these require integration with existing practices in pre-service education, education practicum, teachers' professional development evaluation, and the teaching and mentoring teacher system, and they await the completion and issuance of TPSs, including the systematic planning of the specialization course and the transitions to various stages. Therefore, with over a century of practice in teacher education, the following topics concerning Taiwan's experience may be valuable to other countries. At the same time this experience can also serve as guidelines for Taiwan when the country reviews and makes adjustments of its own teacher education policy and practices.

Insights from the history of state-controlled and market-oriented teacher education

During the course of the country's teacher education development, Taiwan was moving back and forth between government control and market-oriented practices, and attempts have been made to find a balance between the two extremes. This experience offers the following insights.

The function of the state in identifying the role of teachers

Judging from Taiwan's own experience, the choice between state-controlled and market-based teacher education models depends on how the government views the role of "teachers" and what they can do for the country. From the time Taiwan was under Dutch and Japanese rule, teachers have played the role of promoting the national ideology for the country and a model for the society. In this respect, the government imposed control over teachers' everyday life and the course of their teacher training. The government manipulated the meanings behind the education policy and expected teachers to adhere to the policy's values, thus making teachers' work part of service to the nation.

In examining the course of teachers' status toward professionalization, a teacher's role is to a large extent influenced by the government, which has indeed become the body charged with defining teachers' roles and responsibilities. For example, in the early twentieth century in the United Kingdom, the government advocated that teachers should "act professionally". The emphasis was that teachers should become professionals and a model for society in terms of how they conducted themselves. In addition, teachers should also be patriotic individuals who take action to effect social progress. Teachers should never voice their discontent, nor should they complain about the legitimacy of education. The concept of teachers behaving and acting professionally thus became an ideology, a symbol of obedience to the authority (Sykes, 1990, pp. 76–7). Therefore, when the government expected teachers to behave in a certain manner, a kind of rhetoric aimed at control and manipulation under the guise of the "teaching profession" easily became a pretext for the government to demand or inhibit specific behavior from teachers. The so-called "teaching profession" under these circumstances represented an empty proper noun with no substantive meaning.

However, by the mid-twentieth century, the teaching profession in the UK had achieved "reasonable independence" under the British government. Not only did this independence appear in teacher education curricula, teachers' autonomy was also asserted in the classroom, and the emphasis was placed on teachers' devotion to teaching (Hoyle and John, 1995; Lawn, 1996). The relationship between teachers and the government became that of a partnership. The government respected teachers' autonomy, thus helping teachers to create self-respect for their profession, shaping an image of the country's fine teachers, and establishing a professional status for teachers. These were the conditions made in exchange for teachers' political and economic roles on behalf of the country. They were also designed to prevent the power from being taken by other political parties and also to prevent teachers from acquiring a leftist ideology (Hoyle and John, 1995; Ozga, 1995). The professional status and autonomy of teachers are considered "licensed professionalism". Given the consistency of school curricula, identical subjects and time, as well as formal examination, teachers have very limited professional autonomy. As a result the professional status of teachers does not stem from their irreplaceability but is granted by the government. This status is also affected by the political and economic landscapes (Ozga and Lawn, 1981). Thus the establishment of the teacher's role was deeply influenced by the government, especially in the context of the era's political, economic, and social climate where teachers were on the same side as the state, and the state required the support of teachers who could function as a stabilizing force in society.

This type of relationship between teachers and the national government, as happened in British history, has also occurred in the history of Taiwan. As described in Chapters 1 and 2 of this book, before 1949 Taiwan was subject to the indoctrination of Japanese imperialism. Local Taiwanese teachers were trained in accordance with the Governor General's Normal School Regulations established under the Taiwan Education Act of 1919. As the Japanese government considered the political orientation of teachers very important for its Kōminka (Japanization) movement in education (Lee, 1997), teachers were part of the strategy in communicating the government's will in education to the people. At the time, due to political considerations, the Japanese government imposed restrictions on the way Taiwanese teachers received training. Local teachers were only allowed to participate in teacher education programs conducted by the teacher education division of the Japanese School and to become elementary school teachers, who were less likely to influence the political thought of the younger generations. Not until 1942 did the Taiwanese gain the opportunity to receive teacher education for the purpose of obtaining teacher qualifications at the secondary school level (Tsau and Liang, 2002).

Especially during the mid-twentieth century, the general consensus in Taiwan was that teachers represented a spiritual national defense and they were the media through which a cohesive national identity was forged (as explained in Chapter 3 of this work). As a result, the national policy on teacher education remained conservative and rigid. Only the "normal education system [was] allowed to train elementary and secondary school teachers, and the government [was] responsible for establishing teacher education institutions to implement educational programs based on the Three Principles of the People" (National Construction Planning Commission, 1970, p. 31). At that time teacher education policies were dominated by a unitary ideology under strong political control (Syoug and Ji, 2002), which was evidently in competition with the market and thus inconsistent with the philosophy of diversity in teacher education.

From Taiwan's experience, teacher education was moving back and forth between state control and market competition, which was obviously the result of how the government viewed the role of the teacher. In addition, it was also related to the political, social and economic conditions of the time. When a society experiences political, economic, or social turmoil, teachers play a core role in stabilizing the country's political and economic conditions. The government then expects teachers' political orientation to be in harmony with the government's political ideology and educational requirements. During economic downturns, teachers are also expected to work together to ride out the tough times and be a role model for society. This meant that teacher education was under the control of the state, and, as a result in areas such as teacher selection and participation in formal and informal courses during the training process, the government closely monitored school curricula, pedagogical approaches, and the rules of examination.

Extent of state involvement affects degree of state control and market-based teacher education practices

According to the social closure theory of New Weberian sociology scholars on teaching professionals (Huang, 2008), it is possible to distinguish the formation of and status and class awareness between professional and non-professional points of view with respect to social boundaries when conducting sociological analysis. According to the perspectives of social closure theory, persons who are qualified may pass through this boundary and become a member of the professional group, and all members of the group must conduct themselves in accordance with the professional body's requirements. Therefore, those who would like to be members within the closure must first meet the standards and qualifications to pass through the boundaries. Those who have been admitted to the elite group must then observe and adhere to the group's regulations, such as practicing professional standards and complying with education ethics in order to jointly shoulder collective responsibility. Thus the social closure must exclude the unqualified, or else the status-group awareness of the qualified is not easy to take shape and be maintained. More importantly, members within the closure are supposed to take on collective responsibility together, and to the teaching profession, continuing to improve teaching, while gaining professional knowledge and putting the interests of students first are objectives that members within the closure must all share. It would otherwise be very difficult to develop the sense of professional status among teachers and not easy for teaching professionals to form the social closure phenomenon.

However, speaking from the perspective of teachers' professional status and culture, it is not enough that members within the social closure share their common responsibilities. It also requires involvement of the government. A profession needs a strong government to act as the intermediary in order to maintain its uniqueness and exclusivity in the market. Under the lawful knowledge authorized by government and support of professional-level differential, experts were allowed to transform their scarce resources (knowledge and skills) into an exclusive form of status and compensation. Compared with individuals or groups that belong to this particular occupation, it is necessary to first acquire the knowledge sanctioned by the government and then apply the knowledge and skills in an appropriate manner to produce and defend the rarity of professional expertise, as well as passing the established standards and procedures required to enter the profession (Larson, 1977, p. 15). Thus the state must be able to allow teachers' professional knowledge to become legally sanctioned knowledge, so that teachers may acquire professional knowledge and skills through the course of the teacher preparation process, transforming their professional status and level of compensation. Moreover, those who become teachers will also be compliant with standards and procedures required by the government and can thus provide professional teaching services.

Apart from the fact that the state must administer professional standards and procedures through licensed professional knowledge and classification, it is also necessary for the state to safeguard the interests of consumers. As there is information asymmetry between professional service providers and consumers, it is necessary for the government to control and regulate the conduct of professional service providers through licensing and certification. This allows national requirements to conform to the public interest theory of regulation (Graddy, 1991; Huang, 2006; Jang, 2003). The state employs the licensing system as a mechanism to protect public interest and to ensure that holders of licensed certificates are able to provide qualified professional services that meet the society's needs. Comparatively speaking, the government may also intervene in the standards and procedures for acquiring professional licenses for the purpose of protecting consumers (Sykes, 1992). Thus one can see that when the state decides on teachers' professional knowledge and the professional standards and procedures for acquiring such professional status, the state's attitude represents the sole basis for the legalization and strengthening of professional services (Larson, 1977). As a result, at the two ends of state control and market-based mechanism, the state's attitude toward teacher certification will affect the determination of the teacher education model, knowledge content, and the standards and procedures for acquiring the certificates.

In terms of Taiwan's experience, judging from the development of teacher education policies (as outlined in Chapter 2) and that of the ideologies and theories of teacher education (Chapter 3), during the years in which the country was shrouded in political and economic uncertainty, the mechanism for state control of teacher education was quite clear. Whether it was viewed in terms of the unitary avenue for training teachers, implementation of the concept of competency-based teacher education or the awarding of teacher certificates, teacher colleges and normal universities were the only route to obtain teacher certificates. It can be seen that the Taiwan government has been conscientious and careful about protecting the teaching profession. Complete control by the state would ensure that only sanctioned knowledge, qualification and procedures were administered in teacher education programs, and that teachers' ideology was being imposed as well. With Taiwan's democratic movement came liberalization and openness of teacher education. However, the attitude pervasive in Taiwan toward the teaching profession did not seem to have much effect on the control mechanism despite the proliferation of teacher education institutions. Teacher pre-service programs (Chapter 5 and Chapter 8), education practicum curricula (Chapter 6), teacher qualification examination approaches and teacher education evaluation (Chapter 11) are the government's control mechanisms in teacher education under diverse market models. As a matter of course, the reduced demand for teacher education in the market has forced some universities to give up their teacher education programs. However, as far as the quality of teacher education programs is concerned, the government is still in control, and the level of teachers' professional expertise has remained the primary concern of the government.

Mechanisms employed by the state in market-based teacher education policy

Following the lifting of Martial Law in Taiwan, the new democratic concepts in society resulted in wider participation and oversight from the citizens. This replaced the past attitudes that blindly advocated teachers' professional autonomy or teachers' major responsibility for maintaining social order. As mentioned in the Introduction of this book, the choices, competition, and supervision required as the operational logic in a neoliberal market also apply to the work of teachers. This causes the original priority of the teaching profession to facilitate citizens' compulsory education and their well-being to shift to the new idea that teachers must also be subject to market competition, so that the teaching profession will also comply with market order in a changing time and will also accept control or oversight management (Whitty, 1997). Taiwan also developed the competency-based teacher education model (Chapter 3), which is an approach to overseeing teachers' pedagogical abilities through a licensing strategy, thus allowing the government to gain legitimacy in monitoring teachers' teaching competences (Jones and Moore, 1993). Compared with the level of control imposed by the government initially, apparently the competency-based teacher education model has strengthened the government and society's ability to oversee individual teachers' teaching competences.

However, with the spread of neoliberal philosophy, the logic behind market management has made it possible for the government not to expand its authority directly. Instead a national standards and oversight mechanism can be established to promote various reforms that meet the government's expectations (Popkewitz, 1991). This new mechanism for teacher education management includes not only the design of the rules and regulations (e.g. awarding of teacher certificates, teacher evaluation, teachers' professional development and teacher education evaluation) but also symbolic control of the government via the use of agents (Jones and Moore, 1993). Similar to teacher education evaluation (Chapter 11), the Higher Education Evaluation and Accreditation Council of Taiwan has been established to provide evaluation and accreditation services on behalf of the government, which acts only on the results of the evaluation process carried out by professionals. The role of the "agent" has now become a mechanism for government control and enforcement. In addition, Taiwan has employed the use of information processing strategies for the purposes of monitoring and control of teacher education. For example, publications and Internet resources such as the *Statistics Yearbook of Teacher Education* and the *In-service Teacher Education Information Web* utilize statistical functions and social science research capabilities (Popkewitz, 1991) to establish a mechanism to monitor the status of teacher education development. Real statistical data is provided as a reference for the system's adjustment and rectification.

Furthermore, the number of teachers prepared via the market-oriented approach in teacher education has underscored the issue with unstable teacher quality, and the government must consider a new control system design in addition to replacing the traditional route for teacher education. For example, the teacher evaluation system (Chapter 9) has been resisted by teachers in Taiwan, and, as a result, this proposed practice has yet to be adopted into law, which prompted the government to modify the practice of the teachers' professional development evaluation system (Chapters 7 and 9) and to become the facilitator for promoting teachers' current professional development. This allows teaching observation processes and tools that are familiar in teacher evaluation, portfolio assessment, and TPSs operating procedures to be included in teacher evaluation, which also helps with the subsequent incorporation of teacher evaluation into the Teachers' Act. In addition, teacher education evaluation (Chapter 11) has entered the accreditation system of the second cycle. The number of teachers prepared by teacher education institutions can be controlled via teacher education evaluation. At the same time, the reduced demand in teacher education will no doubt be an important consideration for some teacher education institutions in their decisions to exit the market.

Therefore, despite the country's move toward a market-oriented teacher education model, Taiwan's experience tells us that the government remains in control of teacher education. In response to this new market-oriented teacher education model, strategies employed by the government include layers of control mechanisms imposed on the process of teachers' professional development. They also include a network of symbolic control units that the government utilizes to control market-oriented teacher education quality and the quantity of teachers via oversight and management.

The design of the teacher education system is susceptible to imbalances in supply and demand

After the advent of compulsory education in Taiwan, the shortage of available and qualified teachers was once a serious issue. To solve this problem, the government recruited a large number of substitute teachers via recommendation, application, and examination. These temporary teachers were then required to participate in short-term training programs and workshops to rectify shortcomings in professional knowledge and skills (Huang, 2014). Indeed, many difficulties were encountered in maintaining teacher quality during years in which there was a shortfall of available teachers, and in-service training for teachers and an examination process had to be introduced as a stopgap measure. However, the issue of teacher shortages was readily solved upon adoption of the market-oriented education model.

Following Taiwan's democratization, ideas of liberty and democracy became widespread. Market-based competition and operation logic has also been reflected in the teacher education policy. Since the promulgation of the Teacher Education Act in 1994, there were once as many as 74 teacher education institutions in Taiwan that offered teacher education programs. However, only 52 institutions remain at present (Chapters 8 and 11). The universities withdrew from the teacher education market either because they were judged to have provided substandard curricula, or because the market for teacher education has simply shrunk and it became too costly to continue to administer the program. Some universities withdrew due to mergers with other institutions. All these factors have contributed to the current stable quantity of trainees in the teacher education programs.

In terms of Taiwan's experience, whether the country was experiencing teacher shortage or a surplus supply, the end result always involved uneven teacher quality, which had a negative impact on the design of the teacher education system. As teachers' professional status and image are still valued in this country, the problem associated with the supply and demand of teachers via the education system may offer a few pointers to other countries with similar issues.

Standards-based teacher education policy seeking balance between state control and market-oriented models

The development of standards-based teacher education policies in Taiwan is based on the premise of stabilizing the number of teachers supplied through the education system, followed by the teacher quality enhancement plan. In particular, determining the professional standards for teachers (as described in Chapter 4) is the core task. The next step is the development of teachers' professional performance at various stages. Corresponding assessment methods are then designed as the basis for awarding a teacher license or certificate. Taiwan's participation in developing standards-based teacher education policy has been consistent with international trends. Adjustments are made to the development process based on Taiwan's political and social context, and attention is paid especially to teacher education institutions and teachers' opinions, which have an impact on the design of related systems of practice.

As Taiwan has liberalized the teacher education market, the government remains in control of teacher education in general. The only difference is that the government has lifted the restrictions on available teacher education avenues, although professional education courses and the education practicum are still under the administration of the government. The authority to approve education curricula in a state-controlled setting (Chapter 5) was inconsistent with the spirit of autonomy. As a result the government eventually returned the authority of planning and designing professional education curricula to individual higher institutions. With respect to the implementation of educational practicum programs (Chapter 6), teacher education institutions must comply with government regulations and carry out a variety of learning and assessment activities. In addition, in-service teachers continue to resist the implementation of the teacher evaluation program, causing the government to face challenges when enforcing state control over teacher education in a market-oriented and pluralistic scenario. Under these circumstances, standards-based teacher education policy represents the efforts of the government in its attempt to seek a balance point in the face of diverse teacher education institutions.

Standards-based teacher education policies are therefore guided by TPSs, allowing the results of the evaluation of teacher quality to be the object of government control. The authority to approve professional teacher education curricula in the teacher education process will likely be shifted to universities offering teacher education programs. However, on reviewing the results of teacher education, it can be concluded that the same also applies to practicum curricula. It is advisable to award teacher certificates based on the results of assessment rather than imposing a large number of hurdles along the teacher education process. The government will then be able to strike a possible balance between state control and market competition.

Systematic institutions planning and establishing adjustment process

From the perspective of historical development, changes in a system imply a design failure in the old policy or system which caused it to fail to adapt to the new social environment. The government has thus developed an alternative measure of governance (Huang, 2008). The purpose of the design of the policy or system is to develop a deliberate strategy for solving the problem. The value of the system itself and its response to the social environment's context facilitate the production of desired results (Chien, 2004; Chou, 1995). Thus the design of a policy or system does not only involve techniques of the problem resolution strategy but also the philosophy, value, and significance of the supporting policy or institution behind it (Schneider and Sidney, 2009). Therefore, during the planning and adjustment of a system, the implications include the philosophy and value of the results expected by the government as well as the approaches in response to the social context. Furthermore, the purpose of the design and adjustment of the system is to resolve institutional problems arising from the social and cultural context. Basically the strategies themselves for solving the problem are neither right nor wrong. The institution itself is constantly changing and evolving; the system's designers and viewpoints of the analysts also affect it. Thus a single issue cannot be solved by a single strategy; it is necessary for the policy or institutional decision-makers to conduct systematic analysis and form a structural design of the system (Huang, 2013).

From the perspective of the system's historical development, Taiwan's teacher education policy or institutional change was not only consistent with the institutional design being affected by political, social, and economic factors, but also influenced by how the government viewed the teaching profession and its value. In the era of state-controlled teacher education, from the selection of teachers in the workforce to curricular implementation and the awarding of teacher certificates, a single teacher education model monopolized the teacher education market. With subsequent changes in society, the teacher education market was liberalized and the number of teacher trainees proliferated. As the government continued to emphasize the importance of teachers' professional expertise, even though comprehensive universities have since been allowed to offer teacher education programs, the government has retained the right to review and approve teacher education curricula and the education practicum. The change was made to certifying teachers through qualification examinations and imposing quotas on the teacher education enrollment based on teacher evaluation results, which resulted in a control strategy for reducing the supply of teachers via the education system. It can be seen that the initial idea was to end the monopoly of the state-controlled teacher education market and to institute a free market competition model to solve the unitary teacher education model. However, the end result was that market competition created an excessive supply of teachers with uneven teacher quality. In order to solve the problem of uneven teacher quality, qualification examinations and teacher education evaluation were created. The teacher qualification examinations, however, were unable to truly test teachers' practice performance, while the teacher education evaluation failed to reflect the diversity of programs offered by teacher education institutions due to the unitary teacher education process. Efforts to create institutional designs to resolve these issues have led to new problems with their implementation, causing linear thinking-based problem resolution to be tackled by means of systemic thinking strategies.

As mentioned in Chapter 10, it is necessary for teacher education to generate a collaborative network that ties together central government, local governments, teacher education institutions, schools, and other academic societies in order to make the quality of teacher education and teachers the central focus for cooperation among members of this network. In turn, this will allow teacher education institutions to adapt and respond to the expectations of government and society, and to address the education requirements of local governments in their design of pre-service teacher education curricula. To be sure, schools should also closely cooperate with teacher education institutions to provide internship and practicum opportunities. The academic societies can also develop a teacher evaluation system based on individual school and local government requirements. The system planning shaped by this network also includes the core requirements of TPSs at the national level and divides the teacher specialization process into stages, with the stated aim of providing guidance to teachers at all stages of their professional development. This network also facilitates cooperation between local governments, schools, and teachers in order to improve teachers' professional knowledge and capabilities (as further detailed in Chapter 7). Based on Taiwan's experience in teacher education, it is apparent that systematic decision-making is one of the key factors to the successful implementation of teacher education policy.

Conclusion

The development of teacher education in Taiwan has over a century of history, from Dutch and Japanese rule up to and including the current administration. Teacher education policies and the associated institutions have become more diverse and complex. The most critical issues concern the quantity of teachers supplied through the teacher education system and the overall quality of teachers. From the effects and implementation of teacher education philosophy to the current standards-based teacher education, the government has established professional standards for teachers and planned a comprehensive, multi-stage process to increase the professional level of teachers. A number of systems have also been designed to solve the current problems associated with education curricula, education practicum programs, and the professional development of teachers. In addition, the development of universities offering teacher education programs, and control and management designs such as teacher evaluation, teacher education alliances, and teacher education evaluation as well as the management and design of such programs, are also the basis on which a balance between state control and market-oriented models can be struck. In Taiwan, the teaching profession is still highly valued; one possible key to improving teacher quality in the proliferation and liberalization of teacher education institutions lies in the standards-based teacher education approach, which is the temporary objective at the current stage.

However, during the implementation of the standards-based approach, it is necessary to emphasize the development of teachers' professional capacities and to achieve a concept of post-standardization reform to enhance their professional status. Decision-makers must first be concerned with this approach, i.e. teacher education policy and system design must be based on trust for teachers and on the belief that teachers have the ability and are capable of taking responsibility. They should also acknowledge teachers' position and commitment to change their teaching (Hargreaves and Shirley, 2007). This will ensure that the implementation of standards must be flexible and possess guidance as an attribute, rather than simply restriction or control. Only in this way will the standards-based approach be spared the historical mistake of the competency-based approach, which has restricted itself to concrete behaviors that are observable and assessable. Taking New Zealand as an example, although New Zealand has adopted a standards-based teacher education policy, no research evidence has suggested that the quality of teachers may be improved by adopting a specific set of standards. For example, in terms of New Zealand students' achievements in international competitions, such as the Programme for International Student Assessment (PISA) and Progress in International Reading Literacy Study (PIRLS), students from New Zealand performed better than those from England, with teachers from New Zealand conducting teaching based on a student-oriented approach (Thrupp, 2006). The reason behind New Zealand's adoption of a standards-based teacher education approach was a response to the diverse teacher education market. Thus the government adopted the standards-based approach as a quality assurance mechanism to provide guidance to teachers in developing their teaching practice. However, the professional standards have not been used as a requirement to compel teachers to produce a certain level of output. Therefore, the standards associated with the standards-based teacher education policy must be able to encourage teachers to willingly enhance their professional knowledge and skills, rather than employing the standards as a means of control, to apply political pressure, or to compel teachers to produce in order to achieve a certain level of performance. This is a key factor that any country should take into consideration when contemplating the adoption of the standards-based approach for the purposes of controlling teacher education quality and the quality of teachers.

References

Chang, D. F. (2002) "Exploring the teacher education policy and the feasibility of establishing a supply and demand mechanism," in Teachers Education Society of ROC (ed.), *Teacher Education Policies and Reflections*. Taipei: Pro-Ed Publishing, pp. 51–72 (in Chinese).

Chen, K. H. (1998) "Analysis of changes of teacher education system in Taiwan," *Bulletin of Educational Research*, 23: 171–95 (in Chinese).

Chien, H. C. (2004) "The implementation predicament and the solutions of the Grade 1–9 curriculum policy," *Educational Policy Forum*, 7 (1): 19–40 (in Chinese).

Chou, C. T. (1995) *Public Policies: Study of Contemporary Policies and Scientific Theories*. Taipei: Chu Liu (in Chinese).

Graddy, E. (1991) "Toward a general theory of occupational regulation," *Social Science Quarterly*, 72 (4): 676–95.

Hargreaves, A. and Shirley, D. (2007) "The coming age of post-standardization," *Education Week*. Retrieved from: http://www.bc.edu/bc_org/rvp/pubaf/07/Hargreaves_EdWeek.pdf.

Hoyle, E. and John, P. (1995) "The idea of a profession," in E. Holy and P. John (eds), *Professional Knowledge and Professional Practice*. London: Cassell, pp. 1–18.

Huang, J. L. (2006) "A historical analysis of teacher certification in Taiwan since 1990," *Journal of Educational Research and Development*, 2 (1): 63–91 (in Chinese).

Huang, J. L. (2008) "The change of political rationalities for management of teacher quality in Great Britain: an analysis of governmentality," *Chung Cheng Educational Studies*, 7 (2): 129–61 (in Chinese).

Huang, J. L. (2013) "Structural logic analysis on the education practicum institution design in Taiwan," *Journal of Educational Research and Development*, 9 (3): 79–90 (in Chinese).

Huang, J. L. (2014) "The institution of obtaining teacher qualification since 1949 in Taiwan: perspective from historical institutionalism," *Chung Cheng Educational Studies*, 13 (1): 1–43 (in Chinese).

Jang, C. L. (2003) "An empirical examination of the political economy of occupational licensing in the US healthcare system," *Journal of European and American Studies*, 33 (1): 1–56 (in Chinese).

Jones, L. and Moore, R. (1993) "Education, competence and the control of expertise," *British Journal of the Sociology of Education*, 14 (4): 385–97.

Larson, M. S. (1977) *The Rise of Professionalism: A Sociological Analysis*. Berkeley, CA: University of California Press.

Lawn, M. (1996) *Modern Times? Work, Professionalism and Citizenship in Teaching*. London: Falmer Press.

Lee, Y. H. (1997) *Normal Education System of Taiwan During the Japanese Colonial Period*. Taipei: SMC Publishing (in Chinese).

National Construction Planning Commission (1970) *Study of How to Improve Normal Education in Taiwan*. Taipei: Editors (in Chinese).

Ozga, J. (1995) "Deskilling a profession: professionalism, deprofessionalisation and the new managerialism," in H. Busher and R. Saran (eds), *Managing Teachers as Professionals in School*. London: Kogan Page, p. 21–37.

Ozga, J. and Lawn, M. (1988) 'Schoolwork: interpreting the labour process of teaching," *British Journal of Sociology of Education*, 9 (3): 323–36.

Popkewitz, T. S. (1991) *A Political Sociology of Educational Reform: Power/Knowledge in Teaching, Teacher Education, and Research*. New York: Teacher College Press.

Schneider, A. and Sidney, M. (2009) "What is next for policy design and social construction theory?" *Policy Studies Journal*, 37 (1): 103–19.

Sykes, G. (1990) "Fostering teacher professionalism in schools," in R. F. Elmore and Associate (eds), *Restructure Schools: The Next Generation of Educational Reform*. 59-96) San Francisco: Jossey-Bass, pp. 59–96.

Sykes, G. (1992) "Teacher licensure and certification," in M. C. Alkin (ed.), *Encyclopedia of Educational Research*. New York: American Educational Research Association, pp. 1352–9.

Syoug, R. M. and Ji, J. S. (2002) "The influence mechanisms in the policy domain of the Teacher Education Act," *Taiwanese Sociology*, 4: 199–246 (in Chinese).

Thrupp, M. (2006) *Professional Standards for Teachers and Teacher Education: Avoiding the Pitfalls*. Retrieved from: http://img.scoop.co.nz/media/pdfs/0604/avoiding_pitfalls.pdf.

Tsau, R. D. and Liang, J. M. (2002) "A study of the teacher education system in Taiwan," *Journal of Taitung Teachers College*, 13: 211–40 (in Chinese).

Weng, F. Y. (1996) "Reflection on the teacher education system reform in Taiwan in early 2000s: dialogue between structure and policy," in Chinese Education Society, Chinese

Comparative Education Society, and Teachers Education Society of ROC (eds), *The New Issues Facing Teacher Education System*. Taipei: Shi Ta Books, pp. 1–24 (in Chinese).

Whitty, G. (1997) "Marketization, the state, and the re-formation of the teaching profession," in A. H. Halsey, H. Lauder, P. Brown, and A. S. Wells (eds), *Education: Culture, Economy, Society*. Oxford: Oxford University Press, pp. 299–310,

Yang, S. K. (2002) "Exploring the revisions to the Teacher Education Act in Taiwan based on new developments in professional beliefs," *Journal of Education Research*, 98, 79–90 (in Chinese).

Name index

Archer, Margaret 63

Bell, T. H. 77

Campbell, Hugh Ritchie W. 27
Chen Yonghua 24
Chiang Ching-Kuo 52
Chiang Kai-Che 75
Chiang Kai-Shek 45

De La Chalotais, Louis-René 69
Duncan, A. 81
Durkheim, Émile 3

Emperor Guangxu 26
Emperor Shunzhi 24

Fichte, Johann Gottlieb 3
Friedman, Milton 6
Furlong, J. 197, 213

Georgius Candidus 72
Goodson, I. F. 206, 207

Han Yu 109
Hans Olhoff 22
Hargreaves, A. 204, 206, 210
Herbart, J. Fr. 136
Heylen, A. 72
Hursh, D. 82
Hwang Shu-Ling 129

Izawa Shuji 4, 18, 73

Kabayama Sugenori 28
Kangxi Emperor 18
Keynes, John Maynard 6
Kobayama, Admiral Viscount 73

Koxinga 17
Kublin, H. 73

Latouche, S. 71
Leibbrand, J. A. 206
Li Dan 17
Li Ting-hui 52
Lin Chen-Yung 128
Liu Mingchuan 26
Lynch, K. 79

Mahon, R. 79
Manabu Sato 130, 132
Maxwell, James Laidlaw 27

Pan Chen-Chiu 47
Purple, D. E. 209

Reagan, Ronald 77
Robertus Junius 72

Shao Youlian 27
Shapiro, S. 209
Shi Lang 18
Smith, Adam 5
Sun Yat-sen 8

Thatcher, Margaret 6
Toyotomi Hideyoshi 22
Tsurumi, E. P. 73

von Hayek, Friedrich A. 6

Weber, Max 8
Wei Chien-Kung 43
Whitty, G. 207
Wise, A. E. 206
Wu, W.H. 73

Name index

Yang, T.-R. 75
Yasuyuki Iwata 131

Zheng Chenggong 71

Zheng Jing 24
Zheng Zhilong 20

Subject index

12-Year Basic Education 121, 127, 129, 130
1984 Scheme of Reforming School System 77
410 Education Reform Association 53

A Nation at Risk 77
a taskforce for the Promotion of Professional Development Evaluation of School Teachers (the promotion taskforce) 203, 204, 208
Aichi Prefectural Normal School 18
American Association of Colleges for Teacher Education 82
"assimilation and Kominka" policy 28
Assimilation(doka) policy 74
Australian Institutes for Teaching and School Leadership 82

Batavia 20
Bayrische Lehrerzeitung 69
Benshengren 43
Bureau of Administration Office in Taiwan Province 75
Bureau of Education Affairs of Taiwan 18, 28

Catechism 68
Central Design Bureau 75
Certificate of Successful Completion of Pre-service Teacher Education 141, 142
Changhua Advanced Girl's School 35
Changhua Youth Normal School 35
Chihshanyen School 29
Chihshanyen School Affliated with Japanese Schools 29
Chihshanyen Student Affairs Department 29
China Youth Corps 46
Chinese Comparative Education Society-Taipei 78
Chinese Cultural Renaissance Committee 45
Chinese culture education 76
Christian Doctrine in the Tamsui Language 23
Chuxianguan 24
Civil Affairs Bureau 28
closed system 8
colonial imperialism 71
colonialism 71
Committee of Promoting Chinese Language 75
competence-based; competency-based 2, 44, 76, 77, 94, 113, 115, 120, 219, 266, 267, 272
Consultation Committee on Education Reform 81
contract employer–employee relationship 9
Cultural Revolution 45

Das Edikt zur Allgemenen Schulpflicht 68
decentralization 172, 173
De-Japanisation 42, 76
Deliberation Plan for Amending the Teacher Education Act of 1994 124, 126, 127, 128, 131, 132
Democratic Progressive Party (DPP) 52, 78
Department of Educational Affairs of the Government-General of Formosa 73
deregulated; de-regulated/competitive market 6, 7, 9, 79, 80, 81, 129, 131
dufu 18
Dutch 17, 71
Dutch East India Company 20

École Normale 67
Education Department of Taiwan Provincial Government 77

Subject index

Educational Fundamental Act 53, 91, 101
education practicum(s) 58, 91, 98, 113, 119, 123, 124, 125, 132, 135, 136, 137, 138, 139, 140, 141, 142, 143, 144, 145, 146, 147, 148, 149, 151, 152, 153, 262, 266, 269, 270, 271
education practicum courses 140, 145
education practicum institution(s); education practicum-related institution(s) 136, 139, 142, 143, 144, 145, 146, 147, 148, 150, 152, 153
education practicum system 136, 137, 138, 139, 141, 148, 149, 152
Elementary School Teacher Certification Regulation 43
Enhancement Program(me) for Elementary and Secondary Teachers' Quality 55, 147, 148, 151, 152, 162, 163, 164, 174
Enhancement Program(me) for Teacher Education Quality 55, 82, 89, 91, 101, 147, 151, 152, 153, 242
enlightenment 68
Essential Points for Enacting Competency-based Education in Junior Teacher Colleges 77
Establishment Alliance for Elementary School Teacher Education 150, 153
Establishment Guidelines for the Council on Education Reform 53
Europe of Knowledge 80
European Higher Education Area 80
European Region of Education International 2014 Special Conference 80
European Research Area 80
European Union 80

Final Consultation Report on Education Reform 54, 79, 81
Five Classics 18
For Provintia 22
Foucauldian caring technology 76
Four books 18
Four Books 76
French National Convention 68
Fukien Province 72
fuxue 18

General Administration Report to Provincial Assembly in Taiwan 75
General Agreement on Trade in Services 80
General Medical Council 64
General Teaching Council 64
German Weimar Constitution 69
government-regulated market mechanisms 191
Governor General of Taiwan 27, 18, 19, 33, 37, 39
Guidelines for Evaluating Teacher Education at Normal Universities and Teacher Training Colleges 193, 194
Guidelines for Improving the Quality of University Teachers Subsidisation Project 192, 196
Guidelines for the Evaluation of Teacher Education Centres in Universities 57
Guidelines for Universities with Teacher Education in Developing Exquisite Characteristic Development Subsidization Project 150
Guidelines for Universities with Teacher Education to Organize Education Practicum 141, 143, 144, 147, 148, 152, 153
Guoyu 45
gymnastics 76

Halle University 67
Hamada Yahyoue incident 19
Higher Education Evaluation and Accreditation Council of Taiwan 242, 243, 267

Imperial Descript on Education 34
Imperial Ordinance 73
Imperialization (kominka) 74
Implementation Guidelines for Education Practicum Guidance Provided to Students Having Completed Students 137
Implementation Guidelines for Ministry of Education to Subsidize Universities with Teacher Education in Consolidating Education Practicum Guidance 141, 146, 152
Implementation of the Pre-service Teacher Education Courses and Credits Table 188
Intellectual Youth Party 46
intern(s) 138, 139, 140, 142, 143, 144, 145, 146, 147, 148, 149, 150, 152, 153, 154
Interstate New Teacher Assessment and Support Consortium 81, 94
IUFM 70

Jakarta 20
Japanese colonial period 4, 12, 17, 18, 28, 30, 34, 35, 36, 181, 182, 195
Jinshan 23
Junior College Act 50

Kaohsiung Female Normal School 46
Keelung 18
Kingdom of Tungning 17
Kogakko 73
kokumin gakko (elementary school) 74
Kuomingtang 45
Küster- und Schulmeister Seminarium für Kurmark 68

La loi du 2 mai 1982 dans le cadre de la décentralisation 70
La loi du 22 juillet 1983 relative á la repatrition des compétences entre les communes, les départments, les regions et l'État 70
Le décret de 17 mars 1808 de Napoleon Ier 70
learning community 130, 132
Les écoles supérieurs de professorat et de l'éducation 70
Lo loi d' orientation sur l'éducation du juillet 1989 70
low birth rate 87, 90, 190, 191, 216, 220, 223, 224, 235
Luzon 23

Madou 20
Manila 23
market mechanism 171, 180, 186, 189, 190, 191, 192, 195, 238
marketization professionalism 170, 171
market-oriented teacher preparation; a market-oriented model 135
Martial Law 3, 7, 8, 42, 50, 51, 52, 62, 64, 71, 76, 77, 78, 79, 112, 113, 182, 195, 260, 266
mentor(s) 136, 138, 139, 142, 143, 144, 145, 146, 147, 148, 149, 150, 151, 152, 153, 154
Military Drill 76
Ming dynasty 17
Ministry of Education Outstanding Education Practicum Performance Award and Incentive Guidelines 151, 152, 153
Moralia 67
Mujialiuwan 20

National Academy for Educational Research 205, 242
National Assembly 50
National Board for Professional Teaching Standards (NBPTS) 82, 94
National Changhua University of Education 35
National Chengchi University 87, 137
National Chiayi Institute of Technology 57
National Chiayi Teachers College 57
National Chiayi University 57
National College for Teaching and Leadership 70
National Convention 70
National Council for Accreditation of Teacher Education 70
National Dong Hwa University 57
National Hsinchu University of Education 56
National Hualien University of Education 56
National Kaohsiung Normal University 51
National Pingtung Institute of Commerce 57
National Pingtung University of Education 56
National Pintung University 57
National Professional Standards for Teachers 82
National Socialism 69
National Taichung University of Education 56
National Tainan Teachers College 57
National Taipei University of Education 56
National Taitung Teachers College 57
National Taitung University 57
National Taiwan College of Education 35
National Taiwan Normal University 46
National Union of Teachers 63
National University of Tainan 57
nationalism 76
Nationalistic Party (Kuomintang) 75
NCLB Act 70
neo- liberalism and 3, 6, 7, 10, 12, 80, 92, 194, 255, 256
neo-liberal 79
neo-professionalism 3
New Party 78
new professionalism 2, 157, 158, 170, 173, 174, 198, 206, 207, 208, 209, 210, 211, 213, 214
New Weberian 90, 264

Normal Education Law 7, 8, 50, 87, 110, 111, 114, 136–8, 152, 159, 160, 161, 179, 180, 182, 183, 195, 260
Normal Education System 87, 70, 101, 151, 249, 253, 260
Normal School Curriculum Standard 46
Normal School Rules 4, 33, 35, 37, 158, 159, 181, 182

Obama administration's Agenda for Education Reform 81
OECD 79
open system 8
Orphanage House 67

Penghu 22
People First Party 78
performance-based 3, 77, 94, 146
performance-based education practicums 146
Plan for Teacher Education Quantity 88, 194, 196, 241, 251, 261
pluralistic teacher education 10
Postgraduate Certificate in Education 51
Postgraduate Elementary School Teacher Education Programme 60
Postgraduate Teacher Education Programme 60
pre-service teacher education 2, 140, 142, 148, 150, 151, 187, 188
pre-service teacher education courses; pre-service teacher education curriculum/curricula; pre-service education curricula for teachers 109, 110, 111, 112, 113, 114, 115, 116, 117, 119, 120, 121, 122, 123, 124, 125, 126, 127, 129, 130, 131, 132, 138, 139, 140, 141
private interest 8
professional development evaluation; teacher professional development evaluation 59, 89, 90, 96, 101, 163, 166, 168, 169, 170, 173, 202, 203, 204, 205, 206, 209, 210, 213, 214, 262, 267
Professional Development School(s) 136, 148, 149, 150, 153, 154
professionalism 138, 143, 145, 150, 154
Program for Universities with Teacher Education to Develop Outstanding Teacher Education 149, 152
Programme for International Student Assessment 80
Project for Excellence Teacher Education Scholarship 60
Proposal for Improving Teacher Education, R.O.C. 82
Prussian-French War 69
public goods 7

Qing dynasty 17, 72
Quality Improvement Project for School Teachers 47
Quality Improvement Project for Secondary School Teachers 47

Rapport sur Formose 18
Re-Chinalisation 42
regulated/monopolized market 9
Regulation for National School Teacher Certification 44
Regulation for Registration and Certification for Secondary and Elementary School Teachers 51
Regulation for the Pilot Evaluation of Teachers of Secondary Schools and below 59
Regulation for the Registration and Certification of Elementary School Teachers 47
Regulation for the Registration and Certification of Secondary School Teachers 47
Regulations for Establishment Teacher Education Centres in Universities 57, 186, 187, 188
Regulations for Evaluation of Universities with Teacher Education (Program; Center) 57, 116, 192, 239, 240, 241, 242, 244
Regulations for Taiwanese Governor Japanese Schools 29
Regulations of the Establishment and the Academic Faculty of Teacher Education Programs Offered by Universities and Colleges 79, 185, 240
Reichenschulpflicht 69
Renaissance 68
Republic of China 17
Re-Scinization 76
Research Group of Reforming School System 78
Review on Evaluation and Assessment Frameworks for Improving School Outcomes 82
Romantzy 72

Santo Domingo 17
Scheme of Taking Over Taiwan Plan 75

Schizangan School 73
Second World War; World War II 17, 19, 34, 40, 52, 75
Seminarium Praeceptorum 67
separatist education policy 73
Shih fan jiau yü fa 79
Shih tzu pei yü fa 79
Shogakko 73
Shufang 18
Sinckan 17
Sinckan Manuscript(s) 21, 72
Sino-Japanese War 4, 18, 37, 181
social closure 90, 264, 265
Socialism 8
Soviet Union 46
Spain 23, 42, 72
Spanish 17, 18, 19, 20, 22, 23, 24, 37, 38, 71
Special rights and obligations relationship 9
Spiritual national defense force 76
St. Dominic 72
standards-based 2, 12, 91, 116, 239, 271, 272
standards-based teacher education (SBTE) 81, 82, 89, 90, 91, 92, 94, 95, 101, 102, 103, 104, 116, 148, 261, 268, 269, 271, 272
state control 2, 3, 7, 8, 10, 11, 12, 43, 62, 63, 69, 70, 71, 77, 91, 92, 94, 116, 117, 122, 123, 125, 126, 127, 130, 131, 132, 170, 174, 239, 242, 248, 255, 260, 262, 264, 265, 266, 268, 269, 270, 271
State Education Department 82
Sulangh 20
Sun Yan-sen's Thought 76
supervisor(s) 142, 143, 144, 145, 146, 147, 148, 149, 150, 152
Syraya 17

Taichung Normal School 33
Taihoku Imperial University 44
Tainan 17
Tainan Normal School 33
Taipei Municipal University of Education 56
Taipei Normal School 31
Taipei Physical Education College 57
Taiwan Culture Association 43
Taiwan Education Decree 31
Taiwan Education over Ten Years 44
Taiwan Investigation Committee 75
Taiwan Provincial College of Education 35
Taiwan Provincial Education Association 64
Taiwan Provincial Education Division 44
Taiwan Provincial Government 44, 77, 158
Taiwan Provincial Kaohsiung Teacher's College 46
Taiwan Provincial Mandarin Promotion Council 43
Taiwan Provincial Translation and Compilation Centre 43
Taiwan Solidarity Union 78
Taiwanese Governor Normal School Rules 33
Taiwanese Governor Normal School System 33
Tamsui 23
Tamsui Language and Vocabulary 23
Tapuyen 20
Tavocan 18, 20
Teacher Education Policy Proposal 91
Teacher Education Act 53, 78, 87, 88, 90, 109, 110, 111, 114, 117, 124, 126, 127, 128, 129, 131, 132, 135, 136, 138, 139, 141, 142, 143, 146, 148, 152, 154, 161, 180, 182, 183, 186, 187, 189, 191, 194, 195, 196, 239, 240, 254, 256, 260, 261, 268
Teacher Education Act Enforcement Rules 136, 141, 152
Teacher Education Action Plan 136
teacher education institutions 216, 217, 219, 220, 221, 223, 224, 225, 226, 227, 228, 230, 231, 232, 235, 236
Teacher Education Review Committee 54, 87, 186, 188, 240, 241, 254
teacher education strategic alliance 216, 217, 218, 219, 220, 221, 223, 224, 225, 226, 227, 228, 230, 231, 232, 235, 236
Teacher In Service Training Regulation 51
teacher in-service training 157, 158, 159, 160, 161, 162, 163, 164, 165, 166, 168, 170, 171, 172, 173, 174, 175
teacher profession standards (TPSs) 89, 90, 91, 93, 94, 95, 96, 98, 99, 100, 101, 102, 103, 104
teacher professional development 149, 151, 157, 158, 159, 162, 163, 164, 170, 171, 172, 173, 174, 175, 197, 198, 204, 205, 209, 211, 212, 213
teacher professionalism 197, 206
teacher qualification exam(s) 91, 98, 124, 132, 136, 138, 139, 140, 141, 142, 148, 152, 153, 154, 261, 266, 270
Teacher Quality Improvement Project 55

282 Subject index

Teacher Training Agency 70
teachers as researchers 1
Teachers College Regulation Amendment 43
Terakoya 27
The 410 Demonstration for Education Reform 78
The Commercial Training School 32
the evaluation of teacher professional development 162, 163, 164, 166, 168, 169, 170, 171, 172, 173
The First Global Teacher Education Summit 82
The Imperial College of the Ming dynasty 24
the Implementation Project for Professional Development Evaluations of Teachers 204, 205
the National Teachers' Association 200, 201
The Pilot Implementation Project for Professional Development Evaluations of Teachers 201, 202
The Pilot Project for Excellence Teacher Education Scholarship 60
The Regulations Governing Teacher Qualification Exams and Education Practicum for K-12 Schools 138, 139
The Report on Education in the ROC 148, 150, 152, 153
The Resolution on the Impact of Neo-liberal Policies on Education 80
The Security Maintenance Secretary 46
The Shoo King (The Book of Historical Record) 67
The Taiwan Provincial Teachers College 44

The Teacher Act 205
Three Principles of People 75
Tokyo Higher Normal School 28
Tokyo Technical School 32
Training and Development for Schools 70
Treaty of Shimonoseki 18

UK 2002 Education Act 80
Unified normal education 10
United Nations 49
University Act 140, 141, 142
University of Taipei 57

Vienna-Budapest Declaration 80

Waishengren 43
White Book of Teacher Education in R.O.C. 82
White Paper of Teacher Education 56, 82, 89, 91, 95, 109, 111, 116, 123, 136, 148, 152, 153, 157, 163, 164, 166, 168, 172, 174, 179, 180, 205, 212, 213
World Bank 79
World Trade Organization 80

xiangxue 18
xianxue 18

Yearbook of Teacher Education Statistics 60
yixue 18

Zeelandia 19
Zheng dynasty 17
Zhongli Incident 51
zyuku 27